NASHVILLE: THE FACES OF TWO CENTURIES

A COMMEMORATIVE VOLUME
IN HONOR OF NASHVILLE'S FIRST TWO CENTURIES,
PUBLISHED BY THE EDITORS OF NASHVILLE! MAGAZINE
FOR THE METROPOLITAN NASHVILLE-DAVIDSON COUNTY CENTURY III COMMISSION
RICHARD H. FULTON, MAYOR

NASHVILLE

THE FACES OF TWO CENTURIES *1780-1980*

WRITTEN AND EDITED BY	John Egerton
WITH A REMINISCENCE BY	Robert Penn Warren
PERIOD PIECES BY	Wilma Dykeman John Hope Franklin Dewey W. Grantham Sam B. Smith
PORTRAITS IN TIME BY	David Wright
A GALLERY OF NASHVILLE COMMERCE	Louise Littleton Davis

PLUSMEDIA INCORPORATED

STAFF FOR THE BOOK

DESIGNED BY
JAMES A. BATEMAN AND HARRIETTE HUGHEY BATEMAN

EDITORIAL AND RESEARCH ASSISTANTS
SHARON MACPHERSON, CHARLES F. BRYAN JR., JAMES A. HOOBLER

RESEARCHERS
ELEANOR GRAHAM, MARY GLENN HEARNE, LEE ANN THORNTON

BILL LaFEVOR, *Principal Photographer*
LESLIE PRITIKIN, *Photographic Copyist*
RONNIE THWEATT, *Production Director*
DANNY PROCTOR AND GAIL STEPHENS, *Production Coordinators*
KAY KERSTEN NICKELL AND VICKI SENSING, *Copy Editors*
TINA ADAMS ECHOLS, *Typographer*
TERESA MOON HAVERLY, KENT HUNTER, DON MILSTEAD,
AND BOB PARSONS, *Production Assistants*

Lithography by COMMERCIAL ENGRAVING & LITHOGRAPHY INCORPORATED
Binding by NICHOLSTONE BOOK BINDERY
Printed by WILLIAMS PRINTING COMPANY

PRODUCED BY NASHVILLE! MAGAZINE, A DIVISION OF PLUSMEDIA INCORPORATED
C. TURNEY STEVENS JR., *President*
WILSON P. BURTON JR., *Vice President*
MARY RUTH TEMPLE, *Secretary-Treasurer*

Contents

1780-1820 AN INTRODUCTION BY WILMA DYKEMAN 9

NASHVILLE: Cumberland Frontier 13

1820-1860 AN INTRODUCTION BY SAM B. SMITH 59

NASHVILLE: Jackson's Town 63

1860-1900 AN INTRODUCTION BY JOHN HOPE FRANKLIN 109

NASHVILLE: Division and Reunion 113

1900-1940 NASHVILLE: Twentieth-Century City 165

A REMINISCENCE BY ROBERT PENN WARREN 203

1940-1980 AN INTRODUCTION BY DEWEY W. GRANTHAM 233

NASHVILLE: An American Song 237

A Gallery of Nashville Commerce 301

INDEX 369

CREDITS 372

APPRECIATION 375

A Dream of New Ground

Wilma Dykeman

Land.

Land was the dream and the reality. It seduced rootless adventurers, quickened shrewd speculators with their blueprints of empire, compelled irresistibly those men and women whose yearning was simply and fiercely for home, for a place on earth.

When they turned inward to the land of the Western Waters, surmounting the Appalachian barrier, they left the sea behind them. It was a definitive transition. In the countries most of them or their immediate ancestors had known—England, Scotland, Wales, Ireland, Germany, France, Holland, coastal Africa—they were seldom far from the sea. Distant horizons extended thoughts and awareness to other lands. For the colonies strung along the Atlantic shoreline the sea was an umbilical cord joining them to the motherland. Inland, however, the aroma of salt and ocean spray gave way to fresh winds from the hills, to the smell of forests rich with the mulch of centuries and the raw scent of open, succulent grasslands.

Westward the explorers and surveyors and settlers reached into this new country. Its vastness challenged their powers of measurement. Its abundance whetted the appetites it fed. From the nettle of its dangers and the blossom of its beauty and bounty, the fruit of personal and community freedom was plucked in blood-stained hazard and boundless hope.

Along trails opened by the muscled shoulders and heavy trampling hooves of buffalo and smaller beasts, on rivers surging with perils and bounded by death, a spearhead of those with the westward vision walked, rode, hacked, floated, shoved, fought, drudged, endured their way to the place on the Cumberland called the French Lick. It was new ground.

Above all it was a green land, a land alive. It was alive with the beat of a billion wings, the thunder of a million hooves, the rush of nourishing waters flashing with the iridescent sparkle of fish, the splendor of apparently limitless virgin forests, the dark unseen reach of roots and rivulets and an underground web nurturing a vital and delicately balanced variety of visible life. And all of that life was interrelated, interdependent. Even the archaic past was not past—it was present in the very soil determining the crops that would flourish, the livestock that should increase, the commerce that could develop.

In one sense those who had turned from the familiar ocean and its decisive influence had only turned to another, an unfamiliar sea whose influence was of daily, permanent, inescapable consequence. This land they were committed to claiming, to holding, had been in large measure created by inland seas millions of years ago in the dim dawn of earth's formation. During the Ordovician period and the later Mississippian period when folds and upthrusts born of stress deep within the earth wrinkled the landscape with mountains and faults and valleys, a quiet inland sea covered much of the interior continent. Size and depth of a succession of such seas

9

shifted from one era to another, while in the warm shallow water of the Mississippi Valley simple forms of aquatic life, especially tiny shellfish, laid down deposits that eventually formed great beds of limestone.

This was limestone country to which the settlers and founders of Nashville came. Grasses and trees, animals and humans, the whole spectrum of life was influenced by this underlying foundation of the soil. Weather, too, played its role in the patterns of habitation in this place: extreme enough to permit changes of the seasons but temperate enough to allow occasional mild interludes loosening winter's grip and refreshing periods of coolness relieving summer's heat.

The forests were the initial astonishment, as they had been in so many encounters with newcomers to the American land. Lofty, virgin, creating in their shade a sort of luminous green darkness even at midday, they dominated the landscape. To some of the settlers these forests represented "a howling wilderness" set in opposition to human civilization, a thing to be conquered and subdued as quickly as possible. To others the forests were a welcome haven inviting exploration and understanding, a reserve to be used in the course of necessity and developing foresight.

The trees yielded up their unique qualities fulfilling special needs. Cedar, with its rich, blood-pink color and pungent aroma, flourished in the Middle Tennessee country and on the bluff above the French Lick. It probably provided logs for the first homes; it certainly provided wood for the pails that were a pioneer necessity and for the churns that were the pride of every housewife. Tall and straight poplar, the numerous oaks, stout hickory, rich black walnut, maple, ash, beech, chestnut, dogwood, sycamore—each offered some special asset, some singular value, to the settlers in their midst.

To a greater extent than in many regions, however, the country around the French Lick consisted of more than forests. Equally distinctive were the canebrakes and the expanses of wild pea vine and nutritious grasses. Along the banks of streams and the river some of the cane had grown through the years to a height of twenty feet or more. Wild muscadine grape and jasmine vines were only two of the fruits and flowers that added to the bounty of the woods and fields.

Cane, grass, water: These had attracted herds of wild game to the land the pioneers claimed. During that first Cold Winter of 1779-1780, many lean deer starved, but that was an exceptional experience. As other newcomers joined the earliest settlers all marveled at the teeming multitudes of birds and fish, of buffalo, elk, deer, bear, turkeys a hundred in a flock, wild geese, and smaller game. It was free for the taking and take they must, take they did. One hunting party returned after a five-day trip only twenty or thirty miles from the bluff with a count of 105 bears, seventy-five buffalo, and eighty-seven deer slaughtered. Within five years, a young German visitor to Nashville observed that in the surrounding countryside the buffalo were greatly diminished in numbers and that during his stay he saw "but a single elk, and that, too, at a distance." Predatory animals flourished along with the game, of course. There were panthers and wildcats, but the most feared were the wolves, whose lonely howling must have sometimes seemed to be the very voice of this immense and often hostile place.

10

For the main part, the men and women who sought out this land were a restless people who longed to sink deep roots, ready with a rifle, an ax, or a Bible. They were a hearty, praying, singing, remembering people who turned their history into family chronicles, their hardships into tall tales, and their longings and disappointments into ballads—all the while clearing fields, building homes and barns, establishing dominion over the kingdoms of fur and feather and fin.

Native red hunters who had cherished this land as a source of game and legend, sustenance for body and spirit, now saw herds of cattle taking the place of buffalo, rooting hogs replacing deer and elk, forts and cabins rising on old campfire sites, corn growing where wild cane once flourished. Above all they saw the surveyors measuring off the open spaces and parceling out the land. For possession of the land the red hunter and the European settler fought and killed in relentless warfare. The toll was tragic and wasteful beyond reckoning.

The land remained. To some—the speculators, the lawyers staking claims with paper rather than lives, the bold and the shrewd who held on and survived—it brought fortune. To others, including many of the first comers who risked all but were forced to move elsewhere when the county was established and overlapping claims conflicted, it brought despair. To still others—the quiet, determined, rooted citizens—the land was the dream made real.

Between the self-sufficiency characteristic of the small, independent East Tennessee farmer and the single-crop wealth of the West Tennessee planter, Middle Tennessee land and climate and attitude encouraged both self-sufficiency and money crops. Horses and hogs and sheep, corn and wheat and cotton, plants as different as turnips and iris: All flourished on that Bluegrass soil that was more extensive than neighboring Kentucky's fabled Bluegrass. From the region came walking horses and lamb's wool that won international prizes. Commerce found the site favorable and the village became a city. Politics found the situation central to the state and the city became a capital.

Memory of the land remained, and remains today. It rides on the west wind whipping the sting of snow across eyes and face even as it did during that first Cold Winter. It stirs with the smell of freshly cut cedar as it did for those first builders of cabins and homes. It pierces through the plaintive call of a ballad limning the endless search for home, for the security of love as well as legalities. Perhaps today the memory is not so far removed from the land itself, that same land that was the dream and the reality for seekers two centuries ago.

Among Wilma Dykeman's thirteen books (three co-authored with her husband, James Stokely, and one with her son, Jim Stokely) are an impressionistic history of the French Broad River valley in the Tennessee-North Carolina mountains and Tennessee: A Bicentennial History, *published in 1976.*

11

Nashville:
Cumberland Frontier
1780-1820

NOBODY KNOWS what the Mound Builders called the river. Even the Shawnee elders, who knew of their nation's tenure in the valley from the middle of the seventeenth century, had no recollection of the people who had preceded them here and left their dead in stone coffins buried beneath gracefully curved earthen mounds.

What would in time become Middle Tennessee was until early in the eighteenth century a home for the Shawnees, but their presence was never secure. It was a region of primeval beauty, an undisturbed wilderness garden of nature, and many besides the Shawnees coveted it: the Iroquois in the north, the Cherokees in the east, the Chickasaws in the west, the Creeks and Choctaws in the south. Eventually, the Shawnees were driven out, leaving little behind except their name for the river: Warioto.

For nearly three-quarters of a century, it was understood among the various Indian tribes and the handful of French trappers and traders who ventured here that this park-like expanse of forest and streams could be hunted and fished by all, but possessed by none. The Iroquois did in fact claim it but did not occupy it; until well past 1770, no one did.

The few French traders who came (perhaps the earliest of them being a man named Charleville, in 1714) followed the Mississippi to the Ohio and the Ohio to the mouth of what they called *le Riviere des Chauouanons*—the River of the Shawnees. South and east from there, they paddled their small boats two hundred miles upstream to a canebrake-bordered sulphur spring and salt lick beside a high bluff, and they gave the place a name: the French Lick.

Sometime around 1769, a young French-Canadian backwoodsman and trader named Jacques-Timothe De Montbrun came to the French Lick from Kaskaskia, Illinois, near the confluence of the Mississippi and Ohio rivers. The furs he obtained from the Indians here were soon to bring him a handsome profit in the market at New Orleans, and De Montbrun decided on the basis of his gain to spend his winters trading at the French Lick. Neither the American Revolution nor his later appointment as lieutenant governor of the Illinois Country would keep him from occasional extended visits to what became his favorite spot in the Western wilderness. (By 1790, when he was generally known as Timothy Demonbreun, he had moved here permanently, and he remained an honored "first citizen" until his death more than thirty-five years later.)

But Demonbreun was not alone—probably not even the first—among Europeans to be en-

1750

An adventurous group of Virginia gentlemen rode through a fine valley in the southwestern part of the state to discover what sort of country lay beyond their wonted horizon. The outline of some mountains took form against the western haze. The leader of the party was Dr. Thomas Walker. One of his favorite noblemen must have been the Duke of Cumberland. So he gave the name "Cumberland" to the mountains. They rode on and in time came to a great gap in the mountains. Dr. Walker christened it "Cumberland Gap." The Duke of Cumberland was being made immortal that day. The party made its way down the tortuous side of the mountain, and at its foot, they came to a beautiful river. Dr. Walker made the series complete by naming it the "Cumberland River." The beauty of the name has pleased the people from that day to this.

And yet there is a massive irony in the colonists' acceptance of those christenings. The Duke of Cumberland, favorite son of George II, was in charge of the English troops at the battle of Culloden. The battle was a massacre, told of in tragic story and heartbreaking song. Dr. Walker was surely aware of the Duke's consequent reputation among the Scottish people. The Butcher, they called him, and with reason. One may be excused to regard somewhat oddly the Scotch-Irish settlers' willingness to accept it. The poetry of the name must have obscured its bloody associations.

ALFRED LELAND CRABB, in
Nashville: Personality of a City

chanted by the lands within this river basin in the decade or so before white settlers came to stay. There was Uriah Stone, who gave his name to a tributary of the river a few miles upstream from the salt lick; there were Isaac Lindsey, and Isaac Bledsoe, and a Dutchman named Kasper Mansker; there was a bear of a man named Thomas Sharpe Spencer, the one they called "Big Foot," who is said to have lived for several months in a hollow sycamore tree; and there were others, perhaps a dozen or more in all. With the possible exception of Spencer, none of these so-called Long Hunters appeared to have permanent settlement in mind; what they were after were furs and food, and in their sporadic comings and goings they managed to keep a relatively peaceful relationship with the Indians.

It was to be a temporary peace. Englishmen had long since come through the great mountain pass west of the Blue Ridge and named it Cumberland Gap, and they had changed the name of the Shawnee River to the Cumberland. The colonies of North Carolina and Virginia, from which the Long Hunters had come, were clearly eager to stretch their borders farther west, to the Mississippi and beyond. By the early 1770s, a pioneer settlement had been established on the Watauga River in the Virginia-Carolina mountains, and the Kentucky territory was being explored with an eye to settlement. England was nearing a state of war with its American colonies; the French and the Spanish had their own territorial ambitions; land speculators and would-be settlers in the border regions longed to make their own way without restraint by national, colonial, or native interests. And as for the Indians, they could only know that while the whites contended fiercely among themselves, what they contended *for* was the vast sweep of wilderness lands that innumerable tribes had claimed for centuries. The

14

Forty-five years before he traded away the Cherokee claim to Middle Tennessee, the diplomatic chieftain Attakullakulla (extreme right) went with six other young Cherokee chiefs to be entertained by King George II of England. This engraving, made in London in 1730, is the only likeness of Attakullakulla known to exist.

Indians were confused, saddened, angered. Some of them were honor-bound not to yield without a struggle; others were willing to talk and listen, to make treaties.

At Sycamore Shoals on the Watauga in March 1775—just one month before the Revolutionary War began—several hundred Cherokees met with a delegation of colonial whites headed by Richard Henderson of North Carolina. They bargained for four days; in the end, the chief warrior of the Cherokees, Oconostota, and their chief diplomat, Attakullakulla, relinquished their people's claim to most of the land between the Ohio and Cumberland rivers in Kentucky and Tennessee. In payment, they accepted six wagonloads of guns and ammunition, rum, blankets, and assorted goods.

In truth, it was not the land of Oconostota and Attakullakulla to sell, or Henderson's to buy. Others claimed some or all of it— the Chickasaws, the British, the Virginians, the

North Carolinians, scores of land agents and warrant-holders and squatters. There would be lengthy disputes, claims and counterclaims, and no little bloodletting, but there would be no stopping the westward movement. The beginning of Cumberland settlement was at hand.

Within a year, the Cherokees had joined with the British in the war against the colonies and attacked settlements on the Holston River and the Watauga. Another treaty was needed—this time a peace treaty—and it took place at Long Island on the Holston in July of 1777.

The Long Island parley produced another tenuous armistice between the Cherokees and the Wataugans, but something of greater significance to the history of the West also happened there: Richard Henderson, who seemed in danger of having his western territorial purchase voided by the North Carolina and Virginia governments as well as the Continental Congress, met for the first time with the two men

15

———

. . . The long-hunting-soldier-farmer-borderer was an unloved figure; Washington praised his skill with the long rifle, but found him difficult. He was; he didn't mind fighting but hated soldiering, and had an innate distaste for drills, standing armies, and all other aspects of the military life. New Yorkers and New Englanders found him uncouth and even silly with his long shirt and "rifled barreled firelock," though even Boston made him welcome as long as he was needed. The British also hated the borderers for they found the "shirt-tail men, with their cursed twisted guns, the most fatal widow-and-orphan makers in the world."

They were; they hated war. Fighting was a business they would be done with, and the only way they knew to end it was to kill as many men as possible. They could then return to the real struggle for more and better land on which to raise their families and get ahead in the world. Their many-handedness was typical of the times when a man had to be a world within himself: make a poem; sing a song; mend a gun; preach a sermon; shoot buffalo, Indians, British; make a moccasin or a boat; teach school; but always able to live in the woods if need be. It wasn't so much that he was completely master of a hard world and hence fearless, but rather it was his ability to believe in himself and the world around him. Seneca snakeroot may never have cured a single case of snake bite, but a man with faith and a bit of dried Seneca was never afraid to sleep in rattlesnake country.

HARRIETTE SIMPSON ARNOW, in *Seedtime on the Cumberland*

——— ———

who subsequently saved the Cumberland country for him.

One of them was James Robertson, the thirty-five-year-old leader of the Watauga settlement. He was experienced as a farmer and a fighter, an explorer, a surveyor, and a fair-handed agent among the Cherokees.

The other was John Donelson, who at age fifty-one was a veteran land speculator and surveyor and a former member of the Virginia colonial legislature.

Henderson had expected his purchase of the Kentucky and Tennessee lands from the Cherokees at Sycamore Shoals to be challenged, but he had not expected government repudiation of the treaty. He had advertised for settlers in 1776, apparently without much response. In the face of growing opposition to the speculative venture, he and his associates were by 1777 keenly anxious to send settlers to the West, knowing that in any disputes over land titles, those in possession would have a decided advantage. Henderson needed a large number of settlers and able men to lead them; in Robertson and Donelson, he found just such men.

The following year, after Virginia had voided the Kentucky portion of his purchase, Henderson apparently renewed his contact with Robertson and Donelson, engaging them to organize a large settlement on the Cumberland. Favorable reports had already come in from the Long Hunters at French Lick. Henderson knew that a survey to extend the North Carolina-Virginia border through their western territories would soon be made; believing that the French Lick region would be shown by the survey to be south of the boundary, he wanted to get settlers there quickly before North Carolina repudiated his claim, as Virginia had done.

By late 1778, Donelson had made plans to move from Virginia to Watauga and then to direct the construction of a flotilla of boats at

Remarks on the Management of the Scalped-Head. By Mr. JAMES ROBERTSON, *of Nashville, in the State of Tenessee. Communicated to the* EDITOR, *by* FELIX ROBERTSON, *M.D., of the same place.*

In the year 1777, there was a Doctor Vance, about the Long-Islands of Holsten, who was there attending on the different garrisons, which were embodied on the then frontiers of Holsten, to guard the inhabitants against the depradations of the Cheerake-Indians . . . . In March of the same year, Frederick Calvit was badly wounded, and nearly the whole of his head skinned. Doctor Vance was sent for, and staid several days with him. The skull-bone was quite naked, and began to turn black in places, and, as Doctor Vance was about to leave Calvit, he directed me, as I was stationed in the same fort with him, to bore his skull as it got black, and he bored a few holes himself, to show the manner of doing it. I have found, that a flat pointed straight awl is the best instrument to bore with, as the skull is thick, and somewhat difficult to penetrate. When the awl is nearly through, the instrument should be borne more lightly upon. The time to quit boring is when a reddish fluid appears on the point of the awl. I bore, at first, about one inch apart, and, as the flesh appears to rise in these holes, I bore a number more between the first. The flesh will rise considerably above the skull, and sometime raise a black scale from it, about the thickness of common writing paper . . . . These scales are often as large as a dollar, and sometimes even twice as large.

It will take, at least, two weeks from the time of boring for it to scale. When the scale is taken off at a proper time, all beneath it will appear flesh, like what we call proud-flesh, and as if there was no bone under it.

The awl may, at this time, and, indeed, for a considerable length of time, be forced through the flesh to the bone without the patient's feeling it; but after any part has united to that portion of the scalp, which has remaining original skin, it becomes immediately sensible to the touch.

The scalped-head cures very slowly, and if this kind of flesh rise, in places, higher than common, touch it with blue-stone water, dress it once or twice a-day, putting a coat of lint over it every time you dress it, with a narrow plaister of ointment.

It skins remarkably slow, generally taking two years to cure up.

In the year 1781, David Hood was shot, at this place [Nashville], with several balls, and two scalps were taken off his head, and these took off nearly all the skin which had hair on it. [David Hood was shot and scalped near Fort Nashborough in 1781.] I attended him, bored his skull, and removed from almost the whole of his head, such black scales as I have described above. It was three or four years before his head skinned over entirely; but he is now living, and is well . . . .

I never knew one that was scalped, and bored as above directed, that did not perfectly recover. There is always part of the scalped head over which but little or no hair afterwards grows.

(Felix Robertson, son of James Robertson, sent these words of his father to the Philadelphia Medical and Physical Journal *on April 10, 1806. They were published in the journal soon thereafter.)*

Fort Patrick Henry on the Holston. Robertson, meanwhile, had organized a small advance party, and early in the spring of 1779 they made an exploratory trip to the Cumberland.

With his brother Mark, a black slave, and six others—George Freeland, William Neely, Edward Swanson, Zachariah White, William Overall, and James Hanley—Robertson traveled across the mountains to the upper Cumberland and followed the river some 400 miles to the French Lick, seeing no signs of human life along the way. Timothy Demonbreun, Kasper Mansker, and Thomas Spencer were thought to be near the area of the salt lick at the time, but the Robertson party did not see them. Close to the lick, they cleared a small plot of ground and set out a corn crop as a symbolic means of staking their claim to the land. Then Robertson and two others went on to Kaskaskia to inform George Rogers Clark—and through him, the state of Virginia—that they had taken the first step toward settlement.

It was August before they returned to Watauga. What they had seen in the valley of the Cumberland had whetted their appetite for moving, and they were pleased to find that scores of families were as eager as they to get started. With them, as with countless thousands of others in the years ahead, the call of the West was like a fever, contagious and irresistible. The Robertson advance men had seen the Promised Land; they could paint for the Watauga families a glowing vision of boundless possibility. All who went to claim it could have plenty of land—enough to settle and be comfortable, enough to sell and become rich. They would perhaps have fewer problems with Indians than they had experienced around Watauga. They would be far removed from the British, too, and from the war, and from the growing frustrations of politics. Surely they would be able to make a fresh start here, to hunt and fish, raise some crops, build a town, amass wealth. But they would have to hurry, before others beat them to the choice lands around the French Lick.

THEY WOULD NOT WAIT for spring. By the first of November, James Robertson had assembled his company of overland movers—between 200 and 300 younger men—and started for Cumberland Gap with pack horses, food and provisions, and the colony's assorted herd of livestock. Their route would be along the Wilderness Trail to central Kentucky and then southwest, following a succession of streams to the Cumberland. On today's map, it shows as a journey of nearly 500 miles—roughly from Elizabethton, Tennessee, to Danville, Kentucky, to Nashville.

The convoy being readied under John Donelson's direction was also nearing completion. They were to set out soon after Robertson, transporting the older men, the women and children, the servants, and most of the household belongings of the settlement along a crooked river path to Muscle Shoals on the Ten-

nessee, where Robertson was to meet them and lead them the rest of the way overland.

In retrospect, they seem to have been pitifully ill-suited for this migration which one historian termed "a mad venture." The Donelson party in particular seems so. They had crude maps of the rivers, but no one in the flotilla had ever navigated them. Unexpected complications delayed their departure from Fort Patrick Henry until December 22, and soon thereafter they were forced by bitter cold, swift currents, and general discouragement to stop and camp for two months. Furthermore, Donelson appears to have been an unlikely choice for their leader. An English gentleman's son, he had spent most of his life in the settled regions of colonial Virginia, not on the border or in the backwoods, and his acquaintance with Indians and pioneers or with hardship of any sort was limited. He was, in addition, a large, fleshy man, by then fifty-four

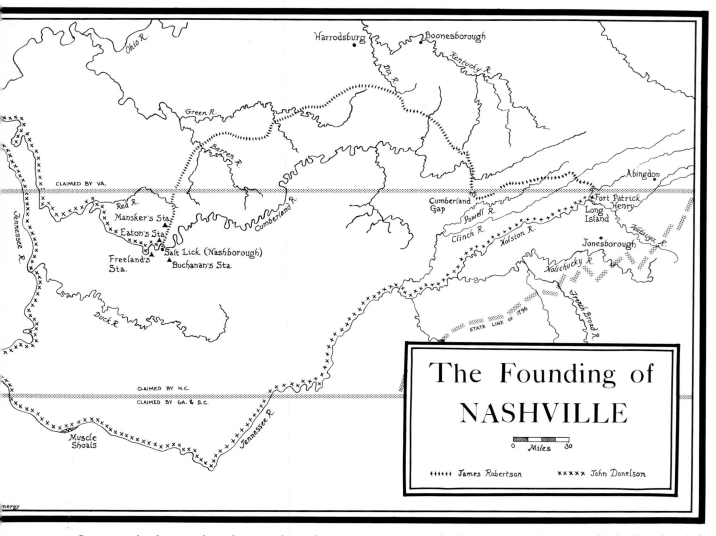

On an overland route of nearly 500 miles and a river journey twice that long, James Robertson and John Donelson led the first pioneer settlers in two parties to the valley of the Cumberland in 1779-80.

years old—hardly of an age or condition to undertake such an arduous journey with more than 200 vulnerable people dependent on his leadership.

The Robertson group had more strengths— and as it turned out, less trouble—but they, too, faced hard traveling. Robertson, however, was an ideal guide for them. Tall and athletic-looking, not yet forty years old, he had been living on one frontier after another since his Scotch-Irish father and his English mother had brought him into the world. Until he married Charlotte Reeves in Wake County, North Carolina, in 1768, he had not taken the time to learn how to read and write, but under her tutelage he learned fast. Of the more essential kinds of knowledge—the knowledge of Indians and pioneers, of woods and mountains, of in-

dependence and self-sufficiency—he had an abundance. And unlike Donelson, he knew where he was going, because he had been there.

Although they started out with no women or children among them, the Robertson party was joined by several families along the Wilderness Trail. John Rains, John Buchanan, John and James Mulherrin, Sampson and Daniel Williams, Thomas Thompson, Amos Eaton, Haydon Wells, Benjamin Drake, and Frederick Stump—all with their families, bound for Kentucky or Tennessee—were among the ones who accepted Robertson's invitation to come along and settle with them on the Cumberland. They traveled not in close ranks but widely scattered along the trail, and by the time the bleak chill of December came, they must have numbered close to 400.

Dressed in unaccustomed finery, young James Robertson sat for this portrait by an unknown artist. The painting probably was done before Robertson came west to the Cumberland.

Robertson's brothers Mark and John were in the group, and so was his oldest son, eleven-year-old Jonathan, whose job it was to help drive the sheep, horses, hogs, and cattle. By the time they passed the central Kentucky settle-ments, snow and ice and bitter cold threatened the livestock and caused great discomfort for the people; even so, they passed the final 200 miles of their journey without catastrophe, seeing neither Indians nor whites along the way.

Charlotte Robertson wore pearls and a lace hood for her portrait, which was done by the same artist who painted her husband. The paintings were acquired in Texas in 1978 by the Tennessee State Museum.

Overleaf: Under snow clouds and Christmas Day sunshine, James Robertson and his companions reached their destination on the Bluff in 1779. Nashville artist David Wright's interpretation of the scene was painted in 1979.

The first members of the party entered what is now Davidson County along a route that was to become Gallatin Pike (Kasper Mansker's station was already built nearby) and proceeded south to a point where White's Creek Pike now parallels the Cumberland. There, Amos Eaton and a few others stopped on Christmas Eve and made shelter; they would soon be at work building a station on the bluff north of the river.

The others went another mile or two farther south, probably to a point between the now-standing Jefferson Street and Victory Memorial bridges. There, across the river, was their destination: the French Lick, the Big Salt Lick, the Sulphur Spring—and a little farther on, the Bluff.

Tradition has it that on Christmas Day, 1779, James Robertson and his weary companions crossed the frozen Cumberland on the ice, driving their pack horses and their livestock before them. That the story lacks proof seems inconse-quential; what matters—and what is certainly true—is that before a new year dawned, the long line of migrants had completed a two-month passage through the wilderness to a new out-post, and they had done it without the loss of a single life.

While the Buchanans and the Mulherrins and others started work on a walled station on the bluff and George Freeland and his companions began a similar task on the opposite side of the spring and lick, James Robertson prepared for yet another trip: a cross-country ride to Muscle Shoals on the Tennessee and the planned rendez-vous with the Donelson flotilla.

But Robertson was to wander off course in the deep snows; he confused the Elk River with the Tennessee, and finally was forced to give up in despair and turn back. His mission could not have succeeded anyway, though, for even as he wandered about lost, the troubled flotilla was aground at the mouth of Reedy Creek on the Holston, just a few miles below its starting point.

Not until two months later, at the end of February, did they start again, with Donelson's flagship, the "Adventure," in the lead, carrying upwards of forty people, and a motley assort-ment of companion vessels following. In the journal he kept of the voyage, Donelson wrote in classic understatement of the perils they faced: a death by frostbite, a drowning, a hunter lost in the woods, two more captured and killed by Indians; twenty-eight persons on a smallpox-quarantined flatboat in the rear of the fleet in-tercepted by Indians and massacred, "their cries distinctly heard"; the constant ravages of hunger and fatigue, of the weather and the water; a baby born, and then found dead after the confu-sion and terror of an Indian attack; the distress at reaching Muscle Shoals and finding no one there waiting; and then the harrowing rush over the shoals, thirty miles in three hours.

21

David Wright ©1978

On the twentieth of March, they reached the mouth of the Tennessee River, nearly 800 miles from their embarking point. The mouth of the Cumberland was ten miles ahead of them up the Ohio, and the French Lick was another 200 miles upstream from there. In his journal, Donelson recorded the convoy's grim prospects—and his own unbending resolve:

Our situation here is truly disagreeable. The river is very high and the current rapid, our boats not constructed for the purpose of stemming a rapid stream, our provisions exhausted, the crews almost worn down with hunger and fatigue, and know not what distance we have to go, or what time it will take us to our place of destination. The scene is rendered still more melancholy, as several boats will not attempt to ascend the rapid current. Some intend to descend the Mississippi to Natchez; others are bound for Illinois, among the rest my son-in-law and daughter. We now part, perhaps, to meet no more, for I am determined to pursue my course, happen what will.

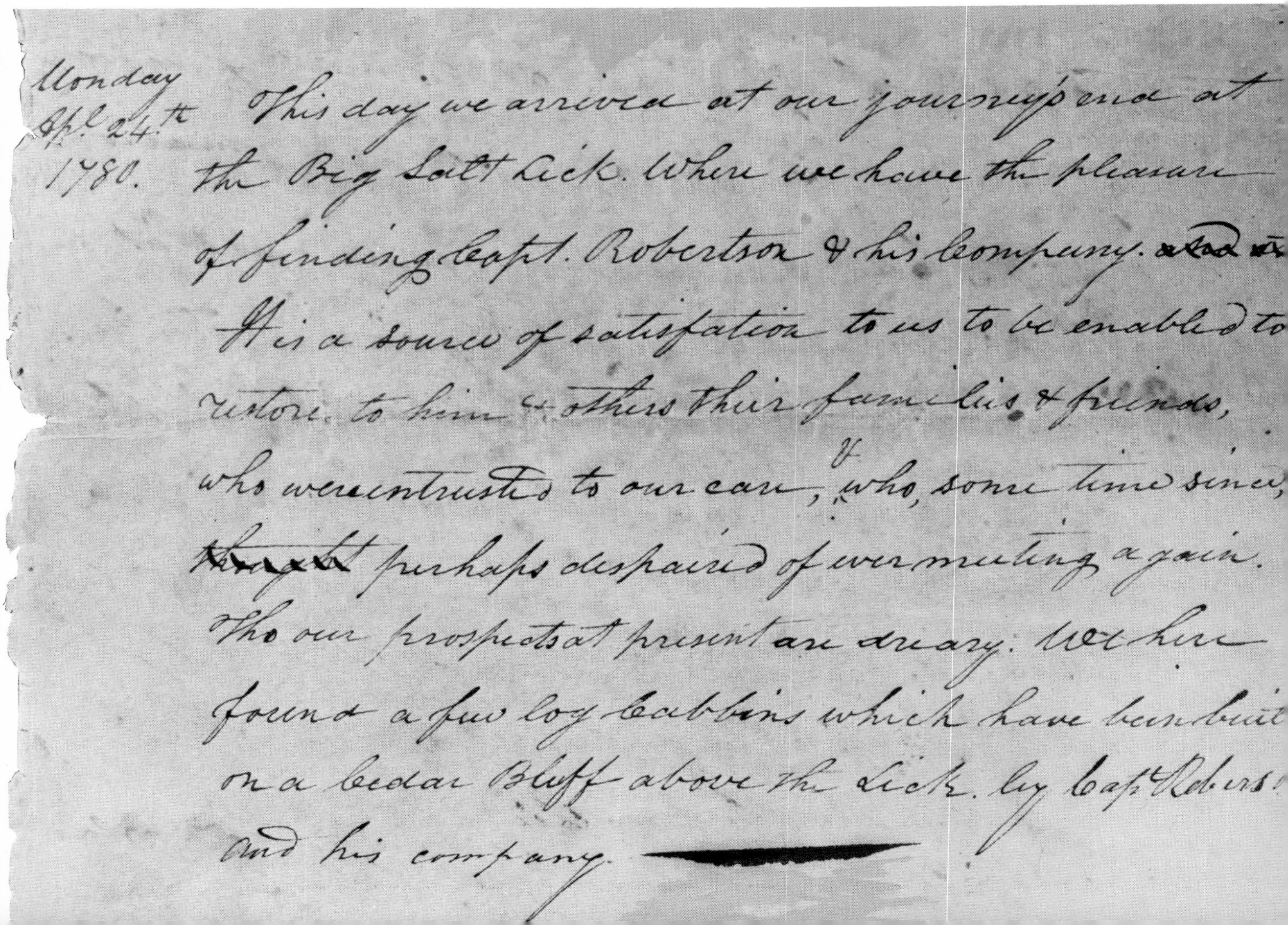

Monday
Apl. 24th
1780.

This day we arrived at our journeys end at the Big Salt Lick. Where we have the pleasure of finding Capt. Robertson & his Company. It is a source of satisfaction to us to be enabled to restore to him & others their families & friends, who were entrusted to our care, who, some time since, perhaps despaired of ever meeting again. Tho our prospects at present are dreary: We here found a few log cabbins which have been built on a cedar Bluff above the Lick, by Capt. Robertson and his Company.

THERE WERE more than 500 settlers in the valley of the lower Cumberland that spring, and they were a more diverse group than was customarily found in most frontier regions. The majority were English or Scotch, but there were also several Germans (most notably Frederick Stump), a few Welsh and Irish, Mansker the Dutchman, Demonbreun the French-Canadian, and Edward Swanson, a member of Robertson's advance party, who was Swedish. Blacks in the various stations may have numbered close to fifty, and not all of them were slaves; one free black, a man named Jack Civil, was wounded and captured in an early Indian battle and was later said to have fought on the side of the Indians.

Women were far less numerous then men and also less visible. With the exception of Robertson's wife Charlotte and his sister Ann, Donelson's wife and daughter, both named Rachel, and Sally Ridley Buchanan, a heroine of one particular battle with Indians, the names of few women are mentioned prominently in the various accounts of early Cumberland settlement. Even so, women in that period—and free blacks, too—enjoyed a measure of freedom that would later be denied them. Until well into the nineteenth century, they could own property, sue in court, and speak their minds. Class divisions were hardly noticeable at first; everyone worked, and all the work was hard, and there appeared to be no favored jobs or favored workers.

The first duty of all was to secure food and shelter. Corn was planted as soon as the weather permitted, and building continued at the main station on the bluff, at Freeland's, Eaton's, and Mansker's, and at four other stations. The land in spring was lush and healing, full of wild game and soaring promise, and the settlers yearned to spread out and claim some of it for their own. As it turned out, they were soon too scattered

Whatever he may have lacked in knowledge, experience, or good judgment in undertaking a thousand-mile river journey through Indian country in the dead of winter, John Donelson apparently did not lack determination—or courage.

Having begun with about forty white men, thirty slaves, and the wives and children of fifty or more would-be settlers—including most of his own family and James Robertson's wife and four small children—Donelson finally arrived at the French Lick on April 24, 1780, counting nearly forty lives lost along the way. Tears of grief and joy must have attended the reunion.

A total of 256 signatures appear on the original Cumberland Compact, which was discovered in an old trunk in 1846 by Tennessee historian A. W. Putnam. Various tabulators over the years have marked their sums on the compact.

for their own safety, but that discovery was awhile in coming. There would be time before that to celebrate a few weddings—James Robertson performed the first one, in June of 1780—and to form a civil government "guaranteeing equal rights, mutual protection, and impartial justice" to the settlers.

Early in May, just two weeks after the arrival of the flotilla, Richard Henderson appeared on the Cumberland to be reunited with Robertson and Donelson and to see how the migration he

had instigated was faring. He was then serving as North Carolina's representative on the team surveying the Kentucky-Tennessee territorial boundary, and he had learned that the Cumberland settlements definitely were on the North Carolina side of the line, safely beyond Virginia's grasp. Back home, Henderson's friend Abner Nash had been elected governor; perhaps the time was ripe for the state legislature to certify the Cumberland purchase.

To speed that process along, Henderson drew

up the Cumberland Compact, a document detailing settler rights and procedures for land transactions, and at a meeting with the assembled colonists at the station on the bluff, he got the names of more than 250 men signed to it. (Only one man marked an X for his signature.) The compact called for the election of a "Tribunal of Notables," or governing body, with equitable representation from each station. Historian Stanley F. Horn has described the document as "a sort of regional counterpart of the Constitution of the United States . . . a bill of rights . . . [and] incidentally, a business contract between Richard Henderson & Company and that company's prospective tenants and land-buyers." James Robertson was elected leader of the first government.

There was one other item of business to be taken care of at that meeting on the bluff. Ten years previously, when Henderson had been a judge in Orange County, North Carolina, the clerk of his court was Francis Nash, Abner's

Graphic detail marks artist Jirayr H. Zorthian's conception of the Battle of the Bluff, painted on a wall in the governor's reception room at the Tennessee State Capitol.

brother. Francis had gone on to become a general in the Continental Army and had died a hero's death on a Pennsylvania battlefield. It would be fitting to honor him, Henderson said, by naming the French Lick settlement Nashborough. Without objection, it was done.

After setting up a land office and assuring the settlers that a much-needed shipment of corn was on its way to them from Kentucky, Henderson left Robertson and Donelson and the others to secure a place for themselves in their remote frontier settlement which the Cumberland Compact aptly described as "in its infancy, unknown to government, and not included within any county within North Carolina, the state to which it belongs . . . ." Ironically, they could look to North Carolina for nothing except a nod of recognition, and even that was not immediately forthcoming.

What *was* immediately forthcoming was trouble. Most of the Cumberland stations were south of the river, on land not included by the Cherokees in their cession at Sycamore Shoals. Other tribes in the region—principally the Chickasaws and Creeks—had never relinquished their claim to any of the Cumberland lands. And to all of the tribes, the Cumberland valley was hunting ground, not settling ground; they had accepted without much hostility the presence of the Long Hunters, but now the sight of women and children, of cabins and palisades, meant permanence, and the Indians fought against that with vengeance.

In September, a group of men harvesting John Donelson's corn crop at Clover Bottom, upriver and east of Nashborough, was fired upon and forced to flee, and several were killed. Soon after, Donelson moved his family to Kentucky. All through the fall, ambushes took a steady toll. In January of 1781, after numerous deaths and departures, only four stations remained occupied—Mansker's and Eaton's north of the

An unknown artist created this steel engraving of an Indian attack on a Cumberland valley station. The engraving first appeared in Amos Kendall's Life of General A. Jackson *in 1843.*

river, and Nashborough and Freeland's on the south—and in that month there was a seige at Freeland's, and two more men were killed. In April, at the Nashborough fort, eleven settlers died in what would be remembered as the Battle of the Bluff. A year after the signing of the Cumberland Compact, only about one-fourth of the settler population remained; more than fifty had been killed, and the rest had left for safer quarters in Kentucky and Illinois.

James Robertson went back to North Carolina that summer, hoping to put before the legislature a petition asking that the Cumberland settlers be allowed to keep their land. (Some of the land was already being granted to soldiers in the Revolution, in lieu of pay.) Robertson waited for several weeks, but the war was so much of a preoccupation that the legislature was unable to meet. He came home empty-handed in January

1782, not knowing whether he would find anyone still alive at Nashborough.

T HE STALWARTS were still here, but they were mostly confined to the Nashborough station, a one-acre fort tucked among the cedars atop the bluff. (On today's map, its exact location can be pinpointed between Church Street and the Woodland Street Bridge, on the river side of First Avenue North.) In the lonely months to follow, the remnant of settlers would find their crops destroyed, their cattle killed, their food and gunpowder nearly depleted. Under the influence of British and Spanish forces—and with motivations of their own—the Indians kept up a relentless pressure to drive the pioneers out. The wonder is that they could not succeed. By one estimate, there

29

were 10,000 warriors within 200 miles of Nashborough; even one-tenth that number would have been ten times as many men as the settlers had in the leanest of their early years here.

And if the Indians did not offer opposition enough, there was always the North Carolina legislature. It did receive Robertson's petition in 1782, but referred it to committee. At that same session, the lawmakers formally dismissed Henderson's Cumberland claim, threw open the territory to speculation by issuing a flood of transferrable land certificates, and—almost as an afterthought—offered each man over twenty-one who had settled here before June 1, 1780, a chance to buy what he had been able to hold. Only a small minority of the whites who had first come to the Cumberland were still around to say what they had claimed, and to pay the state's price for it.

The following year, after the moribund Nashborough governing body was revived and an influx of speculators and new settlers from the East had begun, North Carolina decided to turn Middle Tennessee into a county, the better to keep account of who was getting the land. The Revolutionary War had ended, and the British had lost their claim to the Tennessee territory. Virginia's claim had been dismissed with the fixing of the Kentucky-Tennessee line (although Patrick Henry, William Byrd, and George Rogers Clark would keep trying to get some of it back). North Carolina had ended Richard Henderson's claim. That left North Carolina itself, the Spanish, the Chickasaws and Cherokees—and last of all, the Cumberland settlers—to vie for a permanent hold on the ancient valley of the Mound Builders and the Shawnees.

For all its neglect by the state, Nashborough under James Robertson never broke its ties to North Carolina. When Davidson County was created in October of 1783 (being named for William Davidson, another North Carolina general, killed in battle in 1781), the settlers cheered it as proof that the state did have concern for the area. They left it to Robertson, later to be their representative in the legislature, to gain assurances that the concern would result in clear titles to the land they had fought and bled for.

And once again, Robertson came through for them. In 1784, his petition in behalf of the Cumberland settlers became a bill "for the Relief of Sundry Inhabitants of Davidson County," and it was passed into law. It provided for each of the original white settlers or their heirs a grant of 640 acres of free land.

Robertson was the Cumberland settlement's Everyman; not without reason has he been called "the father of Tennessee." For someone so seemingly indispensable, he has been given less visibility and stature in history than he deserves. Perhaps the reason is that he was not a flamboyant man, not learned, not given to seek credit. But he was a supremely talented, effective, and indefatigable leader—and it seems safe to say that had there not been a James Robertson, there would not be a Nashville, and perhaps not even a Tennessee.

Even when he was of a different mind than his comrades, Robertson had the grace to make the best of it. In June 1783, he opposed the convening of a conference with the Chickasaws on the Cumberland—perhaps because Virginians and not North Carolinians were behind it—but when the settlers voted in favor of the parley, he offered a place on his Richland Creek land in present-day West Nashville as the gathering site. John Donelson, back from Kentucky as one of the Virginia negotiators, took part in the talks; Piomingo, known and respected as the so-called Mountain Leader of the Chickasaws, may also have been present; Robertson was there, but only as an observer for North Carolina and as the

Piomingo, the Chickasaw leader, is thought to have given this beaded bag to James Robertson's wife Charlotte at the Richland Creek parley of Chickasaws and white settlers in 1783.

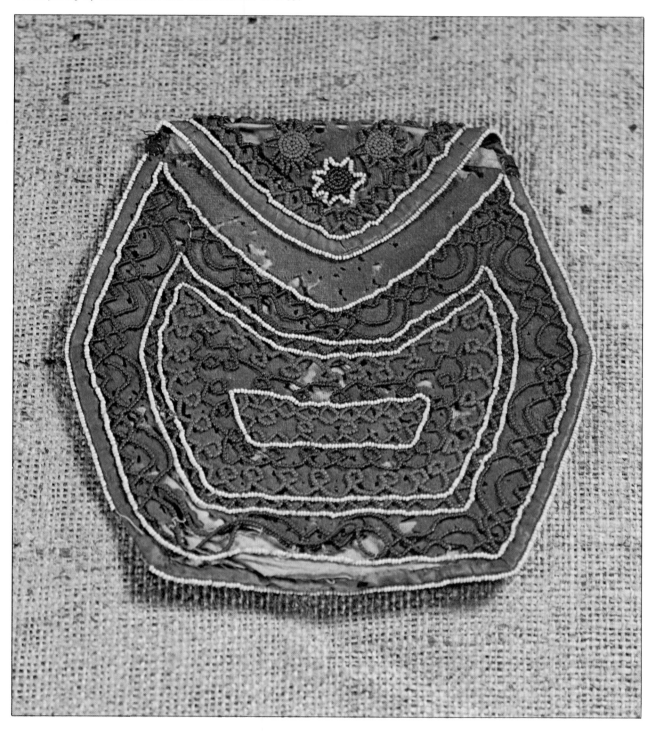

silent host. Nothing of substance was resolved, and Donelson and his colleagues finally left to pursue their land interests elsewhere, but Piomingo and Robertson were to meet many times again, and the bond of mutual appreciation that grew between them resulted in a permanent peace between the Cumberland settlers and the Chickasaws.

Davidson County at its founding in 1783 was the first official government on the Cumberland, and it took in all of Middle Tennessee—more than 10,000 square miles, one-fourth of the present state. Its governing body, the county court, was made up of eight justices appointed by the North Carolina legislature. (Robertson was one of them, but six of the eight were men who had not lived here previously.) The following year, the legislature made formal what the settlers had already done: It gave an official name to the rising village on the bluff. The name would not be Nashborough, though; that smacked of England, and England no longer ruled. Rather, the name would be Nashville, as the French allies of the new United States might say it. Timothy Demonbreun, by then not only a trader on the Cumberland but also Virginia's chief official in the Illinois territory, must have liked that; within two years, he would resign his post across the Mississippi and move to Nashville to live for the rest of his life.

Nashville was laid off in 200 one-acre lots along the bluff above the river, with four acres reserved for a public square on which a courthouse and other structures could be built. Another 200 acres around the salt lick and spring were set aside as a public area for the use of all. Thomas Molloy, a local surveyor, drew the lines, and thus the embryo of Nashville was formed. The first merchant, Lardner Clark, arrived, and soon there was a grain mill, and a whiskey still. Daniel Williams, one of the first settlers, became the first sheriff. A doctor came,

(These have been represented as the words of Piomingo, the Mountain Leader, and other Chickasaw leaders, spoken at a parley with Cumberland settlers held on Richland Creek in November 1783; related in a letter from James Robertson to a North Carolina government official, and published in the State Records of North Carolina, 1784.)

I came here formerly with my King, and have nearly the same talk now as I had then; the talks he gave, for he is since dead, still live in mine and my people's remembrance—the sun shines clear on us all, the children may walk about and not be afraid . . . . I have heard that a settlement is to be made in the bend, & that the Cherokees have given up the Land on Tennessee to the White People, which surprises me, as it is mine and my children's land from which we get our living . . . . I give these Beads as a token of peace & hope they will be accepted.

•

. . . I would not have my Brothers the Americans think their former talks lost . . . . Though we have lost our King I would have the Americans think us as much their friends as before; tho' we were not brought up together yet we are friends and Brothers and though there has been bad talks and War between us I hope it will never be so again. I would have the white people go & kill Buffalo, and we will do the like and not interrupt one another.

•

You came here and thought no harm, and I come now to see you and talk with you. The land on this River we do not call ours and you are settled on it, and are welcome to it. But the land from which we get our living on Tennessee we never gave to you nor no body else, tho' we hear the Cherokees have. I have heard a talk from the Spaniards, advising us to kill you; but do not be afraid of it for they are our old enemies:—we never had anything from, nor never will join them.

I told the Spaniards you were both white people alike, and if they had any quarrel with you to fight their own Battles.

Nashville was still Nashborough and Davidson County belonged to North Carolina when the original county seal, designed by an unknown artist, was made in 1783.

**AN ACT
FOR ESTABLISHING A TOWN ON
CUMBERLAND RIVER
AT A PLACE CALLED THE BLUFF,
NEAR THE FRENCH LICK**

I. Be it Enacted by the General Assembly of the State of North Carolina, and it is hereby Enacted by the authority of the same, That the directors or trustees herein after appointed, or a majority of them, shall so soon as may be after the passing of this Act cause two hundred acres of land, situate on the south side of Cumberland river at a place called the Bluff, adjacent to the French Lick, in which the said Lick shall not be included, to be laid off in lots of one acre each, with convenient streets, lanes, and alleys, reserving four acres for the purpose of erecting public buildings, on which land so laid off according to the directions of this Act, is hereby constituted, erected and established a town, and shall be called and known by the name of Nash-Ville, in memory of the patriotic and brave General Nash.

from Chapter XLVII,
LAWS OF NORTH CAROLINA, 1784

─────── ❧ ───────

Dr. James White was, I think, the first physician who settled in Nashville, in 1784. He came from North Carolina . . . . He had studied, Divinity, Law, and Medicine, and was a man of very distinguished general literature. He possessed a very high order of talents. He excelled in conversational powers on grave or humorous subjects; perhaps no man told a story better, or could, for a great length of time, enchant, by his conversation, a company of friends.

He had a great many eccentricities. He would take occasional sprees of drinking, and sometimes, while in one, he would dress up in buckskin and march through the streets with a gourd of whisky under his arm, and almost compel every person he met with to drink with him. In one of these freaks he met with Maj. Wm. T. Lewis, (a very genteel, respectable gentleman, and wealthy,) whom he asked to take a drink with him. Lewis refused to drink out of his gourd, and White knocked him down, calling him a damned aristocratic rascal. But when not in this state, his manners were so gentlemanly and so kind, that no one would continue offended with him. When he was in his sprees, his originality and humor made him the admiration of the vulgar; when sober, of the learned and talented.

He was the first delegate sent to Congress [from the Tennessee territory], and his active exertions, while there, for the benefit of his constituents, gave him increased popularity on his return. On his way to Congress he went through North Carolina, and met with a young girl whom he determined to take with him. He dressed her in boys' apparel, mounted her on a horse with his portmanteau behind her, and passed her for his body servant. Before they reached Nashville [on the return from Washington], she became unable to proceed, and was delivered of a son.

from a memoir of Dr. Felix Robertson published in the *Nashville Journal of Medicine and Surgery* in 1874

─────── ❧ ───────

and then another. With all the competing interests in pursuit of land, title disputes were inevitable, and that meant lawyers, and a court to settle civil and criminal suits. Yet another treaty with the Cherokees was negotiated, this one for claim to certain land south of the Cumberland. The first school, Davidson Academy, was chartered and endowed with 240 acres of land south of the town, and the Reverend Thomas B. Craighead, a Presbyterian minister and educator, was invited from North Carolina to preside over it. By the end of 1785, Nashville was gradually losing its rude and rustic frontier trappings and taking on the appearance of a back-country village.

HARD TIMES were not over, though, far from it; another decade of skirmishes with Indians, disputes with land speculators, and changes in the ownership and governance of Tennessee lay ahead.

North Carolina in 1786 found it necessary to draft a 200-man militia—its officers elected by the legislature—and march them to Davidson County as a protective force against continued Indian attacks. No less a personage than John Donelson, then contemplating a return to the Cumberland, was waylaid and murdered on the trail from Kentucky, and ambushes of that sort were not uncommon. Davidson was still not a populous region—it had only 372 adult white males on its tax list in 1787 and surely less than 1,000 people all told—and they were widely scattered and vulnerable to assault. The town of Nashville, seat of government though it was, attracted relatively few residents; it had only a handful of houses and cabins at that time, and probably no more than twenty-five families. Whatever the dangers, people chose to live out on the land, for land was the principal source of

The Cumberland River . . . after a course of about five hundred miles, discharges its water into the Ohio . . . . After passing a day at its mouth, we commence ascending the stream with the aid of eight oarsmen, but found the current much stronger than we expected, and thus we passed *fifteen days,* laboring harder than galley-slaves, before arriving at Nashville (Nash's Station) which is two hundred and eleven miles from the mouth of the Cumberland . . . .

Nashville is a recently founded place, and contains only two houses which in true, merit that name;—the rest are only huts that formerly served as a sort of fortification against Indian attacks.

It is only about five years since the country began to develope; and in the civilized portion of the Union, there are at present but few who know even its name.

During the War with the British, the inhabitants of this remote station suffered greatly from the inroads of the Indians, and were almost exterminated, when the peace of 1783 released them at once from their dreadful sufferings and horrid anxieties.

The people resemble those whom I have already spoken of in Kentucky; but their reputation for some time past, has been rather worse than that of their northern neighbors. It is said, however, that since they have come under the laws of North Carolina, their deportment has improved. Some distinguished official personages whose duty required their attendance at this post, have in some degree polished these rough dwellers of the wilderness, who, in their lonely and distant fastness, had in truth begun to live very much like the Indians. Nevertheless, I am sorry to learn that magistrates are occasionally found here with their ears cut off!

from a journal written by Lewis Brantz, a German merchant in Baltimore, after he visited Nashville in 1785

Campbell Co., Va., 4th September, 1785

Dear Johny,

I have the happiness to inform you that I am in health at present, with the most sanguine hopes that by the first opportunity I shall be made happy by hearing of the health, happiness, etc., of yourself and our dearest connections.

I entreat you to take particular care so to provide that no waste may be made in my corn at Cumberland. A plentiful stock of provisions is the main chance. Give every assurance to your dear mamma that I shall use every endeavor for her happiness, and for every branch of the family.

Your mamma's ease and happiness in every comfort of life, your and your brothers' and sisters' well-being and happiness, and more, if I could say more, is the constant petition and most ardent desire of

your most affectionate father,
JOHN DONELSON

(What is thought to be the last letter John Donelson wrote was addressed to his son John in Kentucky; soon after, the elder Donelson was killed while riding alone on the trail in south-central Kentucky.)

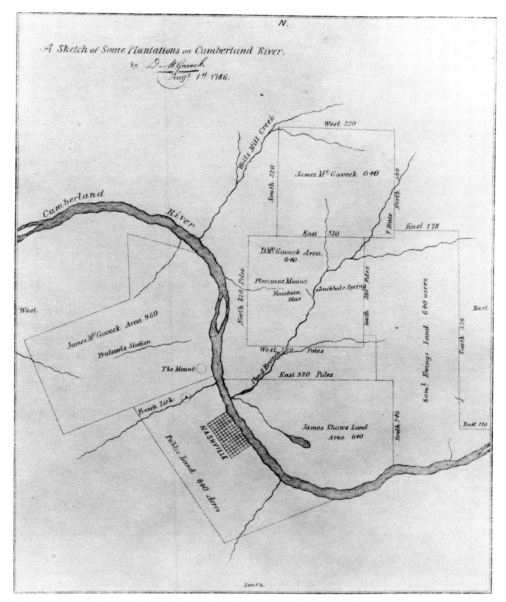

When he drew this map in 1786, David McGavock and his father claimed 2,240 acres of prime Cumberland land, including much of what is now North Nashville, East Nashville, and Madison.

wealth, and it was certain to become ever more valuable.

How many people died seeking to claim a share of that wealth, it is impossible to say, but the toll was heavy. Of the nine men in the advance party to the Cumberland in 1779, only James Robertson and Edward Swanson were still alive a decade later; George Freeland, William Neely, Zachariah White, William Overall, Robertson's brother Mark, and the slave, his name unrecorded, had all been killed by Indians by 1787, and James Hanley had simply disappeared. Another of Robertson's brothers and

two of his sons were also killed, and Robertson himself was twice wounded. Many died without ever gaining title to a piece of ground, or recognition for their part in making settlement possible. At considerably less risk were the ones who came later; they may not have been as diverse or as self-sufficient or as courageous a group as their predecessors, but they had more political power, more influence, and more money to begin with—and they got the land.

David McGavock is a good example. A civil engineer and land surveyor, son of a prominent Virginia magistrate, McGavock emigrated with

Daniel Dunham's cabin beside the Natchez Trace was built in the 1780s and rebuilt after Indians burned it in 1792. It was the first structure on what later became Belle Meade Plantation, and it stands there now.

When he built this log house late in the eighteenth century, pioneer settler Frederick Stump was already past seventy. He married a second time twenty years later, and finally died in 1822 at age ninety-nine. The house may be the oldest still occupied in Davidson County.

38

Hand-hewn of red cedar, the logs in Frederick Stump's house on White's Creek have withstood the wear of almost 200 winters.

his brother to Nashville in 1786. Before the year was out, they had bought for themselves and their father more than 2,000 acres which today make up a large portion of North and East Nashville and the Madison area. The McGavocks remained to become strong and influential figures in the building of Nashville.

Rapid change continued. A road was opened from East Tennessee in 1788, and the first wheeled vehicles followed it to Davidson County. That same year, a part of Davidson on the northeast became Sumner County, and two years later a sizable tract on the northwest became Tennessee County (later Robertson and Montgomery). For a while, the three jurisdictions would be known as the Mero District, in honor of the Spanish commandant of New Orleans—a hint, perhaps, that national loyalty was not yet a settled matter. By 1790, North Carolina was nearly bankrupt and growing weary of trying to control the swelling ranks of settlers and speculators in its territory beyond the mountains; after much hesitancy, the state finally decided to cede all of what is now Tennessee to the United States.

The principal effect of that change in Nashville and Davidson County was to accelerate further the rapid growth that had started with the opening of the road from East Tennessee. By 1791, the Mero District had 7,000 residents—half of them in Davidson County—and Nashville was showing a few signs of growth outside its forted structures.

Tennessee was then known as the Territory of the United States South of the River Ohio (more commonly, the Southwest Territory). President George Washington had commissioned William Blount as its governor and James Robertson as brigadier general of the Mero District militia. (Robertson wore many hats, as he always had; in addition to his military role, he was also Blount's agent to the Chickasaws and manager

In 1832—the year of his death—seventy-three-year-old John Buchanan was portrayed by John C. Grimes. Forty years earlier, his station had withstood the last major siege by Indians in Davidson County.

of the governor's own extensive land interests.) In effect, the territory was very much like a province of the United States, a colony in the continental interior. Shortly, it would move to attain statehood.

Before that happened, though, there would be one final desperate and bloody clash with Indians. It took place on September 30, 1792, at Buchanan's Station east of Nashville, where Elm Hill Pike now crosses Mill Creek.

John Buchanan, a strong, thick-set Scotsman, had come early to the Cumberland. He was twenty years old when he, his mother and father, and his two brothers crossed the frozen river with the first party of settlers in 1779. The Buchanan men were the principal builders of the first station at French Lick, and they fought to defend it at the Battle of the Bluff. By 1786, John Buchanan's father and both of his brothers had been killed.

Buchanan was one of seventeen militiamen at his station on Mill Creek on the night when it was stormed by several hundred warriors, most of them Creeks and Chickamaugas. The story of that all-night battle has survived in several versions, but this much is consistent: The fort was held, without the loss of a single defender. Sally Ridley Buchanan, John's wife, a tall, big-boned woman who weighed more than 250 pounds, is remembered as a heroine of that long night. It was she who kept watch over the women and children, some of them hysterical with fright, and it was she who kept the men supplied with powder and bullets, even as she drank from a bottle of whiskey to keep her nerves steady.

Handmade in 1781, this schoolbook of young John Buchanan's is the oldest surviving symbol of education—and book publishing—in Nashville.

The surveys of Daniel Smith were the basis
for most of the early maps of Tennessee,
including this one, published in 1795. Smith
was one of the first settlers in what is now
Sumner County. Smith and Richard
Henderson were in the party of surveyors
that fixed the boundary between Kentucky
and Tennessee, a line that shows on this map
as straighter than it turned out to be.

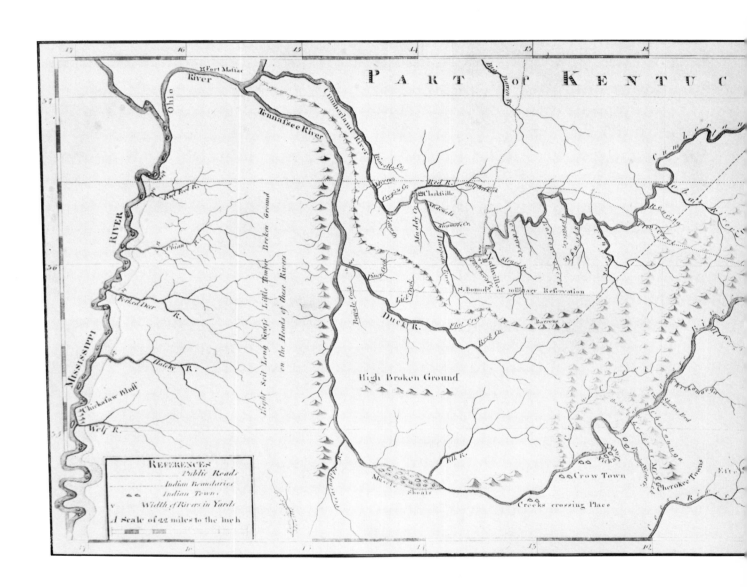

42

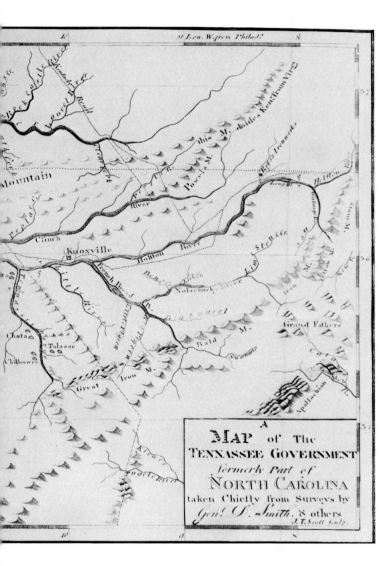

That was to be the last great Indian battle in Middle Tennessee. In 1795, a treaty with Spain—chief supplier of weapons to the Indians—signaled the end of warfare in this region of the frontier. The Mississippi was soon opened to Tennessee traders, barges and keelboats began to reach the Cumberland settlements, and the growth that had been steady since 1788 became a swift, swelling tide. When Tennessee was admitted to the Union in 1796, Davidson County had 3,600 people; in the census of 1800, it had 9,600, even though Wilson and Williamson counties had been carved from it in the interim. The growth was still in the countryside, not in town—Nashville in 1800 had fewer than 400 residents—but the little village on the Cumberland was firmly in place, and its day was coming.

John Overton looked out these Travellers' Rest windows at two winters before the nineteenth century began. The convex mirror between the windows dates to the Federal period.

FOR THE FIRST twenty years of its life, Nashville had been nothing more than a string of small forts scattered along the river and its tributaries. The people who came to build those shelters and live in them were, in the main, neither the sons and daughters of the colonial aristocracy nor the landless and illiterate poor; rather, they were the eighteenth-century equivalent of today's middle-class and working-class population. They were farmers, craftsmen, soldiers, surveyors; they aspired to be merchants, lawyers, politicians, landowners. Many of them loved books and music. They loved to talk, and their language was direct, specific, clear, and unadorned. Perhaps because violence and death were so constantly near them, they were an emotional people, often laughing, crying, cursing, shouting. Some of them sought solace in the religion of the frontier, delivered to them sporadically by circuit-riding evangelists who were the harbingers of the Great Awakening. Many of them found some release from the harshness of their lives in the distilled spirits they began making as soon as corn was plentiful enough. (In 1795, thirty-nine men and one woman were licensed in Davidson County to make whiskey; among the largest producers were Frederick Stump, John Buchanan, and the schoolmaster, Reverend Craighead.)

In those first two decades, local government—the notables, the justices, the magistrates, the militia—constituted the only visible and continuing institution; everything else, even religion and education, was home-centered, for the fort and the cabin were the only sanctuaries. For settlers and speculators alike, land was the one consuming preoccupation—it, and the security to tame it unmolested. In the main, the practical, resourceful men and women who struggled and often died to seize and hold the land would not be the ones who eventually turned it into a center of commerce and culture.

The transition from pioneer colony to established town did not happen overnight; it came with traffic on the road and the river, with the defeat of the Indians, with statehood. Nonetheless, it happened quickly, and when the new century dawned and the little village on the bluff was twenty years old, there was already an abundance of signs that the wilderness frontier had been pushed farther west toward the Mississippi.

By 1800, Nashville had a post office, a newspaper, several stores and taverns, and a

May 9, 1797

. . . The whites first planted sweet corn in the Cumberland Valley in 1779; but the influx of settlers took place later. Nevertheless there are some who have been here fifteen or sixteen years. Only since the last peace with the Indians, which is to say since two or three years ago, has emigration toward this region increased significantly. One of the considerable drawbacks to the Cumberland Valley is a lack of salt . . . . all salt is imported from Kentucky in wagons, and sells for four dollars a bushel, and everyone complains that there is none to be had . . . .

In Nashville we lodged at Captain Maxwell's. We would have been comfortable enough there if court had not been in session; as it was, the house was full, and even sleeping on the floor there was hardly room. We spent two full days there to rest our horses and bring our diaries up to date, which was not easy among such a mob. We bought a horse to spell our others. (He was a good one, as in general all horses are in this area, and dirt cheap.)

(LOUIS-PHILIPPE, DUKE OF ORLEANS, *later to be King of France, spent four nights in Nashville, sharing one bed in the crowded town with his two younger brothers and a manservant. His journal,* Diary of My Travels in America, *was first published in France in 1976.*

sizable hostelry, the Nashville Inn, opened in
1796 by William T. Lewis. The Davidson
Academy, located at Reverend Craighead's
Spring Hill meeting house on the road to Sumner
County, was about to erect a building on its land
just south of the Nashville boundary. The
Methodists had a church on the Public Square (a
temporary meeting place, as it turned out), and
they later built the town's first stone structure.
Visitors to the community, coming in ever-
increasing numbers, were surprised to find here
and there a touch of luxury in the muddy
streets—a coach or two, some carriages, even
some men wearing silk stockings and brass-
buckle shoes.

It would be another decade before the town
had its first bookshop (John Inston's, founded in
1811), but books and papers could always be
bought in the printers' shops, and literacy was
widespread—as high, perhaps, as it has ever
been. Inventories of personal belongings from
the period included a great many books—
volumes of law and history, Bibles and hymnals,
collected works of Shakespeare and John Locke
and Thomas Paine, practical books on cooking
and doctoring and measuring land. The
academy served a relative handful of young people (charging "five pounds hard money . . . for
each scholar per annum"), but most people apparently felt that reading and ciphering were im-

47

portant and necessary skills, and children customarily used goose-quill pens and pokeberry ink to practice their letters and numbers at home.

Keelboats and flatboats took cotton and tobacco and a variety of goods downriver to New Orleans (the boatmen returning overland via the Natchez Trace), and some boats were being poled up the Cumberland, bringing supplies from as far away as Pittsburgh. Governor John Sevier presided over Tennessee's fortunes at the capital in far-away Knoxville, but Nashville had representation in Congress (George W. Campbell and William Dickson were to serve there on and off for several terms), and at home it had a rising class of wealthy and influential citizens, as well as a growing number of skilled craftsmen, merchants, and professional people.

The community also had some white farmers who were dependent upon large landowners for work and lodging—and it had, from the beginning, slavery.

Black slaves had come to the Cumberland with Robertson and Donelson, and their number was steadily increased. They constituted one of every five residents of Davidson County in 1791, one of every four in 1795, one of every three in 1800; for a long time thereafter, they made up forty percent of the population. Accounts of their lives as chattel are difficult to find. What does show up in the record are some revealing insights on the conflict slavery caused in some people's thoughts and actions, and some interesting profiles from the small community of free blacks.

There is, for example, the newspaper advertisement placed by Goodrum Marshall in 1805, offering a fifty-dollar reward for his stolen or runaway slave, Booker Griffen, "fair complected with roman nosed, thin visage," who

Winter sunlight and an open fire warm the living room of the Hayes-Kiser house in Antioch. Built about 1796, it may be the oldest brick house in Davidson County. According to legend, the girl in the portrait was dead when it was painted; her parents had her body exhumed so they could have a picture to remember her by.

WOMANS HARD FATE.
By a Lady.

How wretched is poor woman's fate,
No happy change her fortune knows;
   Subject to man in every state;
How can she then be free from woe?

   In youth, a father's stern command,
And jealous eyes controul her will;
   A lordly brother watchful stands,
To keep her closer captive still.

   The tyrant husband next appears,
With awful and contracted brow;
   No more a lover's form he wears:
Her slave's become her sov'reign now.

If from this fatal bondage free,
And not by marriage chains confin'd:
   If, blest with single life, she see
A parent fond, a brother kind.

   Yet love usurps her tender breast,
And paints a Phoenix to her eyes:
   Some darling youth disturbs her rest,
And painful signs in secret rise.

   Oh cruel power's since you've design'd,
That Man, vain Man, should bear the sway,
   To slavish chains add slavish mind,
That I may thus your will obey.

Tennessee Gazette,
September 16, 1801

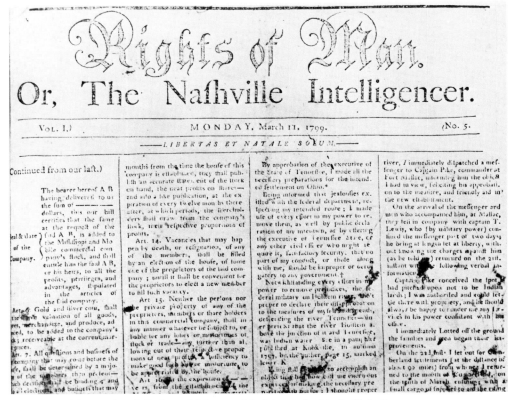

Though its life was brief, Rights of Man *could claim to be Nashville's first newspaper, beginning publication early in 1799.*

FROM THE MINUTES OF THE MERO DISTRICT
[MIDDLE TENNESSEE] SUPERIOR COURT,
1801

Henry Beeler, late of the county of Davidson, labourer, who stands convicted of Horse Stealing, was again led to the Bar in custody of the Sheriff of Davidson county—and thereupon it being demanded of him if anything for himself he had or knew to say, why the Court here to judgment and execution of and upon the premises should not proceed, he said, he had nothing, but what he had before said—therefore it is considered by that the Court, that he be hanged by the neck until he is dead, and that execution of this judgment be made and done upon him the said Henry Beeler by the sheriff of Davidson county, on Tuesday the twenty ninty day of December next, between the hours of twelve in the forenoon and three in the afternoon of the same day, at the public gallows of the county of Davidson—and that the said Henry Beeler be remanded to jail.

Joel Childress, who stands convicted of Manslaughter, was again led to the Bar in custody of the Sheriff of Davidson county; and thereupon it is demanded of the said Joel Childress if he hath or knoweth anything to say, wherefore the Court here ought not upon the premises and verdict aforesaid to proceed to judgment and execution against him; and the said Joel Childress prayeth the benefit of Clergy, which is alowed him in this behalf—Whereupon all and singular the premises being seen it is considered by the Court here, that the said Joel Childress be burned in his left hand with the letter M, and that the Sheriff of Davidson county put the Judgment in execution immediately, and he is immediately burned in the left hand with the letter M.

THE NEGROES COMPLAINT.

Published at the request of a number of Subscribers.

Forc'd from home & all its pleasures,
   Afric's coast I left forlorn,
To increase a stranger's treasures,
   O'er the raging billows borne.

Men from England bot' & sold me,
   Paid my price in paltry gold—
But tho' their's they have enroll'd me,
   Minds are never to be sold.

Still in thot' as free as ever,
   What are Englands rights I ask,
Me from my delights to sever,
   Me to torture, me to task?

Fleecy locks and black complexion
   Cannot forfeit nature's claim—
Skins may differ, but affection
   Dwell in white and black the same.

•

Is there, as you sometimes tell us,
   Is there one who reigns on high?
Has he bid you buy and sell us,
   Speaking from his throne, the sky?

Ask him if your knotted scourges,
   Fetters, blood extorting screws,
Are the means which duty urges
   Agents of his will to use?

Hark! he answers! wild tornadoes,
   Strewing yonder sea with recks,
Wasting towns, plantations, meadows
   Is the voice wherewith he speaks.

He, forseeing what vexations
   Afric's sons would undergo,
Fix'd their tyrant's habitations
   Where the whirlwinds answer 'no!'

•

Deem our nation brutes no longer,
   Till some reason you shall find
Worthier of regard, and stronger
   Than the colour of our kind.

Slaves of Gold! whose sordid dealings,
   Tarnish all your boasted powers,
Prove that you have human feelings,
   Ere you proudly question our's.

Tennessee Gazette,
October 7, 1801

"took with him my wife Sally Marshall . . . ."

In wills and other court documents, there are some instances of slaves being freed by their owners. Thomas Molloy, the surveyor who laid out Nashville, provided in his will in 1802 for the emancipation of a girl, Sophia, for her "Great Attention and faithfull Services," and he left two-thirds of his property to three prominent Nashville men to be used for her "benefit comfort and Education." Sophia was not only Molloy's slave; she was also his daughter.

Free blacks in Davidson County, of whom there were never more than one or two hundred before 1820, show up frequently in the record, and their presence served to accentuate the contradictions of slavery. There was Philip Thomas, a barber, who also ran a livery stable and advertised his hackney coach for hire. When his daughter was married, several of Nashville's leading white citizens attended the wedding and danced with the bride. Another black man, known only as Caesar, was for several years a tavern-keeper near the public square.

And there was also "Black Bob" Renfroe, perhaps the best-remembered of all. His popular tavern on the square, praised by its patrons as "never a disorderly house," is known to have been in continuous operation for at least a dozen years before and after the turn of the century. Renfroe had come west on the Donelson flotilla, perhaps as a slave; he fought in the defense of Renfroe's Station on the Red River in 1780.

Free blacks at the beginning of the nineteenth century had voting and property rights under the Tennessee Constitution, and there were no laws prohibiting their education. Those restrictions would come later, when whites decided that freedom for blacks—any blacks—was too much in conflict with their maintenance and defense of slavery.

Nashville and Davidson County were not much concerned with conflict of any sort in the first two decades of the new century, however. Instead, progress was the keynote, and there was plenty of that. The community's leaders were driven by a common aspiration to make money and to be recognized favorably in the East. In 1806, Davidson Academy was reincorporated as Davidson College, and in 1809, when Thomas Craighead was replaced by James Priestly as president, the name of the school was changed again, to Cumberland College. It was a long way from being a stable and effective institution of higher learning, but its continued presence was a fair indication of the ambitious hopes of its leaders.

Nashville was also incorporated as a town in 1806, electing six aldermen and a mayor, Joseph Coleman, who held the office for three years. Over the next decade, his successors in office included Benjamin Bradford, editor of the *Tennessee Gazette*; Joseph Elliston, a silversmith; and Felix Robertson, a physician and a son of Charlotte and James Robertson, having been born at Freeland's Station in January of 1781, just before its siege. He was the first white child born in the settlement.

Four years before Felix Robertson was elected mayor in 1818, his father died at the Chickasaw Bluffs (later the site of Memphis), where with Charlotte he had lived for several years as the government's agent to the Chickasaws.

In Felix Robertson's recollections written some forty years later, he recorded that his seventy-four-year-old father had died "after ten days of painful disease ending in mortification of the face and throat . . . . He suffered with the greatest patience and died perfectly composed,

Benjamin J. Bradford remained in the newspaper business in Nashville from 1800, when he began The Tennessee Gazette, *until he died in 1814. Typical of advertisements in his paper was this notice of a traveling wax museum:*

WAX FIGURES

Dabenport & Street

Respectfully acquaint the ladies and gentlemen of Nashville, that they have opened in Mr. C.A. Parker's ball room, a NEW and ELEGANT collection of WAX FIGURES, as large as life, among which are the following characters:

1ST, A striking representation of the Late Unfortunate DUEL, between **Col Burr**, Vice-President of the U. States, and Gen. **Alexander Hamilton**.

2D, a striking likeness of the late **Gen. Washington**.

3D, His Excellency **Thomas Jefferson**, President of the U. States.

4TH, the Honorable **John Adams**, late President

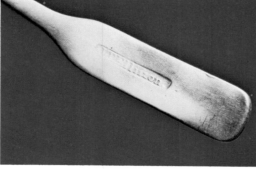

Silversmith Joseph Elliston, an early mayor of Nashville, was in middle age when Washington Cooper painted this portrait of him. A few of Elliston's signed silver pieces have survived.

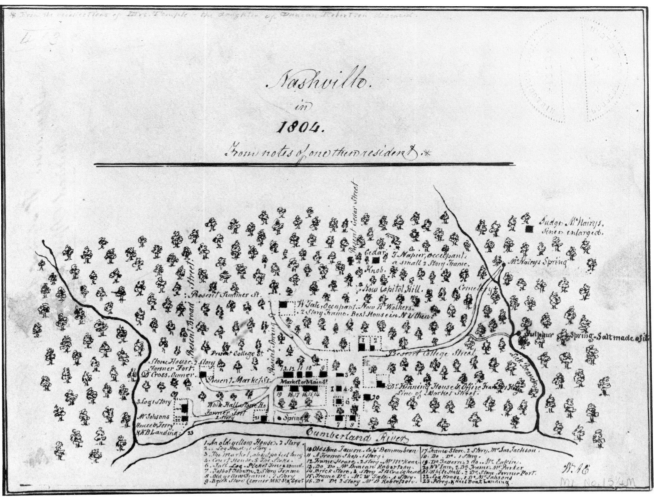

William A. Eichbaum, Irish-born of German parents and a Nashville resident for fifty years beginning in the 1820s, drew this map in 1857 to show what Nashville looked like when it was still a frontier village.

his wife the only relation present." James Robertson was buried there among the Chickasaws, unsung by the Nashville beneficiaries of his courage and leadership; his remains were reinterred at the City Cemetery in Nashville in 1825.

With Robertson's death, the first chapter of Nashville's history was almost finished. A few of the old guard remained—John Rains, Edward Swanson, Timothy Demonbreun, and of course Charlotte Robertson—but the days of privation and danger in the primeval forest were fast receding from memory. More and more, people looked to the future, for the past was full of pain, and the future was full of hope.

. . . in the morning, people came from all directions, telling the same story of their houses being badly shook. While discussing the matter, father set out on the table some brandy and water, and asked his frightened neighbors to drink . . . . Every key shook in its lock. Then it shook the water and brandy on the table. No one tasted them. While the gathered neighbors stood by the door in the yard, afraid to go in the house, a distant heavy murmur, like low-down thunder, was heard. All eyes turned to the south-west. The house began shaking. The boughs of a tree in the garden shook, while the air was still. Water in vessels ran over. Some said the end of the world was nigh; others, that it was a sign of war with England. The meetings, directly after, were well attended. Some went who never had gone before. By day and night men sought God . . . .

(In his autobiography, the Reverend Joseph Tarkington recalled the effect in Middle Tennessee of the 1811 earthquake that formed Reelfoot Lake; Tarkington, a native of Nashville, was the novelist Booth Tarkington's grandfather.)

Rebecah Foster of Nashville sewed her name and a date—October 5, 1808—in this earliest known Tennessee quilt. The seventeen stars above the eagle represent the first states of the Union, through Ohio. The names of the states are sewn in the lengths of the oval chain (below).

RECONCILIATION AGREEMENT

Conditions of reconciliation, Between Mr. George M. Deaderick, and his lady Mrs. Mary Deaderick, Viz.

Mrs. Mary Deaderick, do solemnly agree and promise: that she will live a chaste and upright life, and that in no instance will she deviate from Virtue prudence and discretion She further promises to be a dutifull and obedient wife to George M Deaderick—and that she will not invite to the house of him the said George M Deaderick, any person or persons whatever, without first knowing, whether such invitation will be agreeable to him the said George—and lastly doth agree and promise, that she will not resort, or visit any assemblies private dance or entertainment, without first obtaining his approbation and consent—and the said George M. Deaderick on his part, do most solemnly promise and agree, that his conduct towards his lady Mrs. Mary Deaderick, shall be Strictly, and uniformly upright—and further does engage, that he will not debar her from privileges that are proper for a Virtuous, prudent and obedient wife to possess and enjoy. to all of which things we promise and agree—and have hereunto set our hands in the presence of our Mutual friend.

GEORGE M DEADERICK
MARY DEADERICK

Test:
ANDREW JACKSON
JOHN MARR

(GEORGE DEADERICK, *Nashville's first banker, wrote to his friend and counselor that his wife was "fetter'd to the will of her Father and relative mother," that "they advocate the going to private dances, in and out of Town, Assemblys, Inviting Gentlemen & Ladies to my house all without my knowledge or consent," and that he and his wife had separated. Their "mutual friend" brought about this reconciliation in the spring of 1807.)*

THE PEOPLE'S MINDS were on culture and agriculture, on commerce and banking (the Bank of Nashville was chartered in 1807), on government (the Tennessee legislature met in the town for four years, beginning in 1812), on the comings and goings of the celebrated and notorious Aaron Burr, former Vice President of the United States, who visited Nashville several times on much-discussed missions of intrigue.

The people's minds were on the War of 1812, and on the election of James Monroe to the Presidency in 1816. Their minds were on growth: Undaunted by the Panic of 1819—the first national depression to be felt west of the mountains—Davidson County was about to record in the decennial census a population of more than 20,000 (including more than 3,000 in Nashville), and that was more than twice the total in 1800, even though large areas of the county on the southeast and the southwest had been carved off since then to form new counties. (Only one other jurisdictional subdivision would be made—to form part of Cheatham County in 1856—before Davidson County would reach its present shape and size of 533 square miles.)

The people's minds were on the founding of Nashville Female Academy in 1816, on the lively competition among three weekly newspapers, on the beginning of a theater, an agricultural society, and an antiquarian society. Their minds were on schools for instruction in fencing and dancing and the French language, and on the arrival of a noted portrait artist, Ralph E.W. Earl, to live in Davidson County.

And their minds were on horse racing. At the Nashville Turf and at Clover Bottom—where John Donelson had set out his first crop of corn—high-bred racing horses ran for supremacy, and high stakes were bet on them. Two celebrated races between Truxton and Ploughboy, champions worthy of any competition, caused large sums of money to change hands, grown men to engage in fist fights, and two notable gentlemen to fight a duel to the death.

The people's minds were on President Monroe's visit to Nashville in 1819, and on the honor and prestige his visit brought to the bustling, thriving village in the West, just a few decades removed from the primitive stillness of the wilderness.

Their minds were on the flush times Nashville and Davidson County were enjoying then, and vaguely on what they must have assumed would be even greater times in the future.

In the March 13, 1819, edition of the *Nashville Whig and Tennessee Advertiser*, a brief and inconspicuous notice of that impending future appeared. The article announced the arrival, two days earlier, of a steamboat from New Orleans, "having run from that place to Harpeth Island (20 miles below this place) in 21 days, 6 hours. She remained there for several days waiting the rise of the water and had nearly unloaded when the river on Wednesday night took a rise."

When the steamboat reached Nashville, the paper reported, "a sight so novel at this place . . . attracted large crowds of spectators." It had come around the bend past Eaton's Station, long since only a faded memory, and steamed on past the bluff to its berth at the foot of Broad Street, Captain Smith at the wheel—tugging, no doubt, on the boat's whistle. Just a stone's throw downriver, James Robertson and his companions had walked across on the ice forty years before.

The arrival of that first steamboat marked the end of frontier isolation for Nashville and ushered in a new age. As surely as railroads and airplanes would later transform the town again and shrink the distance between it and the rest of America, the steamboat did that, though few

The goods and services of a thriving community are found advertised in this 1815 edition of The Clarion & Tennessee State Gazette, *a Nashville newspaper.*

. . . Friday we came away late to Nashville, stopping on our way to speak to the widow Bowen, the daughter of my ancient friend, the late General Russell; this lady hath three daughters who profess religion; surely we have not prayed in vain. We found the river high on Saturday; Mr. Hobbs, the jailer, kindly took us in; but we are not prisoners, but of hope—but of the Lord.

Sabbath 31. I preached in the new, neat brick house, thirty-four feet square, with galleries. Twelve years ago I preached in the old stone house, taken down since to make a site for the state [court] house. The latter house exceeds the former in glory, and stands exactly where our house of worship should by right have stood; but we bear all things patiently . . . .

from the journal
of BISHOP FRANCIS ASBURY, 1812

could have realized it at the time. They did know, however, that the man for whom the steamboat from New Orleans was named—a local citizen, one of their own—was already famous the country over, and celebrated in Europe as well. It may have been the boat's name, as much as anything else, that drew spectators to the Nashville dock for the arrival, on its maiden voyage up the Cumberland, of the *General Jackson*.

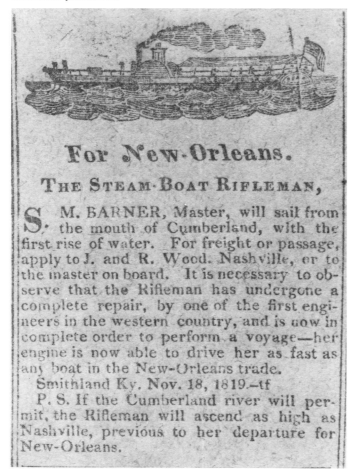

The Rifleman, *unable to cross the Harpeth Shoals, invited passengers to board at the mouth of the Cumberland for this early trip to New Orleans.*

December 18. Nashville, like everything else, sounds louder at a distance than when it draws near. At a distance of a mile from the town you see a board with a hand painted on it as large as life, and the fore finger pointing, with the following inscription in large letters underneath—"Look and see the Town!" Upon looking down the road you see the town sure enough. It has a beautiful appearance when viewed from this point. As you approach it you are so much engrossed by its lofty looks, from which it is so difficult to avert your eyes, that you would be apt to plunge into the narrow Cumberland which flows between you and "the Town." We, however, did not happen to do so; but preferred a boat which met us in good time.

Nashville is built on a high bluff, and the houses look very much like tumbling on your head as you cross the river in a small boat at what is called the middle ferry. The citizens have, with much labor and expense, cut a passage through this bluff large enough for carriages to pass and repass . . . . I was much disappointed in the size of this far famed Cumberland river. Although the large barges on it seem to indicate that there is much water, yet it is narrow and steals softly along, its blue smooth waters making not the least noise.

. . . . I am afraid my brave Tennesseans indulge too great a fondness for Whiskey. When I was in Virginia it was too much whiskey—in Ohio, too much whiskey—in Tennessee, it is too, too much whiskey! . . .

Nashville is principally built of bricks and is very handsome, and does much business. In size it is nearly as large as Lexington . . . . The citizens of Nashville in their dress and manners exhibit much taste and opulence . . . .

I am sorry I am obliged to leave Nashville so soon; were it not for this I might write again from this place.

(ANN ROYALL, *later to become noted as a Washington journalist and author, "the first woman journalist of America," visited Nashville in 1817—with "three slaves as attendants, two men and a maid, in addition to a courier"—and wrote about her brief stay in one of her books,* Letters from Alabama.)

A Spirit of Reform

Sam B. Smith

The swift ascendance of Andrew Jackson to the pinnacle of public renown in the early years of the nineteenth century had an important if somewhat less spectacular parallel in the rise of Nashville, his adopted home, to a place of permanence and stability in the young nation.

In 1800, when Jackson was a frontier lawyer of great promise but limited recognition, Nashville was just twenty years removed from its beginning as a rude settlement in the wilderness. By 1828, when Old Hickory was elected as the seventh President of the United States, his little village on the Cumberland had become a thriving town noted for its charm and hospitality.

The spirit of Jacksonian Democracy that spread across the land during his years as the nation's chief executive was full of promising implications for an expanded franchise, for public careers open increasingly to talent, and for a growing pattern of upward social mobility. Along with it, there developed a kindred spirit of reform that reached beyond politics into the realms of economics, religion, and the general welfare. With its conscience pricked by intellectual ferment and religious exhortation, the United States between 1820 and 1860 manifested a rising concern for underprivileged citizens and victims of misfortune. It was Jackson's effort to democratize the political process, as much as anything else, that helped to stimulate this concern. The people of Nashville and Tennessee, in moving with the rest of the nation to address unmet social needs, thus joined in the reform movement that their own favorite son had done so much to initiate.

A new state penitentiary was built in Nashville in 1830 and expanded in 1857 to bring about much-needed improvements in the housing of prison inmates. In the late 1840s, a state hospital for the mentally ill was constructed near the city as a direct result of the prodding of Dorothea L. Dix, the New England philanthropist whose crusading efforts helped to rescue the nation from its medieval conception of insanity.

A public school system was launched in Nashville in 1852 after Alfred Hume, an eminent teacher, studied school systems in northeastern cities and helped to devise a local plan of educational development. By the end of the decade, one high school and several grammar schools had been established in the city.

Interest in education for the blind was stirred by an exhibit at a downtown church of a blind person's ability to read raised letters through the sense of touch. From this example the community was aroused to make subscriptions for the creation of a special school to serve sightless persons.

The American Lyceum movement contributed directly to the beginning of adult education in Nashville. A group of professional men led by Wilkins Tannehill and Gerard Troost started the movement by sponsoring public lectures on subjects ranging from literature and American history to geology, architecture, and "the philosophy of the human mind." A direct consequence of their efforts was a community library, and by 1832 it had 830 volumes. In those years, the Nashville bookstore of W.T. Berry stocked a wide variety of finely printed and bound volumes from as far away as London and Edinburgh.

Public health reform came slowly to Nashville, and cholera remained a dread disease. But Dr. Felix Robertson, the first president of the city's board of health, introduced quinine to the community in 1827 for the treatment of malaria. Robertson, a wise and distinguished physician for more than a half-century, kept a poster in his office which read, "Never use medicine except when absolutely necessary."

The care and protection of orphaned children was another area in which local initiative produced favorable results. Women active in local churches sponsored the Protestant Orphan Asylum, which was built in 1845 at the corner of McLemore (now Ninth Avenue) and Church streets, and over the years it sheltered more than five hundred children. Catholic laymen established St. Mary's Orphanage in 1863.

Two reform movements that developed elsewhere in the country during the mid-1800s—anti-slavery and temperance—did not find fertile ground in Nashville. Temperance was preached fervently by some ministers, but abolitionism had few adherents, and it would remain for later generations to face the consequences of these unresolved social problems.

From 1820 onward, Nashville grew steadily as a religious community. By 1860, the city had sixteen Protestant churches, a Catholic diocese, and a small but active Jewish community. Religious publishing was by then a major local enterprise, with presses of the Methodist and Baptist churches in the forefront.

The men who provided spiritual leadership in those formative years laid the foundation for Nashville's continued development as a religious center. A representative early leader was Robert B.C. Howell, pastor of the First Baptist Church. When he arrived in Nashville in 1835, he found at least ten separate Baptist groups, all refusing to take communion together. He remarked after a few weeks that "Baptists in Tennessee have been ever since the state was settled, the victims of religious demogogues." Slowly but deftly, Howell led most of the Baptists of the area into a unified and progressive church during the quarter-century of his work. He regularized the ministry and instruction of the church, built support for home and foreign missions, and helped to establish Sunday schools, a state Baptist convention, and an educated ministry.

By mid-century, Nashville was maturing into a city of broad cultural opportunities and interests. Its architecture was distinguished by the work of William Strickland and Adolphus Heiman. The botanical gardens of the Nashville Horticultural Society featured greenhouses, shrubs, fruit trees, evergreens, and flower-lined walkways. Gaslit streets added a touch of romance to the city, and there were splendid steamboats to ride, many of them with lavishly adorned cabins and public rooms where guests might dine, drink, gamble, and dance to their hearts' content. In the vicinity of present-day Eighth Avenue and Demonbreun Street, Nashvillians flocked to the Vauxhall Garden, a splendid structure modeled after its famous London predecessor of the same name. The building contained a large assembly hall, a circular railway, winding promenades, and many features for the recreation and amusement of guests. There the multitudes attended conventions, heard great orators, and generally enjoyed the "green groves, and wilderness of lamps which dimmed the stars."

For some time the city had had theaters, but when the beautiful and ornate Adelphi Theater opened in 1850, it attracted national and international musical and dramatic talent. In 1851 the great Swedish soprano Jenny Lind sang there, and in 1854 an Italian opera company gave Nashville its first taste of grand opera. Five years later, Edwin Booth's portrayal of Hamlet captivated the city.

By 1860, the University of Nashville had a respected medical school, a reorganized liberal arts department, and a new law school. The city's public school system was firmly in place, and several commercial schools and schools for young ladies were operating successfully. In substantial measure, Nashville shared in the economic well-being of the nation as it grew, developed, and prospered. Railroads entered the city from four directions, and a hundred steamboats called regularly at the Broad Street wharf. Turnpikes radiated from Nashville to Kentucky, to Gallatin and Charlotte, to Franklin and Murfreesboro. Telegraph wires brought news from the nation and the world.

In just forty years, Nashville had been converted from a frontier town to a thriving city. The spirit of progress and reform that Andrew Jackson had helped to create had brought great benefit to his home community. But in spite of its gains, Nashville still faced serious problems, and some of those problems would soon be brought into sharp focus. For Nashville and the nation, 1860 was the eve of tragedy.

Sam B. Smith has served as the Tennessee State Librarian and Archivist, as chairman of the Tennessee Historical Commission, as a professor of history in the University of Tennessee system, as the editor and compiler of Tennessee History: A Bibliography, *and as the editor of* The Papers of Andrew Jackson.

62

Nashville:
Jackson's Town
1820-1860

ANDREW JACKSON'S figure looms so large in the early nineteenth-century history of Nashville—not to say the history of the United States—that the story of his life completely dominates the chronicle of his adopted town in that time. He had ridden west from North Carolina in 1788, a tall, slender, twenty-one-year-old lawyer with blazing blue eyes and a thick crop of reddish hair, and from the day he arrived in Davidson County until he died here fifty-seven years later, he was a singular presence, a man too forceful and commanding to be denied, much less ignored.

If overcoming adversity is a mark of character, Jackson had met and exceeded the measure before he was old enough to shave. A few days before he was born in the Waxhaw settlement on the border of North and South Carolina in March 1767, his Scotch-Irish father died suddenly. He lost both of his brothers in the Revolutionary War. By the time he was fourteen, he had been wounded and captured in the war himself, suffered from smallpox in a Tory prison, and learned of the death of his mother from cholera after she had nursed wounded Continental Army soldiers on a prison ship in Charleston harbor. Passed among relatives for the remainder of the war, young Jackson bore the scars of his childhood openly. Even when he

was a small boy, he had been regarded disdainfully as a wild, reckless, foul-mouthed bully with a trigger-quick temper and a fondness for bare-knuckle brawling; as a military veteran in his early teens, he showed few signs of having been tamed. He was exceedingly bright, but his schooling had been brief and fragmented, and he was more inclined to apply his intelligence to gambling, horse racing and cockfighting than to other more widely encouraged pursuits of the mind.

When he was sixteen, he mustered enough interest and self-discipline to try his hand at teaching school, and a year or so later, stirred by the discovery of his ability to use words, he moved to Salisbury, North Carolina, to begin tutored preparation for a career in law. He was by then brimming with cocky self-assurance and obsessed with an ambition to make for himself a life of wealth and comfort. All the same, he still found time for rambunctious drinking sprees and randy escapades in the taverns of Salisbury; with fellow law student John McNairy and others, he made an impression in the town that lingered long after he was gone.

McNairy was a man with intimate ties in North Carolina politics, and he subsequently was elected by the North Carolina legislature to be judge of the Superior Court in the state's

64

Between wars and political campaigns, the master of the Hermitage enjoyed looking after his land and horses. This painting of Jackson wearing a planter's hat was done by resident artist Ralph E. W. Earl.

His reputation as a duelist and gunman having been indelibly established when he killed Charles Dickinson in 1806, Andrew Jackson would be remembered for his pistols long after he had put them aside. During a restoration of the Hermitage in 1968, this Kentucky-type flintlock pistol, an 1812-era weapon with maple stock and thirty-caliber octagon barrel, was discovered hidden in the attic. The initials A. J. are stamped in the metal underneath the barrel.

western district. In 1788, Jackson persuaded the new judge to hire him as his public prosecutor, and in the company of a few young lawyers of their acquaintance, the two men set out for the Cumberland. They stopped first in Jonesboro, staying long enough for several court appearances and for the volatile Jackson to engage in a pistol duel with another attorney. (Fortunately for both duelists, neither man was hurt.) Then, in October, Jackson and McNairy rode on to Nashville on the newly opened road across the mountains.

The Cumberland settlements were almost nine years old by then, and their permanence was all but assured. Jackson and McNairy represented a new wave of westward migrants intent on converting land to wealth and power, and unlike the ones who had come before them, they had political influence, a knowledge of the law, and a relatively safe field in which to maneuver. For McNairy, those assets would bring modest wealth and a quiet career on the bench; for Jackson, they would lead to national and world prominence.

Jackson lost no time in establishing himself. By chance, he found lodging at the home of John Donelson's widow—she having returned to Nashville since the death of her husband—and the Donelson family's social connections were soon turned to his advantage. Jackson fared well in the legal realm, too, first as public prosecutor and then as attorney general for the Mero District under Governor William Blount. Those

As a young attorney in Nashville beginning in 1788, Andrew Jackson established himself in the inner circle of political and social prominence before he was thirty years old. This engraving by an unknown artist is from that period.

positions, together with his active private practice, allowed him within a few years to accumulate substantial land holdings.

Another young lawyer and boarder at the widow Donelson's was John Overton, and the two men became fast friends. Overton's support and counsel would serve Jackson invaluably for thirty-five years. And there was someone else in Mrs. Donelson's home who would be of paramount importance to Andrew Jackson for the rest of his life: Rachel Donelson Robards, the widow's daughter. As a thirteen-year-old girl she had come to Nashville in the Cumberland flotilla with her parents; now she was a vivacious, dark-eyed, raven-haired woman and—for the moment—the wife of Lewis Robards of Kentucky. Her marriage was already on shaky ground when Jackson arrived, and his presence did nothing to shore it up. In 1791, after Robards and Rachel had separated and she had gone to stay with friends in Natchez, word circulated that he had divorced her. Jackson soon went to join her in Mississippi, and when they returned to Nashville, they announced that they were married. Two years later, it became known that Robards had only recently obtained the divorce. That news prompted Andrew and Rachel, with Overton's urging, to have a civil wedding ceremony performed in Nashville.

The complications of the marriage notwithstanding, Jackson found—as he apparently had anticipated—that his formal entry into one of Nashville's most prominent families solidified his social and political position in the community. He became a trustee of Davidson Academy; he represented Davidson County (with James Robertson, John McNairy, and two others) at the convention called to draft Tennessee's first constitution; he was the new state's first member of Congress, serving in the House of Representatives in 1796; and the following year he was elected by the Tennessee legislature to a seat in the United States Senate.

All the while, often in partnership with John Overton, he was acquiring property throughout the state, and like every canny land speculator, he had a knack for buying low and selling high. One especially fertile and appealing tract of about 500 acres located on the Cumberland twelve miles east of Nashville became his home plantation, Hermitage. He bought it for a little more than five dollars an acre.

But some of his financial transactions turned sour on him in the mid-1790s, and Jackson found himself strapped with heavy debts for several years. His preoccupation with personal financial problems may have been a factor in his decision to take a leave of absence from the Senate a few months after his election and then to resign his seat altogether. In any event, by the spring of 1798 he was back home in Tennessee, and soon thereafter he had secured an appointment to the state's Superior Court, a post which paid him a respectable salary, kept him well-connected politically, and left him time to look after his land and business interests.

In six years on the bench, while he looked the part of a wise and dignified judge in his flowing black gown, Jackson compiled a record that was adequate but undistinguished; one man described his opinions as "short, untechnical, unlearned, sometimes ungrammatical, and generally right." If his demeanor was satisfactory in court, however, it was at times injudicious elsewhere: He still had a penchant for finding trouble in his personal relationships. He quarreled with his old friend John McNairy and with the immensely popular Governor John Sevier. Jackson was a tempestuous man, blunt and abrasive, easily offended; he was a tangle of contradictions, by turns crude and charming, cold and compassionate, defiant and fiercely

66

When he was past sixty and his friend Andrew Jackson had gone to the White House, John Overton sat for this portrait by an unknown artist. Overton died in 1833. Jackson never had a closer or more supportive friend.

loyal. He was not a man to leave others indifferent to his personality; people seemed either to love him or to hate him.

One who hated him was Sevier, and the feeling was mutual. Jackson outmaneuvered him to win the office of major-general of the Tennessee militia in 1802; Sevier retaliated by getting the legislature to split the prestigious post into eastern and western commands; Sevier accused Jackson of "taking a trip to Natchez with another man's wife"; Jackson called Sevier "a base coward and poltroon" and challenged him to a duel. The wild and riotous affair degenerated into a show of swords and pistols that ended miraculously without injury to either party, and Jackson came away from it more feared than ever as a man not to be trifled with.

His notoriety had just begun. In 1804, he resigned his judgeship, built a two-story log house on the Hermitage land, and turned his attention to such interests as horse breeding, storekeeping, cotton production, whiskey-making, and trading in land and slaves. In 1805, he entertained Aaron Burr at the Hermitage, and some of his enemies suspected him of conspiring with Burr to plan a military invasion of Spanish-held Louisiana. And in 1806, after a quarrel over a horse race bet, he fought a sensational duel with Charles Dickinson, a renowned marksman. Jackson walked away from it with a bullet forever lodged near his heart. Dickinson was less fortunate; he was left bleeding to death on the ground.

For the next six years, Jackson's star seemed in eclipse as he kept himself occupied with personal matters of property and family. He had in Rachel not only a wife of long-suffering devotion but an excellent manager as well, and she helped him to increase the worth and productivity of their land. Though they were childless themselves, the Jacksons raised several of the children of their nieces and nephews; one boy,

Andrew Jackson Donelson, remained close to the elder Jackson throughout his life, and another, christened Andrew Jackson Jr., was legally adopted. As he passed the age of forty, the mature Mr. Jackson caused some to wonder if his impulsive combativeness might perhaps be softening a bit. That must have been wishful thinking; he was in fact as keenly ambitious as ever and as much feared—by his enemies, his subordinates, his slaves, even at times by his friends and family. He may have been temporarily out of the center of battle, but all he lacked was a cause to fire his passions anew.

George Catlin, noted for his portraits of American Indians, was also interested in Andrew Jackson. It is not certain when or where he executed this painting of the General. Nashville financier Rogers Caldwell acquired the portrait at a New York auction in the 1920s.

68

AN OLD SOLDIER'S ADVICE TO GENERAL JACKSON

Nashville Febary 1st 1806

Sir

    if I have wandred in aney maner from the true line of Frindship, will you pass it over as an Errore of one who wishes you well from the bottom of my hart . . . . this with other Reasons Compels me to drop you these incorect scrrals, hoping you will Reflect on there Contents, and not suffer pation to git the upper hand of your good Sence . . . . will you pardon me my frend when I tell you that I have bin longer in the world than you have and ought to have heard the opinions of people more that you have. and do heare the fals honer of dueling Redeculed by most of thinking persons and I assure you that your frends do think a man of your standing ought to say littel about dueling . . . . if your bravery was in the smallest manner doubted I should not have gon to such lenth once for all let me tell you that you will have more than ten to one which will applad your prudance in avoyeding a duel . . . . I readely agree that in former days I might have suffered my pation to have over Ruled prudance and in haste have taken the life of my fellow mortal, but . . . I have of late vewed Duelling with abhorance. Sir I feare I have all Ready truspased on your patiance and conclude with my best wishes for your heth and sucsess while

        I am your most Humb. Sevt
        JAS. ROBERTSON

THE CAUSE WOULD BE WAR. When Congress declared war against Great Britain in the spring of 1812, Andrew Jackson could claim virtually no experience as a military leader. He was still a major-general of the Tennessee militia, but that post was more political and social than military; he had not directed men in any major battles or even spent much time in uniform.

Nevertheless, he stepped forward to seize prominence as a soldier, and looking back on his exploits, it seems almost as if the War of 1812 was made for him—and he for that war. The reckless bluster of his youth had given way to a controlled rage, a tightly disciplined view of men—of life—as objects to be prevailed against and systematically conquered. Jackson was intensely, reverently patriotic; he believed in sacrificial service for the good of his country, as he saw that good, and he had the magnetism, the energy, and the aggressiveness to inspire other men to follow him. There would be twentieth-century soldiers (George Patton and Douglas MacArthur come quickly to mind) who would find instruction and inspiration in Jackson more than a century after his sword had been sheathed.

His brief and brilliant military career has been told and retold so often that it would seem redundant to describe it here. It should be sufficient to say that between 1813 and 1818 he waged unrelenting war against the British and their allies, the Creek Indians and the Spanish, throughout a vast triangular region stretching from north Alabama to New Orleans to the Florida peninsula. The men he enlisted and exhorted to follow him into battle—Tennessee volunteers, Louisiana free blacks, Mississippi Choctaw Indians, and others—admired him extravagantly, when they were not in total fear of him. He was tough, one of them said, as tough

Head quarters Fort Strother
Decbr 29th 1813 ½ past 11 oclock at night

My love
 . . . before I lie down . . . I take up my pen to Say to you that I am well, my arm mending I hope I will be able to wear my coat Sleeve on it Soon. I have been much pestered and vexed with the Shamefull retrograde of the Volunteers and mounted gunmen . . . . fireside Patriots will Sink the reputation of our State—and I weep for its fall—and with it the reputation of the once brave and patriotic Volunteers . . . to keep whom from open acts of mutiny I have been compelled to point my cannon against, with a lighted match to destroy them . . . . There abandonment of the Service may destroy the campaign and leave our frontier again exposed to the Tomhawk of the ruthless Savage . . . .
 Please write me how my little andrew is and whether, his little Indian Lyncoya was taken to him by Major Whyte of Gallatine. if he had got him how & what he thinks of him. Keep Lyncoya in the house. he is a Savage but one that fortune has thrown in my hands . . . . I therefore want him well taken care of, he may have been given to me for some Valuable purpose—in fact when I reflect that he as to his relations is so much like myself I feel an unusual Sympathy for him. tell my dear little andrew to treat him well. and kiss andrew for me, and with love to all friends accept the blessing of your affectionate husband
      ANDREW JACKSON

(In this letter to his wife, General Jackson wrote of his recovery from a gunshot wound and the threatened mutiny of some of his soldiers. Lyncoya was an infant Jackson took from the arms of its dead mother in a Creek village his men had decimated. The child lived at the Hermitage until his death from tuberculosis at age seventeen.)

On his way to military glory at New
Orleans, General Jackson received
frequent letters of encouragement and
longing from Rachel:

Nashville, April 12, 1814.
**My Dear, once more you have been
Led from The feild of battle in safety and
one of the most Daingerous interprizes of
aney History Ever recorded murcifull God
how he has Smileed on us and Crownd
your patriotic Zeale with unequealed
successes with Glory and Honour for
yourself and Country. I received the News
with so much pleasur when I herd the first
Cannon oh never Can I desscribe but
when ther was nineteen or twenty I was
sure you wer safe . . . . remember I have
Clame on you That nothing but Death
will Desolve . . . . when you write againe
Saye to me when you think you will
Commence your returne march oh the
Dear Idea how it Springs through my
miend with joye and Hope . . . . farwell
my Dearest may we meete againe is the
prayer of your affectionate wife**

as hickory—and ever after, they regarded him reverently as "Old Hickory."

Even in the midst of war, Jackson seemed unable to avoid controversy and personal conflict. In Nashville in the spring of 1813, he served as a second for one of his officers, William Carroll, in a duel with another of his soldiers, Jesse Benton. In the exchange of shots, Carroll somehow managed to strike his opponent in the buttocks, and the embarrassment was such that Thomas Hart Benton, Jesse's brother and a colonel in Jackson's command, angrily blamed his general for the entire affair. Stung by the accusation, Jackson vowed to horsewhip Colonel Benton. A few days later, on the Public Square in Nashville, the two men met by chance. The en-

suing fight involved no less than seven men armed with guns, swords, knives, and sticks. Jackson was shot in the shoulder and almost bled to death. The speed and skill of several doctors (one of them being Boyd McNairy, brother of Judge John McNairy) saved his arm from amputation, but the bullet was left embedded in his flesh. The Bentons quickly left town for Missouri. (Thomas Hart Benton eventually was sent to the United States Senate from Missouri; he served with distinction in Washington—and there renewed his acquaintance with the gentleman from Tennessee.)

Before he had fully recovered from his gunshot wound, Jackson led his men into battle. They ruthlessly laid waste to the Creek Nation in Alabama, devastated a British invasion force at New Orleans in the most overwhelming victory ever won by an American fighting force, and drove the Seminole Indians into the swamps of Spanish-owned Florida. Along the way, Jackson was rewarded with the rank of major-general in the United States Army, and after the Battle of New Orleans he was swept up in a tidal

wave of national praise and hero worship. He had driven his men relentlessly, obsessed with a determination to end British and Indian resistance to white American continental dominion finally and for all time. The nation's citizens had never known a more devoted general or one more in tune with their collective will. They showered him with admiration, and the gaunt, gray General, his cheeks hollow, his hair by then almost completely white, received their praise with composed formality. As he had been ready for war, he was ready for the fruits of victory.

In a nation so dependent upon military strength for its survival, it was perhaps inevitable that the choicest fruit for a war hero would be high political office. Jackson had already been a congressman and a senator. There was only one other position he could aim for: the presidency. After he had resigned his military rank and served briefly as territorial governor of Florida at President James Monroe's request, a small circle of politicians and strategists assembled around him in Nashville. They had one objective in mind: to make Old Hickory the first Westerner to be elected President of the United States.

When he came back from New Orleans a hero, Andrew Jackson was given this ceremonial sword by the state of Tennessee in a ceremony on the steps of the First Presbyterian Church.

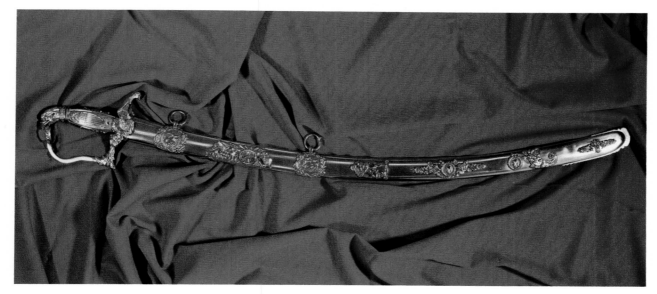

CONSIDERING HOW EXUBERANTLY the rest of the nation poured its praise on Jackson, Nashville seemed to adjust to his celebrity reasonably well. It was not that he was taken in stride—no one took Andrew Jackson in stride—but rather that he was simply better known in his home community, remembered as a lawyer and a planter as well as a soldier, and the aura of mystery that followed him elsewhere was not so thick and impenetrable here.

And besides, the ascending prominence of the General was not the only development of importance to the people of Davidson County. Even as Jackson, by the force of his own personality, was beginning to reshape the mood and character of the country, steamboats and commerce and refinements from the East were reshaping the character of Nashville.

In the early 1820s, Nashville was humming with movement and activity. Shops and stores, inns and taverns, banks and public buildings had sprung up along with houses on the town's streets, and new structures were constantly being built. There were schools of several kinds. The Presbyterians, Methodists, and Baptists had churches, and the first Catholic mass was celebrated in 1821 for sixty Irish laborers who had come from Pittsburgh to help build the first bridge across the Cumberland. There was a library, open "every day to shareholders, citizens and strangers," and oil-burning street lamps glowed in the night. The Nashville Medical Society was organized with seven physicians as members, including Boyd McNairy and Felix Robertson, who was the society's founder and president. (The two men had studied medicine together in Philadelphia and come home to extend the prominence of their family names into a second generation.)

There were other "old faces" in town, people whose names had then been known on the

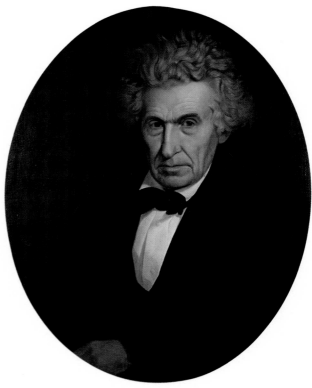

As familiar as he was to Nashvillians, Felix Robertson was sometimes mistaken on the street for Andrew Jackson. Washington Cooper painted this portrait of Robertson sometime in the 1840s.

Cumberland for three or four decades and would be carried on without interruption late into the next century—such names as Hayes, Harding, Cockrill, Gower, Thompson, Trimble, Watkins, Foster. And there were many new faces that would be long rememberd: Ralph E. W. Earl, a noted artist from the Northeast, who came to the Hermitage to paint Jackson's portrait and stayed to marry a niece of Rachel's and live out his life here; Washington Cooper, a Tennessean and a student of Earl's, who opened a studio in Nashville and earned a national reputation with his portraits; Wilkins Tannehill, a businessman and writer, who served twice as the town's mayor and was a national authority on the fraternal order of Masons; Henry M. Rutledge and his wife, Septima Sexta Middleton, both of whose fathers had signed the Declaration of Independence (her Latin name means Seventy-Six); John Shelby, a physician and businessman, who was to build three mansions east of the river and later to found a medical school.

Like a gray ball of lamb's wool, Washington Cooper's remarkable beard highlights this self-portrait by the artist, painted in 1885.

Overleaf: *Wreathed in an early morning fog, the* General Jackson, *first steamboat to call at Nashville's Broad Street wharf, slips upriver past the bluff. David Wright's 1979 painting recaptures the scene from the early 1820s.*

Nashville physician John Shelby left his name on a park and a street in East Nashville, where he lived and built three large homes for members of his family. He also founded Shelby Medical School. The portrait is by Washington Cooper.

The list steadily lengthened as the town spread out in all directions. The new bridge, opened at the northeast corner of the square in 1823 (the Victory Memorial Bridge is there now), was a big improvement over the slow and undependable ferries, and it speeded development in the broad bottomland across the river, an area that soon would be called Edgefield. The courthouse was twenty years old by then, and there were lawyers on almost every block. Nashville had about it a look of modest charm and comfort, of permanence—and it was thriving.

What made it so, more than anything else—including the presence of General Jackson—was the steamboat that bore his name (it was owned by his close friend and fellow soldier, William Carroll) and the others that followed it. Before they came, Nashville had operated in slow motion, its needed goods being poled upriver on barges and keelboats or packed over poor roads and trails by wagon. The steamboat stepped up the pace dramatically. It brought sugar and coffee, china and cutlery, plows and clothing and people—a stream of people—from New Orleans and Louisville and Pittsburgh; it carried back hides and cotton and tobacco to those markets, and soon it would carry iron products, for the heyday of the ore smelting furnaces on the Cumberland was at hand. When the *General Jackson* first reached Nashville, Knoxville was barred from the Mississippi by the Muscle Shoals and Memphis was nothing more than a muddy plain on the river bluffs, an expanse of wilderness that John Overton had bought from the Chickasaws, hoping to start a town there. The steamboat gave Nashville a head start in Tennessee and a fair start in the West.

There were shoals on the Cumberland, too—the Harpeth Shoals, thirty-eight miles below Nashville—and they took their toll in lives and cargo, but they were not as formidable as the Muscle Shoals. The river pilots learned how to negotiate them. They waited patiently for high water or impatiently hogged their boats across; one way or the other, they got through.

73

The introduction of steamboats upon the western waters constitutes an era in the history of Nashville, as it does in that of the whole valley of the West. As steam navigation presented new facilities for trade, the slumbering spirit of enterprise was awakened and Nashville sprang forward if not with great strides, yet with a sure and certain progress. The first steamboat that ever stemmed the Cumberland was the General Jackson, which arrived here in the spring of 1819. The spectacle was a novel one, and as may be supposed the bank of the river was thronged with men, women, and children to gaze at this wonder of the waters, this offspring of the genius of Fulton.

. . . . The arrival of the barge from New Orleans was almost as important an event to the citizens of Nashville as the arrival of a ship from England in the early days of British colonization on the Atlantic coast. We remember upon one occasion a barge made the trip in eighty-three days. This was so wonderful an event in the navigation of the [rivers] that the captain collected his friends on board and gave a "blow-out." He imagined he had done what could never be outdone and it was his pride and boast in those days. He lived, however, to see the triumph of steam by the agency of which New Orleans, instead of being a far distant place, is now regarded as a neighboring city . . . .

from an editorial by Wilkins Tannehill, editor, in the Nashville *Orthopolitan*, October 16, 1845

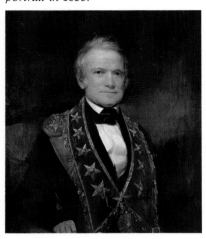

The grand master of the Tennessee Masonic order, Wilkins Tannehill, bedecked in the regalia of the society, sat for this Washington Cooper portrait in 1858.

As early as 1825, no less than nine steamboats called regularly at Nashville, and the commercial and social interchange they made possible lifted the town literally out of the backwater and into the mainstream.

The riverboat also lifted Andrew Jackson. Call it perfect timing or simply good fortune—whatever, it was one more development that came along just when he needed it. He might never have been President without the steamboat; certainly it gave him better access to people all over the country, and it was those people who put him in office. At the Hermitage, he had a boat landing at his back door. And, with a fitting touch of symbolism, it was a steamer that took Jackson from the Hermitage on the first leg of his journey to Washington and the White House in 1829.

Before that happened, though, much preparation was necessary. The Jacksons had moved out of their log house into a grander Hermitage, something more in keeping with an aspirant to national office. Carroll had been elected governor in 1821—the first of six two-year terms he would serve in that office—and with Overton, John H. Eaton, William B. Lewis, and Felix Grundy, he controlled the old Blount faction of Tennessee politics. That group also was the nucleus of Jackson's brain trust, the so-called Nashville Junto, and it induced the Tennessee legislature to nominate the General for the presidency in 1822 and then to elect him to the United States Senate the following year. (In those days, the legislature rather than the electorate performed such tasks.)

Thus, twenty-six years after he had first served briefly in the Senate, Jackson went back—again, briefly—and he spent much of his time there seeking support for his presidential candidacy. He patched up his old quarrel with Thomas Hart Benton, impressed others with his mastery of the political process, and went into the 1824 election with a good chance to win.

Victory eluded him by the narrowest of margins. He actually won a plurality of the popular vote—a margin of 40,000 over John Quincy Adams, the second-place finisher among four candidates—but since no one had a majority of electoral votes, the House of Representatives had to choose the winner (each state delegation casting a single ballot), and the House finally picked Adams by a vote of thirteen to eleven.

Jackson accepted the defeat stoically at first, but on his way back to Nashville, he was already calculating strategy for a return match four years hence. He resigned his Senate seat, reconvened his Junto, and began making alliances with some of his oldest political enemies. That was the beginning of party

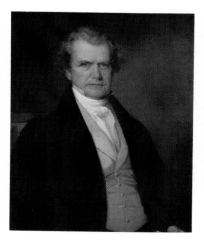

It was a great intellectual feast to hear Booth in Richard the Third, Forrest in Macbeth or King Lear, Miss Cushman in Lady Macbeth, or Jo. Jefferson in Rip Van Winkle, but to hear Felix Grundy in a closely contested case of homicide, when all his fires were burning, his passions aroused; to see his actions, the flash of his gray eyes, the vivid flashes of lightning bursting from his lips; at times to witness his scathing sarcasm, and then his sparkling wit: take it all in all, it was the grandest exhibition any Tennessean ever witnessed. He found himself carried away by a storm of eloquence that was irresistible. He felt that he was aroused by the same feeling and passion that moved the godlike advocate. I have heard Felix Grundy speak a hundred times. If he were alive I would go a thousand miles to hear him again. Under the influence of his magic eloquence, I have seen great assemblies tremble and shudder. I have seen the judge on the bench forget his position, loll out his tongue, and clap his hands for joy, and refined and enlightened galleries have wept and fainted in the excess of feeling.

I have heard most of the American orators, read the speeches of the ancients, as well as the great orators of France, England, and Ireland, and my opinion is that Felix Grundy was the greatest advocate the world has produced.

Grundy died in 1840. What a calamity that so much intellect perished with him, and that eloquent tongue is forever silenced, and will never again stir the American heart. America has produced two great orators, Patrick Henry and Felix Grundy. Their speeches were never written out like those of Cicero or Demosthenes. Their genius could not be chained down, or fairly represented by the copyist. It was a wasteful and ridiculous excess to attempt to report them.

J. C. GUILD, in
Old Times in Tennessee, 1878

Music publishing is an older industry in Nashville than most people realize. The oldest known imprint on the subject is a book appropriately named The Western Harmony.

"I have heard Felix Grundy speak a hundred times," an admiring contemporary said of him. "If he were alive, I would go a thousand miles to hear him again." This portrait is of Grundy in the 1830s. It was painted by Nashville artist Washington Cooper.

Nashville, August 14, 1823, Thursday

My Dear Father:
We have just returned from the Hermitage, General Jackson's residence in the country, 13 miles from town. We went out on Sunday evening and spent a few days there delightfully. The General called upon us in town on the evening of our arrival. He is one of the most hospitable men in the whole state. Mrs. Jackson is not a woman of cultivation, but has seen a great many people, has fine spirits, entertains well, and is benevolent. She is short in her person and is quite fat. The General is lean and has been in ill health, but is now envigorated and promises to live out his three score and ten. He has built him a good brick house in the last three years, and has finished it handsomely . . . . He is a prompt, practical man, with very correct moral feelings . . . .

Nashville is agreeably situated on the Cumberland River . . . . The hills about the town afford agreeable sites for houses, and many are well filled. Cumberland College is about prostrated for want of funds, but an attempt is being made to revive it. Two new buildings are going up, but there are neither teachers nor scholars . . . . Our best love to mother and all the families.

Your son,
Horace

*Luther Holley, Esq.
Salisbury, Connecticut*

politics in the United States, and the emerging coalition of Jacksonians would come to be known as the Democratic Party.

Three months after his painful loss in the House of Representatives, Jackson presided at a massive welcome in Nashville for the Marquis de Lafayette, the venerable French general who had been a hero of the American Revolution and was in 1825 making a triumphant return tour. Jackson was by then almost sixty years old, and Lafayette was ten years his senior. Together, the two old generals led a procession up Market Street to the Public Square, warmly receiving the ovations of the largest crowd ever assembled in the town. After Lafayette had stayed the night at the Boyd McNairy residence and attended a number of public fetes and receptions, he left by steamboat for Louisville. Jackson, rejuvenated by the cheers of the people and inspired by the old Frenchman's praise, stayed behind to resume his quest for the one remaining unmet goal of his life.

Nashville was a comfortable and secure base for a presidential aspirant, and particularly so for Jackson, who had grown with the town for nearly forty years. He must have been fond of the place, with its interesting blend of indigenous settlers and transplanted aristocrats, for he had a little of both in him, or liked to think he did. The languishing Cumberland College had a new president—Philip Lindsley, a Princeton graduate—and it was about to be renamed the University of Nashville and revitalized, and Jackson, as one of its trustees,

Gilbert du Motier, Marquis de Lafayette, was a dashing French general and a hero of the American Revolution in 1781. More than four decades later, when he was almost seventy years old, he made a nostalgic return tour of the United States, and was received everywhere with deep affection and emotion.

Nashville was no exception. When Lafayette's steamboat docked upriver from the Broad Street wharf on a May morning in 1825, a throng of cheering thousands awaited him, and Andrew Jackson was there to escort him by carriage over College Hill and up Market Street to an official welcome in the Public Square.

Revolutionary War veterans from all over Tennessee had gathered for the occasion, and fifteen young men were chosen as a guard of honor to wait on the aging Frenchman's every need. A long day and evening of events and ceremonies followed, the highlight of which was a gala dinner and ball for a select circle of guests who had received coveted invitations hand-lettered by artist Ralph Earl. Among the guests was Timothy Demonbreun, then nearly eighty years old; he was toasted at the dinner as "the patriarch of Tennessee," and his French and American pride knew no bounds.

The home of Nashville physician Boyd McNairy (above left) had been offered to Lafayette for his exclusive use during his brief stay. As the general slept there that night, a member of his guard of honor crept into his room and stole a gold watch from his traveling trunk. It was no ordinary timepiece: George Washington had given it to Lafayette at Yorktown in 1781 to commemorate the British surrender there.

The theft of the watch was never made public by the gracious general. In fact, more than forty years passed before it became known. In 1868, the watch turned up in a Memphis pawn shop and then at a public auction in Louisville. The man who bought it there turned it over to Senator Charles Sumner of Massachusetts in 1874, and it was soon sent to Paris and given to a member of Lafayette's family.

The recovery of the watch prompted a writer for the New York World to search for clues to its mysterious disappearance. In Memphis, he found the name of the woman who had pawned it and traced her to a small town in Mississippi. There, she told him that her grandfather had been a member of Lafayette's guard of honor in Nashville. He had died in 1847, when he was the rector of a Nashville Episcopal church, and had left to his son—the woman's father—a small estate that included his desk and library. The son was killed in the Civil War. His widow and daughter, left destitute, decided at length to sell the desk, but in it they found the gold watch, and in 1868, the daughter pawned it.

When the New York writer came to see her in 1874, the young woman still owned her grandfather's desk. The writer looked it over carefully. In the drawer in which the watch had been found, he discovered a false bottom, beneath which was a letter in the old rector's handwriting, dated at Nashville, December 18, 1846. It contained a full explanation of the mystery of the watch. One of the rector's companions in the guard of honor had come to him late in his life and confessed the theft. Remorsefully, the man had handed over the watch and asked that it be returned after

his death to the heirs of General Lafayette. The rector agreed and then wisely wrote down everything his friend had told him, "as a guide to my heirs," in the event that he should die before his guilt-striken friend.

The rector did die first, and the gold watch lay hidden in the drawer of his desk for twenty-one years until it was discovered and pawned. The confession remained a secret for six more years until it was found by the New York reporter. And the reporter himself left undisclosed the most intriguing information of all: the names of the principals in the forty-nine-year-old case of Lafayette's stolen watch. In his story in the New York World, he changed the names of the individuals he had written about, making it virtually impossible to trace them. Even the writer's name is a mystery since he did not sign his story.

There is no record of the names of the fifteen men who served in the guard of honor for General Lafayette in Nashville. There is, however, one more possible clue to the identity of the rector who heard the confession of his friend: In 1846, when the confession was heard and the letter was written, there was only one Episcopal congregation—Christ Church—in Nashville. According to the records of the church, its rector from 1836 until 1848 was the Reverend John Thomas Wheat. Reverend Wheat's son, C. Roberdeau Wheat, was an international soldier of fortune and a Confederate Army hero before he was killed in battle.

The engraved gold watch remained in the Lafayette family in France from 1874 until 1948, when it was passed on to an American relative, from whom it was inherited in 1963 by its present owner. The watch is now on loan to the Smithsonian Institution in Washington. ✍

One of the few paintings ever made of Rachel Jackson is this unsigned portrait of the President's wife. It was created sometime between 1820 and her death in 1828.

heartily approved. All the same, he still liked a good horse race or a cockfight, still had an instinctive feel for the barroom and the barracks. Those elements were also part of Nashville's makeup, and they, too, must have pleased the General, though he had little time for them.

He only had time for his obsession. As 1828 drew closer, Jackson virtually declared war on President Adams, and Adams fought back savagely. The campaign was vicious and mean-spirited, with both men and their supporters giving and receiving low blows.

Most wounded of all by the political meanness was Rachel. The complications concerning her first marriage were dragged out and twisted into tales of wanton immorality; she was ridiculed for smoking a pipe and for having grown fat; her religious piety was mocked. A younger Jackson no doubt would have responded with a sword or a pistol, but Old Hickory was beyond dueling; his only way to fight back effectively was with the ballots of the people.

More than four times as many Americans voted in 1828 as in 1824, and they turned Adams out of the White House and put Jackson in by a large margin. In Tennessee, the General got all but about 2,000 of the more than 46,000 votes cast.

The triumph gave him more pleasure than his

The death of Mrs. Jackson, consort of General Andrew Jackson, which we hastily announced in our paper of Tuesday, last, came upon our community like an electric shock. Arrangements had been made by the citizens of Nashville for a public dinner and ball on Tuesday, in honor of the General, and he was expected in town that morning, to receive the congratulations of his friends, & to partake with them a parting glass, preparatory to his departure for the seat of the national government. On Thursday preceding, Mrs. Jackson was attacked with severe pain in the arm, shoulder and side, and violent palpitation of the heart. Medical assistance, however, soon afforded her relief, and no serious result was apprehended. On Monday she again complained of pain, and a slight fever returned, but in the evening about 9 o'clock when the physician visited her, she appeared relieved, and was free from pain. No alarming symptoms appeared, nor was it then supposed that her indisposition would be so great as to interfere with the arrangements of the next day. In about half an hour, however, she sent for the physician, who was in an adjoining room, and before he could reach her, had fallen from her chair, and expired in less than two minutes. The immediate cause of this awful event is supposed to have been a sudden spasmodic affection of the heart.

The funeral took place on Wednesday and was attended by an immense crowd from Nashville and the surrounding country.

Most sincerely do we sympathize with our distinguished fellow citizen in the severe and trying affliction. A whole nation sympathizes with him. At the moment of his high elevation, he is suddenly depressed and cast down. His hopes are disappointed, his plans deranged . . . . This is indeed a great and sudden reverse, and affords a striking lesson of the uncertainty of human happiness, a forcible illustration of the mixture of alloy with the richest and purest of human enjoyments.

National Banner and Nashville Whig,
December 26, 1828

victory at New Orleans, but it lasted only a few weeks. On December 17, Rachel suffered a heart attack, and on the twenty-second a second seizure killed her. Jackson was unbelieving, then devastated. He buried her on Christmas Eve in the garden at the Hermitage and then retreated to the solitude of the big house to grieve for three weeks. Finally, in mid-January of 1829, he boarded a steamer and sailed downriver past Nashville, on his way to Washington. Near the town, he heard the sustained cheers of people bidding him farewell. The old man rose slowly, stepped out on the deck, and gravely bowed to the only sovereign he had ever publicly acknowledged: the people.

IN HIS EIGHT YEARS as the nation's seventh President, Andrew Jackson sustained his reputation as an advocate for ordinary citizens against aristocracy and privilege, and in doing so, he showed how delicate was the balance of conflicting forces in the national system of government—and in his own personality. He was a forceful, defiant, ruthless, calculating, inspirational, theatrical, thoroughly political President, a man whose virtues and vices always seemed slightly larger than life. He was the first chief executive to make a serious attempt to apply democratic principles of government—and one consequence was the emergence of a chaotic and unstable spoils system. He was a nationalist, favoring the Union over the concept of states' rights (it is interesting to speculate what he might have done in Lincoln's place), yet on several occasions he refused to assert federal authority against acts of defiance by individual states. He championed the rights of the common man, but his equalitarian ideals did not extend far enough to embrace the rights of Indians or blacks in slavery.

. . . . It was with difficulty he made his way through the Capitol and down the hill to the gateway that opens on the avenue. Here for a moment he was stopped. The living mass was impenetrable. After a while a passage was opened, and he mounted his horse which had been provided for his return (for he had walked to the Capitol) then such a cortege as followed him! Country men, farmers, gentlemen, mounted and dismounted, boys, women and children, black and white. Carriages, wagons and carts all pursuing him to the President's house . . . . But what a scene did we witness! The *Majesty of the People* had disappeared, and a rabble, a mob, of boys, negros, women, children, scrambling, fighting, romping. What a pity what a pity! No arrangements had been made no police officers placed on duty and the whole house had been inundated by the rabble mob . . . . The President, after having been *literally* nearly pressed to death and almost suffocated and torn to pieces by the people in their eagerness to shake hands with Old Hickory, had retreated through the back way or south front and had escaped to his lodgings at Gadsby's. Cut glass and china to the amount of several thousand dollars had been broken in the struggle to get the refreshments, punch and other articles had been carried out in tubs and buckets, but had it been hogsheads it would have been insufficient, ice-creams, and cake and lemonade, for 20,000 people, for it is said that number were there, tho' I think the estimate exaggerated. Ladies fainted, men were seen with bloody noses and such a scene of confusion took place as is impossible to describe,—those who got in could not get out by the door again, but had to scramble out of windows . . . . Ladies and gentlemen only had been expected at this Levee, not the people en masse. But it was the People's day, and the People's President, and the People would rule . . . .

MARGARET BAYARD SMITH, *a Washington society matron, describing the aftermath of Andrew Jackson's inauguration in a letter to a friend*

Yet with all his contradictions, he retained an immense popularity with the masses of citizens. He won re-election easily in 1832 (Tennesseans gave him a victory margin of almost twenty-five to one, and in Davidson County he got about eighty percent of the vote). Jackson gave voice to what had been a silent and subjugated majority of white Americans; he was the cabin-born orphan boy who had scratched and clawed his way to national power, and they could identify with him and love him for it. Jacksonian Democracy extended the ideal of equality, if not the fact of it, from a few people to a great many.

It would remain for other generations to make the ideal a reality for all Americans.

Jackson came home to the Hermitage in 1837, weary but unbowed. He had prevailed in getting Martin Van Buren elected as his successor, but at great personal cost: Hugh Lawson White, a Tennessean, had been the candidate of the new Whig Party, and White, in losing, had carried both Tennessee and Davidson County over Van Buren. If that were not insult enough to Jackson, Whigs in Nashville took the occasion of his retirement to build a strong opposition party, and some of its leading members were old

---

Nashville contains about 6000 inhabitants, has a public square, churches, meeting-houses, markets, &c. &c., and is built upon a lofty knoll of limestone, the fossiliferous flat rocks of which come to the surface; there is also a commodious bridge which connects the town with the northern bank of the Cumberland River, on the road to Kentucky. Some of the streets are steep, and encumbered with sharp pieces of limestone, that punish the feet severely in walking. There is an excellent spacious building in the vicinity called the Penitentiary, and another is erecting for a hospital. Coming from the wilderness, where we have been leading rather a rude life for some time, Nashville, with its airy salubrious position, and its active bustling population, is quite what an oasis in the desert would be; and when improvements are made in the navigation of the Cumberland River, and in the public roads, it cannot fail to become a populous town.

•

No traveller who comes into the country as I have done, can feel anything but respect for what he sees around him in this place. When I first visited North

America, in 1806, the word Tennessee was mentioned as a kind of Ultima Thule. Now it is a Sovereign State, with a population of upwards of 700,000 inhabitants, has given a President to the United States, and has established a geological chair in the wilderness. The first log-hut ever erected in Nashville was in 1780; now there is a handsome town, good substantial brick houses, with public edifices that would embellish any city in America, and certainly, as far as architecture is concerned, one of the most chaste episcopal churches in the United States. Besides these there are numerous extensive warehouses, evidences of a brisk commerce, and an exceedingly well constructed bridge thrown across the Cumberland River. It adds greatly too to the interest of the place, that a few of the hardy individuals who, with their rifles on their shoulders, penetrated here, and became the first settlers, still live to see the extraordinary changes which have taken place.

G. W. FEATHERSTONHAUGH'S *Excursion through the Slave States,* published in London in 1844, contained these observations from his 1834 visit to Nashville.

The only known view of the Hermitage before it was damaged by fire in 1834 is this steel engraving, first published in 1832. The now-familiar face of the house, with its Corinthian capitaled columns and two-story portico, was added when President Jackson had the home rebuilt after the fire.

friends and allies of the General. Most notable among them was John Bell, the congressman from Nashville. He had been elected Speaker of the House of Representatives in 1834, even though President Jackson had given his support to another Tennessean, James K. Polk. In a dramatic speech in Nashville in 1835, Bell had rejected Van Buren (and by implication, the Democratic Party and Jackson), and that was the end of Old Hickory's political dominance in Davidson County and Tennessee, as surely as it was gradually ending in the nation.

The Hermitage had been badly damaged by a fire in 1834, and he had ordered it restored immediately, for he was looking ahead to retirement. Right up to the end of his tenure in the White House, he kept command of the presidency with the same furious intensity he had brought to it in the beginning. Under the watchful eyes of his nephew and personal secretary, Andrew Jackson Donelson, and Donelson's wife Emily, the General worked most of the time, socialized little, slept hardly at all. When he came home to his plantation on the Cumberland, he was seventy years old, mentally sharp but physically infirm, too proud to talk of retirement—and yet too handicapped to rally the home forces for any more crusades.

Just as Jackson was noticeably changed in eight years, so was Nashville. The town's population had reached almost 7,000. There were a half-dozen churches and nearly as many banks; there was a "lunatic asylum," a penitentiary, and a masonic hall. The waterworks, first built in 1823 and then modified and expanded a decade later, gave people convenient access to the flowing Cumberland, still green and clear and pure enough to drink.

Dozens of doctors and lawyers and scores of merchants offered their goods and services. There was much sentiment for making Nashville the permanent capital of Tennessee. Stagecoaches came daily to the Public Square, and more steamboats docked at the foot of Broad Street. New buildings were everywhere, the most spectacular being Vauxhall Garden, a large hall for assemblies and dining, located on the Franklin turnpike south of town; a railway inside the hall moved guests about on cars propelled by hand cranks. And another marvel: The first telegram had arrived, sent by someone in Louisville to a local resident, Henry O'Reilly. What would they think of next!

Jackson came home in his autumn years to find Nashville in the midst of its own budding spring. Everything was changing—and much

BURNING OF THE STEAMBOAT RANDOLPH

Our town has seldom, if ever, been visited with such a disaster as that which occurred yesterday. The Steamboat Randolph, the largest boat on our waters, and the pride of our port, is now a smoking and unsightly mass.

About 3 o'clock yesterday afternoon, as she came within sight of town, loaded with a heavy and costly freight, and springing gaily along as if rejoicing that her goal was so nearly attained, it was discovered that she was on fire. The flame, which broke out through the boiler deck, was small, and at first created but little alarm. The Captain (Miller) thought he had extinguished it, when a puff of wind rekindled it, and in a few moments it became unmanageable. The wind was high, and all hopes of extinguishing the flames being abandoned, the only effort now made, was to run her to shore. This was accomplished by the presence of mind and exertions of the Captain, the Clerk (Baldwin,) and the Pilot, a colored man, by the name of David Crafts. The negro stood firm at the helm, while the flames were raging around him, and actually *until the ropes of his wheel were burnt in two.* Mr. Baldwin manifested the utmost coolness and deliberation. As the boat was nearing the shore, he was seen to issue from the midst of the flames, bearing a trunk, and when he had attained the edge, tossed it into the water, and then . . . he deliberately drew his coat around him, and plunged in after it, and succeeded in reaching the shore.

The boat was at length secured, a great mass of flame, at the landing opposite the old Magazine, and our fire companies and hundreds of citizens were on the spot immediately. Every assistance was rendered, and by extraordinary exertions, the fire was subdued by nightfall, but not until the boat was burnt to the water's edge.

As far as we can ascertain this morning from the most diligent inquiry, three lives were lost, all of whom were slaves. Two were drowned, a male and a female, and the other, a male, died, after being brought on shore . . . .

Nashville Republican,
March 17, 1836

84

The first Tennessee penitentiary building was located on Spring Street (now Church) near the Nashville Female Academy. This drawing of it was printed in Harper's Weekly on June 11, 1887, after it had been in existence for several decades.

had happened in his absence. Volunteers had gone to war again, this time in Texas, and once more, Tennesseans had led the way. The legislature had been meeting in the courthouse in Nashville, and a new state constitution had been written there. John Overton had died, and so had Frederick Stump, Timothy Demonbreun, John Buchanan, John Rains, and all but a few of the founding settlers. (Charlotte Robertson, the "First Lady," would be the last of them to pass on; she would be ninety-three when she died in her daughter's Nashville home in 1843.) Local newspapers were beginning daily publication. A cholera epidemic had hit Nashville, claiming dozens of lives, and fires were a frequent threat, but in spite of the losses, steady growth continued.

Columbia's James K. Polk, a Jackson ally, came home from Congress to be elected governor. Felix Grundy, another of the General's closest associates, had moved from the United States Senate to President Van Buren's cabinet to serve as attorney general. Montgomery Bell, a wealthy and eccentric manufacturer of iron products, had freed fifty of his slaves in a ceremony at the Presbyterian Church on Spring Street and walked with them down to the wharf, where they departed on a journey to Liberia.

Perhaps the most astonishing development in Nashville during the years of Jackson's presidency concerned Sam Houston, another of the

Age was written in the lines of Charlotte Robertson's face when she posed in a baby blue lace bonnet for this portrait by Washington Cooper. It may have been painted after 1840, when she was past ninety and living with her daughter and son-in-law, Lavinia and John Craighead. She died in their house, a two-story Federal-style brick that stands now on Westbrook Avenue in Nashville.

As stone-faced as the Cumberland valley iron ore he made his fortune from, eccentric industrialist Montgomery Bell stood for this photograph sometime in the 1850s. For twenty years before he died in 1855, Bell kept a large number of slaves—and freed an even larger number.

Among the engravings on an 1832 map of Nashville by J. P. Ayers is this perspective of the Public Square. Flanked on the left by the Nashville Inn and on the right by the City Hotel is the courthouse that served the city from 1832 until it burned in 1856.

Gray-bearded, sad-eyed Sam Houston was in his twilight years in Texas when artist Sam Swan Walker painted his portrait sometime in the 1860s.

General's old friends and fellow soldiers. His early career had been remarkable for its diversity. A good student and an avid reader in his youth, he had run away from home at sixteen to live with Cherokees and then had fought against the Creeks at Horseshoe Bend. In Nashville after the war, he studied law, became a district attorney, and—among other side interests—acted on stage in an amateur theatrical company. He was a handsome man, six feet-six inches tall, a stylish dresser, and a favorite with the ladies. With Jackson's backing, he was elected twice to Congress, and in 1827, after riding from one polling place to another—wearing a white ruffled shirt, shining black trousers, a beaded red sash, embroidered silk stockings, and silver-buckled pumps—he was elected governor.

In January 1829, right after Jackson left for the White House, Houston married Eliza Allen of Gallatin. He was at the peak of his popularity, certain to be a candidate for re-election and likely to win, and some of his supporters dreamed of grooming him to be Jackson's successor as President in a few years.

Then came the stunning news: Not three months after the wedding, Eliza Allen left Houston and went home to her parents. Within a week, Houston had resigned as governor and slipped away from Nashville in disguise to live among his Cherokee friends in the West.

The cause of the breakup was not revealed. It stirred a whirlwind of rumors and gossip, but Houston would not explain. "If my character cannot stand the shock, let me lose it," he said. He vowed to punish "any wretch" who ever questioned "the purity of Mrs. Houston," and reaffirmed his love for her. And then he was gone.

The most often-repeated explanation of Eliza Allen's separation from her husband was that she was repulsed by an unsightly and

Mr. Allen:

The most unpleasant & unhappy circumstance has just taken place in our family, & one that was entirely unnecessary at this time. Whatever had been my feelings or opinions in relation to Eliza at one time, I have been satisfied & it is now unfit that anything should be averted to. Eliza will do me the justice to say that she believes I was really unhappy. That I was satisfied & believed her virtuous, I had assured her on last night & this morning. This should have prevented the facts ever coming to your knowledge, & that of Mrs. Allen. I would not for millions it had ever been known to you. But one human being knew anything of it from me, & that was by Eliza's consent & wish. I would have perished first, & if mortal man had dared to charge my wife or say ought against her virtue I would have slain him. That I have & do love Eliza none can doubt—that she is the only earthly object dear to me God will witness.

The only way this matter can now be overcome will be for us all to meet as tho it had never occurred, & this will keep the world, as it should ever be, ignorant that such thoughts ever were. Eliza stands acquitted by me. I have received her as a virtuous wife, & as such I pray God I may ever regard her, & trust I ever shall.

She was cold to me, & I thought did not love me. She owns that such was one cause of my unhappiness. You can judge how unhappy I was to think I was united to a woman that did not love me. This time is now past, & my future happiness can only exist in the assurance that Eliza & myself can be happy & that Mrs. Allen & you can forget the past,—forgive all and find your lost peace & you may rest assured that nothing on my part shall be wanting to restore it. Let me know what is to be done.

SAM HOUSTON

9 Apr. 1829

(What this letter from Sam Houston to his father-in-law sought to prevent—the separation of the governor and Eliza, his bride of twelve weeks—came to pass two days later when she went home to her parents in Gallatin. Within a week, Houston had resigned from office and left Nashville for the Cherokee lands west of the Mississippi. Seven years later, he was elected the first president of the new Republic of Texas.)

Sam Houston was a dashing revolutionary and president of the independent Republic of Texas when an artist—probably George Catlin—painted a miniature portrait of him in watercolor on ivory. Less than a decade earlier, in 1829, he had resigned as governor of Tennessee and left Nashville in anguish after the mysterious breakup of his marriage.

malodorous sore Houston had in his abdomen, a festering arrow wound that he had sustained at Horseshoe Bend fifteen years earlier. An additional revelation from Eliza herself, later in life, was to the effect that Houston was "insanely jealous and suspicious" of his nineteen-year-old bride, that he was cruel to her, and that he was "a demented man." Whatever the truth, the effect of their parting was traumatic, not only for the two principals but for Nashville and the state.

Sam Houston would be heard from again. He lived for a while in drunken sorrow, and then took a Cherokee wife, and in 1832 he passed through Nashville once more, leading a delegation of Indians to Washington. President Jackson received him warmly there, and so did Senator Felix Grundy. The following year he was in Texas, rallying soldiers to a war for independence from Mexico, and not a few Nashvillians would answer the call, including Sterling Robertson, a grandson of James and Charlotte, and George C. Childress, a local newspaper editor, who in 1836 would distinguish himself as the author of the Texas

Declaration of Independence. Houston would find glory too, first as president of the Texas republic, then as a United States Senator from the state of Texas, and finally as governor of the state. He also married again, to a woman from Alabama, and fathered eight children.

Having fought so hard to bind Texas to the Union, Houston could not abide the thought of secession, and when the Civil War broke out, he was turned out of the governor's office for refusing to join the Confederacy. Two years later he died of pneumonia, murmuring "Texas, Texas" with his last breath. That such a giant ever got away from Nashville was a great loss for the community and for Tennessee.

Jackson certainly could have used the counsel of the man who proudly called himself an adopted son of the Cherokees. The General had always favored resettlement of the Indians in the West—voluntarily, if possible, but if not, by force—and while he was still in the White House, a minority faction of the nearly 17,000 Cherokees still living in the Southeast agreed to sell their people's land and move to a reservation in the West.

The Cherokees had developed an advanced standard of living, and most of them wanted to stay in the mountains of Tennessee, North Carolina, and Georgia; only a few left voluntarily. Finally, in 1838, when Jackson was living in retirement at the Hermitage, most of the 15,000 who remained were rounded up by army troops and forced to migrate. They passed through Nashville in the fall of that year, a pitiful train of trudging thousands, walking to Oklahoma territory on what would be known as the Trail of Tears. The previous year, members of the treaty party—the ones who had signed away their land—had passed in wagons through the town, and a journal kept by B. B. Cannon, the conductor of the party, noted that "Reese Star and other of the Emigrants visited General Jackson

Not long before he died in 1845, former President Jackson sat for this painting by George Caleb Bingham, an artist whose celebrated works ranged from river scenes to political rallies.

who was in Nashville." But he was not called upon by any of those in the forced march, nor did he ever hear from any of the thousand or so who hid in the mountains to evade removal. The old General may never have known that about 4,000 of the dispossessed died of disease, starvation and exposure on the march west. He may not have wanted to know. He had closed the book on the Indians.

The rest of his accounts were about to be summed up, too, and some of them would not come out to suit him. Not until after the Civil

Saturday. **Our dear Cherokee breathren prepared seats on one side of the camp ground, where we held a meeting in the afternoon.**

Sabbath. **A Baptist elder offered us the use of his meeting house, about a half mile distant.**

Monday. **The detachment being supplied with tents we proceeded on our journey. We travelled but four miles from Nashville and camped. As the fires began to be kindled, an aged Cherokee, who had been sick all the way, lay down by the fire, when his clothes caught fire, and he sprang up, but before he could be releived, he burnt nearly to death.**

Tuesday.

Sat, Dec. 1. **Camped on a branch of Red River, in Kentucky, having travelled during the week about 60 miles. The poor old man who was burnt, we left at a house to be taken care of, but died in a few days. On Wednesday night of this week sister ooskaoni gave birth to a son, and on Thursday two children, one a daughter of our dear sister Ash hopper, were called into eternity. They had been long sick.**

> *entries in the diary of Daniel Buttrick, a missionary who accompanied one group of Cherokees when they were removed to the West on the Trail of Tears in 1838*

War would the political rebellion against the Jacksonian Democrats be overcome in Davidson County. Even in 1844, when former Tennessee governor and Jackson protege James K. Polk—"Young Hickory"—won the presidency in an upset, he failed to carry his home state and was defeated by a large margin in Davidson County. Most embarrassing of all, he lost the Hermitage precinct. Jackson could no longer strike fear in the hearts of politicians. The Whigs delighted in punishing him—they even brought their national convention to Nashville in 1840—and there was nothing he could do to retaliate. But the old soldier could at least take satisfaction in Polk's election and in the admission of Sam Houston's Texas to the Union, and

those final victories allowed him to die in peace, though he suffered much from a complex of physical infirmities.

Late in his life, the General joined the Presbyterian Church (as Polk was to unite with the Methodists a few years later), and he pronounced himself ready to go and meet "my beloved wife . . . when my God calls me to sleep with my fathers." Most of his dearest friends had preceded him—Overton was gone, and Ralph Earl, and so was Felix Grundy, the great trial lawyer and silver-tongued orator. Old Hickory was lonesome; there were no more challenges left for him, no more battles worth the bother. On June 8, 1845, in his bedroom at the Hermitage, he quietly gave up the fight.

TO JAMES K. POLK

June 8, 1845

My dear Sirs: In deep sorrow I address you this hasty note. At 6 o'clock this evening Gen. Jackson departed this life. He retained his faculties to the last hour. I lament that I was denied the satisfaction of seeing him in his last moments. I was unfortunately delayed in ascending the Mississippi, so that I did not reach Nashville till half-past six this evening. I immediately procured a conveyance, and came out with my family—having understood that the General's health was exceedingly precarious, and being anxious to administer, if I could, some comfort in the closing scene of his eventful life. On my way, a few miles from the city, I met the family physician, who informed me that the General was no more. About three hours before his departure he conversed for some time with his family, and took an affectionate leave of them, as also of his domestics. His physician represents the scene as most affecting; and remarks that he departed with perfect serenity of mind, and with full faith in the promises of salvation through a Redeemer. I have seen the corpse since my arrival. The visage is much as it was in life. The funeral will take place on Tuesday next, at 11 o'clock a.m. A nation will feel this loss, as a nation has received the fruits of his toils, during the best years of his life.

SAM HOUSTON

JAMES KNOX POLK was not groomed for the presidency, as Jackson was; he just happened to be in the right place when the call came. He had been elected governor of Tennessee in 1839 but then had lost two successive bids for re-election. His political career seemed finished, but then the aging General Jackson pushed him to a surprise nomination for the presidency, and Polk went on to recapture the White House for the Democrats in 1844.

The Whigs ridiculed him as an obscure politician and a loser, but the quietly efficient Polk was actually well prepared to be President. He had studied law under Felix Grundy in Nashville, represented Maury County in the legislature, and spent fourteen years in Congress, the last four of them as Speaker of the House. (It was Jackson's support of Polk to be speaker over Congressman John Bell of Nashville that had contributed to the birth of the opposition Whig Party.)

In his one term in the White House, Polk presided over a nation eager to expand its borders: Texas was annexed, the War with Mexico was fought, the territories of California and Oregon were acquired. The notion that it was the "manifest destiny" of the United States to own all of the land from the Atlantic to the Pacific was widely supported throughout the country, and with President Polk actively pursuing that goal, Tennesseans were, if anything, the most eager combatants of all. "To Arms! To Arms!" a headline in the Nashville *Union* exhorted when war was declared on Mexico, and 30,000 men offered their services when Governor Aaron V. Brown asked for a volunteer force of 2,800. A million square miles of territory were added to the nation during Polk's tenure in office.

When Polk came home from Washington in the spring of 1849, he was ill and exhausted. He and his wife bought Felix Grundy's home on a

hill near the new state capitol, then under construction, but they had hardly settled in before the ex-President fell victim to the intestinal ravages of cholera and died. (His widow, Sarah Childress Polk, would live on as the grand old lady of Polk Place for more than forty years, receiving callers of all political persuasions with grace and equanimity.)

Cholera had come often to Nashville, and it would return. W. F. Cooper, a local man, wrote to a friend three days after Polk's passing that "Fully two hundred deaths have occurred in the last fortnight—nearly half of them during the three last days. On Friday, there were 38 burials, on Saturday 41, and on Sunday about 15." The lack of effective embalming methods and the sheer number of bodies made speedy burial a necessity. When bodies had to be sent elsewhere for burial, it was not uncommon to store them in barrels of whiskey.

Nashville was not an especially healthy place in those years. Coal, shipped in on the river and sold for about fifteen cents a bushel, was the principal fuel for homes and industries, and smoke from the fires hung in the air of the river basin like a foul cloud. Furthermore, summers in the town were still and humid, and winters were damp. Other diseases besides cholera would add to the inability of local doctors to establish and maintain good health in the community for decades to come.

But it would take more than a cholera epidemic to slow the expansion of Nashville and Davidson County. In the 1850 census, the town counted 10,165 residents; in truth, it was a town no more, but a small city, and it would soon be a large one. Davidson County's population had grown even more impressively, to a total of almost 39,000, and soon it would be organized into twenty-five civil districts, Nashville being only one of them. The others would constitute a

Aaron V. Brown, a Democrat, and Neill S. Brown, a Whig, had in common their Giles County roots, their service in the state legislature, and their last name, and they also served back-to-back terms as governor—but they were not related. Neill Brown is credited with giving the name Edgefield to what is now East Nashville. He was once the American minister to Russia.

92

The steamboat Embassy *called regularly at Nashville in the 1840s, delivering the mail as well as passengers and cargo. This 1848 daguerreotype of the* Embassy *docked at the waterfront in Cincinnati is taken from a panoramic view which is the earliest known photograph of steamboats in America.*

network of country communities built around churches, stores, mills, ferries, and crossroads. The names of those communities are now a mixture of the familiar and the forgotten: McWhirtersville, Donelson, Glen Cliff, Mount View, Couchville, Hermitage, Paragon Mills, Hillsboro, Belle View, Madison, Goodlettsville, Edgefield, White's Creek, Antioch, Ridge Post, Cool Spring. For nearly twenty years prior to the Civil War, District Two (Donelson) would have the only college in the county outside of Nashville: Franklin College.

The focal point of these rural jurisdictions, the center to which everything gravitated, was Nashville. It was, in fact, the center of Tennessee, having been designated as the permanent state capital. Turnpikes radiated in all directions from the city. More than fifty steamboats called regularly at the wharf; *America,* the fastest of them, could make the run from New Orleans in less than six days, and the largest boat, the *Nashville,* was an elegant colossus of 397 tons. A new 700-foot suspension bridge spanned the Cumberland from the southeast corner of the Public Square to Edgefield on the east bank, and it stood 110 feet above the river—high enough to let the big new steamboats pass. The legislature, falling in line with the nation's "iron horse

A steamboat below the bluff and scaffolding around the State Capitol place the time in this mural at about 1850. Jirayr H. Zorthian painted it in the governor's reception room at the capitol in 1938.

fever," had authorized construction of a railroad between Nashville and Chattanooga.

The decade between 1845 and 1855 was a golden age for Nashville, an exciting time crammed with mechanical innovations, major construction projects, far-reaching institutional developments, and an ever-broadening sea of new faces. The city built a plant to manufacture gas from coal, and gas street lights and store lights soon followed. A sparkling new theater, the Adelphi, was opened on what is now Fourth Avenue, and Jenny Lind came to sing there, and out-of-town companies brought in productions of grand opera and Shakespeare. Daguerreotype photographs had made their appearance, and there was an attractive botanical garden in the city, and William T. Berry's bookstore was widely regarded as the best in the West. Nashville's several newspapers received copy from the North and East via telegraph, and church publishing houses had begun to produce journals and other religious materials for an expanding market. Plans were being made for a public school system, and both the Nashville Female Academy and the University of Nashville appeared to be flourishing, the latter having opened a medical school.

The great love of Andrew Jackson—horse racing—had not been forgotten either. For more than a decade, Nashville had been recognized as a premier racing city. It had four tracks, one on each side of town, and they competed avidly for purses, crowds, and prestige. The richest horse race in the world, to that time, took place in 1843 at the Nashville Race Track (now the site of MetroCenter); the race was called the Peyton Stakes, and the winner, a stout-hearted chestnut filly named Peytona, went on to win a celebrated match race in New York two years later. That one was billed as the race of the century.

Horses had something to do with the growth

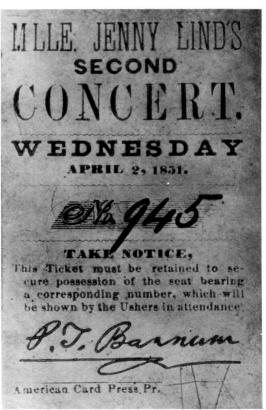

The Swedish soprano Jenny Lind was booked in Nashville's Adelphi Theater by master promoter P. T. Barnum, and overflow crowds came to hear her. Barnum's signature was stamped on the tickets. The Adelphi, designed by Adolphus Heiman, was Nashville's leading theater. It opened in 1850.

Currier and Ives, the noted American lithographers, produced this hand-colored scene showing Peytona, Nashville's favorite filly, beating a New York horse named Fashion in their Long Island "race of the century" in 1845. Peytona apparently was walked or ridden from Nashville to New York for the race.

of plantations around Nashville, particularly Belle Meade, which under William Giles Harding's direction became a renowned thoroughbred nursery. The mansion at Belle Meade was one of several handsome country homes and estates—Belmont, Two Rivers, Clover Bottom, and Riverwood were others—that gave Nashville a reputation for elaborate hospitality among the well-to-do.

Another example of purebred stock raising —and a reminder that for all its new-city sophistication, Davidson County remained a predominantly rural and agricultural entity —was afforded by the story of Mark Robertson Cockrill. A son of James Robertson's sister and her husband, he achieved singular success as a breeder of short-horn cattle and fine sheep. Before he was twenty, he had gone to Washington to buy ten Merino sheep from a

Spanish diplomat who had made known his interest in selling them. Cockrill drove the sheep home overland in 1814; thirty-seven years later, at the great Crystal Palace Exposition in London, his display of wool was judged to be the best in the world.

All in all, these notable individual accomplishments and community developments added to the luster of the first city on the Cumberland. In seventy years, it had become a diverse and substantial place. Five groups of professional people and the institutions they represented were particularly important to Nashville's growing sense of permanence, and in the decades of the 1840s and the 1850s their contributions did much to shape the character of the city. The five were interrelated in many ways, and together they formed the base upon which much of modern Nashville is built.

T HE FIRST GROUP was made up of the architects who designed Nashville's structures—and the engineers, craftsmen, and laborers who built them. There were several architects in the city by 1845, and others came on occasion from outside the state to help shape the face of the city, but two men above all others left a lasting imprint: William F. Strickland and Adolphus Heiman.

When the state legislature finally decided in 1843 that Nashville would be the permanent seat of Tennessee government, a national search was begun for an architect to design a capitol building. William Strickland of Philadelphia, once an apprentice to the designer of the national capitol, was chosen for the job, and in 1845, he moved here to supervise the construction. Before he died nine years later—with the Tennessee Capitol still unfinished—Strickland had designed several other structures, including the Downtown Presbyterian Church, but it was the capitol that would be his masterwork. The Greek-revival structure on what was known as Cedar Knob, the highest hill in the city, was built of limestone quarried a few blocks from the site. Penitentiary inmates and slave laborers did the back-breaking work. The capitol stands now as a monument to the sweat and genius of its builders, and Strickland left his body as his signature in the building: He is buried in a vault in one of its walls.

Adolphus Heiman, a Prussian immigrant, set-

The name of the artist who painted this portrait of William Strickland is not recorded, but it is thought to have been done in the 1840s, while Strickland was at work on the design and construction of the Tennessee State Capitol.

tled in Nashville in 1841 and quickly established himself as a creative man of exceptional talent. He designed the state mental hospital, the main building of the University of Nashville, and the suspension bridge across the Cumberland, all reflecting a Gothic style that was highly popular at the time. When construction on the bridge

Prussian immigrant Adolphus Heiman, an outstanding architect in Nashville for two decades before the Civil War, was a colonel in the Confederate Army when this engraving was made. He died during the war. Among the many Nashville structures Heiman designed was the city's first suspension bridge (below).

From the time it was first opened in the early 1850s, the suspension bridge connecting the Public Square with what is now Woodland Street on the east bank sustained several misfortunes. Part of it collapsed in 1855, and the retreating Confederate Army cut its cables in 1862. The Union Army temporarily repaired it, and the city rebuilt it after the war. This unsigned water color of the bridge and the town is dated 1851.

was not done according to Heiman's specifications, he resigned from the project in protest, and in 1855, after the bridge had been in use just five years, his unheeded warning bore tragic results: A portion of the bridge collapsed, killing one person and injuring several others. Heiman was a prolific designer of Nashville structures for twenty years before he died fighting for the Confederacy in 1862.

With hardwood timber floated to Nashville from the upper Cumberland, with limestone quarried in Middle Tennessee and iron products made in the furnaces of the area, with bricks that had been manufactured locally since 1790, the architects and builders of the mid-nineteenth century gave Nashville much of its proportion, its shape, and its personality.

Philip Lindsley turned down the presidency of Princeton University in order to lift the moribund Cumberland College to new life as the University of Nashville. It was still struggling when he retired after a quarter of a century in 1850, but he had established a tradition of higher education in Nashville. This portrait of Lindsley as a young man was painted in Nashville by John C. Grimes.

A second group of significant leaders in that time were the clergyman and the institutions in their care. Since about 1800, when survival had ceased to be the only preoccupation of the settlers, churches had been growing in influence and importance. Presbyterians, Methodists, and Baptists led the way, to be followed later by Episcopalians, Catholics, Jews, and others. The Presbyterians were closely associated with the University of Nashville and other educational ventures; their leading clergymen were also teachers, and vice versa: Thomas Craighead, William Hume, Philip Lindsley, Obediah Jennings, and John Todd Edgar, the men who institutionalized the Presbyterian faith in Nashville, were also associated with

In the eloquent appeals which he was constantly making in behalf of [the University of Nashville], Dr. Lindsley . . . knew precisely what he was about from the beginning . . . . In carrying forward so great a work, he had expected at one time to secure both the public aid of the state and the private co-operation and munificence of the citizens of Nashville . . . . But finding, after a few years' trial, that he could neither depend on state aid nor secure from individual munificence such endowment as his scheme demanded, he then set to work manfully to make of his university as good an institution as the limited means at his disposal . . . would admit . . . .

It was a favorite opinion with Dr. Lindsley, or rather a great general idea for which he battled bravely through all his presidency at Nashville, that education, while it should be *most distinctly religious and Christian, need not be sectarian or even denominational* . . . but worthy of the confidence and patronage of all evangelical denominations—being at the same time open and free to all others, whether in the church or out of it . . . .

But it was all in vain. The denominational currents were too strong for him. From having no college in Tennessee, colleges got to be the order of the day. His very success at Nashville emboldened many to go and do likewise: colleges sprang up in all quarters faster than they were needed . . . . "When this college was revived and reorganized at the close of 1824, there were no similar institutions, in actual operation, within two hundred miles of Nashville [said Dr. Lindsley in 1848]. There are now some thirty or more within that distance . . . and *nine* within fifty miles of our city."

The writer . . . can bear witness that he has visited no point in all this vast region where the influence of Philip Lindsley has not been felt . . . . But perhaps the most striking illustration of his influence as an educator is seen at Nashville itself—the scene of his longest labors—the home of his adoption—the resting place where his ashes sleep. We have no citizenship at Nashville; and hence cannot be accused of partiality in what we are about to say. But of all we have seen and known, we may safely say, there is no city west of the mountains which seems to us so justly entitled to be called the Athens of the West, as Nashville. And for that distinction we think there is no man to whom Nashville is so much indebted as Dr. Lindsley. If any man ever made his mark, deep and ineffaceable, upon a place and people, he made it at Nashville . . . .

LEROY J. HALSEY, from *A Sketch of the Life and Educational Labors of Philip Lindsley, D. D.* (1859)

The University of Nashville campus included the Western Military Institute when this engraving was made in the 1850s. The building on the left was President Philip Lindsley's home. It and Lindsley Hall, the barracks, are gone, but the classroom building on the right still stands on Second Avenue South, intact except for its tower. Peabody College used this campus until after 1910. Nearby, the university's medical department was housed in a building designed by Adolphus Heiman.

Cumberland College and the University of Nashville. The Methodists, more hierarchical in their structure, looked mainly to one man—William McKendree, the first bishop of their church west of the Blue Ridge Mountains—as the founder of Methodism locally. The Baptists honored James Whitsett as their pioneer preacher on the Cumberland, and another early Baptist preacher, Philip Fall, became the leader of a Disciples of Christ faction that split off to form Spring Street Christian Church.

In their early years, the churches were activist institutions. They staged public debates on theology; they summarily excommunicated those who wavered in the faith or wandered from it; they thought little of the notion of separation of church and state, ceremoniously inaugurating governors and sending men to war from their sanctuaries. They also split on occasion into separate bodies—the Cumberland Presbyterians from their mother church as early as 1810, the Disciples of Christ from the Baptists in 1828, the Jewish congregation into three separate synagogues after mid-century, the Church of Christ from the Disciples of Christ after the Civil War—and of course, Southern churches from Northern ones and whites from blacks.

Many of the first Nashville churches were clustered along Spring Street, so many that its present name—Church Street—must have been inevitable. As visible and influential as they were, however, the churches did not have large memberships. As late as the mid-1830s, only the Methodist churches of Davidson County had as many as a thousand members, and all the others combined had fewer than a thousand. There was one small Methodist church for blacks in the 1830s, but customarily the blacks attended the same institutions as the whites; the first Baptist church for blacks was not established until 1848. Fifteen years before that, blacks outnumbered whites in both the Baptist and Methodist churches on Spring Street. And although white males were the leaders of all the churches, females were as noticeably predominant in the congregations as they were subordinate in virtually all dimensions of public life at large.

As surely as the architects and builders defined Nashville's early physical appearance, the clergymen shaped its spiritual character; even the politicians, who operated in another realm, took care to seek the sanctions of the faith.

Physicians made up the third category of professional men whose influence was so important to the early development of Nashville. Beginning with James White and John Sappington in the 1780s and running through the long and distinguished career of Felix Robertson from 1806 to 1865, Nashville was seldom without a cadre of notable doctors. John Berrien Lindsley, son of the University of Nashville's president, organized the university's medical school in 1850, and within five years it had more students and more graduates than all but three medical schools in the nation. Paul F. Eve, William K.

99

Four of Nashville's earliest churches attracted the attention of artists and engravers. First Baptist Church (lower right) on Spring Street—later converted to the Christian Church—appeared on the 1832 map of Nashville by J. P. Ayers. In 1857, William Eichbaum engraved the others (clockwise from lower left): First Presbyterian, which was built on Spring Street in 1849 and still stands there (now as Downtown Presbyterian); St. Mary's Catholic Church, finished in 1847 and still in use (with a steeple added after the engraving was made); and McKendree Methodist, on Spring Street (now Church) from the 1830s to the 1870s.

100

Bowling and William T. Briggs, three eminent members of its faculty, were each to serve a term as president of the American Medical Association, and in 1857, the AMA held its national convention in the city.

The early tradition of eminence in the field of medicine would continue in Nashville into the twentieth century. (Since 1900, five more Nashville physicians have been elected to the presidency of the AMA; of all American cities, only Philadelphia has ever had as many.) Of more importance to the city in the 1850s, however, was the fact that three dozen or more physicians were on hand to struggle against epidemics, to press for higher standards of community health, and to train future doctors for the city, state, and nation.

There was a fourth group of professionals whose efforts were extraordinarily important to Nashville: the educators. Their work had begun with Thomas Craighead. After his academy had faltered in his later years, Philip Lindsley came, and from 1826 to 1850 he struggled to put the University of Nashville on its feet. He wanted to make the institution into an eminent center of learning, one of the few in the country, and to that end he ran a rigorous program, too rigorous for the taste of many. Lindsley was a learned and eloquent man, and he attracted some outstanding scholars to the school (most notably Gerard Troost, a German geologist), but Nashville apparently was not ready for such scholarship: The Univeristy of Nashville at mid-century was poorly supported financially, and its enrollment was small; furthermore, several religious denominations had formed competing insitutions; and worst of all, elementary and secondary education in the city had never been developed for the children of rank-and-file citizens. Ironically, there may have been more illiteracy in Nashville in 1850 than there had been when the Cumberland Compact was signed seventy years earlier.

Still, Philip Lindsley had laid a foundation for general education to begin, and belatedly, in 1852, a system of public schools was authorized by the city board of aldermen to supplement the network of private schools then in existence. Alfred Hume, a son of the Presbyterian clergyman William Hume, was subsequently chosen to be the first superintendent, and Francis B. Fogg, a local attorney, was elected president of the board of education. (Fogg's wife, Mary Middleton Rutledge, granddaughter of the Middleton and Rutledge men who had signed the Declaration of Independence, may have been Nashville's first author of note; she wrote seven books of fiction, poetry, and religious discourse.)

In 1855, after Alfred Hume had died suddenly, the first public school was opened on Broad Street and named for him. (Later, a school was named for Fogg, and in 1912 the two names were combined in a high school that still operates at the corner of Eighth and Broad.) Joshua F. Pearl was appointed superintendent after Hume's death, and served in that capacity until the outbreak of the Civil War. By 1860, Nashville had four public schools. One of them, Trimble School in South Nashville, actually had opened three years before Hume, when South Nashville was still an independent town. After the Civil War, Trimble apparently became Nashville's first public school for blacks. Fifty years before the city established public schools, the state founded Robertson Academy on the Franklin turnpike south of Nashville. It has operated as a public school since 1806.

(An interesting footnote to the evolution of education in Nashville was recorded in the will of Montgomery Bell, the wealthy and reclusive industrialist who died in 1855. He left $20,000 to the University of Nashville "for the support of an Academy or school to be called the Montgomery Bell Academy forever for the education of children . . . who are not able to support and

Alfred Hume (above) son of one of Nashville's leading ministers, could not have been long out of college when this portrait of him was painted by an unknown artist. Later, he was the city's first superintendent of schools. He died before the first school was opened, and it was named for him.

With the clarity and detail that marked his work, Nashville artist George Dury painted this portrait of Francis Fogg (left) a local attorney and a founder of the city's first public school system in the early 1850s.

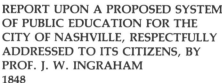

REPORT UPON A PROPOSED SYSTEM OF PUBLIC EDUCATION FOR THE CITY OF NASHVILLE, RESPECTFULLY ADDRESSED TO ITS CITIZENS, BY PROF. J. W. INGRAHAM
1848

Let it first be clearly understood, that the system of schools proposed to you is no experiment. It is a copy of a system in Natchez and in New Orleans in successful operation this very day, and every day becomes dearer and dearer to the citizens of those cities. What is proposed is the adoption of a system which renders Boston the pride of American cities . . . .

Last September, a few days after I came to reside among you, my attention was drawn to the subject of Common Schools by finding in the Sabbath School temporarily placed under my superintendence several children, ten, eleven, and twelve years of age who could not read. Upon inquiring of a citizen if there were no system of Public Schools established in this city, I [was told that] an intelligent and highly respectable gentleman is hired to keep a 'Free School.' Sometimes he has twenty scholars, sometimes he has seventy; and it is a wonder that he should have any, capable as he is as a teacher, for, by some means, the school has unkindly got the name of "The Poor School," and the poor don't like to be labelled too plainly, and they have a little pride, and so had rather their children should run idle and ignorant about the streets than be branded "poor" by attending the Poor School! . . . The result is, people that can pay for private tuition send to the private schools, and those who cannot, get along as they can, move away to other cities which are better provided with schools, or suffer their children to grow up in ignorance and vice.

[I ascertained] the number of children in the city old enough to go to school [to be] 1500 above 6 years and under 20 . . . . The number of schools in the city, not including the existing Free School already spoken of, I ascertained to be thirty-six, of every kind and degree, male and female . . . there [are] 890 Nashville children that attend these 36 schools. Subtracting this number from the whole 1500 . . . there remain 610 children of the city that do not go to school and have no means of school education . . . .

The object of the contemplated school is not to interfere with the other schools, but to build up one for those who have not the means of paying the high tuition fees of private schools, or pay them with great difficulty; and in this category are found not only the laborer and the mechanic but the professional man and the merchant . . . .

My only wish is to see you enjoying the blessing of a system which I have seen producing such good fruits in other cities of the Republic.

educate themselves and whose parents are not able to do so.")

Finally, the fifth corps of professionals to make an indelible mark on Nashville was the legal fraternity. Lawyers had come early and often to the frontier settlement, and in countless ways they influenced the shape and direction of its development. Nashville attorneys dominated local and state politics—and in the cases of Jackson and Polk, national politics as well. The decision of the state legislature to make Nashville the permanent state capital of Tennessee elevated the importance of the legal profession in the city to an even higher plane; it meant that not just the legislature but the courts, the governor's office, and the state bureaucracy would be concentrated here, and lawyers were necessary to those endeavors.

The presence of state government and the swarming cliques of attorneys and politicians made Nashville a magnet for an interesting and diverse mixture of new people who might not have come here otherwise. A new state constitution was written here in 1834, and that was the beginning of the city's importance as a convention center for government, politics, and the professions. Nashville's newspapers were given added visibility and attention because of the government's presence. And through the decades, the government's role as an employer—of lawyers, among others—would expand steadily and become the foundation of the local economy.

The professional men of Nashville in the middle of the nineteenth century dominated life in the community as completely as the Long Hunters and the pioneers and the land speculators had in the 1780s. Unlike the first settlers, however, their impact would be permanent, as permanent as the city itself. More than a century later, the architects, preachers, doctors, and educators—and most especially, the

lawyers—would still be influential out of all proportion to their numbers.

BUT THE PROFESSIONAL MEN and their institutions were not flawless. The legislature at mid-century was not noted as a fount of wisdom, nor were the schools and churches renowned for their all-embracing benevolence. Public health in the city remained generally poor; beggars roamed the streets; dilapidated shantytowns grew in a festering ring around the city's core. Intellectual sophistication often clashed with the stubborn spirit of frontier individualism. Religious intolerance was commonplace, not only among denominations but within them. Nashville had its share of dishonest lawyers, fake preachers, suspicious farmers, greedy merchants, and pretentious scholars; it had, as well, some fugitives from justice and some otherwise respectable citizens who assumed themselves to be above the law. One historian of the period, writing on Nashville's cultural life, characterized the city in 1850 as having "much unwarrantable pretension" and a "tendency to boast and to exaggerate." Pretension—or at least cockiness—must have been almost irresistible for the mixture of people who in three generations had built a city on a wilderness bluff.

However one chose to explain it—as hostility to authority, suspicion of outsiders, perpetuation of unfair advantage, survival of the fittest, or simply the way things were—it was possible to see in Nashville in the 1850s (as in the nation at large) a complex series of fissures and faults running through the fabric of the community. The divisions cut in every direction, some deeper than others: between town and country, rich and poor, churched and unchurched, educated and uneducated, Democrat and Whig, Irish and German and Anglo-Saxon. They divided slaves from free blacks, whites from all blacks, abolitionists from advocates of the "peculiar institution." They separated river men from railroad men, Catholics from Protestants, Christians from Jews.

In 1860, on the eve of the Civil War, the population of Nashville reached 17,000. Sixteen percent of those people were foreign-born whites, recent immigrants, the vast majority being Irish or German. Another twenty-three percent were blacks, and of them, roughly 700 were free and 3,200 were slaves. These combined totals, making up about two-fifths of the overall population, represented in the main an underclass of "different" people whose assigned role it was to make life easier for the ruling majority of established white citizens.

Photographer Joseph Loiseau made this picture of the north side of Union Street in 1859. It is the earliest dated photograph of a Nashville street scene known to exist. The building at left was the Bank of Tennessee.

For the foreign-born whites—most of whom were young males and many of whom were unskilled and illiterate—living conditions were generally poor. The Irish in particular were hard-pressed. The Germans, among whom there were a good many merchants and craftsmen, found more opportunities open to them; some of them were later to build the homes and churches and business establishments that made North Nashville a showplace after the Civil War. For all of the immigrants, even those in the laboring underclass, there was always hope of finding a way up and out of the confining grip of poverty.

But for the blacks—even the free blacks—there was no way out. In an atmosphere of growing national discord over slavery, blacks in Davidson County, as elsewhere, found themselves ever more rigidly bound to the whites under whom they lived and worked. Slavery in the cities of the South was generally less harsh and oppressive than in the rural countryside, and Nashville was no exception—slaves could sometimes learn a skill, hire themselves out, have some freedom of movement—but they could also be sold or traded, and they frequently were. Free blacks were not much better off; beginning in 1834, when the new state constitution took away their right to vote, the difference between slavery and freedom quickly became

even more meaningless for free blacks. In 1856, a decision of the United States Supreme Court effectively removed from all blacks whatever civil rights and citizenship rights they might have had, and from then until the end of the Civil War, they lived in a state of constant uncertainty and danger. Also in 1856, rumors of a slave insurrection in Davidson County led to the banning of all assemblies of blacks and to a series of other repressive measures.

As early as 1850, delegates from several Southern states had met in Nashville and discussed the prospect of a united defense of slavery, but not until the Civil War had actually begun did the voters of Nashville approve of Tennessee's secession from the Union. The city had a good many citizens who vigorously opposed secession (but few who openly opposed slavery). Shortly before the Confederates fired on Fort Sumter and the Civil War began, a referendum in Nashville calling for Tennessee's withdrawal from the Union failed by a narrow margin; in another vote after Fort Sumter, secession was overwhelmingly approved.

All of the other divisions among Nashvillians in 1860—over religion, social class, occupation, politics, and other matters—were minor compared to the issue of slavery. Somewhere along the way, Nashville had ceased to be a Western

Like ducks in a row, steamboats lined the Nashville wharf in the "golden decade" of the 1850s. This 1859 photograph may be the earliest ever taken of the busy scene at the foot of Broad Street.

city in the national scheme of things; it had become Southern, in both fact and feeling, and it lay at the very edge of the fault line along which the nation would soon be divided.

The time when the village on the Cumberland had been a beckoning land for fortune seekers had long since passed. The seekers had come, and a few of them had found fortunes, and they and the less fortunate together had built a city. It had kept its gates open for more than half a century, attracting thousands of newcomers and even sending restless soldiers of fortune on to the next horizon. Sam Houston and Sterling Robertson and George C. Childress were among that restless breed, but there were others: Peter H. Burnett, a Nashvillian who pioneered in the far West and became the first governor of California; William Walker, who became president of

A failure as a physician, an attorney, and an editor, the brilliant and enigmatic William Walker of Nashville became an international sensation as a soldier of fortune. This tintype shows the "gray-eyed man of destiny" in his 1850s prime. He led an invasion of Nicaragua in 1855 and was elected its President, only to die five years later before a firing squad in Honduras.

Nicaragua and was put to death by a firing squad in Honduras; and C. Roberdeau Wheat, a local preacher's son who fought in revolutions in Central America and Italy and died leading the Louisiana Tigers against Union forces in the Civil War.

Nashville had drawn adverturers to it and sent others out in search of new adventures. It had been an open city for all its years of existence. Now it was about to become a garrison, a battleground, and it would be profoundly changed by the experience.

Republican Banner

AND NASHVILLE WHIG.
PUBLISHED BY W.F. BANG & CO.

Monday, December 16, 1850.

THE IRON HORSE ARRIVED AT LAST

The steamboat Beauty, from Cincinnati arrived here on Friday evening with the *first locomotive* for the Nashville and Chattanooga Rail Road. It is from the manufactury of A. Harkness & Son, of Cincinnati, and is a very substantial piece of work. Along with it were brought one tender, and one splendid passenger car from the establishment of Keck & Davenport, also of Cincinnati. Also thirteen freight cars . . . . The passenger car is a very beautiful piece of workmanship, the seats of mahogany with figured plush cushions. We understand from Mr. Stevenson that a much finer one has been ordered, which (we take it) *must be for the especial accommodation of the Editorial fraternity* who have done so much to push the enterprize through. This is truly considerate,—supposing that to be the case.

The road in the vicinity of town is going forward in its completion very fast, the iron rails being laid as rapidly as possible.

NASHVILLE TRUE WHIG.

A.M. ROSBOROUGH, Editor

Saturday Morning, Dec. 28, 1850.

The Iron Horse "in Harness"—The new locomotive, "Tennessee," was put "in gear" yesterday evening, and made a trial trip of a mile out the Nashville and Chattanooga Railroad. The little excursion was witnessed with much interest by a number of speculators, some of whom "took passage." It marks an era in our history.

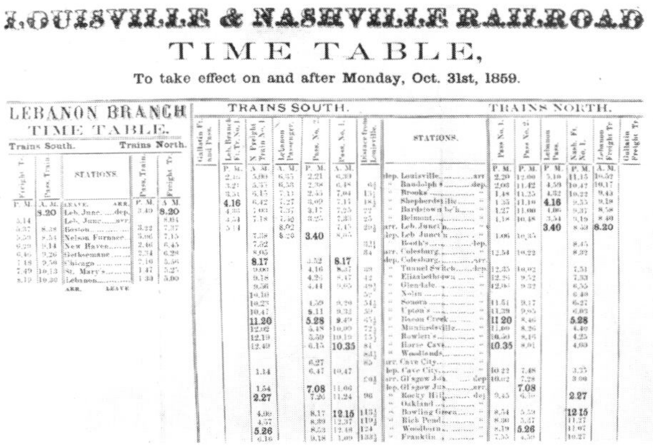

LOUISVILLE & NASHVILLE RAILROAD

TIME TABLE,

To take effect on and after Monday, Oct. 31st, 1859.

LEBANON BRANCH TIME TABLE.

Trains South.			Trains North.	
Freight Tr.	Pass. Train	STATIONS	Pass. Train	Freight Tr.
P. M.	A. M.	LEAVE. ARR.	P. M.	A. M.
	8.20	Leb. Junc. ....dep.	3.40	8.20
5.14		Leb. Junc. ....arr.		8.04
5.37	8.38	Boston	3.22	7.37
5.53	8.54	Nelson Furnace	3.06	7.15
6.20	9.14	New Haven	2.46	6.45
6.46	9.26	Gethsemane	2.34	6.29
7.18	9.58	Chicago	2.16	5.58
7.49	10.13	St. Mary's	1.47	5.27
8.10	10.30	Lebanon	1.30	5.00
		ARR. LEAVE		

TRAINS SOUTH.								TRAINS NORTH.					
Gallatin Ft. and Pass.	Leb. Branch Ft. Tr. No. 1	N. Freight Train No. 1	Lebanon Passenger	Pass. No. 2	Pass. No. 1	Distance from Louisville	STATIONS.	Pass No. 1	Pass No. 2	Lebanon Pass.	Nash. Ft. No. 1	Lebanon Freight Tr.	Gallatin Freight Tr.
	P. M.	A. M.	A. M.	P. M.	A. M.			P. M.	P. M.	P. M.	P. M.	A. M.	
	2.15	5.00	6.35	2.21	6.30		dep. Louisville .... arr	2.20	12.00	5.10	11.15	10.57	
	3.27	5.37	6.53	2.38	6.48	6¾	" Randolph's .... dep.	2.03	11.42	4.59	10.47	10.17	
	3.51	6.15	7.11	2.55	7.04	13½	" Brooks .... "	1.48	11.25	4.32	10.22	9.43	
	4.16	6.42	7.27	3.09	7.17	18¼	" Shepherdsville .... "	1.35	11.10	4.16	9.55	9.18	
	4.33	7.03	7.37	3.17	7.25	22	" Bardstown br'h .... "	1.27	11.00	4.06	9.37	8.58	
	4.54	7.18	7.50	3.25	7.33	25	" Belmont .... "	1.18	10.48	3.54	9.19	8.40	
	5.14		8.02		7.45	29½	arr. Leb. Junct'n .... "			3.40	8.53	8.20	
		7.38	8.20	3.40	8.05		dep. Leb Junct'n .... "	1.06	10.35				
		7.52				33¼	Booth's .... dep.				8.45		
		8.05				34	arr. Colesburg .... "	12.54	10.22		8.32		
		8.17		3.52	8.17		dep. Colesburg .... arr.						
		9.00		4.16	8.37	39	" Tunnel Switch .... dep.	12.35	10.02		7.51		
		9.18		4.26	8.47	42	" Elizabethtown .... "	12.26	9.52		7.33		
		9.56		4.44	9.05	49½	" Glendale .... "	12.06	9.32		6.55		
		10.10				[illegible]	" Nolin .... "				6.40		
		10.27		4.59	9.20	54½	" Sonora .... "	11.51	9.17		6.27		
		10.47		5.11	9.32	59	" Upton's .... "	11.39	9.05		6.03		
		11.20		5.28	9.49	63½	" Bacon Creek .... "	11.20	8.46		5.28		
		12.02		5.48	10.09	72	" Munfordsville .... "	11.00	8.26		4.40		
		12.19		5.59	10.19	75	" Rowlett's .... "	10.50	8.16		4.25		
		12.49		6.15	10.35	81	" Horse Cave .... "	10.35	8.01		4.00		
						83½	" Woodlands .... "						
				6.27		85	arr. Cave City .... "						
		1.14		6.47	10.47		dep. Cave City .... "	10.22	7.48		3.35		
						[illegible]	arr. Gl'sgow Jn .... dep	10.02	7.28		3.00		
		1.54		7.08	11.06		dep. Gl'sgow Jn .... arr.		7.08				
		2.27		7.26	11.24	96	" Rocky Hill .... dep	9.45	[illegible]		2.27		
							" Oakland .... "						
		4.00		8.17	12.15	113½	" Bowling Green .... "	8.54	5.59		12.15		
		4.37		8.30	12.37	119½	" Rich Pond .... "	8.30	5.37		11.27		
		5.26		8.53	12.48	124	" Woodburn .... "	8.19	5.26		11.07		
		6.18		9.18	1.09	133½	" Franklin .... "	7.55	4.50		10.27		

On December 13, 1850, a steamboat called at the Nashville wharf to deliver a locomotive engine to the Nashville and Chattanooga Railroad. The symbolism of that transaction was filled with irony—a steamboat had brought to town the instrument of its own eventual destruction—but it would be years before the significance of it would be fully understood. Before the steamboat and the train could wage their battle for survival, the South and the North had to fight theirs, and the Nashville railroad would play an important role.

The train made its first trip, an eleven-mile run to Antioch, in 1851; three years later, the line was opened to Chattanooga. Then, in 1859, a line was opened between Louisville and Nashville. It was finished just in time for the Union Army to take it over. The dreaded day of civil war had finally arrived for Nashville and the nation.

THE LOUISVILLE JOURNAL

Louisville, Kentucky • October 27, 1859

THE EXCURSION TO NASHVILLE

The Louisville and Nashville RailRoad is open to public travel today, and Louisville is within eight or nine hours distance from the Capital of Tennessee. The whole construction and equipment of the road have been effected in the very best style, and it will compare favorably with any other railroad in the country. Two passenger trains will leave our city daily . . . .

Everything seems to have been prepared with careful foresight, and as we were of the number invited to join the excursion for the first opening of the road, we have an opportunity of inspecting the work thoroughly.

It was after five o'clock before we reached Nashville, and in the golden flood of the sunset, it presented a beautiful appearance—the new Capitol, the most conspicuous object in the distance, and the suspension bridge over the Cumberland River, poised in airy lightness like a telegraph wire . . . . Nashville is emphatically built on a rock, the limestone strat being horizontal . . . . It possesses a great many fine stores and palatial residences, but very many of the citizens occupy cottage houses, a few miles from the turmoil of business. The Lebanon turnpike is filled with these suburban abodes. The press is an institution in Nashville. There are five daily newspapers, and the corps editorial is distinguished.

The Davidson, a wood-burning locomotive built in 1855, was also known as Number 8. Named for Davidson County, it was one of the first engines to make the run between Louisville and Nashville when the L&N line opened in 1859. According to the original timetable, the distance between the two cities was 185½ miles, and passenger trains took nine hours to make the trip.

An Educational Awakening

John Hope Franklin

At the end of the Civil War, Nashville had few things of which to be proud, and her educational institutions were not among them. Whether one looked at public school facilities that did not begin until the mid-fifties, or higher education for whites that was not as good in 1860 as it had been in 1830, or opportunities for blacks that did not exist at all, one could see the need for a real educational awakening. That is precisely what happened in the postwar years.

John Berrien Lindsley was a mere two months old when his father, Philip, resigned his position as acting president of Princeton University in 1824 to become president of the University of Nashville. From that point on, the Lindsleys would do much to verify the characterization of Nashville as the Athens of the West, though others would later place it in a more accurate geographic setting. Soon the university and the Lindsleys prospered, and by the time John Berrien succeeded his father as head of the institution in 1855, he was both a physician and an ordained Presbyterian minister. There always seemed to be time for one more public service; in 1856, he became a member of the city board of education and helped lead the drive for a school system of high rank.

Within months after the Civil War ended, Lindsley was called upon to serve briefly as superintendent of the Nashville city schools. Since the schools had greatly deteriorated during the war, Lindsley's task was extremely difficult. He said that Tennessee had the "meanest, poorest, most fruitless school system in America . . . ." Thus, he was understandably aggravated when some politicians assumed that the schools were just another patronage preserve. In a bold statement that must have startled run-of-the-mill politicians, Lindsley warned them that the schools of Nashville were "above and beyond political manipulation."

Lindsley believed that the public schools were no better than their teachers, whose need for improvement was so obvious. Consequently, he sought support from the Peabody Education Fund for a normal school for the training of teachers. The officers of the fund encouraged him to present a plan that they finally accepted in 1875 for the establishment of an institution, the State Normal College (later Peabody Normal College), that would have the support of the fund, the University of Nashville, and the state board of education. With better schools and a reliable source for well-trained teachers, the youngest students in Nashville's white population had a real opportunity to be trained as Southern Athenians.

Clinton B. Fisk, prohibitionist, abolitionist, and brigadier general, postponed his discharge from the Union Army when Abraham Lincoln was assassinated. Andrew Johnson appointed him assistant commissioner of the Freedmen's Bureau in Tennessee, an appointment which the new President defended with the remark, "Fisk aint a fool, he wont hang everybody." Fisk soon had his hands full trying to calm a restive, dissatisfied, disheartened freedman population. When blacks called a statewide convention to meet in Nashville on August 7, 1865, Fisk thought it wise to accept the invitation to speak as a representative of the federal government. He stressed responsibilities as well as privileges of citizenship and urged the freedmen to seize opportunities to improve their economic well-being.

If Fisk was a moderating influence, he did not succeed in restraining the freedmen altogether. In their resolutions they called attention to an earlier petition they had sent the legislature in which they declared that the government could afford to trust the freedman "with a vote as safely as it trusted him with a bayonet." The legislature had not responded, and now the convention asked Congress not to receive the congressional delegation from Tennessee "if the Legislature of Tennessee does not grant the petition before it prior to December 1, 1865." The legislature, in control of Tennesseans who were unalterably opposed to the enfranchisement of blacks, paid no attention to the petition of the freedmen.

Fisk, however, firmly believed that Negroes should have the vote, and he had stated his views in his speeches. But when they received it, as he was confident they would, he wanted them to use their political power wisely. The best way to prepare them for that day was to educate them. As a part of his general plan to aid the freedmen, Fisk joined with E.P. Smith, Erastus M. Cravath (both Congregational ministers representing the American Missionary Association) and John Ogden in securing land on which to erect a school for freedmen. On January 9, 1866, the Fisk School opened in a group of one-story frame buildings that were formerly a hospital barracks for the Union Army. The following year the institution received a charter as Fisk University, and since Lindsley's city board of education was beginning to make provision for the education of black children, Fisk University was gradually relieved of its responsibility for elementary education.

General Fisk continued to maintain an interest in *his* university even after he became a prosperous New York banker. When the Jubilee Singers went to Northern cities and to Britain to raise funds for the university, they had his blessing, and when Jubilee Hall, constructed with the money they raised, was dedicated in 1876, the general returned to deliver an "able, eloquent, and appreciative" dedicatory address. With Fisk University as the flagship institution, the establishment of other colleges and universities for blacks, such as Central Tennessee College (later Walden University), Meharry Medical College, and Roger Williams University, indicated that black Nashvillians would do much to make good the claim that their city was, indeed, the Athens of the South.

In the early postwar years, there was no really first-class university for whites. The medical school and other departments of the University of Nashville had been all but discontinued, and little remained of the venerable institution except the teacher training school that had become the State Normal College. Obviously, this condition could not long continue, and it was the Methodist Episcopal Church, South, that came to the rescue in 1872 with plans for Central University. But the million dollar fund that the Methodists pledged to raise never materialized.

Holland Nimmons McTyeire, who had been elected bishop of his church in 1866, was both disappointed and distressed over the failure of his beloved Methodists to establish a university in Nashville. While visiting his friend, Cornelius Vanderbilt, in 1873, he told the Commodore of the efforts and failure of the friends of Central University. At dinner one evening, Vanderbilt responded by placing before Bishop McTyeire a proposal to save the university.

Vanderbilt authorized the bishop to procure suitable grounds and erect suitable buildings "for the uses of the university." He would establish an endowment fund of $300,000 and later he would provide additional funds for current expenses. These provisions were contingent upon the bishop's accepting the position of president of the board of trustees with a salary of $3,000 and a rent-free residence on or near the university campus. McTyeire accepted the conditions laid down by Vanderbilt and in appreciation for his generosity the board of trustees secured a charter renaming the institution Vanderbilt University. The philanthropist expressed the hope that it would strengthen the ties "that should exist between all sections of the country."

Holland N. McTyeire, at the insistence of Vanderbilt, enjoyed full veto power over any actions taken by the chancellor or the board of trustees of the university. While he did not abuse his authority, he kept himself fully informed of developments at the university. He lived on the campus and was well acquainted with the officers of administration and members of the faculty. He remained president of the board until his death in 1889, by which time Vanderbilt University had no peers anywhere in the South.

What an array of educational institutions Nashville had by the end of the century! There were professional schools, multipurpose universities, liberal arts colleges, industrial schools, and finishing schools. Some of them had even transcended the region and become national in reputation and influence. Thus, Nashville was not only the Athens of the South but the mecca for so many who sought to raise their own educational and intellectual sights.

John Hope Franklin, president of the American Historical Association, is the John Matthews Manly Distinguished Service Professor of History at the University of Chicago. An honor graduate of Fisk University and later a faculty member there, he has served for thirty-two years on the Fisk board of trustees, including seven years as chairman. His mother and father attended Roger Williams University in Nashville in the 1890s.

"No North, No South, No East, No West, Nothing but the Union," proclaimed presidential candidate John Bell's campaign poster in 1860. Nashvillian Bell (left) and his vice presidential running mate, Edward Everett, were candidates of the Constitutional Union Party.

Nashville:
Division and Reunion
1860-1900

CONFEDERATE Major William Mott was among the last of the Rebel defenders to leave Nashville. On Thursday morning, February 20, 1862, he walked alone through the littered streets and "beheld the most desolate place I think ever existed; those beautiful ladies that I [had seen] at every window had either deserted the doomed city or secreted themselves from view of passers by. Soldiers and citizens seemed to have emulated their example and scarcely a living, moving being was to be seen, not even a dog, in once busy, hustling, thriving Nashville.

What had begun the previous June as a defiant bolt from the Union by the people of Nashville and Tennessee was about to end with the surrender of the city to federal forces. On the evening of February 24, Major General Don Carlos Buell arrived in Edgefield with his Union troops. Nashville Mayor Richard B. Cheatham crossed the river in a rowboat to talk with Buell, and he returned later to assure the citizens who remained that their lives and property would be protected. The next morning, a gunboat and several transports loaded with soldiers of the Sixth Ohio Volunteer Infantry reached the wharf at the foot of Broad Street. Marching to the music of their own small band, the soldiers paraded through the streets to the State Capitol and took command of it in the name of the United States. Soon, an old and famous American flag belonging to Nashville resident William Driver, an avid Union supporter, had replaced the Confederate stars and bars atop the capitol. The last statehouse to withdraw from membership in the nation thus became the first to be captured and returned to Union hands.

Nashville had never been eager for war. If its collective mood at the beginning of the 1860s could be fairly characterized, it probably would reflect general support for the practice of slavery but not a general willingness to secede from the Union or go to war for it. Not many local citizens opposed slavery, and the few who did kept their views discreetly to themselves—but at the same time, slave owners were a minority of the white population, even in rural Davidson County, and not even all of them spoke openly of slavery as an institution worth defending with guns and sabers.

Furthermore, Nashville was too well off economically to have a compelling urge for war. Its population of 17,000 in 1860 made it the eighth largest city in the South. It was a turbulent, energetic river town and a rising railroad town, a rapidly expanding center of commerce and industry. With so much money to be made and so much power to be accrued, the very notion of an all-out fight over any issue must have seemed wasteful and distracting. Nashville was a new city, and it had the rough edges to prove it—it had conspicuous opulence cheek by jowl with abject poverty; it had dirty air and dirty water and muddy streets; it could count sixty-nine houses of prostitution in a four-block-long strip between Spring Street and the Public Square. It may have needed refinement and reform, but it did not need war.

Early in 1861, voters of the city and the state opposed calling a convention to decide the secession issue. The previous fall, Nashville's own John Bell, the Jacksonian Democrat-turned-Whig, had run for President as the candidate of the Constitutional Union Party. Without opposing slavery in the South, he pleaded for preservation of the Union above all. He won the electoral votes of Tennessee, Kentucky, and Virginia, and carried Davidson County with fifty-eight percent of the vote—but Abraham Lincoln, barred from a place on the Tennessee ballot because of his views on slavery, swept the Northern states and won the election. A few months later, after the firing on Fort Sumter, Tennessee Governor Isham G. Harris defiantly rejected Lincoln's call for troops, the state legislature passed a declaration of independence from the United States, and the voters of Tennessee (including the Nashville electorate) ratified the resolution by a wide margin. In a complete reversal of form, Tennessee had become the eleventh and last of the Confederate States of America, having rejected the counsel of Bell and a few other moderates and conservatives who wanted the state, as a last resort, to take a position of neutrality.

In the eight months of its rebellion, Nashville moved with increasing enthusiasm toward a readiness for battle. The city became a strategic center for the manufacture and stockpiling of

PROCLAMATION!

MAYOR'S OFFICE,
CITY HALL, April 24, 1861.

WHEREAS, it is understood that self-constituted Committees, or Individuals on their own responsibility, have notified one or more of our Northern-born Citizens to leave Nashville; and whereas it is the determination of the City Authorities to preserve and sustain the peace and quiet of the City: This is, therefore, to notify all Persons that any complaints or suspicions against Persons of Northern birth can be lodged with me for investigation, and that everything necessary will be done. And all Persons implicated can be assured that they will be protected from unfounded rumors and stories, until properly investigated by the proper Authorities.

AND all good Citizens are earnestly requested to endeavor to quiet the public mind in the present state of excitement, and to aid the Authorities in preserving the peace of the City.

R. B. CHEATHAM,

weapons and supplies. A local powder plant was converted to a munitions factory, women began making uniforms and flags, the Nashville Plow Works started turning plowshares into swords, and a local music publishing company came out with a stirring composition called "Flag of the South." More than a dozen units of volunteer soldiers went through training exercises in the streets; the newspapers and even the churches added their voices to the militant chorus; huge parades and demonstrations were staged. For a time, the legislature and the city council sought support for an ambitious plan to relocate the Confederate capital from Montgomery, Alabama, to Nashville. It was moved instead to Richmond, Virginia, but the Confederate high command did send General Albert Sidney

Officers of Rutledge's Artillery, a Nashville unit, were photographed on July 4, 1861, before they went to fight for the South. The outfit was mustered in at the present site of Watkins Park on Seventeenth Avenue in North Nashville.

Johnston to Nashville to take charge of military forces in the area, and he was welcomed by the resounding cheers of thousands of city residents.

For all their patriotic spirit, however, the leaders of Nashville and Tennessee had given little thought to the city's defense. Emboldened by their own verbal belligerence, they had lost sight of the possibility of attack, and before Johnston could redirect their energies, federal gunboats had swept past Fort Donelson downriver and steamed toward the vulnerable city on the bluff.

General Johnston's stunning announcement on February 16, 1862, that Nashville would be abandoned to the Union Army so terrified the city that total panic and chaos spread like a violent fever. A mass exodus began in wagons, carriages, trains, on horseback, and on foot. Banks and stores were emptied; newspapers ceased publication; military units scattered in disarray. Governor Harris and other state officials departed in haste on a special train to Memphis, bearing carloads of government documents.

Johnston moved his command to Murfreesboro, and in the vacuum of authority left by his departure, frenzied mobs streamed wildly

Hard-eyed, hollow-cheeked Confederate General Nathan Bedford Forrest, a thorn in the flesh of his Union enemies in the Nashville area throughout the war, was a wealthy citizen of Memphis before he became a cavalry officer. After the war, he was an organizer of the Ku Klux Klan.

through the military storehouses, plundering goods and supplies. Confederate Colonel Nathan Bedford Forrest, riding in from Fort Donelson, led a cavalry charge into the midst of looters, hoping to restore law and order and to salvage the contents of the warehouses for his troops.

In less than a week, Nashville was transformed from a wartime boom town and a Confederate arsenal to a ghost town and then a Union stronghold in the Southern interior. The retreating Confederates burned the railroad bridge across the Cumberland and cut the huge cables on the suspension bridge, but the Union soldiers were not long delayed. By the time they arrived at the wharf and marched to the capitol, General Johnston and Colonel Forrest and even Major William Mott had departed from this "most desolate place." Before the national conflict was a year old, Nashville had become a prisoner of war.

February 1862

When I crossed the bridge and reached the square in Nashville I beheld a city upon which the foe was advancing. Those who once witnessed such a scene need no description. To those who have not, no description can give any idea of its wild confusion. The streets were filled with carriages, horses, buggies, wagons, drags, carts, everything which could carry a human being from the doomed city. Men, women, and children, the rich, the poor, white and black, mingled in one struggling mass which gave way for nothing but the soldiers marching through the city.

•

Every store and every shop was closed while the people refused to be seen even at the doors and windows of private residences. The Yankees in the most magnificent uniforms, and with bands which made the city echo to hostile airs, march through the streets tormented and enraged as only a Yankee can be by a total failure to make any impression on the contemptuous Southerners. When on the street we turned our eyes from them when possible, or followed them with looks of silent malediction . . . . We had no pleasure but in insulting our oppressors, but we did not stint ourselves in that.

from the diary of Lizzie Hardin, a teenager in a pro-Confederate family

116

DURING THREE YEARS of occupation by the Union Army, Nashville symbolized a nation at war with itself. It quickly became a vital supply depot and military command post for federal forces. River and railroad traffic supporting the military effort soon reached unprecedented levels. Hospitals for wounded soldiers were set up at the University of Nashville and elsewhere in the city. Military units came and went constantly, and a stream of black refugees from the rural countryside poured into the city seeking shelter from the war. And in the midst of all this activity, there remained a great many resident Nashvillians—a mixture of Union and Confederate sympathizers, women and children, merchants and ministers, opportunists and innocent bystanders. Most of them tried to carry on with their normal activities; some of them succeeded, and a few actually profited from the oc-

cupation. All of them witnessed profound changes in the appearance and character of the city.

In March 1862, President Lincoln sent Andrew Johnson to Nashville to be military governor of Tennessee. A native of East Tennessee, Johnson had been governor before, in the mid-1850s, and he had also served in both houses of the state legislature and of the Congress. He had been a member of the United States Senate when Tennessee seceded from the Union, and he had refused to join state officials in rebellion. His intimate familiarity with Tennessee, its capital, and its people made him a natural choice for the task of guiding the state back into the national fold.

To that end, Johnson offered complete amnesty to the "erring and misguided" supporters of the Confederacy and required all municipal officials, educators, journalists, and clergymen to

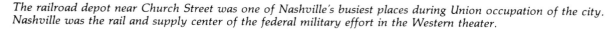

The railroad depot near Church Street was one of Nashville's busiest places during Union occupation of the city. Nashville was the rail and supply center of the federal military effort in the Western theater.

Governor of Tennessee in peace and war, later Vice President and then President of the United States, Andrew Johnson was the third man to go from Nashville to the nation's highest office. His portrait was painted by Washington Cooper in about 1855.

sign an oath of allegiance to the United States. Those who refused were arrested for treason and either jailed or—in the case of several ministers—sent south beyond federal lines. The Methodist and Baptist publishing houses were taken over and converted to Union purposes, and among newspapers, only those which wholeheartedly supported the federal government were permitted to continue publication.

After General Buell moved most of his army out of Nashville to pursue the war on another front, Governor Johnson was left with a garrison of only 2,000 men and a defense structure around the city that was still as inadequate as it had been under the Confederates. Throughout the summer of 1862, Confederate cavalry leaders John Hunt Morgan and Nathan Bedford Forrest continually led raids against Union weak points around Nashville, and as fall approached, the city was virtually blockaded and in imminent danger of recapture.

Overextended both in the field and in defense of the city, Buell seemed to favor abandoning Nashville, but Johnson was firmly opposed. Instead, he turned to what manpower he had available and began systematic construction of fortifications, telling Buell he would burn down the city before he would surrender it. On Capitol Hill and on other high elevations south and west of there, forts were quickly thrown up, with black laborers conscripted to do most of the work. Throughout the city, ancient trees were felled to form barricades and to make easier the sighting of approaching troops. What had been a dense forest in James Robertson's time and a shade-graced town in Andrew Jackson's became virtually overnight an exposed and barren landscape.

A time of privation and near-panic ensued. In the long, humid days of August and September, food supplies dwindled, prices soared, saloons

I had a visit last night from Colonel Moody the fighting Methodist parson, as he is called in Tennessee . . . . He told me this story of Andy Johnson and General Buell, which interested me intensely. Colonel Moody was in Nashville the day it was reported that Buell had decided to evacuate the city. The rebels, strongly reinforced, were said to be within two days' march of the capital . . . . [Moody said he] went in search of Johnson at the close of the evening, and found him at his office . . . . [Johnson approached Moody] manifesting intense feeling and said "Moody, we are sold out! Buell is a traitor! He is going to evacuate the city, and in forty-eight hours we shall all be in the hands of the rebels." Then he commenced pacing the floor again, twisting his hands, and chafing, like a caged tiger . . . . Suddenly he turned and said, "Moody can you pray?" "That is my business, sir, as a minister of the Gospel," returned the Colonel. "Well, Moody, I wish you would pray," said Johnson; and instantly both men went down upon their knees at opposite sides of the room. As the prayer became fervent, Johnson began to respond in true Methodist style. Presently he crawled over on his hands and knees to Moody's side, and put his arm over him, manifesting the deepest emotion. Closing the prayer with a hearty "Amen!" from each, they arose. Johnson took a long breath, and said, with emphasis, "Moody, I feel better!" . . . He then commenced pacing the floor again. Suddenly he wheeled, the current of his thought having changed, and said, "Oh! Moody, I don't want you to think I have become a religious man because I asked you to pray. I am sorry to say it, but I am not, and have never pretended to be, religious. No one knows this better than you; but, Moody—there is one thing about it—I DO believe in ALMIGHTY GOD! And I believe also in the Bible, and I say I'll be *damned* if Nashville shall be surrendered!" *And Nashville was not surrendered!*

ABRAHAM LINCOLN, **as told to F. B. Carpenter at the White House, May 1864, and published in** *Life and Public Services of Andrew Johnson,* **by John Savage (1866)**

Having moved to Nashville from New York in the 1850s after the church split over slavery, the Southern Methodist Publishing House was taken over by the Union Army during the occupation. This photograph from about 1860 shows the publishing house and its bookstore on the east side of the Public Square.

Colonel William Truesdail, head of the Union Army's secret police in Nashville, could have played the part of a spy commander on the basis of looks alone. Not even Union troops escaped his eyes and ears.

closed, general health was endangered, and government at all levels was inept and ineffectual. Finally, late in October, the Army of the Cumberland, a 50,000-man Union force under Major General William S. Rosecrans, marched into the city with orders to shore up its defenses, and the blockade was broken.

Nashville was thus rescued from the danger of Confederate recapture—but it was far from being liberated. In the two years that followed before another external threat to the city arose, day-to-day life in the close confines of this military stronghold grew more crowded and in some ways more dangerous than it had been when the guns of war were cocked and aimed at the city's heart. Counting foot soldiers, hospital patients, civilians, government officials, prison inmates, rural immigrants, and a motley legion of prostitutes and camp followers, the population of Nashville swelled beyond 80,000. An active underground of saboteurs and smugglers worked diligently for the cause of the Confederacy. On the other side, General Rosecrans and one of his subordinates, Colonel William Truesdail, sent spies and agents provocateurs into the streets and taverns to break up the illicit activity. Not even soldiers in the Union Army were exempt from surveillance, and among local citizens, including some of the most prominent, arrest and imprisonment frequently took place.

Drunkenness, prostitution, and crime were rampant. In 1863, military officials arrested 150

prostitutes and sent them away on a steamboat, only to have them promptly returned by city officials in Louisville and Cincinnati. One of the many military hospitals in Nashville was reserved exclusively for patients suffering from venereal disease. A thriving black market in food, clothing, and firearms operated freely throughout the city, and in underworld shantytowns known as Slabtown and Smokey Row, crime was an everyday fact of life. A local newspaper commented in 1864 that Nashville was "filled with thugs, highwaymen, robbers, and assassins. Murder stalks throughout the city almost every night."

Authority—such as it was—was divided in incomprehensible fashion among city, county, state, and military officials, to which could be added the secret police of Rosecrans and Truesdail. In the midst of all the confusion and turmoil and the hazards to health and life, still another perplexing concern arose as legions of former slaves sought refuge in the city.

With the rural countryside in chaos and disorder because of the war, first hundreds and then thousands of blacks began to pour into Nashville in 1863. They came in desperation, often with nothing but the clothes on their backs. As the war dragged on, they huddled under whatever shelter there was, took food and jobs wherever they could find them, and waited in forlorn hope for a better day.

It would be a long time coming. Throughout

Market Street in the Civil War period looked more like part of a Western frontier town than an eighty-five-year-old city. Stone posts at the corners of the muddy streets kept wagons from rolling up on the wooden sidewalks.

the occupation, federal officials regarded the blacks in a variety of confused and contradictory ways—as liberated people, as refugees, as contraband, as potential soldiers, as serfs. The government provided some food, clothing, and tents, a few opportunities for work, and even a little schooling for the children, but all the while they kept the former slaves confined in segregated camps. By and large, the black refugees from bondage were at the mercy of the weather, the military, and the white civilians who had first call on the limited security and sustenance to be found in the overcrowded city.

In the face of these almost overwhelming problems, Nashville struggled to maintain a semblance of normal life. A few churches managed to continue services, but some were converted into hospitals, others were stymied by conflict with military officials, and still others were torn asunder by internal disruptions. Some schools were able to stay open, but the public schools were completely shut down for two years. A good many merchants not only maintained business as usual but made bigger profits in wartime than they had in peace.

The most persistent and determined show of continuity may have been in the regular performances of the Nashville Theater. It had begun long before the war as the Adelphi in a building near the corner of present-day Fourth and Charlotte avenues; under a new name and new management, it provided the only legitimate

Among the many military hospitals in Nashville during the Civil War was this former school at the corner of Summer and Line streets (now Fifth Avenue near Jo Johnston Avenue). Known as General Hospital Number 15, it was used to treat soldiers suffering from venereal disease. A separate venereal disease hospital for women was also maintained.

If I remember rightly there were present Generals Grant, Sherman, Sheridan, Granger, Logan and myself. All of us of the Army of the Tennessee were a hard looking crowd. None us had seen Nashville or any base of supplies since we had marched from the Mississippi river to Chattanooga . . . .

We arrived in Nashville late in the afternoon and General Sherman took us to General Grant's headquarters. General Grant suggested that we should call on the military governor of Tennessee, Andrew Johnson, and pay our respects to him . . . .

After our visit to the Governor, General Sherman suggested that we should all go to the theater that evening, and under his lead we went to the principal opera house to hear the play "Hamlet." We were all strangers in Nashville; even General Grant was not well known. We paid our way in and found the theater crowded with soldiers . . . . General Sherman, who was a great lover of the theater, sat alongside of me, and soon began criticizing the play,

earnestly protesting that it was being murdered. I had to check him several times and tell him that unless he kept quiet the soldiers in the audience would recognize him and there would be a scene.

We had entered late and soon there came the scene where Hamlet soliloquizes over the skull of Yorick. The audience was perfectly still, endeavoring to comprehend the actor's words, when a soldier far back in the audience rose up and in a clear voice called out as the actor held up the skull, "Say, pard, what is it? Yank or Reb?" The house appreciated the point and was instantly in an uproar. General Grant said we had better leave, so we went quietly out, no one discovering the identity of Grant or Sherman.

General Grenville M. Dodge, Sixteenth Corps, Union Army, recalling a December 1863 evening in Nashville; published in *Nashville, The Home of the History Makers,* by Wiliam E. Beard (1929)

local entertainment for war-weary soldiers and civilians alike. Generals Ulysses S. Grant and William Tecumseh Sherman went there more than once on their visits to Union headquarters in Nashville, and Governor Johnson was also an occasional patron.

During a two-week engagement at the theater in February 1864, an actor by the name of John Wilkes Booth performed the prodigious feat of starring in thirteen different plays. Booth already had a reputation as an outspoken advocate of the Southern cause, but he was highly popular with Northern audiences and received generally favorable reviews wherever he went. A critic for one of the Nashville papers wrote that he could not commend Booth because he was "too violent," but in the main the young actor was favorably received on the stage and in the city. He played to packed houses, and after a final benefit performance on February 12—Lincoln's birthday—the *Nashville Daily Union* reviewer wrote: "His genius appears equal to anything the tragic muse has produced; and the time is not distant when he will attain his highest

niche of professional fame." A little more than a year later, Booth produced his own tragic drama when he assassinated President Lincoln at Ford's Theater in Washington.

Nashville staggered under its military burden through the spring and summer of 1864. Then, with Sherman marching through Georgia toward a decisive victory in the war, Lieutenant General John B. Hood led his Confederate Army of Tennessee out of Atlanta and around Sherman's flank for a surprising and desperate dash toward Nashville. Sherman sent Major General George H. Thomas to stop Hood. Thus the only battle of the war to be fought here finally took shape in the last December before Appomattox.

Thomas had nearly 60,000 men behind the fortifications in Nashville. Hood brought his force of 23,000 into the circle of hills south of the city and dug in. Both armies waited through several days of bitter cold, shivering for want of enough trees to fell for firewood. Then, on December 15, Thomas sent his troops out to attack Hood, and while Nashvillians watched from their rooftops, the Union Army used its

The lines were drawn for the Battle of Nashville in this engraving from the December 31, 1864, edition of Harper's Weekly. The view is toward the north, showing the Tennessee State Capitol in the distance.

December 16, 1864

The cannon has been thundering all day yesterday and all today. The battle evidently is raging at last, and will certainly be a furious one under the circumstances—the rebels in sight of their homes will fight with desperation . . . . Yesterday for the first time the rebs returned our fire. Every report shakes the whole house—but we do not mind it, but keep quiet around roaring fires,—for it is bitterly, bitterly cold . . . .

It is wonderful how we could have become so accustomed to this state of affairs as to take it so quietly as we are doing today! I remember when two years ago the battle was raging as far off as Murfreesboro, how excited we all were, and how I started and trembled at the faint, far off sound . . . and was too unnerved to do anything but think of the horrible carnage then going on: while today when the deadly work is going on within a mile of our own doors, within sight indeed!—when the artillery is deafening, we sit before the fire quietly, read, chat & laugh!

from the diary of Maggie Lindsley, a niece of John Berrien Lindsley

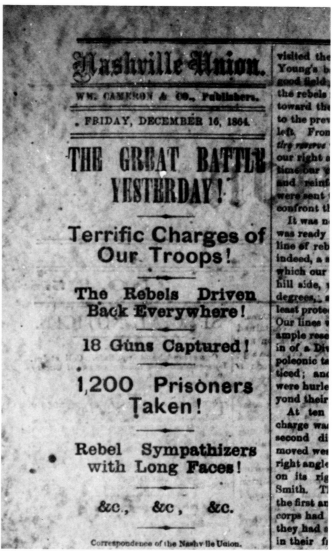

Nashville Union.

WM. CAMERON & CO., Publishers.

FRIDAY, DECEMBER 16, 1864.

THE GREAT BATTLE YESTERDAY!

Terrific Charges of Our Troops!

The Rebels Driven Back Everywhere!

18 Guns Captured!

1,200 Prisoners Taken!

Rebel Sympathizers with Long Faces!

&c., &c., &c.

Correspondence of the Nashville Union.

. . . Nashville . . . was one of the brightest, most wealthy and prosperous cities of the Union. Of all this she is now the exact reverse. Her finest buildings, such as her colleges, churches, and elegant stores, are now used as military hospitals and store-houses. Her streets are dirty, and, where main outlets from the city, they have been cut in two,—dug out, as though a canal was being made through them,—the dirt thrown up on each side, as barricades against rebel attack . . . . Her suburbs are a mournful wreck in many localities,—houses deserted, fences gone, fruit-trees gnawed and disfigured . . . . The groves—the glory of the place—are cut down, and the grounds present the appearance of a new "clearing," a stump-field . . . . The old, wealthy merchants of the city—those who yet remain—are prostrate in the dust of bankruptcy, and new traders—men from the North—are daily rising up in their places . . . . As the Union is more surely restored and its future guaranteed, [Nashville] will revive . . . . She will be purged from the curse that has afflicted her and dragged her down. Slavery will no longer blight and wither her morals, nor will a haughty, unproductive aristocracy prey upon her vitals. Tennessee, with free labor, has the capability of becoming one of the grandest States of the Union; and Nashville is her crown-jewel.

Union officer John Fitch, in the *Annals of the Army of the Cumberland*, Philadelphia, 1864

As soon as I found all was lost, and the enemy closing in around us . . . I ordered the couriers and clerks who were there to follow me, and we rode as we could to where I thought General Stewart and General Hood were. They were gone and in their places were the Yankees.

I turned my horse's head toward the steep knobs and spurred away. It was the only chance of escape left . . . . Finally I reached a place not too steep, and in the midst of a thousand retreating soldiers I turned my horse's head for the ascent . . . . The bullets began to come thick and fast. Now I found my saddle nearly off, and was forced to get down, but on I went on foot. The poor frightened fellows were crying out to me, "Let me hold on to your stirrup, for God's sake." "Give me your hand and help me, please." Some were wounded and many exhausted from anxiety and overexertion.

On I struggled until I, too, became exhausted and unable to move . . . . I twisted my hands into my horse's mane and was borne to the top of the hill by the noble animal, more dead than alive. I was safe, though, and so were my men.

All night long we fled . . . . On we marched through ice and rain and snow, sleeping on the wet ground at night. Many thousands were barefooted, actually leaving the prints of blood upon the ground as the enemy pressed us in the rear.

from a report by Confederate Colonel W. D. Gale, December 1864

superior numbers with devastating effect. After two days of fighting, Hood and his bruised and bloody remnant of an army retreated into Alabama and Mississippi, and the first and only Battle of Nashville was over.

Soon after that, when the Confederate bid for independence was clearly a lost cause, the army of General Thomas was transferred from the city, and Governor Andrew Johnson, having been elected Vice President on the Union ticket with Lincoln, left for Washington to assume his new duties. A new governor, William G. "Parson" Brownlow, was inaugurated. Union loyalists were in command of Tennessee and of the nation. Lee's surrender to Grant, Lincoln's assassination, and Johnson's elevation to the office of President were close at hand.

The war had claimed tens of thousands of lives. One part of the Union, having prevailed against its other half, made a show of celebrating victory, but it was a costly triumph. Wounds had been inflicted that would take a century and more to heal. Many war-torn cities were in ruins. Nashville was among the more fortunate, yet a sympathetic Union officer, John Fitch, described it as "stagnant, prostrate, and in the abject position of a subjugated city." In the chill gray April of 1865, the road to recovery was a narrow path of thorns, and all uphill.

Artist-illustrator Howard Pyle's painting of the Battle of Nashville shows the Seventh Minnesota Infantry charging up Shy's Hill to attack the Confederate fortification there on December 16, 1864. The painting now hangs in the Minnesota State Capitol. The Union Army of General George H. Thomas (right) routed the Confederate Army of General John B. Hood in what proved to be the last major battle of the war.

125

THE EFFECTS of the Civil War upon the institutions and structures of Nashville, upon its homes and businesses and its geography, could be readily seen. The majestic trees were gone, and the hills were scarred with the abandoned remains of Fort Negley and the other military installations. The Nashville Female Academy was closed, never to open again. The University of Nashville had been converted to hospital and barracks use, but it remained and would resume its mission. Hundreds of homes had been commandeered, and some of them had been destroyed.

Still, Nashville was not devastated. It had not been set to the torch, as Atlanta and Richmond had. It had suffered damage, but not destruction. Its downtown area remained essentially intact; it needed renovation more than reconstruction. The physical scars to property could be tended to, and Nashville could be revitalized as a city.

But the personal scars, the physical and psychological wounds, were far more serious. Many of them would be permanent; many more had already been fatal. Only in the anguished faces of the survivors could the awful impact of the war be seen; only in the sundered lives of individual people and families could the full cost of the tragedy be counted. The war's casualties included more than just the dead and wounded.

One such casualty was William Driver, the salty old sea captain whose flag had flown briefly over the Union-held capitol. It was a flag his mother had made for him in 1824, when he was first licensed to command a ship. He had named it Old Glory, and flown it from the mast of his first vessel on a voyage to the South Pacific. Driver had moved from Massachusetts to Nashville in 1837, following two of his brothers here. He had joined Christ Episcopal Church, married, raised a large family, and worked as a salesman. He was a Yankee through and through, and he flew his flag proudly on every holiday and election day. He was called Captain Bill, or Old Glory Driver, and he was well-liked.

When the Civil War began, Driver sewed his beloved flag inside a quilt for safekeeping, but he did not shrink from expressing his deeply felt pro-Union sentiments. When the Ohio Volunteer Infantry occupied Nashville, he solemnly presented the old flag to be flown over the capitol, and thereafter he displayed it regularly in front of his home until his death in 1886.

William Driver lived to see the Union restored, but he did not die a happy man. Three of his sons had joined the Confederate Army, and one had died in battle.

And then there was Felix Robertson: He had been born at Freeland's Station in 1781, born with Nashville itself, in the midst of another war—the war with the native American claimants to the Cumberland country. He had spent his life as a physician, a healer. When the Civil War came to Nashville, he was an eighty-year-old widower; his children and grandchildren were grown and gone, some to wear the Union blue, others the Confederate gray. If Dr. Robertson favored one side over the other, he kept the sentiment to himself; the fact of their division was tragedy enough. Through the years of conflict, he lived virtually as a recluse, shuttered away in sadness. Three months after Appomattox, he died quietly at his home.

And Francis B. Fogg: A lawyer, a Northerner by birth and sympathy, a Southerner by marriage and by choice, he had helped to found Nashville's public school system. He and his wife, Mary Middleton Rutledge, saw their son Henry off to war in a Confederate uniform, and saw him return in a coffin. In the same early battle of the war that claimed the life of Henry

"Old Glory," William Driver's famous flag, had a star for each of the twenty-four states when Driver's mother gave it to him in 1824. Before it flew briefly over the Union-held Tennessee State Capitol in 1862, Driver's family had repaired and updated the flag, adding ten stars and an anchor to honor the old sea captain's sailing days. He was an old man dressed in black—mourning, perhaps, the death of a son in Confederate gray—when his picture was made in about 1880.

Fogg, Nashville journalist Felix Zollicoffer and the son of horseman Balie Peyton also died. The senior Peyton, like Francis Fogg, opposed secession; so had Zollicoffer, until the war came and he went with a sad sense of duty to serve his state and the Confederacy.

Painful family divisions such as these occurred repeatedly. John Berrien Lindsley, who succeeded his father as president of the University of Nashville and founded the medical school there, remained in the city throughout the war and was loyal to the Union. His wife was a sister of Randal McGavock, a former mayor of Nashville and a Confederate officer who died in battle. Joshua F. Pearl, the superintendent of Nashville's public schools, left the city in 1861 because of his Union sympathies and became a captain in the Union army, but his son stayed behind to join the Confederacy. Pearl returned to serve briefly as superintendent after the war.

Tennessee put 167,000 men in Confederate gray and 31,000 in Union blue—more in each case than any other Southern state—and

Nashville exemplified those divided loyalties. Relatively few Nashvillians served in the Union Army, but a good many, including Return J. Meigs, John Trimble, Samuel Watkins, and former Mayor John M. Lea, were steadfastly loyal to the Union cause. The Confederacy attracted an even larger number of the city's leaders, among them John C. Burch, William H. Jackson, John S. Bransford, V. K. Stevenson, Francis McNairy, and the Reverend John B. McFerrin. McNairy, a fourth-generation Nashvillian, lost his life.

Former Governor Neill S. Brown opposed secession, but he refused to sign the loyalty oath required by Governor Johnson; he was arrested for treason and then released, after which he expressed devotion to the cause of the United States.

Judge John Catron had been a Nashville lawyer and Tennessee's first chief justice before Andrew Jackson appointed him to the United States Supreme Court in 1837. Before the war began, he came home from Washington to plead

Handsome, red-haired Randal McGavock, a fourth-generation Nashvillian and a former mayor of the city, sat for this portrait before he went to fight and die for the Confederacy.

In the spring of the year 1869 Andrew Johnson, who had just finished his term as President of the United States, came home to Tennessee, and for some months resided in Nashville. Soon after his return . . . he delivered from a platform erected in the Courthouse square, his defense of his administration, in the presence of thousands of men . . . .

It was a simple, plain, well-constructed apologia, as the philosophers might call it, for his public career . . . . There was a sort of sincerity about it, which, for the time at least, won everybody . . . . I know that Johnson, the man, was to us a very different person from the Johnson about whom we had read and whom we expected to see . . . .

•

We saw Johnson again in September, 1869. On the tenth of that month died John Bell, a man for more than forty years prominent in Tennessee political affairs . . . . He had always been an ardent Whig and was a bitter enemy of his Democratic rival, Johnson . . . . The body of Mr. Bell lay in state in the chamber of the House of Representatives in the State House in Nashville. Sunday afternoon we young fellows made a part of a throng that slowly passed in line by the casket . . . .

It chanced that Andrew Johnson immediately preceded me in the slowly moving line. I watched him with keen interest as he stood before the body of one of his bitterest enemies, and a certain tenseness of feeling seemed to pervade the quiet, halting crowd. Mr. Johnson stood still for a whole minute with his eyes fastened on the face of Mr. Bell, but he made no sign, and his face was during that moment as expressionless as the face of the dead. Then with a sigh he passed on. We went away as if we had a glimpse of a solemn tragedy.

MARSHALL S. SNOW, in the *St. Louis Republic*, **February 28, 1913;** Snow had lived in Nashville after the war.

with Tennessee officials to hold the state in the Union. After secession, he was advised to leave the state. Catron returned in 1865, only to die soon thereafter.

John Bell, the Nashville congressman, moved to the United States Senate in 1847, served there fourteen years, and ran for President in 1860 as an anti-secessionist conservative Southerner. Having given his all to the preservation of the Union, he finally and reluctantly endorsed the Confederacy. Bell left Nashville when the federal army came but stayed in the South, and he died in 1869, described by a friend as "a heartbroken old man."

Andrew Ewing, grandson of the first clerk of the Davidson County court, served in Congress before the war and opposed secession but finally joined the Confederate Army. Adolphus Heiman, the Prussian immigrant who became one of Nashville's outstanding architects, died fighting for the Confederacy. Mark Robertson Cockrill, an old man with strong Southern sympathies, had his livestock confiscated by Union soldiers and retaliated by leading an abortive Rebel cavalry charge when he was seventy-five years old. William Giles Harding, the Belle Meade Plantation owner whose friends thought him peculiar because he bought and kept slaves

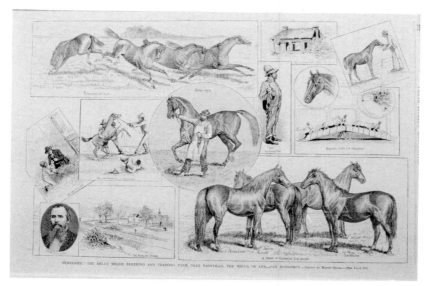

Bearded owner William Giles Harding, head groomsman Bob Green, and the horses that made Belle Meade "the Mecca of American Horsemen" highlight this group of drawings by artist Henry Stull of Frank Leslie's Illustrated Newspaper *in 1882. A photograph of Belle Meade in the 1890s (below) shows an expanse of meadowed upland in what is now Percy Warner Park; the main horse barn is larger than the stud farm's famous mansion, which appears on the far right in the photograph.*

but would not sell them, spent a few months in a Michigan prison for refusing to sign Governor Johnson's loyalty oath. Robert B. C. Howell, pastor of the First Baptist Church and an avid Rebel, went to prison along with several other ministers, and said proudly that it was "all we can do for our country."

The list went on endlessly. The venerable Mrs. James K. Polk graciously received Confederate and Union generals alike at her house, but she was a conspicuous exception; for the multitude, neutrality was not possible. Ordinary citizens, no less than the prominent, suffered division and death with the same certainty, and hordes of dispossessed blacks—landless,

nameless, powerless—could know in their first taste of freedom only more suffering.

Finally, the war's casualty list included the two young men who had been raised by Rachel and Andrew Jackson. Their nephew, Andrew Jackson Donelson, had been nominated for Vice President on the American Party ticket with Millard Fillmore in 1856, and Abraham Lincoln had solicited his support in 1860. Donelson strenuously opposed the secessionist movement, saying it would be the ruin of the South, but his two sons joined the Confederate Army, and both died in the war. His brother and all of his other male kinsmen were also Rebels, yet Donelson remained steadfastly loyal to the

Union. In Mississippi, he denounced Jefferson Davis publicly and called secession a cruel and unnecessary act. He was arrested there and later released. In 1871, he died in Memphis, an outcast and a despondent man who was, in the words of a friend, "overcome by the misfortunes of war."

Andrew Jackson Jr., the adopted son of the late President and his wife, stayed on at the Hermitage until 1855, when his inheritance was dissipated and he was near bankruptcy. He sold the house and 500 acres to the state and moved his family to Mississippi. Jackson maintained a steadfast loyalty to the federal government, but one of his sons, Samuel, joined the Confederacy and died of wounds received in battle, and another son, Andrew Jackson III, also a Confederate soldier, spent ten months in a federal prison camp in the North. In 1865, Andrew Jackson Jr. became one more victim in an age of violence; he died from the complications of a hunting-accident gunshot wound.

Whether by premeditated passion, by sudden outbursts of anger, by accident or inadvertence, death had become a commonplace occurrence and violence a way of life. Such were the consequences of a war among countrymen. Not for a century would the price of it be finally paid or the pain forgotten.

Top: William Giles Harding (seated, center) and his son-in-law, former Confederate officer William H. Jackson (standing, behind Harding), presided at this reunion of the Harding Light Artillery unit at Belle Meade in the early 1880s. Two of the uniformed men in the photograph—one on the left, the other on the right—appear to be blacks. It was rare for black men to wear Confederate gray, but some did.

Above: Soon after the Civil War, the view from Capitol Hill across Nashville's rooftops toward the Public Square and Edgefield took in the darkened rooftops of commercial buildings. The river is visible in the upper right corner of the photograph.

THE PEOPLE who put Nashville back on its feet were, like the ones who had prostrated it, a mixed lot: newcomers and old-timers, peacemakers and troublemakers, carpetbaggers and scalawags, transplanted Yankees and reconstructed Rebels and some who loathed the very notion of reconstruction. It took the better part of a decade for the direction and pace of the city's postwar movement to become fixed, and in that crucial period of transition, Nashvillians could find ample cause for both hope and despair.

With the statehouse tightly controlled by Republican Governor "Parson" Brownlow, the legislature amended the state constitution in 1865 to abolish slavery. (Ironically, Lincoln's Emancipation Proclamation did not apply to Tennessee; only the states in rebellion were affected by it, and Tennessee in 1863 was Union-occupied and thus technically restored to the national fold.) In 1866, when the legislature ratified the thirteenth and fourteenth amendments to the federal Constitution, Tennessee became the first Southern state to be formally readmitted to the Union. The voting rights of ex-Confederates were restored two years later, and Tennessee was exempted from the federal Reconstruction Acts that were to generate such controversy in the lower South.

On paper, the state had put an end to its rebellious past and returned to the good graces of the nation—but in fact, it remained torn and divided. Governor Brownlow, an East Tennessean like Governor Johnson before him, was not kindly disposed to Nashville. He and Johnson had long resisted the steady shift of political power from the eastern mountains to the middle and western districts of the state, and in the 1840s, when Nashville was chosen as the permanent capital, the two men had supported a separatist plan to reorganize a large number of mountain counties into a new state. Their failure only reinforced Brownlow's view that Nashville was in the grip of an aristocratic ruling elite, and when he became governor, he apparently was determined to impose on the city his own plan of reconstruction.

In 1867, Brownlow used his influence to get Augustus E. Alden, a former Union officer, elected mayor of Nashville. Alden was only thirty years old when he took office and was virtually unknown in the city, but the manner in which the governor had advanced him and the reform-minded policies he pursued quickly made him a controversial figure. Alden sought support from the newly enfranchised blacks—two blacks were elected to the city council during his tenure—and in the fields of education, welfare, and public health he began programs for the general improvement of the poor and underprivileged. He was re-elected in 1868, but the following year he was ousted from office when the city was found to be heavily in debt and its treasury almost depleted. Nashville's old guard viewed Alden as a wild radical and his administration—dubbed the Alden Ring—as a corrupt and destructive force. No charges of corruption were ever proved against the young mayor, but he was removed from office nonetheless, and within two years he had left the city.

Alden's impact on Nashville was brief but far-reaching; Brownlow's tenure was longer, but apparently it had less effect upon the city. It is difficult even now to assess either man's motives and intentions, so mixed and complex do they appear. The same can also be said of many of the leading Nashvillians who opposed the Brownlow-Alden regime. But there were two men who worked in very different ways to heal the wounds of war, and they had a significant and lasting influence in the city throughout its long period of recovery.

131

The steamboat Norman, *the rebuilt suspension bridge, and the railroad bridge can be seen in this view of Nashville from the opposite bank. The engraving, a copy of which was later hand colored, was printed in the May 5, 1866,* Harper's Weekly.

Below: After his stormy tenure as Nashville's reconstruction mayor, Augustus E. Alden, a former Union Army officer, left the city. This engraving was made later in Alden's life, when he lived in the Pacific Northwest.

Below right: William G. "Parson" Brownlow was not known for his benevolence toward Nashville during his postwar term as Tennessee's governor. The somber-looking Brownlow was an East Tennessean whom many Nashvillians regarded as a harsh and vindictive man.

132

One of them was John McCormick Lea. As a mayor of Nashville before the war and later as a judge, Lea had earned a reputation as a reconciler, a diplomatic mediator of disputes. The war presented a supreme challenge to such a person, and he rose to the occasion: Lea helped to arrange Nashville's surrender to General Buell's army; he was largely responsible for the favorable treatment accorded most citizens and their property in the occupied city; he influenced Andrew Johnson to make the policies of military control less harsh and vindictive than they might otherwise have been. After the war, when Johnson had become President, Lea continued to advise him, and most of the policy decisions leading to Tennessee's early readmission to the Union were an indirect result of the judge's quietly persuasive counsel.

The other leading advocate in Nashville's behalf operated in a much different manner. John Berrien Lindsley, carrying on a family tradition that had begun with his father nearly fifty years earlier, was an outspoken pleader for local reform and improvement in several areas of pressing concern. He made an investigation of the state penitentiary and issued a report citing inhumane conditions and practices; the institution, he said, "requires a complete remodeling in order to become a fit abode for a human being." Lindsley was president of a local association of citizens chartered "for the purpose of visiting, taking care of, and providing for, the afflicted and destitute." He joined former Governor Neill Brown, John M. Bass, Arthur S. Colyar, Josephus C. Guild and others in denouncing the administration of Augustus Alden, and Lindsley

SANITARY
The Absolute Necessity of Cleanliness— The Hog Nuisance

Our readers will be astonished to learn that only twenty citizens cleaned their premises under the Mayor's proclamation. Such negligence is without a parallel. These are premises that are reeking with filth, which the owners have made no pretense to clean up . . . . It is high time that all those continuing to neglect their duty in this respect, to the jeopardy of the community, should be dealt with as the law directs, and fined so heavily that they will no longer refuse to attend to it . . . .

We were told yesterday by Street Overseer Haslam that there was a hog pen within a stone's throw of the Square, the filth of which was at least half a foot in depth . . . . Citizens should not be notified more than once to comply with the law relative to the removal of all decaying or animal matter . . . . When an alley is cleaned out, the hogs follow in the wake of the scavangers and frequently make its last condition worse than the first. Any one may pass through almost any alley and find from one to a dozen swine rooting it up and making it as filthy as it can possibly be made. Let the hog nuisance be abated.

Nashville Republican Banner,
June 8, 1873

John McCormick Lea, a mayor of Nashville before the Civil War, sought to reconcile the divided interests of Unionists and Confederates in the city during and after the war. This portrait, signed Gagliardi II, was painted sometime in the 1890s.

Concerned with humanitarian reform, John Berrien Lindsley submerged his Union sympathies during the war. Afterward, he devoted himself to medical education, community health, and a variety of social reforms in Nashville. This photograph of the University of Nashville chancellor was made after the war.

went further than the others to charge that Alden was not helping blacks and the poor, as he claimed, but exploiting them, and frustrating their legitimate desire to "become property holders and co-rulers in fact."

Lindsley and his colleagues at the University of Nashville struggled with only limited success to keep the institution in operation, but they had better results with its medical department, which functioned without interruption through the war and entered the 1870s staggered but still intact.

The presence of a strong corps of physicians and medical educators in Nashville made all the more ironic the fact that the city was a very unhealthy place after the Civil War and had been for decades. It was struck frequently by epidemics, the most persistent being cholera; it

had severe and unattended problems of waste disposal, animal control, and water impurity. Between 1833 and 1873, Nashville had seven major epidemics of cholera that in combination claimed more than 2,500 lives; in 1866 alone, nearly a thousand people died of the disease, and in 1873 the death toll may have been even higher.

As the city's chief health officer, Dr. Lindsley called repeatedly for ordinances and voluntary efforts to bring about a general cleanup of the community, but his pleas were unheeded more often than not, and he and his fellow physicians were powerless to do anything more than treat the sufferers while the causes of the disease were not attacked.

Nashville had other serious and debilitating

134

At Nashville [in 1873] the scourge found things favorable for a bountiful harvest of deaths. The city is built on a series of hills and valleys which are drained by creeks emptying into the Cumberland River as it passes the town; the hills are underlaid by a limestone formation which is honeycombed by underground streams and caverns. Waste of every kind, accumulated in the streets, alleys and back yards, were of such a character as to offend all of one's senses not dulled by constant exposure to them.

Human waste was received in various types of outhouses, the almost universal custom of the time. In the lowlands along the creeks where resided the poorer classes the privies were of the surface or shallow pit kinds whose contents were washed with every rain into the creeks. But the senses of the elite of the city, living on the hill, were offended by the foul accumulations of the surface toilets and their individual resourcefulness and genius found a way; they blasted holes into the limestone and the more fortunate obtained pits which opened into underground streams or caverns, thus assuring the owner a privy that today would be the pride of Chic Sale. And some of the oldest residences boasted privies that had never been cleaned and had always remained "sweet and unoffensive." It had occurred to no one that these same underground streams might feed the numerous springs and wells under the hills which supplied the water for those districts.

J. S. Chambers, in
The Conquest of Cholera (1938)

William Strickland's son Francis designed the Greek-columned Davidson County Courthouse in 1857, and it lasted until the present courthouse was built on the same location eighty years later. Hay wagons were a common sight on the Public Square when this photograph was made in about 1880.

The suspension bridge between Nashville and Edgefield was rebuilt after the Civil War. This postwar photograph shows a buggy on the bridge and logs in the river below.

problems in those difficult postwar years. A general condition of unplanned and uncoordinated growth prevailed. The persistent efforts of Lindsley and others to work for the general welfare of the community were exceptional; more common was an attitude of narrow self-interest. Social and economic class divisions were unimproved, if not more pronounced. Some businessmen and industrialists, as well as many government officials, seemed inclined to take whatever advantage they could whenever they could, without regard for the consequences. The few blacks who gained a measure of wealth or influence were as susceptible to corruption as whites, and for the multitude of the poor and unskilled and illiterate of both races, conditions of health and life were in some ways worse than ever. To all this could be added the frightening presence of the Ku Klux Klan, a secret organization of ex-Confederate vigilantes who carried out night-riding acts of intimidation and terrorism for several years after the war. Local Klans from all over the region met in Nashville in 1867 to form a general organization, and Nathan Bedford Forrest, the ex-Confederate cavalry leader, was chosen as the "Grand

Nashville engineer Wilbur Foster drew this intricately detailed demographic map of the county in 1871, fifteen years after Davidson County's present boundary was fixed. The different colors denote civil districts.

136

Self-taught astronomer Edward Emerson Barnard, born in poverty in Nashville, achieved fame in later life as a discoverer of comets and a photographer of the heavens. He also was an early experimenter with electricity.

Wizard" of the "Empire." The local unit of the Klan held regular late-night meetings in the abandoned ruins of Fort Negley.

In spite of its disturbing catalogue of un-addressed and unresolved ills, however, Nashville had some redeeming qualitites, and it offered to most of its people a promise of better times to come.

It had, as a base, the citizens who shared with Lindsley a concern for the general welfare and a willingness to work for community improvement. It also had many young men who had come home from the war to take up the challenge of personal and institutional recovery. They included not only native Nashvillians, most of whom had fought for the South, but a good many former Union officers who stayed in the city, married local women, and rose to positions of prominence.

The achievements of a few Nashvillians, both native-born and transplanted, would make their names familiar far beyond the city's borders. George Dury, a Bavarian-born artist, lived in the city from 1850 to 1895 and painted portraits of such noted figures as Abraham Lincoln, Andrew Johnson, and Robert E. Lee. Henry Watterson, son of a Tennessee congressman, lived in Nashville off and on before the war and came in 1865 for a two-year stay as an editor of the *Republican Banner* before going on to fame as the editor of the *Louisville Courier-Journal.* Edward Emerson Barnard, born in poverty in Nashville, was a self-taught astronomer who became renowned as a discoverer and photographer of comets and planetary satellites. James Braid, a Scottish immigrant and an experimenter in the virgin field of electricity, met Alexander Graham Bell at a scientific convention here in 1877, and the following year used Bell's patented discovery to make a long-distance telephone call from Nashville to Louisville. It may have been the nation's first.

Another resident of some note arrived in the frigid winter of 1864, a seventeen-year-old youth shivering in a linen suit and carrying with him nearly all his worldly possessions. He worked briefly as a telegraph operator and then moved on. When he returned on a cobalt prospecting trip to Hickman County in 1906, his name was a household word throughout the nation, but it was only by chance that a reporter for the *Nashville Banner* found him registered at the Duncan Hotel on Church Street. The visitor and former resident was the famed American inventor, Thomas Edison.

From the beginning of the postwar period, Nashville's gradual recovery was marked by some encouraging developments. In 1866, the suspension bridge was rebuilt, mail delivery was improved and expanded, and horse-drawn streetcars were introduced. In the center of the city, a splendid new hotel, the Maxwell House, was opened in 1869. It had been started a decade earlier by a son of John Overton and occupied in an unfinished state by soldiers and prisoners during the war; now it was completed with much fanfare as a glittering symbol of the city's

"What carpets! What bedding! Oh ye Gods, what looking glasses!" exclaimed a Nashville newspaper reporter on being shown the bridal suite in the new Maxwell House Hotel in 1869. This photograph of the bridal chamber suggests that the furnishings were somewhat more modest than the description.

determination to rise again. It was to become a nationally known landmark, and it would remain for almost a century as Nashville's premier hotel.

The suburban districts of the city—North Nashville, Edgefield, and the university community in South Nashville—were thriving with new growth and vitality. The churches were also active: The convent and academy of St. Cecilia and the Church of the Assumption, having been built by Catholics in North Nashville just before the war, were among the institutions in that part of the city which helped to give many people—especially German and Irish immigrants—a sense of identity and belonging. Nashville's small Jewish community, having within it the roots of Orthodox, Conservative, and Reform traditions, built its first synagogue, the Byzantine-styled Vine Street Temple, in 1876, and it became the Reform congregation as first Conservative and then Orthodox factions split from it and built additional synagogues.

For the Protestant churches of the city, recovery was less rapid. The various denominations had once been united internally across regional and even racial lines, but no longer; all connections with their Northern counterparts

138

Soon after the Vine Street Temple was completed in 1876, Otto or C.C. Giers photographed the first Nashville synagogue with its Russian-style onion domes. It became the Jewish community's Reform congregation when Conservative and Orthodox groups split from it to build additional synagogues. Rabbi Isadore Lewinthal (left) was the spiritual leader of the Temple congregation for nearly thirty years beginning in the 1890s.

Top: The Nashville Banner was in its infancy when this 1876 edition appeared. Front-page advertisements—even whiskey advertisements at the top of page one—were not uncommon. The Banner is now Nashville's oldest continuous newspaper.

Above: Like a jumble of pickup sticks, the gangplanks of several steamboats connect ship and shore at the foot of Broad Street. Water Street (First Avenue North) can be seen in the distance in this 1879 photograph.

had been severed before the war, and black Baptists and Methodists had begun their own churches. With few exceptions, those divisions would be permanent.

The railroads expanded rapidly after the war, systematically hastening the day of the steamboat's eventual demise. Vernon K. Stevenson, the man who had brought the railroad to Nashville in 1850, moved to New York after fighting for the Confederacy, but he still owned controlling interest in the Nashville, Chattanooga, and St. Louis line. He and Edmund W. "King" Cole of Nashville were generally regarded as the leading railroad men of the middle

139

The flag-bedecked Nashville Centennial Exposition Hall, erected at the corner of present-day Eighth Avenue and Broadway, was the focal point of the city's one hundredth birthday celebration in 1880. The United States Court House now occupies the exposition hall site.

South until 1880, when Stevenson sold most of his holdings to the Louisville and Nashville Railroad and control of the line shifted to Kentucky and later to New York.

When Nashville paused in 1880 to celebrate its first 100 years of existence, it seemed suspended between trauma and recovery. It was a study in contrasts, a portrait in light and shadow; for every sign of vitality it showed, it had a corresponding symptom of weakness. It had 43,000 people—almost three times the 1860 total—and for the first time, more people lived in Nashville than in the rest of Davidson County. It was urban in a literal sense, the fourth largest city in the South, an agricultural town no longer—yet pigs could still be found rooting in its streets. It had severe social and economic divisions, lingering political animosities, and the highest death rate of any American city—but it also had some conspicuous signs of wealth, a budding spirit of boosterism, and enough ferment and energy to make almost anything possible.

For more than a month in the spring of 1880, Nashville reveled in an orgy of celebration. It was a century old and in no mood to dwell upon its problems. There was a sprawling new exposition center at the corner of Broad and Spruce streets (now Broadway and Eighth Avenue). In a continuous flow of events and activities—climaxed by the unveiling of an equestrian statue of Andrew Jackson on Capitol Hill—the observance of the city's centennial was carried on in an atmosphere of pride and optimism. Nashville saw itself as having come of age. It bore only the faintest resemblance to the frontier town it had been in Jackson's day—and none at all to its rude beginning as a palisaded station on the bluff. The days of its birth and youth were not only long past but almost forgotten; with the rest of the nation, Nashville was happily and eagerly entering the modern era.

THE NASHVILLE WEEKLY AMERICAN, THURSDAY, APRIL 29, 1880.

1780-1880.

A Memorable Day in the History of Nashville

★★★★★★★★★★★

HER CENTENNIAL CELEBRATED WITH MAGNIFICENT ECLAT.

★

The Most Imposing Procession Ever Witnessed in the South,

★

WHILE THOUSANDS OF SPECTATORS THRONG THE STREETS.

Decorations Everywhere, and the Enthusiasm Unbounded.

Appropriate and Interesting Commemorative Exercises at the Capitol.

The dawn of the one hundredth anniversary of the birthday of Nashville was welcomed yesterday morning with the boom of one hundred guns that shook the earth and aroused to new life the enthusiasm of all the organizations and the persons that had determined to participate in the grand demonstration of the day.

Overleaf: Looking south on Granny White Pike somewhere near its present junction with Tyne Boulevard, David Wright's 1979 painting recreates the scene as it might have appeared early on a summer morning in the mid-1880s, after two decades of healing had hidden the scars of war.

One of the highlights of the Nashville Centennial celebration was a long and colorful parade around the Public Square. Walter Goater sketched it, and an engraving of the scene, later hand-colored, appeared in the May 15, 1880, edition of Frank Leslie's Illustrated Newspaper.

People swarmed over Capitol Hill—and some even mounted the roof of the capitol itself—on May 20, 1880, when the equestrian statue of Andrew Jackson was unveiled. The event was part of Nashville's centennial celebration. The statue was given to the state by the Tennessee Historical Society.

141

Before George Peabody College for Teachers moved to its campus on Twenty-First Avenue South, the site belonged to Roger Williams University, an American Baptist Church-affiliated institution for blacks. This engraving shows the main building of Roger Williams in the 1880s. It was destroyed by fire in 1905.

THE SUREST and most permanent indication of Nashville's emergence as a modern American city could be seen in its development of colleges and universities. Between the close of the Civil War and the celebration of the city's centennial, no fewer than a dozen institutions were restored to service or opened for the first time. The tradition of interest in education that had begun with the founding of Davidson Academy in 1785 reached full maturity in the postwar era.

Davidson Academy had evolved into Cumberland College and then into the University of Nashville in the early 1800s, and its medical and literary departments were still functioning after the war, but they were in precarious condition. With the support of the state government and the Peabody Education Fund, a national endowment, the literary department became a separate institution known as Tennessee State Normal College in 1875 and continued operation in the University of Nashville campus facilities on Market Street (now Second Avenue South).

With the Freedman's Bureau, the Peabody Fund, and the missionary divisions of several Northern Protestant churches leading the way, education for blacks became an important development after the war, and Nashville benefited from that movement when three new institutions were created here.

One of them was Nashville Normal and Theological Institute, an American Baptist school. After twelve years of struggle, the school purchased a mansion and thirty acres of land on the Hillsboro turnpike (later to be the campus of George Peabody College for Teachers) and moved there in 1876. Under a new name—Roger Williams University—it remained in that loca-

A YANKEE SOLDIER RETURNS

Nashville in detail is not a beautiful city. It seems less so now than it did twenty years ago, when it had a sort of shady dignity and grace about it, in spite of war and trouble. Now there is too much of a mixture of hovels and palaces; too much yellow clay and bare rock in sight; but, seen as a whole, it is a very striking and picturesque town. Standing on the high porch of the Capitol, which overlooks the whole city and the valley of the Cumberland until it is shut in by the encircling chains of saw-like hills, I know of few more impressive pictures. Old Nashville lies in a dark mass of roofs, chimneys, spires and treetops, wreathed in a mist of smoke, on the slopes of the capitoline hill. Up and down the river, north and south, stretches the new town, until the houses become scattered and the country begins; but the most impressive feature is the line of public institutions encircling the city like a line of fortifications. First, on the [north], is the great cotton factory; next the massive building of Fisk University; then the three buildings of Vanderbilt University; then the Baptist college for colored people; and thence, on a line drawn toward the river, are Central Tennessee College, a Methodist institution for colored people; the University of Nashville, and the various State asylums. Instead of warlike defenses . . . the city is surrounded by a cordon reared by Business, Education and Charity—good generals they, who march to the rescue of the world.

NOBLE L. PRENTIS, in
Southern Letters, 1881

Dear Pastor:

You have no doubt expected to hear of my welfare before this, but nevertheless you must know I am very grateful to you and the Sunday-School for what you have done. In the first place I am glad to tell you that I have united with the Church here and hope that the prayers of my Sunday-school may help guide me in the path of Christian duty . . . .

Our University is very pleasantly situated, overlooking the city, and the family life is very pleasant indeed. Some mornings as I look about upon the two or three hundred of my companions assembled for morning prayers I can hardly realize they are all my people; that this great assembly of youth and intelligence are the representatives of a race which twenty years ago was in bondage. Although this sunny land is very pleasant, notwithstanding its squalor misery and ignorance spread broad-cast; and although it is a bracing thought to know that I stand among those who do not despise me for my color, yet I have not forgotten to love my New England hills, and I often wish I could join some of your pleasant meetings in person as I do in spirit. I remain

Respectfully yours,
WILLIAM E DU BOIS

(W. E. B. Du Bois, a co-founder of the National Association for the Advancement of Colored People, began his college career at Fisk University.)

Above: A hundred years after it was built, Fisk University's Jubilee Hall was portrayed on a wall of Nashville's Opryland Hotel by mural artist T. Max Hochstettler. Jubilee Hall has been designated a national historical landmark.

MEDICAL DEPARTMENT.

Left: A department of Central Tennessee College when this engraving was made in the 1870s, Meharry Medical School continues now as the oldest predominantly black medical education institution in the nation.

tion until 1905, when a fire destroyed the main building.

Central Tennessee College, another of the institutions for blacks, began operation on Chestnut Street in South Nashville in 1865 and soon moved to facilities on College Street. Under the auspices of the Methodist Episcopal Church, the school developed programs in teacher training, manual and industrial arts, law, and medicine—the latter being Meharry Medical Department, the first such educational program ever established for blacks in the United States. Central Tennessee College changed its name to Walden University in 1900. Fifteen years later, Walden closed, but Meharry Medical College survives and has operated continuously for more than a century.

The third new institution was Fisk University, opened in 1866 and named for Clinton B. Fisk, head of the Freedman's Bureau in the Tennessee-Kentucky area and a former general in the Union Army. (Clinton Fisk was white, as were all of the administrators and most of the faculty of the schools for blacks.) The American Missionary

The Jubilee Singers, students of Fisk University whose concert tours saved the institution from bankruptcy, posed for this painting by Edmund Harvel, Queen Victoria's court artist, during their visit to England in 1873. The portrait is now displayed in Fisk's Jubilee Hall.

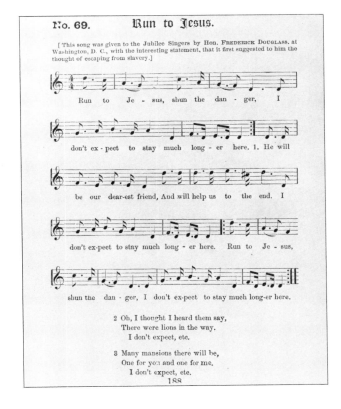

No. 69.   Run to Jesus.

[This song was given to the Jubilee Singers by Hon. FREDERICK DOUGLASS, at Washington, D. C., with the interesting statement, that it first suggested to him the thought of escaping from slavery.]

Run to Je - sus, shun the dan - ger, I
don't ex - pect to stay much long - er here. 1. He will
be our dear-est friend, And will help us to the end. I
don't ex-pect to stay much long - er here. Run to Je - sus,
shun the dan - ger, I don't ex-pect to stay much long-er here.

2 Oh, I thought I heard them say,
There were lions in the way.
I don't expect, etc.

3 Many mansions there will be,
One for you and one for me.
I don't expect, etc.

188

Association, a division of the Congregational Church, supported the institution, and E. M. Cravath, who had been a Union Army chaplain, was named its first president in 1875, after the school had struggled for nearly a decade to establish itself. That struggle was dramatized by the artistry of a group of students, the Fisk Jubilee Singers, whose voices ultimately saved the college from collapse.

The young men and women, most of them ex-slaves, formed a musical unit under the direction of George L. White, the school's treasurer and instructor of vocal music. Ignoring the advice of Clinton Fisk ("I trusted in God and not in General Fisk"), White scraped together funds from the school treasury and his own resources and took the troupe on tour in 1871. After a slow start, they built a moving and melancholy repertoire of spirituals and slave songs that drew cheers and tears—and best of all, money—from audiences in the North and East. They sang "Go Down, Moses" for President Ulysses S. Grant at

The French Victorian Gothic design of Vanderbilt University's first building, shown in this 1875 photograph, gave way to Italianate style when the structure was rebuilt after a fire in 1905. Now named Kirkland Hall in honor of James H. Kirkland, the university's chancellor from 1893 to 1937, the building still houses administrative offices. Vanderbilt is named for Commodore Cornelius Vanderbilt, left, a nineteenth-century railroad magnate and so-called "robber baron" who also had a generous side: He made a gift of a million dollars to launch the school.

the White House and the "Battle Hymn of the Republic" for an audience of 40,000 in Boston, and they returned after eight months with $20,000 for the Fisk treasury.

The Jubilee Singers went on to receive international acclaim. They made two tours of Europe, winning the praise of royalty and the common people alike, and their performance raised more than $100,000 for the university. The funds were used for the purchase of Fisk's present campus in North Nashville and for the construction of Jubilee Hall, a Victorian Gothic edifice that has since been designated as a national historical landmark.

John Berrien Lindsley, who had guided the fortunes of the University of Nashville through war and hard times, noted in a speech in 1875 that "those who are controlling the education of the colored people are wide awake to the advantages of these schools, while those who control the education of the white people do not seem to have turned their earnest attention to the sub-

ject." He added: "I want to see the black man educated, but I do not want to see the white man neglected."

Two years before that speech, Southern Methodists had obtained a charter to establish the Central University of the Methodist Episcopal Church South, but they lacked the funds to start it. The bishop of the church, Holland N. McTyeire, had an opportunity to describe the proposed institution to railroad magnate Cornelius Vanderbilt (the two men having married cousins), and the crusty old Commodore, who was known to be ruthless and domineering in his business dealings, made a million-dollar gift to the school on the condition that Bishop McTyeire be named president of its board of trustees for life. The trustees readily agreed; in gratitude, they changed the name of the institution to Vanderbilt University, purchased seventy-five acres for a campus in the west end of Nashville, and enrolled the first students in the fall of 1875. Landon C. Garland

147

Vanderbilt was at bat against Cumberland University when this photograph of the first baseball game on what is now called Curry Field was played in 1892. Minor league professional baseball had been started in the city seven years before that, in the downtown park that would be known as Sulphur Dell.

September 29

. . . There is something very mysterious working its way or rather has already made its inroad into the hearts of a majority of the Vanderbilt students. It is this—they voluntarily & calmly violate the pledge which was given in good faith to keep the by-laws of the University. The by-laws positively forbids a member of the U. to be a member of any Secret Fraternity, & yet in the face of this many—yes no doubt—a big majority—have pledged themselves to a fraternity. How this can be I am utterly unable to see . . . . This is about the way they look at it. "I must be on the majority & what the majority does is right, therefore I must join." . . . They would & do sell their self-respect.

October 31

Chanceller Garland announced this morning that the executive committee had repealed the law forbidden the organization of "Fraternities" in the U. It was received with much applause & the Fraternities, of which there are 6 already organized, not withstanding they were positively forbidden, will have a banquet soon on the strength of this.

from the 1883 diary of T. Leigh Thompson, a Nashville resident, a Vanderbilt student, and in later years a vice president of National Life & Accident Insurance Company; before he graduated from Vanderbilt, Thompson had joined a fraternity himself

was chosen to be the first chancellor, and by 1880, almost 500 students were enrolled.

Medical education was revitalized in the postwar period, so much so that by the late 1870s, Nashville had five medical schools—in name, if not in fact. In addition to the medical departments of the University of Nashville, Vanderbilt University, and Central Tennessee College (Meharry), there were also Shelby Medical College and Nashville Medical College. In time, Shelby and Vanderbilt would merge, sharing facilities with the University of Nashville, and the latter institution would be joined with Nashville Medical College and moved to Memphis as the medical school of the University of Tennessee. Vanderbilt and Meharry would remain to carry on the tradition of medical education in Nashville.

The city's nineteenth-century effort in higher education did not end there. Ward's Seminary, the successor to Nashville Female Academy, gained notice as a thriving institution after the war. Another school for young women, Belmont Junior College, was founded in 1890, and later it would merge with Ward's to form Ward-Belmont and continue for almost forty years as a finishing school for girls. Samuel Watkins, an orphan who became first a bricklayer and then a major contractor in the city, would be remembered for founding Watkins Institute, a tuition-free vocational school for adults, and J. F. B. Draughon would likewise be recalled for starting a business school bearing his name. Another new institution, Nashville Bible School, owed its existence mainly to a Church of Christ minister named David Lipscomb, and the college would be named for him after his death when his farm south of the city became its campus.

148

Otto or C.C. Giers, of a well-known family of Nashville photographers, made this picture of the city skyline, undistinguished except for the State Capitol, sometime in the 1880s. His vantage point was the Vanderbilt University campus. The Giers photographers (Otto in inset) left a large collection of photographs as a visual record of Nashville in the last third of the nineteenth century.

Nashville's public schools, including separate schools for blacks, went through a period of growth and improvement after the war, and a large number of private academies also continued to operate. Education was a substantial enterprise in Nashville. It had prompted Philip Lindsley's biographer in 1859 to refer to the city as the Athens of the West and a Union Army quartermaster in 1864 to call it the Athens of the South; in 1897, Tennessee's governor would repeat the phrase, and it would stick. Nashville would always point with pride to its colleges and universities, and go on calling itself the Athens of the South.

149

BEFORE it built a Parthenon to symbolize its Athenian aspirations, Nashville would pass the final two decades of the nineteenth century without giving much thought to planning or coordination or regulation. The problems caused by rapid growth were all but ignored. Some fascinating inventions and diversions had come on the scene—the telegraph, the telephone, electricity, machines of all sorts, cameras and phonograph records and dozens more—and they attracted wide public interest. Neither the city's centennial in 1880 nor the state's in 1897 would hold people's minds for long on the past, or on the future; what mattered most was the present.

The growth continued. Edgefield was annexed, bringing 6,500 people from that suburban district into the population of the city. It and other nearby residential neighborhoods north and south of the central business district—as well as the more distant Davidson County villages such as Goodlettsville, Madison, Donelson, Antioch, and Bellevue—stood in sharp contrast to the city itself, as did another large suburban section that was beginning to develop around Vanderbilt University on the west. Nashville still had a mixture of homes and businesses within close range of the Public Square, but its waterfront and its railroad depots gave the downtown district an air of turbulence and transience. Taverns and brothels dotted the area, crime was pervasive, and a squalid cluster of overcrowded shacks housing mostly black and Irish laborers had grown up in a ring that began along the waterfront and ran around the base of Capitol Hill, through the long gulch west of town, and back to the river south of Broad Street.

The inclination of the more affluent segment of the population was to deplore the poverty and crime and vice in the downtown

Across the river . . . is the city of Edgefield, or, as it is sometimes called, "Little Brooklyn." . . . It is, perhaps, one of the loveliest resident places in the South, or in the United States, for that matter; and during the Spring and hot Summer months, it is a pleasant retreat for the business man, whose labors and interests lay in Nashville. It is connected with the city by a magnificent wire Suspension Bridge . . . Edgefield is remarkable for the elegance and taste of its buildings, the spaciousness of its avenues, and the intelligence and refinement of its people. Its population, for the most part, is resident, a large number of people doing business in the city having their residences there. Property . . . has so increased in value, that space has become a costly luxury, only to be enjoyed by the more extravagant. In fact, the many persons who constitute a moving power, and a large proportion of our commercial world, are compelled to seek homes in this and the many suburban towns that cluster around the metropolis, and are vitalized by its proximity. Therefore, the daily emigration and exodus is large.

CHARLES R. ROBERT, in
Nashville and Her Trade, 1870

150

Intricate detail distinguishes this unsigned watercolor of the Nashville skyline. Probably painted sometime in the 1880s, it was owned by C.C. and Otto Giers.

Towers capped the buildings of Church Street when this 1889 photograph was made from Capitol Boulevard looking toward the river. The tallest tower was on Watkins Institute, a vocational school for adults.

The contrasts of affluence and poverty are sharply drawn in these two Nashville photographs from the 1890s. In one, black children play a game of marbles in front of an unpainted frame house. In the other, a son of William H. Jackson of Belle Meade plays in his toy carriage in front of the mansion.

One of the largest and most impressive of Nashville's many mansions of the nineteenth century was Oak Hill, the home of Van Leer Kirkman. It bristled with towers and turrets like a Victorian-era French chateau. First Presbyterian Church on Franklin Road occupies the site now.

district—and whenever possible, to escape it. Nashville's economic base was concentrated in the heart of the city—industry and banking, retail and wholesale trade, transportation and professional services were all there—but many of the people who provided those goods and services were beginning to move to the suburbs, and the problems they left behind in Black Bottom and Hell's Half Acre and the rest of the urban center grew worse.

The most conspicuous contrast to the shacks that ringed the downtown area was provided by the country mansions that had risen in all directions a few miles from the city. Belle Meade and Riverview and the Hermitage were among them, but the most spectacular of all was Belmont—and its mistress, Adelicia Hayes Franklin Acklen Cheatham, was the second woman in Davidson County ever to gain prominence on her own, rather than as the wife of a powerful man. (The first was Lucinda "Granny" White, a legendary tavern-keeper in the early 1800s.)

Adelicia was a Nashvillian by birth, a daughter of local attorney Oliver Bliss Hayes, and from early age she was noted for her intelligence as well as her beauty. She attended the Nashville Female Academy and at seventeen was engaged to marry a banker's son, but he died of typhoid fever. Then she met Isaac Franklin, an enormously wealthy planter and fifty-year-old bachelor; she married him in 1839 and bore him four children. By 1846, three of the children and Franklin himself had died of various illnesses, and Adelicia was a widow before she was much past thirty years of age.

She was also the principal heir to what may have been the largest fortune in the South, and three years after her first husband's death she married another bachelor, Joseph A. S. Acklen. Together, in the early 1850s, they built Belmont, a hilltop mansion of Italian and Greek design and gargantuan proportions. It stands now at

the crest of Sixteenth Avenue South, on a hill that was then the center of a 170-acre estate two miles from the city, surrounded by park-like woods and formal gardens.

Six children were born to the Acklens, but by 1855, the only surviving Franklin child had died of diphtheria and two of the Acklen daughters were dead of scarlet fever. The war was coming, too, and in the midst of it, Joseph Acklen would succumb to pneumonia. In a little more than thirty years, Adelicia Acklen had lost a fiance, two husbands, and six children—grim proof that the diseases of the age were no respecter of class. But in time to come, the mistress of Belmont would be remembered less for the tragedy in her life than for her role as the leading social hostess in a region that treasured such designations. She would also be remembered for her shrewd and independent management of the enormous fortune she had inherited.

From 1850 until well into the 1870s—with hardly a pause for the Civil War—she made Belmont the social center of Nashville, the state of Tennessee, and much of the South. She married

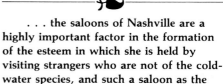

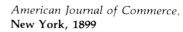

Crisscrossed by the electric wires that brought bright lights to
Nashville, the city's notorious Southern Turf saloon on Cherry Street
(now Fourth Avenue) shows its tall and narrow exterior in this
photograph from the 1890s. The building still stands.

. . . the saloons of Nashville are a
highly important factor in the formation
of the esteem in which she is held by
visiting strangers who are not of the cold-
water species, and such a saloon as the
Southern Turf [at 222 Cherry Street, now
Fourth Avenue North] does more to
enhance the reputation of the city than all
the speeches that were ever made and all
the descriptive articles which were ever
written.

The Southern Turf is located . . .
almost opposite the Maxwell House, and
he who has not been in this tavern knows
not what a paradise it is. It is a
handsome, four-story structure, built of
brick, with white marble front. Its area is
36 by 170 feet, and it was erected in 1895,
by Marcus Cartwright, who is one of the
richest and best-known bookmakers in the
Western hemisphere. It is a veritable
glittering palace of mirth and merriment.
No croaking cares are there, no weariness
or pain . . . . No institution administers
so ably to the pleasures and wants of its
patrons. Their products are of the highest
standard—fine imported and domestic
liquors and wines and the choicest brands
of cigars. The management of the
establishment is conducted by Mr. Ike
Johnson, one of the best-known citizens
of Nashville. He is stout, jolly and always
happy, and his motto is: "Let us eat,
drink, and be merry; for tomorrow we
die."

American Journal of Commerce,
New York, 1899

again after the war, to William Archer
Cheatham of Nashville, then separated from
him after eighteen years, and died at the age of
seventy-four in 1887. Even when she was past
her prime, her hospitality was said to be as
matchless as her wealth. In a society that provided few opportunitites for women to
distinguish themselves, she had made sure her
name would not be soon forgotten.

Adelicia Acklen may have been a little too independent for the prim and proper Victorian
culture that dominated Nashville social life in
the waning years of the century. Among the affluent, those were years of teas and lectures and
recitals for the women, a little discreet whiskey

and gambling for the men (the Southern Turf on
Cherry Street being the favorite saloon), parties
and debutante balls for the young, and revivals
for everyone. Horse racing seemed to be losing
favor (even the livery business was suffering
from the arrival of bicycles), but baseball was a
big attraction in the sulphur spring bottom
where James Robertson had once planted corn,
and riders on the new electric streetcars flocked
to Glendale, an amusement park south of the
city.

It was told around town that the James boys,
Jesse and Frank, had operated their outlaw gang
of bank and train robbers from farms in the
Bordeaux-Joelton section of northwest Davidson

Lodging cost a quarter, lunch a dime when these photographs of the Silver Dollar Saloon at Market and Broad streets were made in the 1890s. The brick streets are gone, but the Silver Dollar is still there, housing Historic Nashville Inc. at street level and the Historical Commission of Metropolitan Nashville-Davidson County upstairs.

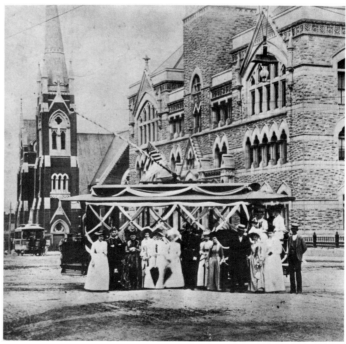

B. Burdette, a member of the Nashville Bicycle Club, signed this 1893 photograph made by Herstein and Mahon, a local photography enterprise. Bicycling was an enormously popular outdoor activity in the 1890s.

The first electric streetcar in Nashville, decked out with flags and ribbons, stopped at Eighth and Broad for an 1889 photograph of its well-dressed passengers. In the background are the Customs House, First Baptist Church, and one of the horse-drawn streetcars soon to be replaced.

155

THE CHICAGOS WIN THE GAME AT THE NEW PARK YESTERDAY

Excepting the Sunday games last season, there has probably never been a larger attendance upon a baseball game than turned out yesterday afternoon to see the Chicagos, a National League club, against the Americans of this city. The number of ladies present was quite a compliment to the management and to both clubs. At the beginning of the game it was evident that the visitors thought they had a soft snap, and hoped to win by daring and bulldozing, but they soon found they had misjudged the ability of their antagonists, and then came down to hard work and careful playing. The home team led off at the bat and made two runs—all they ever made.

The Chicagos made two runs in the second inning and two in the sixth, all of which except one was on account of errors by the Americans. Before and during the game the odds were in favor of the Chicagos. They are the stronger club, but the Americans held their own well, putting their best foot forward. Nearly all the Chicagos are good batters, and if they hit the ball at all it was most always a two-bagger.

Nashville Banner, **April 11, 1885**

(The same year it joined the first minor league in professional baseball, the Nashville team—later to be called the Vols—inaugurated the ballpark to be known as Sulphur Dell in the bottom where James Robertson and the first settlers had arrived in 1779. The centerfielder for the Chiago team in this first exhibition game was Billy Sunday. He returned in later years as a fire-and-brimstone revival evangelist.)

Photographed when it was under construction in 1891, the Union Gospel Tabernacle was first an auditorium for religious revivals and temperance lectures, then a hall for cultural and artistic performances, and finally the home of the Grand Ole Opry.

Captain Tom Ryman, owner of thirty-five Cumberland River steamboats in the freewheeling postwar years, devoted much of his time and money to temperance and Christian evangelism for the last twenty years of his life. He built the Union Gospel Tabernacle, later called the Ryman Auditorium. Ryman's Victorian house on Rutledge Hill (South Market Street) gave him a clear view of the river.

County for a number of years after the Civil War, but nobody wanted to believe that. It was also known around town that a secret political organization called the American Protective Association was stirring up ill will against Catholics and foreigners, but nobody liked to talk about that.

It was more inspiring to talk about Tom Ryman, the last of the Cumberland River steamboat barons. He had risen from humble beginnings in Nashville to control thirty-five riverboats, and he was in his free-wheeling prime in 1885 when he dropped in on a tent meeting being conducted by evangelist Sam P. Jones.

The experience transformed Ryman. He was converted to the Christian gospel, and he opened a temperance hall on Broad Street that year. In 1889 he started building the Union

Reverend Sam P. Jones, the evangelist who converted Tom Ryman, had an overflow audience for this revival meeting in Ryman's Union Gospel Tabernacle in about 1895, before a balcony was added to the building in 1897 and called the Confederate Gallery. This panoramic picture was made by William Gustav or Andrew Joseph Thuss, members of a well-known Nashville photographic family.

Gospel Tabernacle, a cavernous hall where Jones and other evangelists of all faiths could hold revivals. Ryman shouldered more than $85,000 in debt for the building and carried it without complaint into the next century. The riverboat captain died in 1904, and when Sam Jones preached his funeral to a packed hall on Christmas Day, he suggested that the name of the building be changed to the Ryman Auditorium.

Over time, the religious purposes to which the auditorium had been devoted were enlarged to take in a variety of speakers and performers, from Theodore Roosevelt and Booker T. Washington to Enrico Caruso and Sarah Bernhardt and—in the 1940s—the cast of the Grand Ole Opry.

In the Victorian age of guarded morality and extravagant piety, Nashville seemed to see itself as a changed community, but it remained in

The First Tennessee Regiment attracted more than enough volunteers to fight in the Spanish-American War. Their enlistment camp was in Cherokee Park in West Nashville.

When the circus came to town sometime around the turn of the century, the horse-drawn cages of animals attracted a crowd to the viaduct that bridged the railroad gulch.

158

many ways the same city it had always been. It was intensely patriotic, sending more than its share of volunteers to the Spanish-American War in 1898, as it had to all previous wars. It had a diverse economy that was resilient enough to weather the Panic of 1893. Its air and water were still polluted, its streets still dirty, its health still poor. It looked upon inequalities of race, class, and sex matter-of-factly, as if they were providential. Its journalistic and political rivalries were monumental and unceasing. It accepted "New South" segregation with the same casual ease it had once shown for Old South slavery. And it was still a church town, with a majority of its citizens in active membership. (More of them were Methodists than anything else, but surprisingly there were more Catholics than Presbyterians and Baptists combined and more Jews than Episcopalians.)

Nashville was a city of extremes. Its virtues

When this photograph was made in 1894, Hillsboro Pike was a narrow dirt road through farming country. At the same location now, Belcourt Avenue meets Twenty-First Avenue South in the center of Hillsboro Village.

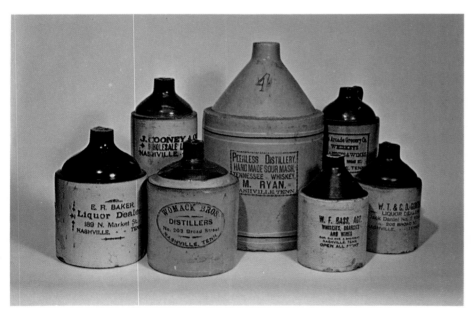

The William Gerst Brewing Company on Sixth Avenue South, a Nashville enterprise from 1890 until 1954, predated and survived Prohibition, and Gerst was not the first: Nashville brewers and distillers made the city a major alcoholic beverage manufacturing center from its earliest days as a town until intoxicants were outlawed in 1919. While waiting for the constitutional amendment to be repealed, Gerst made "near beer," a non-alcoholic beverage. Bottle and jug collectors in Nashville have many representative containers.

and vices were displayed extravagantly, in grand manner and heroic proportion. Sporting events and saloon celebrations no less than revivals and temperance meetings attracted large and emotional crowds. With the slightest provocation, Nashvillians could be heard praising and condemning with equal fervor the perceived saints and sinners of the day.

There could have been no better place, then, for a celebratory extravaganza such as the Tennessee Centennial of 1897, an exposition to commemorate—one year late—the 100th anniversary of Tennessee's admission to the Union. It lasted six months, cost more than a million dollars, attracted 1,786,000 people, and turned a modest profit—a result virtually unheard-of for such events.

The exposition grounds were in Nashville's West Side Park, later to be renamed Centennial Park. Exhibit halls, midway attractions, lakes and fountains and glittering lights drew visitors day and night; there was even an exotic troupe of camels and turbaned merchants and belly dancers from the Middle East. President William McKinley led a train of prominent visitors to the fair, but the primary attraction was a building, not a person. It was the centerpiece of the show, painstakingly constructed of wood, plaster, and

West Side park, the site of the Tennessee centennial celebration, was a country race track when this photograph was made in the 1880s. The West End Avenue entrance to Centennial Park is now in the same place as this entrance to West Side.

stucco: a full-size replica of the ruined pride of Greece, the Parthenon.

Nashville liked the Parthenon, liked the symbolism of it, liked the park in which it stood. When the fair was over, all the other buildings were either moved or torn down and sold for scrap, but the Parthenon was left standing. Within ten years, it had begun to deteriorate; within twenty, it was near to being like the original—a ruin. In 1922, the city would decide to replace the replica with a permanent structure built of reinforced concrete, and a local engineering firm, Foster and Creighton, would win the principal job of reconstruction. Nine years later, Nashville would have a permanent and lasting symbol for its self-styled image as the Athens of the South.

The inspiration for that symbol and for much of the entire exposition came from Eugene C. Lewis, a consulting engineer with close ties to the railroad industry, to the local press, and to the political and economic powers of the city and state. The Tennessee Historical Society originated the idea for the centennial celebration, but in reality, it was a promotional exposition planned and executed mainly by railroad

The Parthenon and an Egyptian pyramid representing Memphis are reflected in the waters of Lake Watauga in this night photograph of the Tennessee Centennial Exposition. Eugene C. Lewis (below), an engineer and railroad executive, directed the fair.

My father was the lawyer for the Arabs when they came here, and of course they paid very special attention to me because I was a girl, and Father would take me over there . . . . One of the men took me riding on a camel. First it was on a donkey and then he put me on a camel. Of course, he got up on the animal too. We went out on West End Avenue and scared the horses nearly to death. Of course, everybody had a carriage. No cars. And the police forbid us going back on the highway anymore because of a near accident. And we would ride all around Centennial Park on a camel. Oh, I felt like I was the biggest thing in the world.

. . . coming from Egypt and bringing all the animals must have been quite an expensive thing because they had no planes to fly them. They had to come by ship, and then be transported by trains to Nashville . . . .

There were overwhelming crowds. I had never seen such crowds . . . . I can remember how tremendous the crowd was and Mother said, "Now do not turn my hand loose because if you get lost, they might take you off to some foreign country." I can always see myself being dragged off to some foreign country.

MRS. JEANETTE NOEL *of Nashville, recalling the 1897 Tennessee Centennial in an interview with Jane King, 1976*

men—and particularly by officials of the Nashville, Chattanooga, and St. Louis line, then a subsidiary of the Louisville and Nashville. Lewis and John W. Thomas, the president of the centennial, were the top officials of the NC&StL.

Before the fair, the railroads were in dire need of public favor and support; in thirty years of postwar operations, their well-documented abuses of power had created a reservoir of cynicism and distrust. The centennial smothered much of that ill will under a blanket of euphoric celebration, and the railroads, encouraged by the result, moved forward with plans for a magnificent new downtown terminal building as a further show of their benevolence and public concern.

But it would take more than Union Station to secure the reign of the railroads. To be sure, they had numbered the days of the steamboats, but horseless carriages were coming (one was demonstrated at the exposition), and there was even talk of flying machines. And in any event, the railroads were too deeply involved in industrial rivalries, journalistic clashes, political power struggles, and competitive strife within their own ranks to find safe harbor in turn-of-the-century Tennessee.

Before the twentieth century had even begun, Nashville would witness the first salvo in a war between power blocs and pressure groups. The participants and the issues would change occasionally, but the struggle would keep its own momentum, and it would go on for decades. When it began on an October day in 1900, the setting and the subject for the initial confrontation were one and the same: Union Station.

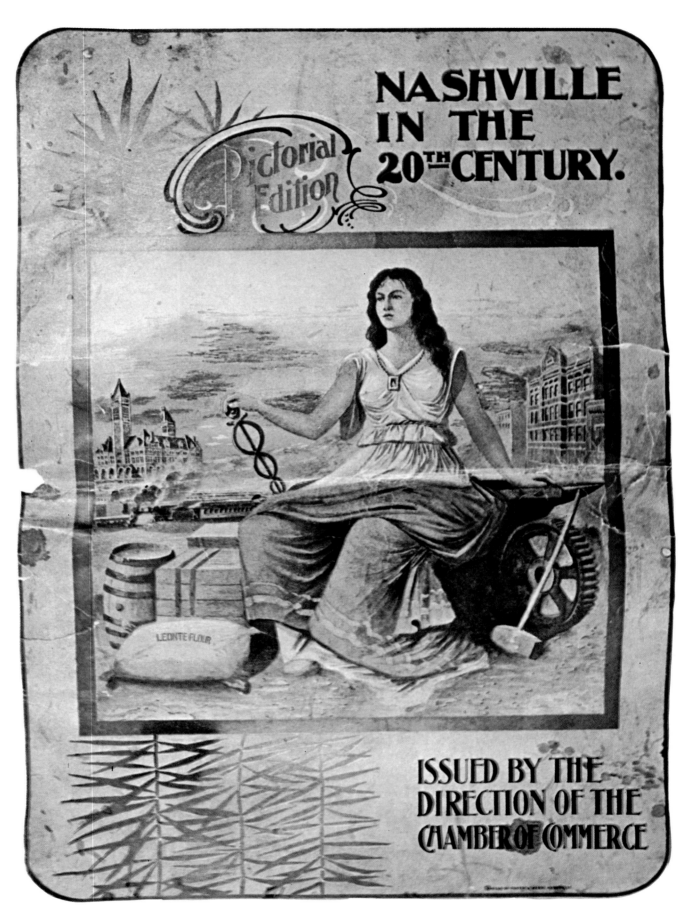

Nashville:
Twentieth-Century City
1900-1940

UNION STATION was a splendid structure, as impressive as any Nashville had ever seen. It had been designed in a Romanesque Revival style by the chief engineer of the Louisville and Nashville Railroad, Richard Montfort. His superiors had wanted a lavish and imaginative structure; Montfort made it nothing less than monumental.

Its tower, looming 220 feet above Broad Street, was topped by a nineteen-foot copper statue of Mercury, the Roman messenger of the gods. (Digital clocks, a genuine mechanical novelty, would be installed later to show the exact time on all four sides of the tower.) The gray stone exterior of the building was dominated by heavy arches and high, narrow windows, and the slate roof bristled with sharply peaked gables and soaring chimneys. Inside, the cavernous central waiting room, with its barrel-vaulted ceiling sixty-three feet high, was an artist's menagerie of wood, wrought iron, stained glass, and ceramic tile. A massive stone fireplace was at one end of the room, and there were bas-relief figures in the walls and brilliantly colored designs in the skylight.

Beneath the station, under a 500-foot-long shelter of steel and timber and slate, the trains rumbled in and out along arteries that tied

Nashville to the nation's major railroad centers. Here was the new hub of a thriving city's transportation industry, a central complex that spelled doom for the steamboats and promised growth and prosperity to Middle Tennesseans in the modern industrial age. In every detail, from the ribbons of steel below street level to the tip of Mercury's outstretched hand atop the tower, Union Station was a showcase symbol of the opulence and power of the railroad industry at the beginning of the twentieth century.

Had it not been for Nashville Mayor James M. Head, the splendor of Union Station and the official ceremony of dedication that marked its opening on October 9, 1900, might have disguised completely the mood of discontent and resentment that had shadowed Nashville's railroads for two decades. Top officials of the railroads dominated the ceremony: August Belmont of New York, chairman of the Louisville and Nashville Railroad's board of directors, was the guest of honor; John W. Thomas, president of the Nashville, Chattanooga and St. Louis Railway, took his turn at the podium; and Eugene C. Lewis, president of the terminal company created by the parent L&N to operate the new station, also addressed the crowd. But protocol demanded that the mayor be given a place

THE BUILDING WE CELEBRATE

AN epoch will this day be made for Nashville. The great stone edifice at Broad and Walnut streets is the matchless monument to record the fact, and this is the day of its formal unveiling. The epoch is one of larger progress and more persistent enterprise. The monument is typical of all that is comprehended in these two words. Erected on the threshold of a new century, it holds aloft a light by which the people of Nashville and this section of country may look upon all the future has in store for them. The beacon points along a great, broad path of promise, generous with the rewards of intelligence and sustained effort. Its beams sweep the enlarged boundaries of Nashville that are to be and bring into strong relief the vast multitude of its greater population.

Nashville is proud to-day, and to the many visitors within her gates points out with conscious pride the reasons why. To them she speaks: "Henceforward my people will approach nearer and nearer to the standard there set for them, and the oncoming years shall find me established in my own—the first city in the Southland."

Such are this day's auguries for our fair city. Mark it well, you scores of thousands of her people, soon to be swelled to many thousands more! In the short years and the longer decades to come, you will find pride and satisfaction in recalling it and giving it to the memories of those who come after you. The ninth day of the month of October in the year of our Lord Nineteen Hundred! . . .

Among those who are her guests to-day, Nashville finds especial pride in welcoming the coterie of gentlemen to whom she acknowledges a debt of gratitude. In her greeting to the conceiving geniuses and moving spirits in the building of the new Terminal Station, there is the expressed hope that they may not find her wanting in appreciation or worthiness.

Nashville American,
October 9, 1900

On one of the ten tracks under the Union Station shed, the first train pulled out in 1900 before the station was formally opened. The L&N and NC&StL railroads soon were running dozens of trains a day through the station, making it one of the busiest in the South.

Nashville Mayor James M. Head, a supporter of Jere Baxter and his Tennessee Central Railroad, admonished the executives of the L&N and the NC&StL not to look upon Nashville as "a lemon to be squeezed," but they squeezed the TC out of Union Station anyway.

166

Stained glass, wrought iron, and ornamental sculpture highlighted the decor of the new Union Station's central waiting room from the vaulted ceiling to the tile floor. The maidens flanking the clock represented Louisville and Nashville.

on the program, and when James Head spoke, his words were in jarring contrast to those of the railroad executives:

> . . . . Let us hope that these public spirited men who have put their money in the enterprise will be big enough and broad enough and bold enough to come to look upon Nashville, not as a lemon to be squeezed, nor even as a rich harvest to be gathered, but as a fertile field to be cared for and cultivated . . . . Let us hope that these terminal advantages, erected for the benefit and accommodation of the public, may be used to still further accommodate the public, and when other railroads come knocking for admission at our gates, the doors of the Terminal Station will be thrown wide open for all comers . . . .

The "other railroads" to which Mayor Head referred actually meant only one: the Tennessee Central, chartered in 1893 by Nashville attorney Jere Baxter. It had been blocked from access to Union Station, the very name of which implied openness to one and all. Furthermore, the L&N and its subsidiary, the NC&StL, would not agree to cooperative handling of freight cars with the Tennessee Central—a standard practice among railroads—and those refusals were viewed as hostile acts by Baxter and his supporters. Even as Union Station showed its sparkling new face to the city, Head's words made it clear that the great Nashville railroad war was in full fury.

The opening shot in that war had been fired twenty years earlier by Vernon K. Stevenson. In 1880, when the two principal railroads in Nashville were in a race to open a direct route from the East and South to the Midwest, Stevenson had stunned the city's business community by selling his controlling interest in the NC&StL to the rival L&N.

Stevenson had been the driving force behind the Nashville and Chattanooga Railroad in the 1850s. After serving as a Confederate officer during the Civil War, he had moved to New York and made a fortune, but he had kept financial control of the railroad. Edmund W. Cole of Nashville had run the line for him, and in 1873 they had changed its name to the NC&StL and set their sights on beating the L&N to St. Louis and the lucrative markets of the Midwest. Just when the goal seemed almost within Cole's grasp, Stevenson sold out to the competition.

In the eyes of many Nashville businessmen, the effects of that transaction were disastrous. Not only did it leave Cole, a popular and respected local leader, without a railroad to run; it also left Nashville, for all practical purposes, with only one railroad, a consolidated line owned and managed by outside interests, and it raised the dreaded prospect of higher freight rates and poorer service.

When John W. Thomas became president of the L&N's new subsidiary, he made an effort to show that the NC&StL would provide genuine competition to the parent company's main line. For a few years, the plan appeared to be working. With the Midwest route open, the NC&StL made Nashville the grain distribution center for the South. There was so much freight to be moved, in fact, that not only the two railroads but even the steamboats carried record tonnage in 1889.

Even so, the L&N's absentee owners reaped most of the profits, and in Nashville the railroad was widely regarded as an insensitive giant in an age of unrestrained business monopoly. Jere Baxter likened it to an octopus, strangling Nashville with its steel tentacles.

The ill will lingered through the remainder of the century, and the L&N's reputation scarcely improved. Business interests in Atlanta and other Southern cities charged in court that the railroad had seized an unfair and illegal advantage to corner the grain market. Steamboat owners quarreled among themselves as the trains took away more and more of their trade, and some of them claimed angrily that the L&N was keeping Tom Ryman in business as token competition while it drove the others farther up the Cumberland in search of trade the railroads could not reach. In Nashville, the railroad spent large sums to ward off government regulation, gave away thousands of free passes to lawyers, journalists, and legislators, and in general exerted heavy influence over politicians and the press.

Not even the building of Union Station was seen as an unalloyed blessing. Demands for a new passenger and freight terminal in the city had been made for years, but the L&N had put off the expenditure, clinging instead to its outdated and inadequate depot. Finally, when the new station was opened, its tracks were placed north and south through a deep gulch that lay like an open wound across the face of the city, and that became a cause of further disenchantment with the L&N.

In 1893, Jere Baxter decided it was time someone confronted the railroad Goliath. He hoped his Tennessee Central line could be extended from East Tennessee through Nashville and on to Western Kentucky, where it could be linked with an existing route to St. Louis. Baxter was soon caught up in a national financial panic and his personal resources were soon exhausted, but in 1896 he persuaded a group of St. Louis businessmen to back his venture, and the project was revived.

Jere Baxter, the Nashville lawyer whose Tennessee Central Railroad took on the mighty L&N and its subsidiary, the NC&StL, was honored posthumously with this statue at Broadway and West End Avenue. It was later moved to Baxter School in East Nashville.

The following year, officials of the L&N and the NC&StL used the Tennessee Centennial Exposition as the springboard for a campaign to build public favor for their lines, and soon thereafter they announced the start of the long-delayed Union Station project, but they were too late to stop the Tennessee Central. At a mass meeting in the Union Gospel Tabernacle on October 1, 1900—a week before the new railroad terminal was dedicated—Baxter and Mayor Head won support for a referendum on a million-dollar public bond issue that would, in effect, make the city a major stockholder in Baxter's railroad.

The L&N wisely chose to use its local resources in the power struggle with the Tennessee Central, and in John Thomas and Eugene Lewis, Baxter faced adversaries as formidable as any the railroad could have enlisted from Louisville or New York. They were Nashvillians, powerful figures in the city, widely known and respected for their creative and managerial skills. More than any others, they had made the state centennial celebration a smashing success, and Union Station was a monument, however belated, to their vision and their imagination.

When the bond referendum was held two months after the new terminal opened, the voters approved Baxter's proposal in spite of an opposition campaign organized by the other railroads. A group of taxpayers then went to court seeking an injunction blocking the bond issue (it was later revealed that the NC&StL had financed the suit), and the litigation was to continue without pause for years. The city's two major newspapers—the *American*, of which Lewis himself was publisher, and the *Nashville Banner*, published by former L&N official E. B. Stahlman—vigorously opposed Baxter and his bond-issue proposal. Baxter, having no outlet for his side of the story, founded a paper of his own, the *Daily News.* He also got himself elected to the state Senate, where he pushed through a bill ratifying the Nashville bond referendum.

The seemingly interminable conflict took its toll in health and friendships on all sides, but in the end, Baxter simply lacked the resources to match the powerful L&N. In the spring of 1903, he resigned the presidency of the Tennessee Central, implying in a statement that his departure might clear the way for the railroad to gain access to the Union Station and make a cooperative freight handling agreement with the other lines. In spite of his departure, however, the L&N refused to make the concessions.

In 1904, Baxter was suddenly stricken with gallstones, and within a month he was dead. Appreciative local citizens and others along the Tennessee Central line had his likeness cast in

170

The fallen statue of Mercury, 1952

bronze and erected it at the junction of Broad Street and West End Avenue (it was later moved to Baxter School in East Nashville). Eugene Lewis, seeking to have the last word, installed a monument in Centennial Park in honor of John Murrell, a famous horse thief in Tennessee's past. The clear implication was that Lewis considered Baxter's bond-issue plan to be nothing more than a scheme of thievery.

By coincidence, Tom Ryman also died in 1904, and his disappearance from the river scene foretold the imminent departure of other names—Lovell, Tyner, Rhea, Bryan, Buttorff—that had reigned there for generations. Ironically, the United States Army Corps of Engineers completed the first lock on the Cumberland River just before Ryman's death, giving more speed and safety to the steamboats that were already in eclipse.

The Tennessee Central struggled on without Baxter, but it was little more of a competitive threat to the L&N and the NC&StL than the few remaining riverboats. Nashville's railroad war was over. For the better part of a half-century, the L&N and its subsidiary lines would dominate the rails in Nashville and much of the South. Their competition would come not from other railroads but from trucks and airplanes, and by mid-century, all the nation's trains would be in trouble. Then, a final note of symbolism would be recorded in Nashville: One morning in 1952, a windstorm would topple Mercury from the tower of Union Station, and the copper messenger of the gods would lie in a twisted sprawl on the tracks below.

IN THE FIRST DECADE of the twentieth century, Nashville showed some unmistakable qualities of a rising American city. Its achievements as well as its conflicts—of which the railroad war was only one—were of a scope and volume and level of complexity that only an urban center could produce. Physical features—buildings, streets, open spaces—provided the broad canvas. Large and growing institutions—government, business, education, the church, the press—provided the medium. Men of talent and power—and increasingly, women too—grasped the opportunities and made things happen. The results were impressive, awesome, and at times frightening.

The list of positive achievements began with sheer growth. In 1900, Nashville counted 80,865 people, and another 40,000 lived in Davidson County. Twenty years earlier, the city population had been barely more than half of 80,000; by 1910, it would be above 110,000. To be sure, Nashville was no teeming metropolis, no New York or Chicago, but it was among the largest and fastest-growing cities in the South.

Along with the growth came many new buildings: two twelve-story "skyscrapers" downtown (one still bears the name of its principal stockholder, E. B. Stahlman); the Hermitage Hotel, to rival the Maxwell House; a public library jointly financed by the city and Andrew Carnegie, and named for the Pittsburgh philanthropist; and the Arcade, a block-long mall housing more than fifty shops on two levels under a gabled glass roof.

Several of the city's leading business institutions of the present day were founded in the first decade of this century, among them the National Life and Accident Insurance Company, the Life and Casualty Insurance Company of Tennessee, and the Cain-Sloan department store. (Castner-Knott, another large department store, had its beginning in the 1890s, and the city's oldest con-

When these streetcar tracks were laid on Fifth Avenue in the early 1900s, the electric-powered public conveyance had already been serving Nashville for more than a decade. Streetcars would be the principal means of mass transit in the city for almost fifty years.

172

After Andrew Carnegie helped Nashville build this turn-of-the-century library at Eighth and Union, Mary Hannah Johnson (right) was its first director. The present main library of Nashville-Davidson County is located on the same site.

When the Arcade was opened in downtown Nashville in 1903, more than 40,000 people came to stroll beneath the flags and other decorative banners that hung from the balcony and the gabled glass roof.

At the end of its line in South Nashville, the Nashville Railway and Electric Company, operators of the city's streetcars, built an amusement park and zoo. The attraction, known as Glendale Park, was located between Granny White Pike and Lealand Lane.

tinuing financial institution, First American National Bank, was chartered in 1883 as the American National Bank by Edmund W. Cole, the deposed former president of the Nashville, Chattanooga and St. Louis Railway.) One Cent Savings Bank, the first black-owned bank in Tennessee (and the second in the nation), was organized in 1904; it continues now as Citizens Savings Bank & Trust Company.

The twentieth century brought a steady flow of innovations and significant developments to Nashville: the city park system, the annual state fair, the Shelby Street and Jefferson Street bridges, the Nashville Union Stockyards, two amusement parks (Glendale for whites, Greenwood for blacks), an efficient electric streetcar system, the conversion of many street names to numbered avenues, the annexation of several suburban districts, a thousand automobiles and ten times that many telephones, miles of brick streets, two successive Southern Association baseball championships for the Nashville Vols, and a revolutionary entertainment medium called the movies. (A young businessman named Tony Sudekum opened Nashville's first movie theater, a nickelodeon called the Dixie, on Fifth Avenue in 1907; he went on to establish a chain of theaters that reached into several states.)

Before the decade was over, Presidents Theodore Roosevelt and William Howard Taft would visit the city, Roosevelt to stay at the Maxwell House (and call its coffee "good to the

The students and faculty of Peabody Normal College turned out in force when President Theodore Roosevelt visited the South Nashville campus in 1907. Roosevelt addressed the crowd from the back seat of the automobile.

"Time and again a single man does something that grips this whole great country," declared this Maxwell House Coffee advertisement in a national magazine. The man being praised was Nashville's Joel Owsley Cheek, "a genius for flavor" whose blended coffee and skillful promotion made him rich and famous.

Serious rioting between students of Vanderbilt University and the University of Nashville was narrowly averted yesterday morning, the trouble growing out of the intense feeling between the football teams of the two universities. A detail of police was called to the scene at 9 o'clock, and later another detail, and finally the entire department was ordered to report for duty. In the rioting that occurred a number of students and officers were struck with stones and other missiles.

The feeling was made more bitter, it is said, Thursday night when the Vanderbilt students paraded the streets, making great demonstrations over the victory Thursday, when the University of Nashville team was defeated by a score of 10 to 0. Guards were kept on the campus because of rumors and fears that the fences would be painted black and gold by the Vanderbilt students.

The first clash was at 9 o'clock in the morning, when about forty Vanderbilt medical students started to parade through the grounds of the University of Nashville . . . . The medical students were met at the gate of the Nashville campus by Nashville students, who prevented them from entering the grounds . . . .

Nashville American,
November 30, 1901

last drop") and Taft to be honored at a lavish Hermitage Hotel banquet. Judge Horace H. Lurton would be appointed to the United States Supreme Court, following two other Nashvillians (John Catron in the 1830s and Howell E. Jackson in the 1890s) and preceding a fourth, Vanderbilt University graduate James C. McReynolds, who would be named to the high court in 1914. Another Nashville judge, Jacob McGavock Dickinson, having served as United States attorney general and president of the American Bar Association, would become secretary of war in the administration of President Taft.

Vanderbilt would have the largest sports stadium in the South and, under Coach Dan McGugin, the best football team in the region;

Donau, a racehorse belonging to Nashville beer-maker William Gerst, won the Kentucky Derby in 1910—by which time it had been declared illegal to make or drink beer (or whiskey) or to bet on horses in Tennessee.

the governor's salary would be raised to $5,000 a year; school teachers would make thirty-five dollars a month (married women need not apply); the Belle Meade stock farm would be subdivided into a residential community; and a horse owned by Nashville brewer William Gerst would win the 1910 Kentucky Derby—after both brewing and horse racing had lost official sanction in Tennessee. In the competitive field of newspaper publishing, Nashville would see its daily papers reduced to two: the *Banner*, founded in 1876, and the *Tennessean*, first published in 1907 but claiming unbroken ancestry all the way back to the *Nashville Whig* in 1812.

In the marketplace, eggs were selling for seventeen cents a dozen, Tennessee ham for ten cents a pound, and six-year-old Robertson County whiskey (while it was still legal) for two dollars and twenty-five cents a gallon. Nashville had become a major regional trade and manufacturing center—it produced a lion's share of the South's flour and corn meal, roasted most of its coffee, and supplied the region with more dry goods, shoes, groceries, hardware, lumber, and building supplies than any other city south of the Ohio River. In printing and publishing, an industry long associated with the city, more than a dozen firms produced a rich variety of materials, including several popular magazines (*Southern Agriculturalist, Trotwood's Monthly, Southern Lumberman, Confederate Veteran, Bob Taylor's Magazine*), and religious publishing houses were operated by Baptists (white and black), Methodists, Presbyterians, and other Protestant groups.

In one area—labor union organizing—there was relatively little activity. Nashville may have had slightly more consciousness of unions than most Southern cities, but compared to the urban communities of the North it was insignificant. Typographical workers, the brotherhoods of

Librarian and writer John Trotwood Moore (above) and Robert Love "Our Bob" Taylor, three times governor of Tennessee, were also publishers. A merger of their independent journals resulted in Taylor-Trotwood Magazine, *a general-interest monthly.*

Skalowski's ice cream parlor on Fifth Avenue, the pride of a Polish immigrant, claimed in 1910 to have "the world's largest onyx soda fountain." Skalowski's is gone now, but another sweet shoppe, Candyland on Church Street, still refreshes downtown shoppers after sixty years on the same corner. Candyland and the venerable Satsuma Tea Room on Union Street are two of the most enduring eating places in downtown Nashville.

railroad workers, and some of the shops and building trades were organized, but unions could count only a small fraction of the Nashville work force in their ranks. Not even the appearance of Samuel Gompers and his American Federation of Labor for a national convention in the city in 1897 was enough to cause an upsurge in union membership. The unions did help to lobby a few labor laws through the state legislature, but the age belonged to big business, and it would be decades before organized labor would have any appreciable power in Nashville, the state, or the region.

But all in all, there was more than enough to hold the interest and attention of Nashvillians in the first busy years of the new century. There would have been enough even without the railroad war—and it was just one of several emotionally charged controversies of the period. The railroads had staged a dramatic opening scene, but their long struggle was only a portent of the conflicts to come.

Three issues in particular—temperance, suffrage, and segregation—were especially volatile. Each one brought into question a social condition of long duration; each inspired attackers and defenders whose actions were filled with moral certitude; each summoned political, economic, religious, and journalistic forces into a battle for high stakes. Eventually, each issue also brought about basic changes in the character and quality of Nashville life.

NASHVILLE CITY ORDINANCES, 1909

1201. It shall be unlawful for any person, firm or corporation to have, maintain or conduct any house, room, place, den or resort where opium is sold, to be consumed or smoked at said place, room, den or resort, or where people assemble to smoke or consume opium in any manner or form; or to keep, conduct or maintain any room, house, place, den or resort for the purpose of prostitution, illegal commerce between the sexes, or sexual depravity, natural or unnatural . . .

1258. Whoever shall, in this city, appear in any public place naked, or in a dress not belonging to his or her sex, or in an indecent or lewd dress, or shall make any indecent exposure of his or her person, or be guilty of any indecent or lewd act or behavior, or shall exhibit, sell or offer for sale, any obscene, vulgar or libelous book, picture, painting, paper or publication of any character whatever that shall be adjudged vulgar, libelous or obscene, or shall exhibit or perform any indecent, immoral or lewd play or other representation, shall be deemed guilty of a misdemeanor.

1259. Any white male or female found living or cohabiting with, as man and wife, any negro, mulatto or person of mixed blood descended from a negro, shall be deemed guilty of a misdemeanor, and fined not less than twenty nor more than fifty dollars.

1266. It shall be unlawful for any person to wash his or her person or any article in any of the stock hydrants within the corporate limits of the city.

1294. Whoever shall fly a kite, or shall be detected throwing stones or other missiles so as to endanger the breakage of windows or glass, or the destruction of property in this city, shall be deemed guilty of a misdemeanor.

1297. The washing of horses and vehicles on the streets shall be a nuisance, and the person so offending shall be subject to a fine of five dollars.

THE PEOPLE OF NASHVILLE had never been of one mind about whiskey. From the earliest days of settlement, there had been those who made and drank it and those who shunned it. On each side of the issue were politicians and preachers and teachers, doctors and lawyers and journalists, respected citizens and demagogues. Two centuries later, their descendants would still be fighting for or against the right to consume alcoholic beverages.

The first temperance society was formed here in 1829. During the Civil War, heavy consumption of liquor was associated with a general condition of disorder, lawlessness, and crime, and when the war was over, organized groups began to campaign for temperance, a term which came to mean total prohibition of intoxicating drinks.

Throughout the final decades of the nineteenth century, the Woman's Christian Temperance Union and similar organizations of men joined with churches, traveling evangelists, most newspapers, and a scattering of politicians in an effort to suppress liquor, but they had only limited success. In 1880, distillers in Middle Tennessee produced nearly a million gallons of whiskey, and in 1887, the electorate—made up exclusively of males—refused to ratify a "dry" amendment to the state constitution.

By the turn of the century, state laws and local ordinances had effectively removed saloons from nearly all rural districts, but in most of the cities, business went on as usual. Nashville, notwithstanding its place as the seat of government, was regarded as a wide-open town; it had 170 saloons, dozens of gambling houses, a high crime rate, widespread prostitution, and a reputation for lax law enforcement.

Still, the pressure for reform in Nashville continued. Mass meetings were called to demand law and order. A reform mayor was elected in 1903, and another in 1905. A new ordinance confined saloons to an area of about twelve square blocks in the central city, and the police, under heavy public pressure, tried to improve enforcement of laws against Sunday tippling and liquor sales to minors. As part of the general clean-up effort, gambling parlors were raided, and the 1907 legislature outlawed racetrack betting.

With each new development, the conflict between wet and dry forces became more uncontrollable and explosive. Politics and religion, public morality and individual conscience, were thrown together in an arena where emotion had absorbed all logic. Compromise seemed impossible. There would be a war of words and even weapons—and out of it would come a winner and a loser.

Or so it seemed. The explosion came, predictably enough, and in its wake, prohibition was approved as a monument to a fallen martyr. But whiskey remained, and so did the divisions between those who accepted its presence as inevitable and those who considered its removal essential.

The martyr, Edward Ward Carmack, seemed an unlikely candidate to carry prohibition's banner, much less to die for it. He had grown up fatherless and poor in rural Sumner County, had never finished school—yet by the time he met Duncan B. Cooper in 1886, Carmack had made himself a lawyer, won election to the legislature, and demonstrated a masterful command of the written and spoken word.

He was then only twenty-eight years old. Cooper, at forty-two, was an old-school Tennessee cavalier who had knocked about in Central America, worked as a contractor on the Washington Monument, and finally found his niche as a publisher and political king-maker. In Carmack he saw an unpolished gem, a sure bet for journalistic and political stardom. Cooper hired him to edit his newspaper, the *Nashville American*. The two men became close friends.

177

Edward Ward Carmack—editor, senator, champion of the prohibitionist cause—was a leading orator for temperance and a bitter foe of the Patterson-Cooper faction of Tennessee Democrats before he was shot and killed in downtown Nashville.

Carmack moved on in 1892 to edit a Memphis paper and then to serve two terms in the United States House of Representatives and win election in 1900 to the Senate, where his glib and outspoken manner brought him more than passing notice.

While Carmack was in Washington, a young Nashville attorney named Luke Lea—a grandson of John M. Lea, the wartime advisor to Andrew Johnson—had helped Malcolm Patterson of Memphis win election as governor, but the two men soon parted company over the liquor issue, Patterson joining the wets and Lea the drys. Carmack had not been known as a prohibitionist—or a teetotaler—but he and Patter-

178

It was Robin Cooper (bottom) who shot and killed Edward Carmack, but it was Duncan Cooper, Robin's father (right), whose murder conviction in the sensational case was finally upheld by the state's highest court. Governor Malcolm Patterson immediately pardoned the Coopers.

son were political and personal enemies, so when Carmack found it necessary to take a position on the whiskey question, he joined the drys on the opposite shore from the governor. That decision separated Carmack from his old friend and mentor, Duncan Cooper, who stood with Patterson not only as a personal ally but also as an opponent of prohibition.

Politics and temperance thus brought about a fundamental realignment of power in Tennessee. Patterson, Cooper, and several other men who shared their anti-temperance views seemed to have the upper hand. They got former Governor Robert L. Taylor elected to the Senate in place of Carmack in 1906 and Patterson re-elected governor over Carmack in 1908. Luke Lea, who had begun publishing a prohibitionist newspaper called the *Nashville Tennessean*, hired ex-Senator Carmack to be his editor, and the two men headed a faction which opposed the Patterson clique on political issues in general and on the whiskey issue in particular. E. B. Stahlman's *Banner* appeared to side with Lea and Cooper, while the *American*, once owned by Cooper (and later by E. C. Lewis), tended to support the Patterson camp.

As soon as he joined the *Tennessean*, Carmack began to attack the opposition. He singled out Cooper for special treatment, calling to question his former mentor's intelligence and—indirectly—his ancestry. Cooper was then sixty-five years old and long since retired from publishing, but he was still combative, and he took feverish exception to Carmack's provocative words. He sent a mutual friend to Carmack with a warning that if the editor attacked him again in the paper, "one of us must die." The next morning, Carmack outdid himself in ridiculing Cooper.

The day was Monday, November 9, 1908. Late in the afternoon, Duncan Cooper and his son Robin, a young attorney, walked up Union

Street with pistols in their pockets just as Carmack, also carrying a gun, approached Union on Seventh Avenue. There were witnesses to the scene, but there would be no consensus on what took place. Only this much was certain: Carmack fired twice, slightly wounding Robin Cooper, and three bullets from the younger Cooper's gun struck and killed Carmack.

Both Robin Cooper and his father—who never drew his pistol—were charged with murder and held without bond. Their trial began in January 1909 and dominated the attention of people in Nashville and throughout Tennessee for two months. Finally, the jury, after three

Mt. Pleasant Tenn.
Nov. 10, 1908

Col. D. B. Cooper
My Dear Friend;

I can hardly tell you how sorry I am of your unfortunate affair with Mr. Carmack. My heart goes out to you in this trouble and I write to express my deepest sympathy. I am frank to say, that I have been looking for trouble ever since he began to point his brow at you. I knew that a man of your civil could not and would not endure it. His assaults on you were so unjust and so uncalled for, that all fair minded men can but have one opinion of it. I am anxious to see you and hear the true story from your own lips and in the meantime sincerly wish I could be of some help, some comfort to you in some way. The affair is unfortunate and I know that you regret it, but keep up a brave heart all honorable men will be with you and no jury of Tennessee's brave men will ever let you suffer.

Give my love to the brave boy, who defended you and tell him that many thousand hearts beat warmly for you both.

Your friend,
J. B. Boyd

I want to tell you that the killing of Senator Carmack could have been prevented with a word, but it wasn't spoken.

It was a smoky day and how appropriate it was. A smoky afternoon for such a deed—the very day to kill a man who loved the sunshine of the South . . . . O, what a day it was, to take away such a man of sunshine. What will the South do for him, when a "spark of the old South" shoots him down, shoots him in the back like a cowardly assassin?

Those bullets haven't stopped yet. They went on through that smoky day. They went on through that body. They went into the anguished heart of that widow. I can hear her agonized wail. They pierced the soul of a little fellow with a face at the window waiting for the click of the gate latch and the sound of familiar footsteps. Yes, those bullets have gone on and on and will go on into the years. They have put the responsibilities of manhood upon the shoulders of a child. No, bullets never stop in the body of the murdered . . . .

It's with you gentlemen to say whether or not people shall take the law into their own hands. I've done what I could. If my duty's done well, I'm satisfied . . . . It has been said the rich and the influential can't be reached. I say stand up and give it the lie. I know you will do it. I know this jury. I know your hearts. I know my people.

My duty's done. All I can say to the spirit that's gone—gentleman, orator, statesman, patriot, Christian—farewell.

Tennessee Attorney General Jeff McCarn, concluding the prosecution's case in the trial of Duncan and Robin Cooper for the murder of Edward Ward Carmack

An eventful day, one pregnant with developments, has this one, the final day in the trial of Col. Duncan B. Cooper and Robin J. Cooper, proved to be. This morning these two noted defendants learned what their fate was to be at the hands of a jury of their peers, and thus is ended the most noted criminal case perhaps ever tried in the old Volunteer State.

•

The defendants were ordered brought into the court room and arrived at 9:26, two minutes after the twelve jurors had taken seats in the box for the last time after the long, hard grind of the session—exactly two months from the date the trial began.

Col. Cooper came in behind his daughter, Mrs. Beverly Wilson, and Robin Cooper followed close after his father, while he was followed by Mrs. Lucius Burch.

"Everybody be seated; Mr. Clerk, poll the jury," said Judge Hart.

"Well, gentlemen, have you agreed on a verdict?" asked the judge.

When the voice of Foreman E. M. Burke spoke to the court there was considerable noise in the room and the court officers called for quiet.

"We find the defendants D. B. Cooper and Robin Cooper guilty in the second degree and fix their punishment at twenty years in the penitentiary," said Foreman Burke.

"So say you all?" inquired Clerk Romans Hailey.

"So say we all," echoed the jury.

As the verdict was read not a tremor passed over the defendants. The silence was intense.

Nashville Banner,
March 20, 1909

Tennessee Governor Malcolm Patterson rose to power as a supporter of the liquor interests, was swept under by the temperance tide, and attempted a comeback as a reformed convert to prohibition. His pardon of Duncan and Robin Cooper for the murder of Edward Carmack created a storm of controversy across the state.

days of deliberation, convicted both men of second-degree murder and sentenced them to twenty years in prison. They appealed to the state supreme court, and in April 1910, the court upheld Duncan Cooper's conviction but ordered a new trial for his son, citing a technical flaw in the proceeding.

While the judges were reading their lengthy decisions on April 13, Malcolm Patterson used his authority as governor to grant the two men full pardons, saying their trial had not been impartial and their conviction was contrary to the law and the evidence. (In a little more than three years as governor, Patterson had already signed nearly a thousand pardons.)

Carmack's murder, the trial of the Coopers, and their pardon by the governor caused volcanic political and social upheavals throughout the state. The 1909 legislature, meeting while the murder trial was in progress, passed a law forbidding the sale or consumption of intoxicating liquors within four miles of any school, and the practical effect was to extend prohibition to Nashville and the few remaining wet cities. For good measure, the legislature also banned outright the manufacture of alcoholic beverages. Patterson vetoed both bills, but he was promptly overridden. Tennessee thus became the ninth state to adopt complete prohibition, a decade before the nation as a whole would attempt the same reform by means of a constitutional amendment. In death, Carmack had become a more influential factor in politics and social reform than he had ever been in life. While temperance forces eulogized him with emotional outpourings of grief and pledges of vengeance, the legislature ordered that a statue of the fallen editor be erected on the capitol grounds.

And that was only the beginning. Governor Patterson and his principal political ally, Robert Taylor, were ousted from power, the Democratic Party was torn into warring factions, and a Republican, Ben W. Hooper, was elected governor in 1910 and re-elected in 1912. The *Nashville American,* which had shown sympathy for the Coopers, was so damaged by the position it took that Luke Lea was able to buy the paper and merge it with the *Tennessean.* A coalition of Republicans and independent (reform) Democrats elected Lea to the United States Senate in 1911, and the regular Democrats, seeing that their struggle against prohibition was hopeless, decided in 1914 to join the majority in advocating enforcement of anti-liquor laws.

Patterson's decline was the most humiliating

of all. In 1911, his son was committed to a mental institution as an alcoholic. Two years later, the former governor was arrested in a raid on a Nashville house of prostitution, and though the disorderly conduct charges against him were dismissed, he admitted that he had been drunk and was unable to account for his activities. Following the embarrassing affair, Patterson joined the Presbyterian Church, became a teetotaler, and gradually re-emerged as a paid lecturer and a prize exhibit of the Anti-Saloon League.

For the remainder of the decade, the consequences of political power shifts and social reformations would be felt from the Mississippi to the mountains, but much of what transpired was ironic and unexpected. Nashville elected a regular Democrat, Hilary M. Howse, as mayor in 1909, and until he was ousted in 1916, enforcement of the prohibition statutes was lax and ineffective. "I am not a drinking man, but as long as I stay in a free country I will eat and drink as I please," Howse said, and Nashvillians did just that. Some saloons continued to operate in open defiance of the law, others were converted to private locker clubs where members could store their own liquor and have it served to them, and it was common for soft-drink shops and even drugstores to sell whiskey to trusted customers. In 1912, nearly one-fourth of

After he had been a United States senator and a World War I hero, Tennessean publisher Luke Lea was a dynamic figure in politics, publishing, and public affairs. He was at the peak of his career when this photograph was made in the 1920s.

all arrests in Nashville were for drunkenness, and both the proportion and the absolute number of such arrests were greater than in 1908, before passage of the prohibition laws.

Neither the temperance organizations nor a succession of governors and legislatures were able to bring about strict enforcement of the law until the federal prohibition amendment was ratified in 1919—and even then, bootleggers kept the whiskey issue alive and the temperance groups busy in Nashville, as elsewhere.

What may have been the ultimate irony of the era occurred in 1916 when Luke Lea sought re-election to the Senate. The prohibitionists had become disillusioned with him and said his support for the cause lacked sufficient fervor. In the Democratic primary, Lea was accused of being a tool of the liquor interests by his principal opponent—who was none other than Malcolm Patterson, the reformed darling of the drys. While Lea and Patterson staged one more classic battle in roles that were the exact reverse of a decade earlier, a West Tennessee congressman named Kenneth D. McKellar slipped between them to win the nomination and go on to a career of nearly four decades in the Senate. That campaign was Malcolm Patterson's swan song (though he did make a futile run for the governor's office in 1932), but Luke Lea would be heard from again.

184

Anne Dallas Dudley posed for this appealing photograph with her children to counter the anti-suffrage charge that only "mannish" women who were coarse, ugly, and childless were interested in voting. The determination of Mrs. Dudley and others was a deciding factor in ratification of the suffrage amendment by the Tennessee legislature in 1920.

WOMEN HAD PLAYED a major role in the campaign for prohibition in Tennessee, and that was unprecedented. In the past, there had been no place for "respectable" females except in the home and the church; it was, in fact, the threat to home life and morality raised by alcohol abuse and related problems that had spawned the temperance crusade in the first place. Women entered the temperance fight more to protect their sheltered place in society than to escape it.

But as the extended campaign wore on, some women began to see other needs and other possibilities. Without the right to vote, they reasoned, women were at the mercy of the men who picked the presidents, made the laws, ran the country—and drank the whiskey. An all-male electorate had rejected a prohibition amendment to the state constitution in 1887, had put Malcolm Patterson in the governor's office, had made Hilary Howse mayor of Nashville; if women had been allowed to vote, the results might have been different.

In 1911, when the temperance struggle was near its climax, a small group of women met at the Tulane Hotel to form the Nashville Equal Suffrage League. Their leader was Anne Dallas Dudley, a socially prominent young woman whose husband, Guilford Dudley, had helped to found the Life and Casualty Insurance Company. The women were careful to distinguish themselves from the suffragettes, whose militant tactics in other places had stirred controversy and opposition. Far from being aggressive, the Nashville women decided their best weapons in the pursuit of suffrage would be graciousness, charm, and gentle persuasion.

Nashville was not then prepared to take women's suffrage seriously. Men tended to think of politics as a rough-and-tumble affair too coarse for the soft sensibilities of the fairer sex, and many women—including some who were

I do not believe that women of Tennessee *want* the ballot, but even if they do, the question which *men* must determine is not affected in the least. It is not a question of what women *want*, but what they *ought* to have; and as men only now vote, it is a question for men alone to determine . . . .

In fine, the only *guaranties* of good government and peace are "the ballot-box, the jury-box, the sentry-box, and the cartridge-box"—the soldier, the sheriff, the policeman and the gun. This is a *fact*, and on it rests this impregnable proposition:

Only those who can bear arms should have a voice in deciding questions which may lead to war, or in enacting laws which may require soldiers, sheriffs, posses and policemen for their enforcement.

This alone puts female suffrage altogether out of consideration . . . .

Undeniably some women, barren masculine individuals, can bear arms, just as there are some men who cannot. We must deal with both as *classes* . . . .

Female suffrage is a social, as well as a political problem. It involves not only the influence of women on politics, but the effect of politics on women—on the family and on the home . . . .

Female suffrage is a racial and social poison because it tends to disintegrate the family life . . . .

from "An Address to the Men of Tennessee on Female Suffrage," by John J. Vertrees, Nashville, 1916

active in the temperance movement—apparently agreed. But within a few months, Mrs. Dudley and her small group were able to take their low-key message to churches, social gatherings, and even labor meetings, and support for their idea began slowly to grow.

The summer of 1920 was a terribly exciting time for me. I was twenty-three years old, just graduated from the University of Tennessee, and I was a reporter for the *Knoxville Journal & Tribune*. Women were admitted for the first time to the state Democratic convention that summer, and I was elected as a delegate. And when the Tennessee legislature met in special session to ratify the women's suffrage amendment, I was, as far as I know, the only woman reporter covering the session.

I wasn't neutral on the suffrage issue—I was on the side of the women who were working to win the right to vote, and I felt all along that we were going to win. A majority of the people of Tennessee didn't want the women to vote—not even a majority of the women wanted it. The suffragists were a very small minority in this state, and some of them were decidedly unpopular. One of the legislators stood up and attacked them as "petticoat-less, childless women." But the women fought back, and they lobbied the amendment through.

They knew how to handle the men. Anne Dallas Dudley and Kate Burch Warner led the way in Nashville—they and others, many others. Anne Dudley was terrific. She was truly a lady, a Southern lady—but she was a politician

from the word go. She had the biggest wallop of any politician you ever knew. She was beautiful and charming, but she also had a brain.

I'd like to see Governor A. H. Roberts given the credit he deserves for calling the special session and supporting the amendment. He told me in confidence three weeks in advance that he was going to call the session. He had known me since I was a baby—my father took a leading part in one of his first campaigns. When the suffrage issue was so intense and people were lined up outside his office waiting to see him—legislators, lobbyists, reporters from outside the state—I could slip around to the side door, tap lightly, stick my head in, and get a few words from him when others couldn't. I had a direct line. I had sense enough not to do it unless it was necessary—but I made the most of that entree.

It was Tennessee that gave the women of America the right to vote. A handful of women, a bare majority of legislators, and Governor Roberts did it. The governor ran for re-election that fall, and the women voted—but they must not have voted for him because he lost. I treasure a hand-written letter he sent me after the election, thanking me for helping him in the campaign.

MARY FRENCH CALDWELL, in a 1979 interview

Governor Ben Hooper embraced the cause after his nine-year-old daughter sagely deplored the fact that "ignorant men are allowed to vote, while educated women are denied this privilege." Mayor Howse cautiously added his support. In 1912 the Nashville women brought a state convention of suffragists to the city, and in 1914 the National American Woman Suffrage Association met at the Hermitage Hotel. Soon thereafter, a men's support organization was started in Tennessee, and on the national level, President Woodrow Wilson announced his support in principle for the women's efforts as suffragist groups built grassroots leagues in all parts of the nation.

Anne Dudley and another Nashville woman, Catherine Talty Kenny, became leading figures

in the Tennessee League of Women Voters. A separate organization of Tennessee suffragists led by Kate Burch Warner joined forces with Mrs. Dudley and Mrs. Kenny in 1918, by which time there were 4,000 members in the Nashville league and sixty chapters across the state. Mrs. Warner was elected president of the merged groups.

Partly as a response to Mrs. Dudley's urging, President Wilson made a rare personal appearance before the United States Senate in 1918 to plead for passage of a constitutional amendment granting the vote to women, and the following year, Congress approved the amendment. Within four months, seventeen states had ratified it, and by March 1920, the number had risen to thirty-five—one short of the two-thirds

Tennessee women who opposed suffrage, led by Mrs. James Pinckard (left) and Miss Josephine Pearson, enlisted an aged veteran of the Confederate Army to pose for this 1920 photograph in the Hermitage Hotel.

Vamped!

It took thirty-six states to ratify the women's suffrage amendment, and Tennessee, in the summer of 1920, turned out to be the "perfect thirty-six." Cartoonists had a field day with the issue.

majority needed to make the amendment the law of the land. As summer arrived, it became apparent that the decisive battle over suffrage would be fought in Tennessee.

Governor A. H. Roberts was prevailed upon to call a special session of the Tennessee legislature to provide the thirty-sixth ratification vote, and at length he agreed. By the time the legislators convened on August 9, 1920, it seemed likely that the suffragist forces would win handily; they had backing from the *Tennessean* and the *Banner*, from Senator McKellar and Governor Roberts, and from the leadership of both houses. Nashville was thus the center of

national attention, and suffragists from all over the country came to join in the victory celebration.

But trouble was brewing. The liquor interests threw their weight behind the anti-suffrage movement—seeking to strike back, perhaps, at the meddlesome women who had championed temperance—and a hospitality suite at the Hermitage Hotel drew in legislators to be liquored and lobbied. Women of the Tennessee Association Opposed to Woman Suffrage showed up in force. Others who saw the amendment as a blow to states' rights joined them. E. B. Stahlman of the *Banner* changed his mind and opposed ratification, and so did Seth Walker of Nashville, speaker of the lower chamber of the legislature. The state Senate quickly cast its expected vote in favor of the amendment, but what had appeared to be a comfortable majority in the House of Representatives gradually dwindled.

Ninety-six members of the House were present on August 18 when the crucial roll-call vote was finally taken. On a preliminary motion to table the ratification resolution, the vote was an even split—forty-eight apiece. Then, unexpectedly, a rural legislator who carried in his pocket a letter from his mother advising him to vote for ratification switched his vote on the final roll-call and put the amendment over by the slimmest of margins, forty-nine to forty-seven.

The women had won, and last-ditch efforts to reverse the decision proved futile and anticlimactic. Tennessee thus became the suffrage movement's "perfect thirty-six," the state that delivered the right to vote to millions of American women. Anne Dallas Dudley and the other Nashville women who had worked for nine years to bring about that result could take special pride in it. They had challenged an inequity that was deeply embedded in the law, and they had won. It was a new experience—for the women, for Nashville, and for the nation.

Richard Henry Boyd, born in slavery in Mississippi, became a leader among black Nashvillians at the turn of the century. He was the founder of the National Baptist Publishing Board, and members of his family have headed the enterprise continuously since he started it. His son, Henry Allen Boyd, was publisher of the Nashville Globe.

ANOTHER INEQUITY that had gained the sanction of law—racial segregation—was by the 1920s a standard characteristic of American life, and despite the efforts of black citizens to remove that injustice, it would remain for another fifty years.

Segregation had been born out of the ashes of slavery, incubated through the years of Civil War and Reconstruction, and brought to maturity near the end of the nineteenth century in the form of restrictive laws and social policies designed to insulate whites as much as possible from the large and growing non-white population in their midst.

In Nashville, where blacks had made up about one-fourth of the total community before the Civil War and close to two-fifths in the decades after it, the encroaching pattern of segregation developed slowly. After the war, blacks could vote, own property, give testimony in court (but not serve on juries), and hold political office. A few served as councilmen and magistrates; a black lawyer was admitted to the bar in 1870; and at least two merchants—Lewis Winter and Henry Harding—accumulated modest wealth. The black colleges attracted a small professional class, and the black churches were an abiding source of community leadership.

But most non-white members of the community were unskilled laborers, dock workers, servants, domestics; their principal labor was the work whites shunned. As the years passed, it became clear that the relative handful of black preachers, teachers, lawyers, and merchants were exceptions to the general pattern, and would remain so. In the social scheme of things, life went on much as it always had; political and economic power, and all the privileges and benefits deriving from them, were in the firm and complete control of whites.

Blacks voted with the Republicans, the party that had freed them from slavery, and when

Democrats regained political control of the city and the state in the 1870s, a slow erosion of the meager gains blacks had made began to set in. At the Nashville centennial celebration in 1880, the Reverend Nelson Merry, pastor of the First Colored Baptist Church, used his few minutes at the podium to speculate that the white and colored races would live together in greater harmony and peace if they would "simply do right." His words were an admonition and a plea; schools were already segregated, the police force was all white, voting and office-holding by blacks were becoming more restricted, and the state legislature was about to enact a law requiring separate seating of whites and blacks on railroad cars.

In 1889, the legislature made payment of a poll tax a prerequisite of voting, and the effect was to disfranchise most blacks and a great many whites who could not afford the cost. Black voter participation quickly fell to a few hundred, and black elected officials were all but eliminated.

Still, there were some prominent exceptions to the pattern. There were a dozen black lawyers in the city in the 1890s, and twice that many black doctors. There was R. F. Boyd, a doctor at Meharry Medical College, who ran for mayor

189

After he had helped to organize a black-owned bank in Nashville—now Citizens Savings Bank & Trust Company—James Carroll Napier served Presidents Taft and Wilson as register of the treasury. In his Washington office he signed his name to all government treasury notes.

and for the legislature; and there was Charles C. Gowdy, a captain in the fire department, who died a hero's death fighting a blaze in 1892; and there was Preston Taylor, a minister and undertaker, who established Greenwood Park, a black counterpart to Glendale Park; and there was Richard Henry Boyd, founder of the National Baptist Publishing Board, the first black institution of its kind.

And most prominent of all, there was James Carroll Napier. Born a slave in Nashville the day after Andrew Jackson died, he received an education in the North and returned with a law degree in 1872. Napier served for eight years on the city council, aided in the creation of Pearl and Meigs high schools for blacks, and ran as a Republican for a seat in Congress.

In a city of 30,000 blacks and 50,000 whites, the handful of exceptions to the segregationist pattern was exceedingly small, and even the exceptions were not exempt from the limitations, for all blacks were considered to have "their place," and their place was in almost all cases separate and inferior to that of whites.

At the start of the new century, Richard Henry Boyd warned his fellow black Baptist ministers in the state that unless they guarded their interests, white politicians would "turn the hand backward on the political dial a quarter of a century." The legislature was already considering a proposal to extend the separate rail coach law to streetcars, and other Jim Crow segregation statutes might follow. It was, Boyd felt, time to speak out in protest, and many blacks did, at public meetings, in debates and speeches, and in letters to the newspapers.

Even as the limitations on blacks increased, white opposition to their visibility and outspokenness grew louder. In Washington, Senator Edward Carmack protested when President Theodore Roosevelt invited Booker T. Washington to the White House, and he warned

Tennessee Acts, 1905
CHAPTER 150.
HOUSE BILL No. 87.

SECTION 1. *Be it enacted by the General Assembly of the State of Tennessee,* **That all persons, companies, or corporations operating any street car line or lines in the State of Tennessee be, and the same are hereby, required, where white and colored passengers are carried or transported in the same car or cars, to set apart and designate in each car or coach so operated for both a portion thereof or certain seats therein to be occupied by white passengers, and a portion thereof or certain seats therein to be occupied by colored passengers;** *Provided,* **that nothing in this Act shall be construed to apply to nurses attending children or other helpless persons of the other race;** *Provided,* **that large printed or painted signs shall be kept in a conspicuous place in the car or cars, or the parts thereof set apart or designated for the different races, on which shall be printed or painted . . . "This car for white people" . . . [or] "This car for the colored race."**

●

SECTION 3. *Be it further enacted.* **That all passengers on any street car line shall be required to take the seats assigned to them, and any person refusing so to do shall leave the car or remaining upon the car shall be guilty of a misdemeanor, and upon conviction shall be fined in any sum not to exceed twenty-five dollars . . . .**

●

Passed March 30, 1905.
J. J. BEAN,
Speaker protem of the House of Representatives.
E. RICE,
Speaker of the Senate.

Approved April 4, 1905.
JOHN I. COX,
Governor.

that Southern whites had the alternative "of recovering their mastery [over blacks] or abandoning their country."

The mastery had never been surrendered, and the legislature proved it by passing the streetcar segregation law in 1905. But the black community refused to accept it meekly. At mass meetings they vowed to boycott the streetcar system, and a group of young men formed a newspaper, the *Globe*, to publicize the boycott campaign. Richard Boyd, J. C. Napier, Preston Taylor and others, having previously founded a bank to serve blacks, proposed the creation of a black-owned transportation company to fill the streetcar void, and they soon obtained a charter for such a firm. While they waited for delivery on an order of five steam-propelled automobiles seating fifteen passengers each, they set up a temporary network of horse-drawn carriages to move black passengers about the city.

The boycott began on July 5, 1905. By late September, when the steam-driven automobiles had arrived, the Nashville Transit Company's daily passenger count had fallen off sharply and the company was reported to be losing money. But as the months dragged on, the new Union Transportation Company found its cars to be too slow and its revenue too sparse. Harassment from whites and the onset of winter added to their woes. Finally, in mid-1906, after the boycott had lost its force, the company ceased operation and its backers had to absorb the loss.

The *Globe* would continue to publish for almost a half-century, promoting black pride and self-sufficiency; Richard Boyd's religious publishing enterprise would prosper under four generations of family leadership; Preston Taylor's diverse business and community interests would include Tennessee Agricultural and Industrial State Normal School (now Tennessee State University), which he and others helped to launch with a door-to-door fund-raising canvass; and J. C. Napier's long and varied career would be highlighted by a term as register of the United States Treasury under Presidents Taft and Wilson and by nearly seventy years of banking and law practice in Nashville. There would be occasional newcomers to the ranks of Nashville's black elite, such as Moses McKissack III, who with his brother Calvin would build one of the earliest and largest architectural firms in the South.

But the Napiers, Taylors, and Boyds personified a very small number of blacks in Nashville whose successes obscured the deprivation and hardship faced by the multitude. Segregation would stay and spread, and court challenges to its constitutionality would fail. A few blacks would turn in desperation from the Republicans to the Democrats, but would find hardly more concern for their needs. The last black officeholder in Nashville, Councilman S. P. Harris, would lose his seat in 1913, and it would be nearly forty years before another black would be elected.

Segregation was the new order; in truth, it was the old order with a new name. Blacks joined the temperance campaign, but only in segregated circles; they fought in World War I, but again, only in segregated units. They were barred from all restaurants, hotels, churches, and schools attended by whites, and the black schools and other tax-supported institutions were tightly controlled by whites. Even at Fisk University, a private institution for black students, all administration and most instruction remained in the firm and often paternalistic grip of whites for eighty years after its founding. In 1925, when a student strike dislodged Fayette A. McKenzie, a puritanical and autocratic Pennsylvanian, from a ten-year reign as Fisk's president, both the *Tennessean* and the *Banner* warned that the school's financial support would evaporate unless the students ended their

192

Gabriel Moses McKissack (seated, left), son of an African slave, was the patriarch of one of Tennessee's oldest and most prominent black families. In this 1913 photograph, taken at the family homeplace in Pulaski, McKissack posed with a sister, a brother-in-law, a granddaughter, three daughters, six sons, and two daughters-in-law. Two of his sons, Calvin (back row, left) and Moses III (back row, fourth from left), were among the state's first registered architects; the firm they founded in Nashville in 1922 is still in business. Sons of Moses McKissack III have continued uninterrupted the architecture and construction enterprises of their father.

"mutiny" and gave up their demand for "equality of rights."

There was a resurgence of the Ku Klux Klan in Nashville in 1924, and in the same year, a black minister was killed by a policeman, a businessman was shot down by a white saloon-keeper, two young women were attacked and beaten by whites on streetcars, and a young black man was taken from the county hospital by a band of white men and lynched. The incidents outraged the black community but caused hardly a stir in the papers.

Unlike temperance and suffrage, which provoked such passionate controversy among white Nashvillians, segregation was all but ignored as a social issue except by those who were directly affected by it. Only blacks, who daily endured its indignities and inequities, could know how harmful it was, and most of them suffered in silence, seeing any other response as futile if not foolhardy. Another generation would pass before blacks in Nashville, the South, and the nation would make equality of rights and opportunity an idea whose time had finally come.

J.B. Singleton (in chair) and father (standing), 1925

I was born at 1116 Jefferson Street in North Nashville in 1902. There's a hole in the ground at that spot now, where the interstate highway runs through. The house belonged to my parents. My father was a dentist; he had come to Nashville from South Carolina in 1887, and in 1892 he was one of the first graduates in dentistry from Meharry Medical College. I received my degree there in 1926 and my son received his in 1954, so three generations of J. B. Singletons have been Meharry graduates who made dentistry their life work.

The area south of lower Broad Street was called Black Bottom in those days, and old Pearl High School was there, on Fifth Avenue. We could only go through the eleventh grade so I went to Fisk and finished high school and two years of pre-medical training before I entered Meharry in 1922. At that time, Meharry was on Chestnut Street in South Nashville.

There were a good many middle-class black families in Nashville back then—doctors, lawyers, college professors, teachers, Pullman porters, people who were in banking and real estate. There was the *Nashville Globe,* a black-owned newspaper, and the National Baptist Publishing Board. We grew up thinking we were living pretty well—and we were, compared to the many poor

people who had no education and even less money. Nashville never was a real bad town for black people, not like so many places in the Deep South.

But it was far from perfect. The indignities of segregation and discrimination applied to all blacks, regardless of education or position or income. We learned early where we were allowed to go—upstairs in theaters, downstairs on steamboats, in the back on streetcars, in the front on trains. Everything was segregated—schools and churches, restaurants and hotels, restrooms and drinking fountains.

I actually believe that a lot of white people didn't know—they had no interest in knowing. Their knowledge of black people was very limited. They only knew the blacks who worked for them.

After the First World War, when blacks who had fought for their country came home and saw how restricted life was, they became concerned, and I remember that as being the time when black people started to realize what segregation was all about. No doubt the realization had been there all along for some. Still, it was a long time after that before black people in Nashville and throughout the South were able to organize and protest segregation laws, and finally to erase them.

J. B. SINGLETON, D.D.S., in a 1979 interview

IN THE MIDST of all the social issues came the First World War, and Nashville laid aside its local agenda and rallied to the flag once again. More than 15,000 Davidson County men—and for the first time, a few women—marched away in uniform. (The first Tennessee woman to join the United States Navy was a popular *Banner* columnist and poet-novelist named Will Allen Dromgoole, who disguised the fact that she was fifty-seven years old when she enlisted in 1917.) Some of the men, like flying ace Ed Buford, returned as heroes; others, like sixth-generation Nashvillian John W. Overton, did not live to return at all.

On the home front, the city's population was swelled by an influx of factory workers, many of them employed at a huge government munitions plant at Hadley's Bend on the Cumberland (later to be called the Du Pont Plant at Old Hickory). The local German community, grown large and

When the troops came home from World War I, they paraded up Capitol Boulevard under a makeshift arch. More than 15,000 Davidson Countians served in uniform during the war.

THE UNITED STATES OFFERS FOR SALE BY SEALED BIDS

A COMPLETE CITY--"OLD HICKORY"

After it had used the powder plant and built the town of Old Hickory during World War I, the United States Government put them up for sale in 1920. Du Pont, the original contractor, bought the plant and the town; it still owns the plant.

Nashville's first and only automobile manufacturer, Southern Motor Works, turned out eight hundred Marathon roadsters like this one, but the company folded before World War I.

MARATHON

Not Simply a Car   But Car Service

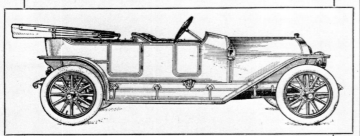

Marathon cars are made throughout in our big plant by skilled mechanics and under the critical supervision of experts. They are the culminating results of the best practice in automobile engineering, together with various improvements suggested by time and a constant effort to better our product, therefore in the 1911 Marathon line we offer what we believe to be the highest development of the Motor Car. In durability, grace of design, efficiency—in all the desirable features of automobile construction, these cars stand pre-eminent at the price.

Southern Motor Works
Nashville, Tennessee

The January 13, 1917, Nashville Banner published an architect's drawing of a proposed office tower to be added to the State Capitol and retopped with the building's familiar lantern tower. The plan must have impressed no one; it was never mentioned again.

prosperous since the Civil War, found itself tarred with the same anti-German brush being used on Kaiser Wilhelm, and as a result, some institutional names were changed—the German Methodist Church to Barth Memorial Methodist, and Edward Potter's German American Bank to Farmers and Merchants (and eventually to Commerce Union).

By the time the war was over, Nashville's first and only automobile manufacturing company, Southern Motor Works, had closed its doors for good, leaving the 800 Marathon roadsters it had built to become collectors' items. Cars were commonplace in the city by then, and even airplanes were a sight to which most people had become accustomed.

In 1918, the year the war was over, a nationwide influenza epidemic struck hard in Nashville, making one in every four residents ill and killing nearly 600 in three months. The same year, two NC&StL passenger trains collided head-on in the western outskirts of the city, killing more than a hundred people in what was described as the worst wreck in American railroading history.

It was July 9, 1918. I had been in Memphis visiting a friend, and she and her young cousin, a boy who was about our age—seventeen or so—were coming back with me. We were in a Pullman car, a steel car, at the rear of the train.

We were running late, and another train, going west, was on the same track. At Dutchman's Curve, near White Bridge Road, the two trains collided head on. The engines just reared up like two dogs fighting, and the day coaches up ahead of us simply crumbled, splintered, and caught fire. They were made of wood.

Our car didn't leave the track, and only a couple of people on it were hurt, but in the day coaches, the carnage was unbelievable. More than a hundred people were killed—most of them Negro laborers who were being brought from as far away as Texas to work in the gunpowder plant at Old Hickory—and I'm sure others died later from injuries.

The rear cars were pulled away from the wreck, and we were picked up in automobiles and taken to town. We didn't see the worst of it, but I can still remember the shock and horror of it all. As soon as it happened, the young boy who was my friend's cousin ran forward and worked like a man to help the injured and dying. But there was a doctor in our car who refused to go and help. I have never seen such scorn as his wife and everyone else showed him. Finally, his wife made him go, and she went with him, but in ten or fifteen minutes he was back. I can see him to this day, stretched out on a seat, refusing to help.

I was facing forward when the trains collided. There was a terrific crash and then a couple of little ones, and I was thrown across to the seat in front of me. I can remember so vividly lying there expecting to die—just waiting to die, waiting to be killed.

JOSEPHINE HUTTON DOUGLAS
(Mrs. Beverly Douglas), in a
1979 interview

When the Eighth Avenue reservoir ruptured in 1912, spilling twenty-five million gallons of water over a wide area, morning-after photographs gave the structure the appearance of a Roman ruin. No lives were lost, but hundreds of people were flooded out of their homes.

The stately homes on Russell Street in East Nashville were spared when a raging fire struck in 1916, but thirty-two square blocks were razed and almost seven hundred homes destroyed in the most extensive blaze in the city's history.

Natural and manmade disasters had sent Nashville reeling earlier in the new century, and others would soon follow. In 1912, the city's reservoir on Eighth Avenue South had split from top to bottom and sent twenty-five million gallons of water rushing through nearby homes and streets, and in 1916, a windswept blaze had destroyed almost seven hundred East Nashville homes and left thirty-two square blocks in charred ruins. Later, on New Year's Day 1927, the Cumberland River would reach sixteen feet above flood stage—the highest level since 1793—and ten thousand Nashvillians would be left homeless by the flood. Finally, in 1933, a tornado, roaring along a 200-yard-wide path through East Nashville, would kill eleven people and damage or destroy more than fourteen hundred homes.

Between disasters, Nashville's postwar years in the so-called Roaring Twenties were filled with big business deals, bootleg booze, gambling, growth, and revivals. Gipsy Smith and Billy Sunday drew great throngs of worshipers to their evangelistic meetings in the city. Sunday conducted a long revival here in 1924, forty

198

In the most devastating flood in Nashville's history, giant steamboats floated out into Broadway and First Avenue. On New Year's Day 1927 the Cumberland River crested at sixteen feet above flood level. It had been that high only once before—and never since.

"I remember very well, don't you," he began, in the most leisurely and casual tone imaginable, "when streetcars ran along Broad Street and all the way out West End? There was nowhere you couldn't go on a streetcar when you and I were growing up. And streetcars had their points; they were lovely things in their way." He paused here, and, with his eyes fixed momentarily on the toe of one of his shoes, he smiled rather foolishly and even apologetically. Then presently he looked up and let his eyes meet mine directly. After that, he continued . . . .

"Things happened on streetcars that couldn't happen now. Why, the governor of the state himself used to ride downtown to the capitol every day—right in the car with everybody else. Once (it was a long time ago), the governor and the governor-elect sat side by side going to town one morning. It may even have been in the days of mule cars, but no matter. The young governor-elect, in his pride, sat up very straight, showing everybody how much taller he was than the old governor, who was on the dumpy side. But just before they got to town, the young governor-elect turned toward the window beside him and spat tobacco juice. He had thought the window was open, and it turned out not to be. Everybody was watching. They say the old governor laughed until he cried.

"My grandfather who remembered mule cars so well said that the mule cars weren't very different from the electrics. Only not quite so noisy. He *liked* the noise, though. It gave him a sense of privacy, he said. With all that noise, he could talk out loud to himself without feeling such a fool. I remember his doing it, too. After he got to be very, very old and couldn't even hear a peal of thunder, he claimed he could still hear the rumbling of the streetcars from up in his room at night. And it comforted him to know they were still running out there on West End. I suppose it was somehow comforting to know that there were people out there awake with him when the rest of us in the house were asleep."

from "Nerves," a short story by Peter Taylor about Nashville in the 1930s, published in *The New Yorker*, September 16, 1961

Russell and Rice, 1952

Grantland Rice had been gone from Nashville for about twenty years when I became sports editor of the *Banner* in 1930, but he certainly hadn't been forgotten. He was the best known and most respected sports writer in the country. I didn't know him personally then, but I read him regularly and admired him very much. I thought of him as a Nashville boy who had made it big, and I idolized him, as most sports writers did.

Rice was born in Murfreesboro, but he was raised in East Nashville. He went to the old Wallace University School, a prep school on West End Avenue, and then to Vanderbilt, where he graduated in 1901. After college he went to work for Jere Baxter's newspaper, the *Nashville Daily News.* He did everything—sports, news, criticism, odd jobs, and of course poetry. He was truly a poet, and a romantic—he just had that feel for verse. The concluding lines of one of his poems have become a famous quotation, known the world over:

For when the One Great Scorer comes to write against your name, He writes not that you won or lost, but how you played the game.

In 1907, Rice went to work for Luke Lea as the first sports editor of the *Tennessean.* He stayed for about three years, and it was during that time that he penned the name Sulphur Dell for the local baseball park. It had been called Athletic Park, and then Sulphur Springs Bottom—years later, they still sold sulphur water from the spring there—but Rice changed it. He said it was easier to write rhyming couplets with Dell than it was with Bottom.

He didn't get back to Nashville very often after he left in 1910 and achieved great fame as a syndicated columnist, but he still thought of Nashville as his home, and he liked to talk about it and even write poems about home. When I first met him in the 1930s, our common ties to Nashville became the basis for a close friendship.

I remember one special occasion in the 1940s when he was here. It happened that Jack Dempsey was also in town, working with a circus, and we all got together for an evening. During the conversation, Rice suddenly came out with a little line he remembered writing in 1927, when Dempsey was the heavyweight champ:

Hail the conquering hero comes, surrounded by a bunch of bums.

Dempsey remembered the line too, and loved it.

Over a period of more than twenty years, Grantland Rice and I covered a great many sports events together. Of all the men I have known, he came closest to combining the qualities of decency, compassion, humor, and creative genius. Nashville may never have fully appreciated what an extraordinary person he was.

FRED RUSSELL, in a 1979 interview

To popularize flying after World War I, the army sent flyers around to towns and cities that had landing fields. They came to Nashville in September 1919. I was a reporter for the *Banner,* and I had a car, so I drove my brother Jimmy and the two pilots out to Hampton Field (some called it Stokes Field) on Hampton Avenue.

Men from both newspapers were there, but I was the only woman. Marmaduke Beckwith Morton, the managing editor of the *Banner,* was the first one to go up—and he urped all over the side of the plane. It gave him a very low opinion of flying, and when Jimmy wrote the story, old Mr. Morton hid it under a one-column headline back on page seventeen.

When they had taken all the men up and it was getting toward late afternoon, I said to one of the pilots, "Aren't you going to take me up?" He looked at me kind of funny and said, "Oh, lady, we have orders not to take women." I said, "What do you think I brought you out here for? My brother said if I drove you out here, you'd take me up." He went over and talked to the other pilot, and they agreed that if I would sign my name M. C. Stahlman instead of Mary, they'd let me go. So they gave me the headgear and goggles, and I climbed in the rear cockpit and we went up.

We flew out over the Cumberland River and came back. It was nearly dark by then, and of course there were no lights on the field and none on the plane. The pilot brought us down on that old stubble field, but it was so short that he couldn't stop, so he had to pull up above the trees and try again. It took four tries before he was able to land.

I was twenty-four years old then, and that was a great thrill. Then a little later, I flew again at the fairgrounds with Jersey Ringle and his Flying Circus. They had been hired to do stunts over the state fair. When I was in the plane, the pilot made a nose dive with the engine shut off. We plummeted toward the crowd—thousands of people—and at the last moment, he pulled out. We came so near the people, if you had been there I could have waved at you and known who you were. They were daredevils—and of course, they were endangering the lives of all the people on the ground.

I wasn't terrified, though—I didn't have sense enough to be. When we landed, I told the pilot I was disappointed he hadn't done any loop-the-loops. He said, "I did four. You just weren't looking over the side."

MARY STAHLMAN DOUGLAS (Mrs. Byrd Douglas), in a 1979 interview

years after he had first come to town as an out-
fielder for the Chicago White Stockings to play
an exhibition game in the sulphur springs
bottom.

Less well-known but no less active was a
Nashville evangelist, Marshall Keeble. A black
minister in the Church of Christ, Keeble became
an apostle of interracial harmony when segregation was in full sway. He started more than 300
churches in the South and baptized more than
40,000 people, many of them whites. (One of his
white benefactors was A.M. Burton of Nashville, a founder of the Life and Casualty Insurance Company of Tennessee.) Keeble initiated the Nashville Christian Institute, an ap-
prenticeship program for young blacks, and ran
it for almost thirty years. When he died in 1968
at the age of ninety, his funeral at the Madison
Church of Christ was attended by more than
3,000 mourners of both races.

Higher education in Nashville after World
War I reflected the growth and ferment that had
come to characterize the city. Ward-Belmont
was known as a leading girls' college in the
South; Meharry Medical College was producing
a majority of the nation's black doctors and dentists; David Lipscomb College was rising as a
monument to its principal benefactor, the
Church of Christ minister whose name it bore.
Across town, the name Trevecca (adopted from
a Welsh school) had been given to a college affiliated with the Nazarene Church. Fisk University would come through its internal crisis to
enter a period of extended productivity; one of
its most noted faculty members in the 1930s
would be James Weldon Johnson, a poet and
lyricist whose prolific works included a song
known as the Negro National Anthem: "Lift
Every Voice and Sing."

Another new school in the city was Scarritt
College, an institution of the Methodist Church,
which moved to Nashville from Kansas City in

202

When Woodmont Boulevard, Nashville's first concrete
street, was paved in 1920, it was considered a broad
avenue. Now it is a busy and narrow cross-town artery.

Ward's Seminary, successor to Nashville Female
Academy and predecessor of Ward-Belmont College,
assumed the task—depicted in these 1902 yearbook
cartoons—of turning "ugly ducklings" into "beautiful
swans."

James Weldon Johnson had been a leading figure in the black literary movement known as the Harlem Renaissance before he joined the Fisk University faculty in 1931. A versatile and prolific writer, Johnson is perhaps best known for God's Trombones, a book of poems published in 1927 with illustrations by Fisk artist Aaron Douglas.

With bristling mustache and piercing eyes, Vanderbilt Chancellor James H. Kirkland posed in cap and gown for this photograph. Kirkland was the university's leader from 1893 until 1937.

Bearded, white-haired David Lipscomb, chief benefactor of the college that bears his name, is shown with Bible in hand in this posthumous portrait by Lee Watts.

1924. Roger Williams University, the black Baptist school on Hillsboro Pike, remained in Nashville for a while after its main building was destroyed by fire and then merged with a Memphis college. Tennessee State Normal College, the successor to the University of Nashville, had changed its name to Peabody Normal College in 1889 and then to George Peabody College for Teachers in 1907, after which it bought the Roger Williams property and moved to that campus. Tennessee Agricultural and Industrial State Normal School was designated by the federal government as a land-grant institution for blacks.

And Vanderbilt University, the largest and most comprehensive of Nashville's institutions, overshadowed all the others. Under James H. Kirkland, who would serve as its chancellor for

Rolling meadows and fenced fields once separated Vanderbilt University from the city of Nashville, but by the 1920s, fashionable homes on West End Avenue stood just outside this Twenty-Third Avenue gate to the campus. The fifty-year-old university, already highly regarded in medicine and the sciences, gained additional stature in the decade of the 1920s through the work of a resident and off-campus colony of writers—the Fugitives.

forty-four years, the school had gained prominence in medicine, the sciences, and literature. A Vanderbilt pathologist, Ernest W. Goodpasture, would become world-renowned as a developer of disease-fighting vaccines; another professor, William L. Dudley, had made his mark in the field of chemistry and as an administrator of intercollegiate athletics (Dudley Field was named for him).

It was through poetry, fiction, and literary criticism, however, that Vanderbilt would find its name placed in the front rank of American higher education. Two English professors—John Crowe Ransom and Donald Davidson—became the principal figures who drew to Vanderbilt a glittering array of scholars and students, and their creative works stirred a national literary renaissance.

They came in two waves and adopted two names: the Fugitives in the 1920s and the Agrarians in the 1930s. Ransom and Davidson

were identified with both groups, and so were two other writers, Allen Tate and Robert Penn Warren. At least a dozen writers who were associated with Vanderbilt in that fertile period would subsequently make important contributions to American literature.

And of them all, none would be more eminent than Warren. He won the Pulitzer Prize for fiction in 1947 with his novel, *All the King's Men;* in 1958, his volume of poems called *Promises* won for him both the Pulitzer Prize and the National Book Award. In 1979, just before he celebrated his seventy-fourth birthday, Warren was awarded a third Pulitzer Prize for another book of poems, *Now and Then.*

At his Connecticut country home, Robert Penn Warren also wrote in the spring of 1979 a reflective account of his years as a student and teacher at Vanderbilt and his experiences in Nashville, the city he had first encountered as a small boy.

ROBERT PENN WARREN
A Reminiscence

NASHVILLE BELONGS to my earliest childhood memories. I was born in the little town of Guthrie, Kentucky, just over the Tennessee line some fifty miles north of the city, and I can remember going there with my father, first on the Kentucky and Edgefield Railroad and later by car.

Of the train ride I can remember only the thrill of going through a tunnel, the sensation of being plunged into darkness and then being delivered from it. The trip by car was a different experience. It was practically a half-day's journey in those days, and you could always count on having at least one or two blowouts.

Of the city itself, I remember more. I lived in a small town and spent my summers on a farm, a very remote farm, with my grandfather—a Confederate veteran, a captain under Forrest, a lover of history and poetry—and in my country boy's eyes, Nashville seemed like a perfectly huge city to me. I was much impressed by its grandeur and size and scale, by its hurry and bustle. The most remarkable place to me was the Arcade, a strange and exotic structure. There was certainly nothing like that in Guthrie. And no football games there, either—my father took me every Thanksgiving to Nashville to see the Vanderbilt game.

But I didn't really see Nashville then, except in a superficial way, and even when I was a student at Vanderbilt in the 1920s, I had only surface impressions of the city. It no longer awed me. It was simply there, and I took it for granted, without giving it any thought. I had other things on my mind.

I finished high school in Guthrie when I was fifteen, and since I was a little too young for college, I spent another year at the high school in Clarksville, hoping for an appointment to Annapolis, for to be an admiral of the Pacific Fleet had been my romantic boyhood dream. I did receive the congressional appointment, but then I had an eye injury from an accident, and so I turned in disappointment to my second choice, which was Vanderbilt, and enrolled there in 1921, when I was sixteen.

My intention was to study chemical engineering, but that notion lasted only three weeks or so. Chemistry was taught primarily for pre-med students— it was very deductive, having nothing to do with the nature or philosophy of science—and that turned me away. The English classes were much more interesting. Edwin Mims taught literature one class a week—Tennyson the first term—and John Crowe Ransom taught grammar and composition two days, and they got me started. I enjoyed writing English themes and I began to dabble a little in poetry, and it didn't take me long to find out where my true interests lay.

I've always been grateful to Dr. Mims for demanding that every student memorize hundreds of lines of verse. His old-fashioned method was total immersion in poetry. It should be the new-fashioned method.

But the two people who influenced me most at Vanderbilt were John Crowe Ransom and Donald Davidson. They were young men in their early thirties; they had been in World War I; they were writing poetry I could identify with and understand. With both men I would maintain a lifelong friendship.

Ransom's house later became almost a second home to me. He was a splendid teacher and a fascinating personality. He was a classical scholar, had been to Oxford, and he was the first real poet I had ever seen—his first book, *Poems About God*, had only been out a couple of years. When I read it, I saw Ransom making poetry out of the life and objects of my boyhood. He had grown up, as I had, in the rural upper South—his father was a very learned country parson—and Ransom had found in that familiar setting the stuff of poetry. It was strange and even disturbing to me, that discovery. In his poetry and in his performance as a teacher, I saw a first-rate mind at work. He could be distracted and uninspiring two days a week, but on the third day he might catch fire, like a man possessed, and pursue a thought into fascinating nooks and crannies, creating fresh ideas before your very eyes. That's what education should be—seeing a first-rate mind catch fire. And with all that, Ransom could also be very witty and amusing.

Donald Davidson was different—a superlative teacher, very systematic, humorous only in his intensity and in his utter seriousness. He was a darkly handsome man with an intense gaze, passionate in his convictions but kindly and generous in human relations. Davidson was particularly fond of folk balladry. His father was, I think, a county school superintendent in Middle Tennessee, and Don had spent much time in the country, as I had, but he really woke me to the special beauty and poetry of the country tongue. And that's only one example of the broad impact of his teaching. Years later, I would realize how deeply he had made me feel a pleasure, a necessity, in writing, for he allowed me to write an "imitation" of an author being studied—say, a new episode of Beowulf—instead of the regular bi-weekly critique.

We had certain fundamental disagreements, Davidson and I—on poetry, on social questions. When, in later years, we would meet, there would be the first warm greeting, then I would get a stirring lecture from him on the error of my ways. That done, old friendship and old discussions were revived, and I found again the kindliness, the warmth, the keen critical sensibility. Looking back, I see a man somewhat divided against himself—on one hand a remarkable and gifted prose writer, on the other a poet whose gift was often distorted by a literary theory and several passions. But I remember most the superlative teacher and warm-hearted friend who meant so much to me. I saw him last on a visit to his bedside at Vanderbilt Hospital, a day or two before his death. The visit was prearranged and purely personal, but brutally interrupted and taken over entirely by a stupid scholarly interviewer, notebook on knee, asking fool questions for some fool book he was writing. So the parting with Davidson was only an exchange of glances, and his grip still firm but dying.

In their quite different ways, Davidson and Ransom touched part of my experience and opened up my mind. I learned from others too—from Walter Clyde Curry, who taught Shakespeare with a real dramatic sense and a sense of scholarship. But I suppose my real university was not Vanderbilt as such—it was classmates and friends I had the good fortune to know, people whose intellectual and philosophical interests and literary tastes were sometimes far more sophisticated than my own. A peculiar feature about the little university that was the Vanderbilt of the 1920s was an active and spontaneous interest in literature and in writing among a great many students. There were two official writing clubs, "Blue Pencil" and "The Calumet," but even more unusual were the informal groups, one of which issued a book of poems, some of which actually resembled poems—though I doubt that mine did.

I recall that Charles Moss and I were admitted to "Blue Pencil" at the same time. Charlie was a very handsome young man, a romantic, a humorous fellow, wonderful company, and he was also a very promising poet, but he turned instead to journalism and was for years editor of the *Nashville Banner.*

Another fellow who pops into mind was Ralph McGill, who had no interest in poetry whatsoever, not the slightest, but who was a marvelous companion. He lived on West Side Row, where a good many of the students were considered "offbeat." McGill worked as a sports writer at the *Banner*—he and Moss were both part-time reporters. The association is what I remember. We used to sit around telling tales, sharing a bottle, arguing. McGill could not have dreamed that he would become publisher of the *Atlanta Constitution.* Years after our time at Vanderbilt together, he helped me with the background material for a book I wrote on race relations in the South.

And there was William Bandy, a dashing young man, a great dancer, popular with the ladies—and mad for them. He had the air of a Frenchman, and though only an undergraduate, he was already a French scholar, especially of the poet Baudelaire. Bill Bandy ran a sort of informal French seminar in his living quarters, a kind of competing university in French. The sessions sometimes went on until four o'clock in the morning—lubricated, as often as not, with a jug of corn whiskey. He had already begun collecting the works of Baudelaire, the first step toward the famous collection he has since given to the university.

Bandy also had the only Stutz Bearcat on the campus. About three o'clock one morning, with several of us as passengers, he undertook to climb the great story-high stone flight of entrance steps to Wesley Hall in the Bearcat. He succeeded, and then made a hair-raising descent, bouncing back step by step in reverse as astonished theological heads popped out of the upper windows of the building. Bandy leveled off at the bottom and we sped away. The culprits were never identified.

Wesley Hall (now long since burned down) was an enormous brick building of Early Methodist architecture, you might say, dating back to the dark ages of the founding of the university. It was an imposing building, ugly as sin, but the theological school. However, non-theologians had crept in as rooms became vacant, for it was a wonderful place for privacy. I lived in Kissam Hall, but in my sophomore year I got into Wesley.

Ridley Wills lived there. He was a senior who had returned to finish his degree after fighting in France in World War I, and after we became acquainted, he invited me to move in with him. I was overwhelmed with pleasure and flattered beyond belief. He impressed me greatly, not just with his age and rich experience but with the fact that he was the only undergraduate who had actually published a book, a real novel in a real publishing house in far-off New York. Not only that, but he was marvelously amusing and full of anecdotes.

Soon Allen Tate, that genius of a poet, moved in with us. He was six years my senior, returning from a siege of illness to finish his degree. (For several years, Tate could not force himself to do freshman chemistry and math; finally, in spite of his aversions, he graduated *magna cum laude*.) A fourth young man, William Cobb (later to be an editor at Houghton Mifflin) came to occupy the last of our two double-decker beds. The room was a sty—dirty shirts in the corners, match stubs and cigarette butts over the floors, empty or half-empty bottles—but there was also the conversation and the poetry. Both Ridley Wills and Allen Tate were members of the Fugitives, a group of young philosophers and poets whose presence was already being felt around Vanderbilt (though the group, as such, had no relation to the university), and they were willing to look at my attempts at poetry and give me detailed criticism and long lectures on the subject.

Our room became an informal gathering place for others of like inclination, and all enjoyed the irony of a little Bohemia in the citadel of a divinity school. Merrill Moore, another member of the Fugitives, lived on the floor above us. Before the year was out, Ridley and Allen had taken me as a guest to a meeting of the group. Later, I published a poem in their magazine, *The Fugitive*, and I was invited to join. My cup truly ran over.

THE FIRST ISSUE of *The Fugitive* had appeared in 1922, during my freshman year, with an introduction declaring whimsically that the Fugitives fled from various things but from nothing more speedily than the "magnolia and moonlight" type of Southern poetry. In fact, the magazine was primarily a manifestation of modernism, or rather a battleground for debating modernism and traditionalism. The group had been founded long before my time—before the war, in fact—but after the war there were new faces and new interests.

The original group had been more interested in philosophy than poetry. It brought together a few young professors (principally Ransom and Davidson), some local businessmen, a banker, and a Jewish sage—I have no other word for him—who presided at the meetings. The sage was Sidney Mttron Hirsch, who in younger wanderings was reputed to have been heavyweight boxing champion of the Pacific Fleet. He had lived in the Orient and in France. He was a mystic, a man of brilliant and undisciplined intellect. He was the catalyst, the magnet to whom the others were drawn. Those first meetings were held at his apartment on Twentieth Avenue South.

Hirsch and his brother, Nathaniel, and James M. Frank, who married their sister, and the Starr brothers, Alfred and Milton, were all young Jewish men in Nashville who would be identified with the Fugitive group for as long as it lasted. Sidney Hirsch and James Frank and Alfred Starr were the principal off-campus members—they and Alec B. Stevenson, a banker, whose father had taught Semitic languages at the university. From the faculty came Ransom, Davidson, Walter Clyde Curry and Stanley Johnson, and the students were Tate, Ridley Wills, Merrill Moore, Jesse Wills (Ridley's cousin), William Yandell Elliott, William Frierson and me. Laura Riding, the only woman, came late into the group from outside Nashville. There were sixteen of us in all, over the years, who were actually members and whose poems were published in the magazine.

I was an eighteen-year-old sophomore when I became acquainted with the

Tennessean, *May 27, 1923*

Fugitive group in 1923, and it was an exhilarating experience to be suddenly involved in an intellectual exchange with men twice my age. It was anything but a college club. That's where I got my education, where I began to find my way in the world—and Vanderbilt was both incidental and essential to the experience.

For the remainder of my undergraduate years, *The Fugitive* was my main interest. The magazine prospered—that is, it attracted attention nationally, and even in England. It was poetry or death for me then, and some of the others shared that passion. We usually met at James Frank's home on Whitland Avenue, each of us in turn reading our poems and having them criticized by others. Among my contemporaries in the university, I became especially close to Tate and Ridley Wills, and also to Merrill Moore, who was a fascinating young man. His father was John Trotwood Moore, well-known in Nashville as a writer and a librarian. Merrill became a psychiatrist, but in those days, as ever after, he wrote sonnets.

Merrill was unique in the history of literature. Even during the Fugitive days he had settled on the sonnet form as his special concern. It became such a natural form of thought for him that even while waiting for a traffic light to change he could compose one in shorthand—or later, in the course of technological change, dictate one to a recorder. At his death in the 1950s he left several remarkable volumes in print and some 50,000 items in manuscript, shorthand or tape, in code of some kind, at the Library of Congress. He was unique as a psychological curiosity. He once joked to me, "I am my most interesting patient." Or was it a joke?

The remarkable thing is that Merrill was a highly gifted poet, not merely a peculiar prodigy. Naturally in such a massive work the percentage of really fine achievement would be relatively small, but a small percentage would constitute the life work of many a man of reputation. He had splendid flashes in his characteristic form, and the challenge to scholarship and criticism waits in those pages and tapes at the Library of Congress. He will be a discovery.

I made other friends at Vanderbilt outside the Fugitive group: Cleanth Brooks, with whom I later wrote several textbooks, and who is now generally recognized as one of the foremost literary critics of our age; and Andrew Lytle, with whom I later attended Yale; and Bill Bandy the French scholar, and Charlie Moss and Ralph McGill and others. I have often looked back on the 1920s in Nashville and at Vanderbilt and wondered how it happened, how this land-locked and then small and provincial university assembled the students and faculty who, with the off-campus Fugitives, so profoundly shaped my life. Why should a small university like Vanderbilt, drawing primarily from young people of the region, become a center of such creative ferment? (The ferment, by the way, was so insidiously widespread that even an all-Southern football player wrote, as I later learned, little poems like A. E. Housman's—but never read them aloud in the locker room. A kinsman of his betrayed him to me in 1932, and showed examples.)

Maybe the best answer is the most obvious: Ransom and Davidson. They were such extraordinary teachers—two particular accidents in a certain place and time, with no explanation for the fact. They drew talented people to them, and drew out talent in many who didn't know it was there. They were bright and literary and accomplished; they had fought in the war, yet they were still young, still in their thirties. I in my teens felt no great separation in age from them (only in experience and wisdom and achievement), and between us in age were Tate and Wills and others. When we sat down together to discuss poetry, we sat as equals. It was one long seminar, and I was getting a priceless education writing boyish poems. I *was* a boy. Ransom and Elliott had been Rhodes Scholars, Frierson had studied at the Sorbonne, Hirsch had been around the world—and I had been to Nashville, and almost nowhere else. We were all Southerners, coming together around a common interest—poetry—but it was Ransom and Davidson who gave us purpose and direction.

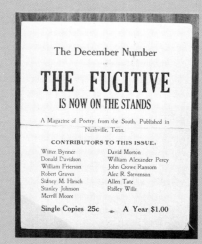

1924

I had another friend at Vanderbilt in those days, Saville Clark, who was far ahead of most people—a generation or two ahead—on a subject that was to become the dominant issue of our time: race. For a time I shared an apartment with Saville and his brother, Cannon Clark, on Grand Avenue. Saville had gone over to Fisk University and become acquainted with a good many students, and he brought one or two of them—to the horror of the landlady—to our apartment for conversations. This was in 1925, I believe, during a big student-administration clash at Fisk. I remember what an eye-opener it was for me, that small beginning in conversation across racial lines. I would think of it often in the 1950s and 1960s, and wish there had been more Saville Clarks.

SOCIAL ISSUES didn't interest me then. Still, other things besides literature were happening at Vanderbilt. Football, for instance. Vanderbilt was a football power in those days. As I remember it, there were two all-Americans in my class—Hek Wakefield and Lynn Bomar—not to mention Gil Reese and Alf Sharp, who were all-Southern. I think Reese starred in the first game ever played at Dudley Field, in about 1922.

1924

And of course, there were girls. Female enrollment at Vanderbilt was limited, I think, to ten percent, and in chapel each Wednesday morning the segregation was maintained, with the girls sitting in a balcony at the rear of the assembly hall, surveying the goings-on among their betters below. Once or twice a year when we (the males) entered the hall and saw the balcony empty, we were prepared to give more attention than usual to the business of the day, for an empty balcony meant it was time for what we called "the clap talk." On this occasion, some member of the medical faculty described in technical detail, sparing no horror, the ravages of venereal disease, and always added that beneath the finest, fairest flower—my metaphor—"the viper might lurk." The doctor would tell us that even that smiling and smartly dressed secretary or telephone operator might have loved not only too well but too widely, and we should be wary of them. I do not recall that the speaker ever touched on morality, or gave instructions for preventive measures. Perhaps he was forbidden to do so, or perhaps he trusted common sense and a mother's prayer in such matters. In any case, the clap talk was welcome and titillating and even provocative. I can't be sure that the female ten percent were given any equivalent admonition; at that time, there wasn't even a dean of women in that purlieu of purity.

Occasionally, greater drama broke routine. A classmate of mine became convinced that he was in the wrong pew—his real passions were not a B.A. and a respectable position, but girls and motorcycles. In those old days before any hint of progress had changed the campus, it was in spring a bosky place full of the chancellor's iris and magnolia blossoms in profusion, and toward late afternoon, ladies from the city would flock there in their black electric automobiles to breathe the clean air and admire the beauties of nature.

One afternoon my nameless friend must have reached the breaking point. His great Harley Davidson, or whatever it was, exploded into action and, as reported to me, began to twine in and out among the automobiles from West End and Belle Meade. That was bad enough to bring well-bred shrieks from the ladies—but worse, according to report, my friend was wearing scarcely a stitch—if even that. He may have been the first streaker. On he wove among the screams of fear and outrage to his doom and destiny. Back then, Vanderbilt University had only a single cause for expulsion: "conduct unbecoming a gentleman." It must have been applied in this case. (A footnote about expulsion in those days before the worldwide exfoliation of professional administrators: Our dean was a classical scholar noted for sweetness of nature and a halo of white hair. It was generally understood that if he even called

212

you in and, affectionately but sadly, laid his arm across your shoulders, your goose was cooked. And he suffered far more than you.)

How long ago it seems since a freshman with a hat cocked on one side of his head and a cigar in his mouth entered a poolroom with a friend and began to chalk his cue, and how long ago the sophomore's first transaction with a bootlegger. I have one vivid memory of a summer job as an American Express truck driver, and briefly as a money guard with a sawed-off shotgun and a gray felt hat with the brim pulled low and sinister. Candor forces me to say that the boss who appointed me to that post drew me aside and said, "Warren, I'm giving you this job because you're expendable—you're the worst driver I've got. All you have to do is close your eyes and pull both triggers if anybody sticks his head in the back of the truck." To my eternal disappointment, nobody did.

By the time I graduated from Vanderbilt in 1925, *The Fugitive* had almost run its course. Its final issue was published in December of that year. The members of the group were beginning to scatter in all directions, and though the effort was made, there was no hope of holding us together. The university had given no recognition or encouragement to the magazine—Chancellor Kirkland had ignored it as best he could—yet the reputation of the journal was substantial. It was called "the most distinguished poetry magazine in America." In retrospect, I think it is fair to say that it was a modest historical document in American literature—not so much for what it contained as for the school of poets and writers it spawned. The creative ferment around Vanderbilt at that time made it a rare place, the only place of its kind.

I went on from there to graduate school at the University of California at Berkeley, to more poetry writing, and to fiction writing, into which I rather stumbled. I found Berkeley to be blank as far as the world of modern literature was concerned, but full of Marx and Freud, about whom I knew nothing. I thought Marx was simply one of a firm of suit makers; I had never heard his name mentioned in my economics class at Vanderbilt.

I dreamed of living the life of a poet in Greenwich Village or on the Left Bank, but after I had seen California and New York and Paris and after I had been to Oxford, an older dream returned: It was a dream of the green hills of Middle Tennessee, of a farm there and a teaching position at Vanderbilt, with time to write about the region I knew best. In 1930, I turned down a better job in California to go to Southwestern in Memphis, and the following year I jumped at the chance to teach in John Crowe Ransom's place at Vanderbilt while he was away on leave.

I had no thought of *taking* his place—who could?—but I filled his physical space. I enjoyed my courses, tried to learn how to teach, and then the following year, when Donald Davidson was on leave, I filled in for him. It was such a delight to be back among old friends and new, inside and outside the university. In addition to Ranson and Davidson, there were so many others: Lyle Lanier, who was back teaching psychology; Andrew Lytle, who was working at his fiction and his biography of Forrest; Frank Owsley, in the history department; John Donald Wade, an exquisite writer with no ambition except to live a civilized life with good friends; and of course Allen Tate, who had lived in Greenwich Village and in Paris, had married novelist Caroline Gordon of my hometown of Guthrie, and had come back to live on the river near Clarksville.

Wade and Lytle were marvelous storytellers, the most amusing and entertaining companions. I have since learned that in the North they tell jokes, they even make joke books, but in the South, at least in the South of that pre-television time, they told tales—elaborate, winding, wandering creations that might never wear out, stories full of human perception and subtlety, told with a richness of language and expression. They told tales that were the essence of Southern fiction—not idle, gossip, not diversions, mind you, but tales of wit and character, of pathos, of scope. Yankees (except in back-country Vermont) don't really know about tales. What I'm getting at is a regional difference, a Southern gift that springs from the pores of the society. It's a classless gift, as apt to be heard in the conversation of a Tennessee tenant farmer or an Alabama plantation lady or a Louisiana fisherman as in the eloquence and art of Eudora Welty or William Faulkner or Katherine Anne Porter. Television may be the death of the tale.

Anyway, it was these people, the Vanderbilt and Nashville friends I have been talking about, who formed the nucleus of the second literary group to gain wide attention there: the Agrarians. We published a book of essays in 1930 called *I'll Take My Stand*, a controversial book that still provokes some argument. I'll come back to that later, but first I'd like to say some more about Nashville in that period, and the people I knew there.

Alfred and Milton Starr were still around, and we became close friends, and I came to appreciate deeply their wisdom and generosity, and the kindness they and their wives showed me. Likewise Charlie Moss and his wife, and another newspaperman, Brainard Cheney, who had married Frances Neel; we became very firm friends. The Cheneys have lived in Smyrna for years, and their home has been a gathering place for kindred spirits interested in books and writing. Lon Cheney—we've always called him Lon—has written some very good novels, and Fannie was for many years a librarian and a leader in the American Library Association.

Tom Zerfoss, the university physician, and young Lucius Burch were also very important to my life in those days. I can't recall how we first became acquainted, but Zerfoss and I used to ride horses in that Middle Tennessee countryside that I loved so much, and Burch gave my wife and me a place to live. Those were the Depression years, the early 1930s, and I felt fortunate to have a job at all, much less one—however temporary—that put me with people I loved in a place I wanted to be. I had come back because being gone had made me miss the South, had made me want to live in Tennessee.

When I had left Nashville in 1925 it was the time of the Scopes trail, but I was too busy with John Donne and Baudelaire—I had no interest in the world around me, and I wouldn't have crossed the street to find out what was happening. Nashville's history and its problems didn't interest me then, but in the 1930s they did. The bankruptcies, the constant melodrama, the fascinating careers of Rogers Caldwell and Luke Lea all made me keenly aware of a Nashville I had never known. It was in many ways a painful awareness, but absorbing, and with the discoveries my life began to change.

I TAUGHT AT VANDERBILT for three years, beginning in 1931. Edwin Mims was still chairman of the English department; he and I were never close, to put it mildly, and after the second year, when Davidson had returned, Mims fired me. Then, just before Christmas, John Donald Wade, who didn't get along with Mims either, made a visit to my house to say that he had just resigned with the stipulation that I be returned to my old post. But I was "let out" the following year. I had come back deliberately, and I didn't want to leave, never wanted to leave, but there was no way I could stay. I hated to give up Nashville and Middle Tennessee, hated to part with the friends—we seemed to have so much to say to one another—but the next fall I left for Louisiana State University, where I had found a job and where my close friend Cleanth Brooks, with whom I had overlapped at Oxford, already was teaching.

Tom Zerfoss had wanted to buy a farm where I could live, a place where he could keep his horses and I could keep a garden and write, hoping the combination would be enough to put something on the table. I made a search and did find such a place, a perfect little farm in Williamson County, and he subsequently bought it, but by then I had been fired and my dream of Middle Tennessee country was gone. Before all that had happened, an old black carpenter named Carpenter and I had fixed up the little house at Riverwood, the Burch place, and I had whitewashed it, and my wife and I had lived there for two years. It was perfectly situated and had its own cranky charm, and leaving it was not easy.

One of my most vivid memories from that house is of the tornado that struck in East Nashville in 1933. A good many people were killed by that storm, as I recall, and the devastating effect of it was everywhere to be seen. I was propped up in bed reading papers when it hit. I heard a noise like a freight train passing over my head, and then a crash. The tornado had picked up part of a brick barn not far off and hurled it through the air. The next morning I walked through the village outside the gate of the farm. It looked like a bombed-out town.

A week later, another storm came. I was in the car when suddenly it got very dark, like turning off a light switch. A tree fell in front of me, and I got stuck trying to get around it. When there was a lull I got out of the car, but the wind returned and literally pinned me against the door. That was one of the most frightening experiences in my memory.

The little whitewashed house was several miles from the university, and I drove back and forth first in a Baby Austin and then in a big old Studebaker we bought from Harriet and Frank Owsley for fifty dollars.

The Owsleys were special friends. Frank was an Alabamian, a tall, sandy-haired, high-spirited man with a warm sense of humor and a great natural dignity. He was a historian who also had a passion for William Faulkner in the early days when the Mississippian was a young and little-known writer, and one of our constant topics of conversation was Faulkner and his work. Frank and Harriet had a camp on a bluff overlooking the Cumberland River, and I remember well the square dances, the summer swimming, the whiskey breakfasts on frosty mornings, all interlaced with ferocious but good-natured arguments about politics, history, and literature. Once when I had a sudden and unexpected operation, it was the Owsleys who took me in for recuperation, and did it with such matter-of-factness and grace. Generosity was the hallmark of that household.

The other home I knew best was Ransom's. He was no longer my freshman English teacher but a close friend, and at the same time a kind of model of human worth. John and his quite beautiful wife, Robb, had two growing children (and later a baby, whom they affectionately called Alibi), and theirs was a place of enormous energy—for work and play and study, for poetry and talk, for writing, even for watching sunsets. They were full of games. My wife and I often disastrously played bridge with the Ransoms on Saturday night. I remember one marathon performance that began early one Saturday afternoon and continued until Sunday night, with only short breaks for necessary food and drink and a little sleep. It seemed scarcely less than natural that the Ransoms rented a bankrupt country club for a year before they settled in the country and invited friends to share their tennis courts and billiard tables.

Many of the people I have been talking about—Ransom and Davidson, Lytle and Lanier, Wade and Owsley and Tate and others—were members of the Agrarian group, a spinoff of sorts from the Fugitives (a few of us had belonged to both), but a different group in many ways, more concerned with economic and social questions than with poetry. The Agrarian movement was an umbrella, a tent, with a big menagerie of arguing animals under it. It was not a cohesive group at all. We were Southerners asking old questions as if they were new, questions about the nature of modernism and technology as they related to the South's economy. We had begun to see that modernism meant a shift in the sense of man's relationship to nature and to his fellow man. There were questions about race for some of us, and others mourned the demise of the Confederacy and wanted to raise again the dream of Southern nationalism, and in many of those matters we disagreed sharply among ourselves. But I think all of us were concerned about the consequences of mindless and uncontrolled change—what most people call progress.

1948

To my mind, the questions were fundamental ones. They had to do with the destruction of the family, the isolation of the old, the loss of a sense of continuity and fellowship, the absorption of the individual in mass society. Today, in all the public debate about oil and gas and energy, about nuclear power, about ecology and environmental quality, the questions are still the same—only the vocabulary is changed. Will man run technology, or will technology run man? Now, as then, there are no ready answers.

When I came back to Nashville in 1931, *I'll Take My Stand* had just appeared to as many jeers as cheers, and some of the cheers depressed me as much as the jeers. In the anthology, I had written an essay on race, a piece called "The Briar Patch." I learned later that some of the brethren didn't want the piece in the book—they thought it was too liberal. It certainly couldn't be considered liberal now. It was a plea to make the separate societies of whites and blacks truly equal. I couldn't see then, as I do now, that the very separateness of the societies was at the heart of the inequality.

The race issue continued to be a preoccupation in my fiction and poetry, and in two other books I wrote—*Segregation: The Inner Conflict in the South* and *Who Speaks for the Negro?* But back then, in 1930, I saw it as merely one aspect of a larger question. How long ago that old book seems, that Agrarian anthology. Race has been the most serious domestic issue of

217

this century in the United States, and it's not settled, not yet. If it is ever resolved, the South may do it first, and best. I've heard many blacks and whites say that, and I believe it too.

FOR ALL THE DIFFICULTIES of those three years I spent at Vanderbilt in the 1930s—the Depression, the temporary status of my job, the Agrarian controversies—I think of them as very happy years for me. So many of the friendships have been lifelong friendships. And so many of the writers who were there went on to have distinguished careers. I wrote one novel in Nashville (fortunately, it was rejected), but years later, my second published novel, *At Heaven's Gate*, was suggested by the Nashville of the period of Rogers Caldwell and Luke Lea. I hadn't known that I was living in the midst of suggestions there, but my life during those years was full of suggestions, full of melodrama. Nashville appears quite often in my work, and I can't write fiction at all except about the South. Not specific facts—imagination doesn't work that way—but suggestions out of what I know and what I am.

With Ransom and Davidson still there to work their magic, the very active literary life around Vanderbilt continued. But there were some students who brought their own magic with them. One, now dead, was a brilliant poet, a Nashville boy from Hume-Fogg High School named Randall Jarrell. My first year there I taught a small section of sophomores who had been selected as the brightest and best prepared, and Randall was among them, though he was only a freshman, because it was already quite clear that no freshman class could hold him. He was so gifted that he terrorized my bright group of sophomores, not out of malice but with the cruel innocence of a baby. Finally I told him that he was scaring them to death.

"What am I doing?" he demanded in sincere innocence.

I suggested that he put his mind to helping them, that being more productive than withering criticism. He did. He was already writing extraordinarily beautiful poems. He was in fact a genius.

Randall and I became very good friends. He would come out to my little whitewashed house and talk poetry and philosophy and brutally criticize my poems. I listened carefully. He was often right and more often amusing, so amusing that it didn't matter much that it was at my expense.

Later, he followed Ransom to Kenyon College. Then, I believe, he washed out as a flyer in World War II, but remained in that branch of service, and the

218

From left: Allen Tate, Merrill Moore, Robert Penn Warren, John Crowe Ransom, and Donald Davidson at 1956 reunion, Vanderbilt

experience gave him some of his finest poems, some of the finest poems ever written on the subject of war by an American. I treasure a letter he wrote to me a few weeks before his tragic death.

To the same period at Vanderbilt belongs Jesse Stuart, a man remarkable in his way and in a very opposite way from Jarrell's. He was a product of Eastern Kentucky mountain schools, and he had absorbed the life and speech and folk sense of his region and had a fanatical drive to write about them. In one of his courses (not mine), he handed in a term paper that became a 350-autobiography, later to be published as a book, to a very good reception. After the autobiography, story followed story and poem followed poem into print. As the volume of his work increased, one reviewer said of him that he had something of the value of a national park. Flannery O'Connor once remarked that Jesse's ego was like the light on the front of a train.

He came often to my house, and I liked nothing better than to catch him in an anecdotal mood and listen to him discuss the world he came from and the raw material of his poems. He was often better in conversation than on the printed page. His poems and stories were simple, sometimes too simple, but many of them contained flashes of true poetic perception, and they always revealed his flawless ear for language, for the poetic terms of folk speech and the characteristic detail of his native region.

Other outstanding students came to Vanderbilt after my time there, and went on to become fine writers. One was Peter Taylor, who was descended from Bob and Alf Taylor, brothers who had run against each other for governor of Tennessee. I knew Peter at Louisiana State, where he went after leaving Vanderbilt. He has become one of the finest writers of short stories in the country in our time. Another notable example is James Dickey, a poet of tremendous power and of promise even beyond the power he has exhibited. There is no doubt that some of his work will be permanent, and he will be one of Vanderbilt's most valuable advertisements.

And it was not at Vanderbilt alone that creativity flourished in the Nashville of the 1920s and 1930s. Among the writers who led the literary renaissance of black America in that period were James Weldon Johnson and Arna Bontemps, both of whom were to teach at Fisk University. Nashville has always been a good book town, too, with its church publishing houses and especially its bookstores. Mills and Zibart's have been there for decades, and there was Stokes and Stockell, and early in the nineteenth century there was a famous bookshop, Berry's, and others before that.

Nashville was to me an interesting place full of interesting people in the 1930s, and I didn't want to leave it. I haven't suffered from being forced out,

REMEMBRANCES

The Fugitives

They cannot here their youth renew.
Reversing years, again review
Old meetings and the plans they drew.

These yellowed pages, scraps of rime,
Detritus of a far gone time,
What once was live, can only mime.

If one seeks sources, verity
Is here, mementoes, history,
But still remains the mystery

Of how and why in those few years
Unequals formed a group of peers
And from brief verse built fame, careers.

No cairn, this is a dwelling place
For script or printed words that trace
Evolvement of an inner grace.

These halls that proper honors give,
Maintaining forms, are like a sieve;
The spirit still is fugitive.

> Fugitive poet Jesse Wills,
> in *Nashville and Other Poems* (1973),
> dedicated "To the Fugitives still at large"

but I haven't forgotten how special those years were. I have gone back often for visits, but there are fewer and fewer old friends left. Early in 1979 I went for the funeral of Allen Tate, my greatly admired friend who had been really a combination of older brother and tutor to me. Some years ago I remember Tate saying he wondered what would have been the result if the poets and writers around the Vanderbilt campus had been scattered among the great Eastern universities of that period. He would have made his way anywhere, of course, and maybe some of the rest of us would have too—but Tate called Nashville a happy accident for us all, and it was.

The little Nashville of fifty years ago was my first big city. I don't even know my way around the new Nashville, not even around the Vanderbilt campus, but I carry the old Nashville in my head, grateful for the friends it gave me and for so much else. How remarkably lucky I was to have been there. I have often thought that for me and my purposes and aspirations, it was the best place in the world. I couldn't want it to have been any different from what it was.

THE NASHVILLE that Robert Penn Warren left behind in 1934 would have been almost unrecognizable to its long-departed residents of the 1830s, except in one respect: The city displayed the most extreme contrasts of atmosphere and appearance, of belief and behavior—as it had throughout most of its century and a half of existence. Whatever else it was or had been, Nashville was no cozy union of like-minded people; in fact, it seemed to thrive on its contradictions and its differences.

In the decades between world wars, Nashville exhibited two profiles. Its progressive side sparkled with economic growth before the Depression and with New Deal optimism after it. Pursuit of affluence and culture and a determined spirit of boosterism marked the period, and as the city began to free itself from the ravages of the Depression, there was much hope and even some concrete evidence that happy days were indeed here again.

But the profile from the opposite perspective was far more grim. It was deeply lined by the effects of the financial crisis, both national and local, and by incessant political and personal conflicts.

Before the Depression, Nashville's diversified economy and its cluster of banks and investment companies had lifted the city to the front rank of American financial centers. Several new office buildings appeared in the downtown area; a Greek-style public building, the War Memorial, was erected to honor the state's military servants, and its open central portico highlighted a heroic statue to "Victory" by Nashville sculptress Belle Kinney.

Hand in hand with the growth and prosperity came a transportation boom—automobiles and airplanes enhanced the city's status as a regional trade center, and the railroads, in addition to hauling a record volume of freight, operated forty passenger trains a day, many of them carrying commuters to and from outlying towns in Middle Tennessee.

Money and leisure time made Nashvillians eager to be entertained, and the Ryman Auditorium and several downtown theaters accommodated them with such diverse talent as Will Rogers and Charlie Chaplin, W. C. Fields

Nashville architect Edward Dougherty won a national award for his design of the War Memorial Building near the State Capitol. It was built in 1925.

While she was manager of the Ryman Auditorium, Lula Naff collected posters of the stars who performed there, including this one featuring Amelita Galli-Curci, the renowned Metropolitan Opera soprano.

and the Ziegfeld Follies, Caruso and Paderewski, live theater and the Metropolitan Opera. Local talent was not lacking, either: The Nashville Symphony, conducted by F. Arthur Henkel, was formed in 1920, and the Nashville Conservatory of Music, directed by the longtime head of Ward-Belmont College's vocal department, Signor Gaetano S. De Luca, was founded in 1927.

Maestro De Luca was famed as a maker of opera singers. In Nashville he prepared several students for outstanding operatic careers, among them tenor James Melton, mezzosoprano Blanche Campbell, and Joseph Macpherson, a bass-baritone who made a sparkling debut with the Metropolitan Opera in 1926. Another Nashvillian who aspired to a career on the stage of the Met was Francis Robinson. He had begun as an usher for Lula C. Naff, manager of the Ryman Auditorium, and as a reviewer for the *Banner*; his fame would come not as a singer but as a biographer of Caruso and as the assistant manager of the Metropolitan for more than a quarter of a century.

High culture also played a prominent part in the early programming of Nashville's first major radio station, WSM, which went on the air in 1925. (Five other modest broadcasting enterprises had obtained call letters in Nashville before WSM.) The station's inaugural program on October 5, 1925, included musical performances by Joseph Macpherson, the Fisk Jubilee Singers, and the orchestras of Beasley Smith and Francis Craig. Classical music was the station's major form of entertainment, but a lighter musical offering called the WSM Barn Dance was added in November. A year later, station manager George D. Hay followed an hour of classical music with this announcement: "We have been listening to music largely from Grand Opera, but from now on we will present the Grand Ole Opry!" Then Hay opened the Barn

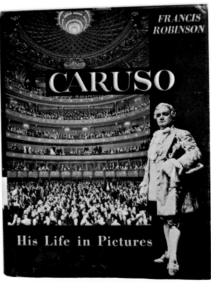

Once an usher at the Ryman Auditorium, Francis Robinson longed to sing at the Metropolitan Opera. He never made it, but became instead the Metropolitan's assistant general manager and wrote this biography of Enrico Caruso.

222

GREAT SUCCESS

Voice of the Athens of the South Speaks to Whole Nation

Nashville suffered an acute attack of "radiolitis" Monday night—and liked it—when WSM, the new $50,000 broadcasting station of the National Life & Accident Insurance Company, went on the air with a "non-stop" program which began shortly after 7 o'clock and ended at 2 o'clock this morning.

The first announcement that the new station was on the air came shortly after 7 p.m. when Edwin W. Craig, vice-president of the company, told the world that "This is station WSM—we shield millions—owned and operated by the National Life & Accident Insurance Company, Nashville, Tennessee." From that time on there was something doing every minute . . . .

The first musical number . . . was the national anthem by Al Menah Shrine band . . . .

Joseph T. McPherson, baritone, was next on the air, with Miss Hattie Paschal as accompanist.

. . . the Fisk Jubilee quintet . . . rendered six of the old-time favorites, including "Swing Low, Sweet Chariot" . . . .

Then came Beasley Smith's orchestra from the Andrew Jackson Hotel, and this collection of jazz artists kept the ether all "pepped" up for more than half an hour. During this period George D. Hay, WLS, did a little announcing, using his famous steamboat whistle.

The Knights of Columbus put on a few numbers of popular music . . . .

Those who like to dance were delighted when Francis Craig's Columbia recording orchestra took command of the ether from midnight until almost 1 a.m. . . . .

Hundreds stood for hours in Union street and Seventh avenue and heard the artists, while radio sets were placed in practically every radio shop, the drug stores, and cigar stores for the convenience of the public . . . .

Nashville Banner,
October 6, 1925

Dance with an introduction of a diminutive black musician, a harmonica player named DeFord Bailey, and thus began the radio show that would be enjoying national popularity more than fifty years later.

The Depression caused the Nashville Symphony to be silenced for fourteen years, disrupted the operation of the Nashville Conservatory, interrupted the careers of several outstanding individual performers, and generally brought Nashville culture—not to mention the economy—to an abrupt standstill. When recovery began, the emphasis was on politics, business, employment, and public works; it would be years before Nashvillians could find the money, the leisure time, or the inclination to concentrate on aesthetic or cultural or recreational pursuits.

The New Deal brought a blizzard of acronyms to the scene—WPA, CWA, CCC, FERA, PWA, NYA, and most notably, TVA. The Tennessee Valley Authority, technically speaking, did not reach to Nashville or Memphis, since neither

Vanderbilt University's Dudley Field was full to overflowing when the Commodores took on the Tennessee Volunteers in 1930. The University of Tennessee won, 13-0. When it was built early in the 1920s, Dudley Field was the largest sports stadium in the Southeast.

Built with WPA funds during the nation's recovery from the Depression, Nashville's Berry Field was served first by American Airlines and then by Eastern Airlines after it was opened in 1936.

city was in the valley of the Tennessee River and its tributaries, but political necessity dictated their inclusion, and the agency's electric power was ceremonially extended to Nashville in 1939. The WPA—Works Progress Administration— was administered in Tennessee by Harry S. Berry, and when Nashville got a much-needed new airport from the program, it was named Berry Field in his honor. The federal program also provided funds for construction and improvements in Edwin and Percy Warner Parks, a wooded expanse of hills and valleys southwest of the city that incorporated gifts from Percy Warner's son-in-law Luke Lea, from Warner's brother Edwin, and from other sources.

Nashville also got a new post office, a state supreme court building, other state office buildings, and a new courthouse in this period, all with the help of federal funds. The courthouse was dedicated in 1937; it occupied the same Public Square site as each of its predecessor buildings, dating back to the 1780s.

Davidson County had voted Democratic in fourteen straight presidential elections from 1872 through 1924; it turned to Herbert Hoover and the Republicans in 1928, but then gave Roosevelt an overwhelming victory in 1932 and

The Tennessee State Fair midway in 1931 looked very much like the midways of the 1970s. The fair's grandstand and Women's Building burned after this postcard photograph was made; they have been replaced with less impressive structures.

continued to support him strongly as long as he was in office. (Only once since then, in fact, has the county failed to give its support to the Democrats, and that was in 1972, when Richard Nixon won by a huge majority over George McGovern). Roosevelt's New Deal offered Nashville and the nation a rescue from economic quicksand, and the city grasped the government's outstretched hand and climbed out to recovery. Eleanor and Franklin Roosevelt were welcomed with praise when they came to Nashville in 1934; the president was to return twice (once for the funeral of the district's veteran congressman, Speaker of the House Joseph W. Byrns), and his popularity would remain high among all factions of Democrats in the city and the state.

Nashville entered the 1940s less damaged by the Depression than most Southern cities. Its population had more than doubled—to 167,000—in forty years, and Davidson County's population of just over a quarter of a million had also doubled in the same period. With the Depression a fading memory and economic growth again the slogan, most people seemed eager to forget the hard times and look ahead.

When President Franklin D. Roosevelt and his wife Eleanor came to Nashville on November 17, 1934, at the invitation of local Congressman and House Speaker Joseph W. Byrns, they were greeted at Union Station by a huge throng. Governor Hill McAlister (seated right) rode with the Roosevelts in an open limousine to the Hermitage, and the newspapers reported that "the largest crowd in Nashville's history" lined the entire route.

225

Cheekwood, one of Nashville's many mansions, displays the elegance and opulence of upper-class life in this 1934 photograph. Built during the Depression by Mr. and Mrs. Leslie Cheek, the home now contains a permanent art collection and is open for a variety of public functions.

The intersection of Eighth Avenue and Church Street was one of Nashville's busiest when this 1937 photograph was taken. Sears, Roebuck and Company later relocated; the Paramount Theater is gone, and so are the streetcars.

A fleet of Chevrolets and Plymouths, equipped with bulletproof glass and windshield gunports, was put on display in front of the War Memorial Building in 1935. Harold Roland (left), an assistant to the chief of police, posed beside one of the vehicles with two men whose identity is uncertain; they were either police officers or car salesmen.

WHEN ALL the monumental conflicts of the early twentieth century in Nashville have been recalled and recounted—the railroad wars, temperance, suffrage, Jim Crow segregation—there remains yet another power struggle to be examined before the picture is complete. It was a war of politics and personalities; it embraced the newspapers, elected officials, captains of finance; it started early and continued without letup, from the first years of the century into the 1940s and beyond. No issue, no principle, no theme or theory explains or clarifies what happened; nothing does, except this: Powerful men, dominating personalities, met and clashed repeatedly, gambling for high stakes in a city that had drawn such gamblers to it since the day of its birth.

V. K. Stevenson and Edmund W. Cole; John W. Thomas and Eugene C. Lewis; Jere Baxter and James M. Head; Anne Dallas Dudley (proving that not all the forceful figures had to be males); Edward Carmack and Duncan Cooper; Luke Lea and E. B. Stahlman; Hilary Howse, Robert Love Taylor, Malcolm Patterson: In no other period of the city's history had so many strong characters contended for power. Even the black community, shackled as it was by law and custom and the reality of white domination, produced J. C. Napier and Richard Henry Boyd and the combative editors of the *Nashville Globe*.

One more towering figure—in some ways, the biggest of them all—came along soon after the war. He was Rogers Caldwell, a money wizard who built a Nashville investment banking firm into the largest financial empire in the South—and saw it collapse in a thundering heap when the Depression swept through the land.

Hilary Howse, an anti-prohibitionist mayor of Nashville from 1909 to 1917—when the temperance movement was at high tide—returned to the office in 1924 and stayed in power

When he was in his prime as "the J.P. Morgan of the South," Nashville financier Rogers Caldwell (right) paused for this photograph with his father, James E. Caldwell. The elder Caldwell, a wealthy man himself, once observed that "Money isn't worth a damn, but getting it is fun."

for fourteen more years. Hill McAlister of Nashville lost a Democratic gubernatorial primary to Austin Peay in 1926 and another to Henry Horton in 1928, but rebounded in 1932 and 1934 to become the first (and to this date, the only) native Nashvillian to be elected governor of Tennessee. Howse and McAlister were aligned with the Democratic Party faction controlled by Edward H. "Boss" Crump of Memphis; Peay and Horton were in the Luke Lea-Rogers Caldwell wing of the party. Issues came and went, economic conditions changed, Republican presidential candidates even carried the state twice in the 1920s, but nothing was more dominant or more permanent than the power of personality.

The baron of the Banner, *Edward Bushrod Stahlman (right), pledged allegiance to no political party. His grandson, James Geddes Stahlman, continued the tradition of personal journalism when he took over the paper in 1930. When Silliman Evans (below, right), a New Deal liberal, bought the bankrupt* Tennessean *at a public auction in 1937, he and fiercely conservative James Stahlman signed an agreement to publish their papers on the same presses—but their personal and political philosophies remained poles apart.*

It showed up early in the newspapers. Edward Bushrod Stahlman, son of a German Lutheran school teacher, had come to Tennessee as a youth during the Civil War. By 1893, when he was a vice president of the L&N Railroad, he had also bought the *Nashville Banner*, and for thirty-seven years he ran the paper not as a party organ but as an independent expression of his own personal convictions. (His grandson, James Geddes Stahlman, would publish the *Banner* for forty-two more years, never wavering from the hard-line style of personal journalism that was the paper's trademark.)

E. B. Stahlman mourned the death of Edward Carmack, supported the senatorial election of

Luke Lea, joined the battle against lawlessness that finally brought on prohibition. But somewhere along the way, the friendship between Stahlman and Lea soured, and in 1916, the *Banner* threw its support to Kenneth McKellar, and Lea became an ex-senator and a permanent foe of Stahlman.

Lea organized a volunteer regiment and went off to fight in World War I, but before he left he accused Stahlman of trying to have him relieved of his command. For his part, the German-born Stahlman accused Lea of branding him an "alien enemy" of the United States and prodding the government to confiscate the *Banner*. Neither man's effort succeeded, but the accusations were

228

After his conviction and imprisonment for banking law violations in the 1930s, Luke Lea lived quietly out of the limelight in Nashville. The Tennessean, *which he had founded and published for almost twenty-five years, printed this picture with Lea's obituary in 1945.*

heated and emotional, and the enmity hardened between Lea and the *Banner* publisher, who was thirty-six years his senior.

When Lea returned from the war—his last and most daring exploit having been a post-armistice attempt to kidnap Kaiser Wilhelm from a castle in Holland—he aligned himself with Rogers Caldwell, captured control of a wing of the Democratic Party, and resumed his feuds with Boss Crump of Memphis in the other wing and with E. B. Stahlman, who had little use for either faction.

In the *Tennessean*, Lea owned a newspaper that had borne his personal stamp since he founded it. He was not afraid to employ writers who had strong personalities of their own—he had hired Edward Carmack, after all, and his sports editor was Grantland Rice, already a famous journalist (and poet)—but in political matters, the *Tennessean* was every bit as much an extension of its publisher as the *Banner* was of Stahlman.

Stahlman did not live to see the downfall of Luke Lea and the *Tennessean*—he died in 1930, three years before the rival paper went into federal receivership and four years before its publisher ran into serious trouble with the law—but as long as the two men were alive and free, they waged unrelenting war against each other in the pages of their papers.

When Silliman Evans bought the *Tennessean* at a public auction in 1937 and moved to put the paper back on its feet, one of his first acts was to negotiate a joint operating system with James G. Stahlman and the *Banner*. The two papers moved into the same building, pooled their circulation, advertising, accounting, and printing operations, set up an independent corporation to manage those business matters—and forthwith resumed their editorial and political hostilities.

Luke Lea had been a boy wonder—publisher of the *Tennessean* at the age of twenty-eight, United States senator at thirty-one. He was a man of great personal magnetism, a dynamic and aggressive leader who made devoted friends and bitter enemies and left few people indifferent to him. He must have been impressed in 1920 to see another Nashville boy wonder, Rogers Caldwell, make a million dollars as an invest-

Early Nashville gasoline stations bore little resemblance to the service stations of later years. "Uncle" Bob Gary's East Nashville establishment was typical of the 1930s.

ment banker by the time he was thirty—and do it with a flair that could not fail to attract notice.

Caldwell was a Nashville banker-businessman's son who dropped out of college to enter the money business. He was twenty-seven when he chartered his own firm, Caldwell and Company, in 1917; within three years he was a millionaire, and by 1929 he controlled more than a hundred banks, insurance companies, newspapers, hotels, and other enterprises with assets in excess of half a billion dollars. So phenomenal was his rise in the reckless boom years of the 1920s that he was hailed as "the J. P. Morgan of the South."

It was probably inevitable that Caldwell and Lea should join forces; their only other option was to fight, there being no way they could ignore each other. Together they bought the *Memphis Commercial Appeal* and the *Knoxville Journal* and almost gained control of the *Atlanta Constitution* and the *Kansas City Star.* Lea

dreamed of a journalistic-political empire, and Caldwell caught the political fever too. With a little more prudence, they might have been able to ride out the Depression, but when the stock market crashed, Caldwell and Company was too overextended to meet the financial demands upon it. The company went into voluntary receivership in November 1930. The newspaper chain and 120 banks in seven states fell with it.

On the political front, a depression of a different sort took hold. A legislative investigation of the company's ties to Governor Horton led to an unsuccessful attempt to impeach the governor. Caldwell was indicted by grand juries in Tennessee and Kentucky on a variety of financial manipulation charges. He was tried and convicted in a Davidson County case, but the state supreme court reversed the ruling, and no retrial was ever held; he never stood trial on the Kentucky charges.

The financier's palatial home near Franklin

230

Road, modeled after the Hermitage and built in 1927 for $350,000, was tied up in litigation for ten years before the state obtained a judgment against Caldwell and eventually got the house. (It is now the Ellington Agricultural Center.)

Caldwell was only forty years old when his empire collapsed. He lived for thirty-eight more years without ever returning to the limelight.

Luke Lea was less fortunate. He and his son, Luke Lea Jr., were indicted in North Carolina and convicted of conspiracy to violate the state's banking laws. After a prolonged and sensational legal battle, they were sent to prison in May 1934. Lea's son was paroled after a few months, but Lea himself served two years of a six-to-ten-year sentence before being paroled. He returned to Nashville and lived quietly for nearly ten years before his death in 1945.

While they were in active pursuit of their financial-political-journalistic dreams of glory and power, Luke Lea and Rogers Caldwell were a formidable pair, easily a match for any of the other powerful personalities who rose to prominence and notoriety in that period. But finally, they seemed to inspire an excess of acquisitive ambition in each other. "If Luke Lea and Rogers Caldwell had never met," a common friend once remarked, "they both would have been better off."

Luke Lea and his son, Luke Jr., had been convicted in 1931 of violating the banking laws of North Carolina. They were released on bond, and when their appeals were finally exhausted, they left Nashville in January 1933 and went into hiding. Nobody knew where they were. It was a big mystery.

I was a reporter for the *Banner* at the time, and I had been covering the Lea-Caldwell story. I got a tip that the Leas were hiding out with his old war buddy, Sergeant Alvin York, up near Jamestown, so I went up there to see if I could find them.

They weren't at York's house so I went to see W. A. "Bully" Garrett, a Jamestown lawyer who had been close to Lea. Garrett slammed the door in my face when I tried to talk to him, but as I was leaving I looked back and saw Luke Jr. looking out the window at me.

That was all I needed to know. I found a telephone and called in a story just in time to make the last edition. That night and the next morning, newspapermen poured in from all sides.

Having been discovered, Lea came out of hiding and changed his strategy. He had his bodyguards deputized by the local sheriff, who ate out of his hand, and while appearing to be under arrest, he was actually searching for a judge who would free him on a writ of habeas corpus. Luke and his boys moved into the Mark Twain Hotel in Jamestown, where I was staying, and for several days it was like a comic opera, with the Leas looking for a judge, the North Carolina authorities trying to extradite him, and the press just watching and waiting.

Luke Lea was a character, a very self-conscious public actor—and an enterpriser, full of manipulations. While we were at the hotel, he came to my room two or three times and argued his case with me. He felt he was being wronged. His supreme belief in himself was remarkable.

Finally, Lea and his entourage left Jamestown in the middle of the night and went to Clarksville for a court hearing, but the judge wouldn't free him. He appealed that ruling too, and it was more than a year later, in May 1934, before he and his son finally went to prison.

I saw him several times after he was paroled. He was always very pleasant to me, and I don't think he ever held it against me that I had smoked him out. He kept his sense of humor, but he never regained power. After he had been in prison, he seemed a lonely man, a beaten man.

BRAINARD CHENEY, in a 1979 interview

Long after his financial empire had toppled, Rogers Caldwell was noted for the breakfasts and luncheons he served to a diversity of guests at his Franklin home. With Caldwell (left) in this 1966 photograph are (from his left) John Siegenthaler, Harry Howe Ransom, John J. Hooker Jr., and John J. Hooker Sr. No alcoholic drinks were served, and the only house rule was posted in view of the guests: "While in this house please do not say anything unkind about anyone."

WHEN NASHVILLE boarded the Twentieth Century Express at its sparkling new Union Station in October 1900, it was bound for bigger and better things. Through four decades, the pace never slackened. There was war—at home and abroad—and very little peace. Depression, disasters, political power struggles, social conflicts, economic boom and bust, religious fervor—the unending chain of events and developments tumbled one upon another.

By the time 1940 arrived, the railroads that had promised Nashville a prosperous future had fallen into a steep decline. It would lead in time to the end of passenger trains and leave Union Station a deserted stone cavern holding only echoes of a glorious past. Nashville had new vehicles—cars and trucks and airplanes—to carry it on the continuing journey. The trains had not been fast enough, and speed was what counted.

If the pace of change in the first forty years of the century had seemed swift, it was so only in comparison with previous times. The modern era, ushered in by World War II, would transport Nashville at an ever-accelerating speed into a world of promise and peril that could not have been imagined when the twentieth century began.

Change and Tradition

Dewey W. Grantham

No aspect of Nashville's recent history is more striking than the far-reaching changes that have taken place in its size, structure, and institutional life. Indeed, the range and intensity of Nashville's social change since 1940 have made it a "new city." The population of the city and surrounding county has doubled during the last four decades, the local economy has grown and become more diversified, the city's residential and business expansion has created a configuration of suburbs, and its governmental and political structure has been reorganized and modernized. The prewar pattern of racial segregation and discrimination has virtually disappeared, and hardly any feature of life in the community has been left untouched by the civil rights movement. Many of these changes were disruptive and painful, and some of them were tenaciously resisted.

Change came as a result of various circumstances and forces. Some developments, such as the spectacular growth of the new suburbia, reflected the acceleration of older trends. Other causal factors were external events, such as World War II. The war rejuvenated and strengthened the economy, stimulated the movement of people into and within the city, and provided a context for more rapid social change. Technological and scientific advances also encouraged change, for they led to great productivity and promoted the growth of the "new consumerism." Communications technology helped pave the way for Nashville's emergence as the center and major dispenser of country music.

Pressures from the outside also brought change. The civil rights movement confronted the city with a series of dramatic and urgent demands. Local leaders and organizations played a vital part in working out acceptable solutions to some problems, and in some instances traditional attitudes and practices helped smooth the transition from the old to the new. Innovations in race relations, for example, were adopted more easily because a measure of interracial contact and accommodation had existed in the prewar period.

There were times when change came amidst social crisis. As Arna Bontemps of Fisk University said, in recalling the freedom movement, "We were in the middle of it in Nashville. Our little world commenced to sway and rock with the fury of a resurrection." The crisis in race relations was manifested in school desegregation disturbances, massive sit-ins, and numerous encounters between the proponents and opponents of racial change. The strident voices, bitter recriminations, and occasional violence that attended the racial confrontations of the late 1950s and the 1960s disrupted the city's civility, permeated its politics, and tested the patience and capacity of its leaders.

Nashville also faced an "urban crisis" in the postwar period. It was rooted in the swift and disorderly growth of the city's suburbs, in the neglect and deterioration of its inner sections, and in the enormous strain placed upon its facilities and institutions by a sprawling and fragmented population. The structure of local government itself was part of the urban crisis, since overlapping agencies, piecemeal policy-

233

making, and divided authority had made it almost impossible to meet area-wide problems.

One consequence of the momentous changes after 1940 was the city's declining insularity and the blurring of its traditional image. As the years passed, Nashvillians steadily converged in their behavior and ideological outlook with the inhabitants of other cities, in and out of the South. The economy of the Tennessee city became more fully integrated into the pattern of national economic activity. At the same time, Nashville contributed to the transformation of Southern politics—the disruption of the one-party system, the emergence of a competitive Republicanism, the enfranchisement and political involvement of black people—and thereby became less distinctive in the national political arena. Changes in race relations and in the status of blacks also gave impetus to the convergence of North and South—and to the opportunity for Nashville and other Southern cities to play a more constructive role in American life. The same was true of cultural developments, particularly in the realm of mass culture, where Nashville became an important creator and exporter—not merely an importer and consumer—of cultural products.

In some respects, Nashville was undergoing a process of modernization. The result was a new and healthier urban environment and a more adaptive and creative social system. In economic affairs, for instance, new opportunities and initiatives brought self-sustaining growth and a more mature economy. The consolidation of the city and county governments in the early 1960s provided a single governmental entity which, with the streamlining of the city's administrative structure, centralized decision-making, facilitated comprehensive planning, and made the political process more coherent and workable. There were also modernizing innovations in local politics: the broadening of the franchise, the equalization of representation, and the coming of more competitive elections.

Reform in race relations meant that ordinary life for blacks was no longer influenced by legal segregation and discrimination, that Negroes were enjoying greater opportunities in education and employment, and that they had achieved a kind of cultural and psychological emancipation. The reorganized metropolitan government and the greater sensitivity to human needs demonstrated in the programs of several public and private agencies encouraged more effective interaction between individual citizens and the major institutions. The role of public opinion was enhanced in the activities and decisions of these institutions. And in a limited way Nashville became a *participant* society.

Although many of these developments have strengthened the city and improved the lives of its people, change has not always been beneficial. Life in the "new city" has many harsh aspects, ranging from ghetto housing to the rising crime rate. The spirit of urban boosterism has fostered an uncritical approval of economic growth. Nashvillians are still differentiated by race and social class as well as by geographical dispersion and the distrust that the "old families" often have for newcomers. Many

234

local residents have no voice in the decisions that affect them most directly, there is a pervasive feeling of powerlessness in dealing with large, bureaucratic organizations, and the old sense of community seems to be disappearing.

Despite its transformation over the last four decades, Nashville has not succumbed entirely to the homogenizing influences of modern American life. There is, in other words, an old as well as a new Nashville. The city remains in many ways a traditional society: in the ruralism that infuses much of its social thought, in an extreme individualism that is frequently evident in public affairs, and in the prevalence of paternalistic attitudes toward blacks and women. Life in Nashville still moves at a more leisurely pace than that of Northern cities, the accent one hears in the street is noticeably different, and people are perhaps more polite and helpful than in other regions. The local culture retains a kind of personalism that finds expression in friendship and kinship relations. It is also made distinctive by the nature and extent of religious beliefs and practices, by an awareness of the past in the present, and by a sensitivity to the unique aspects of the community.

Thus it is not surprising that, while the era since 1940 has been dominated by the experience of change, it has also been filled with paradox, ambivalence, and the clash between continuity and change.

Dewey W. Grantham is the Holland N. McTyeire Professor of History at Vanderbilt University, where he has taught since 1952. His fields of special interest are twentieth-century United States history and the history of the modern South. His most recent book is The Regional Imagination: The South and Recent American History.

Missouri artist Thomas Hart Benton, grandnephew and namesake of the man who once dueled Andrew Jackson on the Public Square in Nashville, painted "The Sources of Country Music" in 1974. The mural, commissioned by the Country Music Foundation for the Country Music Hall of Fame and Museum, was finished but unsigned when Benton died in 1975.

Nashville:
An American Song
1940-1980

RECOVERY from the Depression came sooner for some cities and states than others, and Nashville was among the more fortunate; having suffered comparatively less, it regained its economic health more quickly. At the close of 1940, the city's newspapers reported that the business volume of local manufacturers, wholesalers, and retailers had exceeded pre-Depression levels for the second consecutive year, and bank clearings had surpassed the billion-dollar mark for the first time in the city's history.

The economic forecast for 1941 looked even brighter. Because it had been spared the most crippling effects of the national financial crisis, Nashville was in a position to enter a phase of sustained and unprecedented growth. Its diversified economy was creating hundreds of new jobs and dramatically reducing the rate of unemployment. Furthermore, the city's location at the hub of a market area that reached in all directions to a radius of a hundred miles or more provided assurance that both the labor force and the demand for goods and services could be maintained.

Only the dreaded prospect of another war clouded the picture, and the war would not be long in coming—but ironically, it was the war itself that provided the impetus for economic growth. By 1942, many of Nashville's manufacturers had turned their efforts to military production: parachutes and other equipment from Du Pont's synthetic fibers, airplanes from the Vultee plant (now Avco), naval vessels from the Nashville Bridge Company, combat boots from the General Shoe Corporation (Genesco), sandbags from the Werthan Bag Company.

Pearl Harbor made the fear of armed conflict a reality, and Nashvillians were among the first casualties. The death of Ben E. Holt, a black sailor, was the first to be reported locally, and soon the names of two white sailors, Robert A. Bennett and James A. Wauford, were added to the fatality list from the Pearl Harbor raid. In the months and years that followed, reports of combat deaths appeared in the pages of the press with grim and predictable regularity.

Almost 37,000 Davidson County men and women wore the uniform of the United States as volunteers or draftees between 1941 and 1945—and when the war was over, 734 of them were dead. The fatalities included fifty-nine former students of East Nashville High School alone. One of Nashville's losses was twenty-three-year-old Cornelia Fort, the first female pilot to die in the service of her country; she was killed when the plane she was flying crashed on a training flight in Texas in 1943.

The Nashville division of Consolidated Vultee Aircraft Corporation (now Avco) was a major war production plant in the early 1940s. Assembly line workers—about one-third of them women—constructed cockpit panels for the P-38 Lightning fighter plane. Trailer camps such as this one near Vultee (right) helped to ease the housing shortage in wartime Nashville.

Even without the heavy loss of life, Nashvillians could not have failed to see and feel the effects of war. Massive war maneuvers were staged in Middle Tennessee, and the development of Camp Campbell near Clarksville and of an air base at Smyrna brought thousands of men into the city. Public agencies and private civic groups bent every effort to make them feel at home; parties and dances at the Hippodrome arena on West End Avenue were a regular highlight of local entertainment. There was private entertainment, too, and not all of it was sanctioned: Scores of young girls joined old-line prostitutes on the city's streets, and venereal disease reached epidemic proportions unmatched since the Civil War.

Widespread shortages, price controls, and rationing of such basic items as gasoline and meat took effect early in 1942, providing further evidence that military priorities were paramount. The war effort dominated life in the city—as it did throughout the nation—and in that atmosphere, little else of consequence could gain and hold the public's attention.

In state politics, the Memphis-based Crump machine was in complete control, and Nashville seemed to have neither the power nor the personalities to influence government action. Locally, Mayor Thomas L. Cummings had entered office in 1938 after the death of longtime Mayor Hilary Howse, and compared to Howse, the new mayor seemed to have the instincts of a

Werthan's free hotels on Elliston Place

Congressman J. Percy Priest, innkeeper Joe Werthan, Mayor Thomas L. Cummings (left to right)

A HOME AWAY FROM HOME

A drive through Centennial Park one late summer evening, during which Joe Werthan saw men sleeping all over the ground, was the inspiration for the Service Men's Center which Werthan, Nashville manufacturer, opened at 2224 Elliston Place to commemorate the first anniversary of the attack on Pearl Harbor. That first night, seven men registered to share 200 beds among them.

But this unique one-man-financed center has served to sound the praise of Nashville far and wide, where service men gather, and since that December night in 1942 there has been many a night when 600 beds were spoken for in advance and there remained only the pool and ping-pong tables for other service men to stretch out on for the night.

When Werthan took his eye-opening drive in the park he began to investigate hotels, churches, clubs, railroad and bus stations. Everywhere the story was the same—tired men off maneuvers walking the streets and looking for a place to sleep.

Werthan thought of his two adjoining investment property dwelling houses on Elliston Place, and he set about establishing the center which is now famous.

●

The atmosphere of the house did not suggest drinking, and by the same token it did not engender brawls. Werthan considers it to the credit of his institution that there has never been one man to start trouble among the 650,000 who have been guests at the Center . . . . The record of integrity is almost as high. Among the thousands who had checks cashed or borrowed money, only one defaulted . . . .

Nashville Tennessean Magazine,
October 14, 1945

reformer. Cummings was in office when natural gas pipelines and TVA electrical power came to Nashville, and he was credited with initiating long-range plans for urban redevelopment of the slums around the capitol. Until after the war, however, the resources to support major public works projects were not available, and it would remain for another administration in the postwar years to accomplish changes that the Cummings administration could only dream of.

There were a few new developments in Nashville during the war, though—some important, others trivial—and they all reflected to some degree the character and personality of the city. Streetcars were replaced with a more versatile and efficient bus system (and the fare was still a nickel). Downtown Nashville had no competition as the retail trade center for the central South, but the city's first shopping centers in the Belle Meade and Melrose areas were an early signal of the changes that would come soon after the war. The Children's Museum (now the

---

When I came to work for the *Tennessean* in 1934, Hilary Howse was still Nashville's mayor. He was, like almost every city mayor in those days, a boss—he ran a political machine. He was not a complete autocrat, like Boss Crump in Memphis, but he was in firm control of local government. Howse was a very imposing figure, and Nashville under his regime was a wide-open town.

After Howse died in the late 1930s, Tom Cummings was elected mayor in a surprise victory over Jack Keefe. Both men were criminal lawyers, but Keefe was young and very colorful, while Cummings was a quiet, shy, aloof man. Silliman Evans and the *Tennessean* backed Cummings as an anti-machine candidate, while Jimmy Stahlman and the *Banner* supported Keefe. Both papers indulged heavily in vitriolic personal editorials on their front pages, as they traditionally had done. Many people in the community professed to loath that style of journalism, but it was dramatic and entertaining, and it sold papers. I think Stahlman and Evans genuinely liked each other personally, but they made an asset of their philosophical differences. They were self-conscious, deliberate enemies—and it was good for business. That's just how the game of politics—and journalism—was played here.

Cummings stayed in office with the support of the *Tennessean* until Ben West came to power with the backing of the *Banner* in the early 1950s. Compared to Howse, Cummings was a reformer. He promised TVA power to Nashville and he delivered on that promise, to the city's eternal benefit. He established a power board that was pretty well independent of politics. He improved the civil service, supported labor unions, sought out votes from blacks.

But the greatest contribution Tom Cummings made was to initiate planning for slum clearance and urban renewal. With his man Gerald Gimre, who headed both the planning commission and the housing authority, Cummings set in motion the first major urban redevelopment program in the nation. West got most of the credit because the money was available and the work was done in his administration, but it was Cummings who started it. Urged on by John Lentz, the county health officer, who said venereal disease was ruining the city, Cummings and Gimre devised the plan to literally bury the whorehouses and slum tenements behind the capitol, and to move the poor who lived there into decent public housing.

That red-light district was owned and controlled by lawyers, politicians,

churches, universities—and it was high-income property. Illegal whiskey, gambling, and prostitution flourished there, with an upper-class clientele. Cummings was the man, more than any other, who made a commitment to clean the area up.

There was a lot he didn't do. He didn't end the system of ward politics, and in Printer's Alley and a great many restaurants and clubs, liquor by the drink was regularly sold to anyone who could afford it, including politicians, lobbyists, and newspaper reporters. Still, Cummings was more of a reformer than Nashville had been accustomed to having in the mayor's office.

NAT CALDWELL, in a 1979 interview

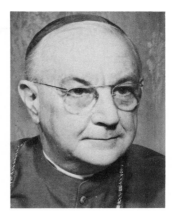

In his thirteen years as Nashville's mayor, Thomas L. Cummings lacked the resources but not the desire to be a reformer. It was his idea to clean up the festering slums near the capitol.

Combining history and fiction, Alfred Leland Crabb of Nashville recaptured a romantic image of the city with his novels about the glories of the Maxwell House, the Belmont mansion, and other nineteenth-century landmarks.

Samuel Stritch, a native of North Nashville, served briefly as a priest in the Catholic diocese here. Later he became the archbishop of Chicago, and in 1945 he was made a cardinal by Pope Pius XII.

Cumberland Museum and Science Center) was opened in 1945, and the Nashville Symphony Orchestra was reactivated the following year. And there was nostalgia for a bygone age of upper-class comfort: Local novelist Alfred Leland Crabb's new books of historical fiction about the nineteenth century glories of the Belmont mansion and the Maxwell House were highly popular, and Belle Meade horse lovers who enjoyed riding to the hounds and racing for pleasure inaugurated the Iroquois Steeplechase in Percy Warner Park. Champagne to celebrate the occasion—and beer for the less affluent—could be found in package stores and taverns, for the state had repealed alcohol prohibition in 1939.

Away from the city, a few Nashvillians gained recognition during the war years—and not all of them were in military service. Claude Jarman Jr., a ten-year-old student at Eakin Elementary School, won a special Academy Award after he starred with Gregory Peck in the 1945 hit movie, "The Yearling." Samuel Stritch, born and raised in North Nashville, capped a lifetime of service as a priest and an archbishop in the Roman Catholic Church when he was elevated in 1945 to the College of Cardinals by Pope Pius XII. Hume-Fogg High School alumnus Johnny Beazley, a pitcher for the St. Louis Cardinals, beat the New York Yankees twice in the 1942 World Series. And at least one Nashville newsmaker attracted unwanted attention: Thomas H. Robinson Jr., a fugitive for nineteen months after he

had kidnapped a wealthy Louisville woman, was finally captured and convicted, and only the intervention of President Harry S. Truman saved him from death in the electric chair.

One of the few colorful personalities in Nashville during the decade of the 1940s was a flashy department store owner, Fred Harvey. Almost from the day he took over a faltering business house on Church Street in 1943, the irrepressible Harvey started giving his conservative competitors a lesson in modern merchandising. He painted the walls of his store in bright shades of pink and purple. He installed escalators—a real novelty. He brought merry-go-round horses and caged monkeys into the store, scattered crazy-house mirrors throughout, and bombarded the newspapers and radio stations with advertising that proclaimed, "It's fun to shop at Harvey's."

The customers loved it. Harvey offered them not only merchandise but entertainment. He also made shopping easier by liberalizing charge accounts and exchanges of goods, opening his store during evening hours, and inviting customers to call long distance—and reverse the charges—to order merchandise.

Within three years, Harvey's had become Nashville's largest department store. Its two principal competitors, Cain-Sloan and Castner-Knott, struggled to adapt their operations to the new pace and style of marketing, but they lacked Fred Harvey's experience—and his flair. A bitter rivalry developed, and after the war, a

Before World War II, streetcars and automobiles ran east and west on Church Street. Twenty-five years later it was a one-way street (right), and Christmas shoppers thronged there. Soon after that, suburban shopping malls began to draw away much of downtown Nashville's retail trade.

conflict over a building lease drew Harvey and Cain-Sloan into a protracted legal battle that went all the way to the state supreme court. When Harvey won a split decision there, his position in the Nashville marketplace was secure.

But the marketplace itself was in dire need of rejuvenation. After World War II was over and Nashville had celebrated the return of its veterans, a wide range of local needs and problems demanded attention. The scarcity of essential goods had ended and the economy had picked up, but inflation, labor unrest, crime, and a variety of social problems were also on the rise and glaring deficiencies were apparent in housing, public health, education, transportation, and government services.

By 1950, the contrasting and conflicting faces of Nashville stood out in vivid detail. The city's population had grown by only four percent during the 1940s (to a total of 174,000), while Davidson County's population outside Nashville had expanded by sixty-four percent, giving the county and city combined a total of more than 321,000 residents. In the inner city, many businesses, homes, and streets were badly deteriorated, pollution fouled the air and the river, and a squalid ring of wooden shacks was crowded around the base of Capitol Hill, while in Belle Meade and a few other suburban locations, fortunes made from banking, insurance, real estate, and manufacturing had built grand estates and country homes. City and county governments were separate, competitive, and wastefully duplicative. An unproductive system of ward politics, particularly in the city, discouraged democratic participation and thwarted change. Neglect and inequity characterized the state of race relations.

Nashville and Davidson County desperately needed a reformation, but they seemed to lack the public and private leadership and the grass-roots pressure to bring it about. The divisions between the city and the county, between white-collar and blue-collar workers, between leisure and labor, between whites and blacks, Republicans and Democrats, conservatives and liberals, put the urban community and its expanding suburban ring in the same class with most postwar cities, particularly in the South. In 1940—after the Depression but before the war—Nashville had seemed on the verge of a renaissance; a decade later, its prospect for distinctiveness had diminished.

The city's daily newspapers symbolized the internal divisions around them. Adversaries in almost every respect, the *Tennessean* and the *Banner* were endlessly preoccupied with arguments of principle and struggles for power. Yet for the sake of profit, they were published under the same roof; when their survival was at stake, they had found a way to coexist productively. In contrast, the metropolitan community they operated in appeared to have neither the means nor the will to reach a similar accommodation within its own divided house.

NASHVILLIANS ROAR JOYOUS WELCOME TO NEWS OF PEACE

The too-young, the too-old, the lame, halt and blind, soldiers and civilians, all victors, shrieked and screamed the victors' song as they thronged the paper-littered streets of downtown Nashville last night in a four-years-pent-up celebration.

It took less than 15 minutes for war-weary Nashvillians to turn the city into a raging inferno of whistles, horns and colorful parades yesterday as the long-awaited V-J Day finally became a glory-ridden reality . . . .

From all over the city and county, long lines of automobiles filed toward the uptown sector and streamed through Church Street with an ever-increasing crescendo of horns and shouts . . . . Unmindful of traffic laws, cars were at times traveling four abreast down Church Street . . . .

All three details of city, county and state police were called to duty immediately . . . . The Nashville fire department also ordered all available firemen into service in the event that any trouble might arise during the long celebration . . . .

The line of automobiles extended far past the Woodland Street bridge in East Nashville; to Twenty-First Avenue across the Broadway and Church Street viaducts; as far as the reservoir on Eighth Avenue South, and as far as Jefferson Street to the north . . . .

Amorous—very amorous—and deservedly inebriated soldiers and sailors milled through the crowds kissing every pretty girl in sight. "Let's celebrate, baby, don't you know the war's over?" . . .

A lone B-29 roared low over the city in reassuring majesty, a reminder of the might that brought Japan to her knees . . . .

Nashville Tennessean,
August 15, 1945

The thrill of victory—and a kiss for a captain

JUST WHEN it appeared that Nashville was drifting aimlessly, the wind shifted. The becalmed city of 1950 was sailing in and out of storms ten years later, and more lay ahead—but it was moving fast.

In 1951, a magazine writer named Rufus Jarman wrote a profile of Nashville for the *Saturday Evening Post* that ruffled the feelings of the city's business and political leaders. Jarman described Nashville as "an old-fashioned city . . . gracious and charming . . . but too leisurely, easygoing, sometimes lackadaisical." It was, he observed, unusually well-off financially, but more interested in banking and insurance than in industry and labor. The aristocratic old families whose succeeding generations had maintained a proprietary claim on the city, Jarman said, were skeptical of progress, resistant to change, cool to upstart newcomers, and disdainful of the Grand Ole Opry—which "has done more to put Nashville on the map than Gen. Andrew Jackson did."

Nashville's greatest charm and its greatest weakness, Jarman maintained, was the determination of its ruling elite to preserve a way of living that had been passed down from the mid-nineteenth century. But, he concluded, "fortunately or unfortunately, a combination of factors seems to be forcing Nashville into an unwilling, halting, resisting sort of progress, whether old-liners desire it or not."

Reluctant accommodation to change may have been barely visible to Jarman when he visited the city, but if he had come back in a few more years, he might have been astonished to see what was happening.

The decade of the 1950s probably introduced more fundamental and permanent changes to Nashville than any other in its history. Some were technological, others physical, still others social; some were quickly absorbed, others resisted and delayed; some were initiated from within, others imposed from without. But without exception, the major developments of the period affected the city fundamentally, and a quarter of a century later it was still adjusting—and still changing.

Modern technology came first, soon after the war, and as it did in every corner of the nation, it altered the way Nashvillians learned, moved about, conducted business, and entertained themselves. The city's airport near Donelson, expanded to more than seventeen hundred acres, welcomed the jet age and made New York and Los Angeles Nashville's neighbors as surely as the steamboat had brought New Orleans and Louisville closer in the 1820s. Computer technology automated and speeded up the flow of everything from news to bills—and also made personal transactions more distant and anonymous. Television was introduced to Nashville by station WSM in 1950, and within two decades it would reach into virtually every home and school in the city. And the interstate highway system, begun in the mid-1950s (and still unfinished a quarter of a century later), affected traffic patterns, neighborhoods, commercial districts, and transportation habits more profoundly than any physical change the city had ever undergone. Nashville was one of a handful of American cities at the crossroads of three interstate routes.

Another of the transformations the 1950s brought to the city was urban renewal. State and local governments, in partnership with the federal government, turned the Capitol Hill slums into landscaped slopes, high-rise buildings, and a tree-lined boulevard, James Robertson Parkway, named in honor of the father of Nashville. The multimillion-dollar project, launched in 1952, took more than six years to complete, and it was only the beginning phase of urban redevelopment in the city; subsequent undertakings affected additional districts and

Outdoor privies, dilapidated wooden shacks, and rubbish heaps marred Capitol Hill until urban renewal cleared the area in the 1950s. Within the residential slum were many once-elegant homes which had become gambling dens and houses of prostitution.

245

continued into the 1970s. The number of public housing units was more than doubled, the state government built several new structures in the capitol area, and a sustained period of private construction in the central city was initiated in 1957 with the opening of the Life and Casualty Insurance Company's thirty-one-story sky-scraper at Fourth Avenue and Church Street.

Urban renewal was not an unmixed blessing; what it added in beauty and usefulness, it sometimes took away through disruption and displacement of neighborhoods and families. The last of the city's redevelopment projects, in the Vanderbilt University district, would still be

unfinished at the end of the 1970s after a decade of bitter wrangles and lawsuits. Similar protests had accompanied the construction of an interstate highway through North Nashville and delayed another interstate project south and west of the downtown area.

The health of Nashville—the physical well-being of its people, the quality of its air and water—was far from satisfactory when electricity replaced coal as the principal source of heat and power in the 1940s, but slowly, the city began to scrub up its sooty face. The thick veil of smoke and smog that had hung over the downtown area was diminished, although

At the time I joined the Vanderbilt University Medical School faculty in 1944, the state of public health in Nashville was very poor. Davidson County had a distinguished public health officer, Dr. John Lentz, but the city of Nashville had no such leadership, and the combination of political, professional, and financial deficiencies was such that the city was not a safe place to live and raise children.

We had at Vanderbilt about two hundred cases of polio a year—we kept twenty or twenty-five respirators going at a time. Diarrhea was common. We still had numerous cases of tetanus, diphtheria, whooping cough, smallpox. We had a typhus epidemic in the mid-1940s, and eight or ten cases of typhoid fever a year. Venereal disease was a serious problem. So was lead poisoning. Nashville had both a county and a state hospital for tuberculosis patients.

The air in the downtown area at that time was so dirty that it was often impossible to see a traffic light from half a block away. The sewer system was dangerously inadequate. The only speech and hearing specialist in the city was an

elocutionist. There were no physical therapy programs at all, and no community mental health programs, and public health education left much to be desired.

In the past thirty-five years, some dramatic improvements have been made. Vaccines and immunization have all but eliminated polio, and antibiotics have wiped out the many childhood diseases that once were so prevalent. Tuberculosis has been virtually eradicated. We discovered at Vanderbilt that much of what was thought to be tuberculosis was actually histoplasmosis, and through drugs and supportive treatment, it too has been almost removed as a serious threat to health. Milk and water are now cleaner, coal smoke is gone from the air, sewer disposal is greatly improved, health education is better. The infant mortality rate in Davidson County is now less than one-third what it was in 1945.

Advances in medical science have helped to bring about these changes, and I'm happy to have been a part of that. TVA, bringing both electric power and innovative social and sanitary programs,

also helped. So did the unification of city and county governments. Nashville's public health is still not as good as it should be, but it's much better than it was. I think we have learned the lesson that good health—a safe place to live and raise children—is purchasable. It takes money, political commitment, professional skill—and those are things a city like Nashville can provide if it values the health of its people.

AMOS CHRISTIE, M.D.,
in a 1979 interview

automobile exhaust fumes soon presented a new hazard. The once-limpid Cumberland River had long since lost its clear appearance and its purity, and probably would never regain them—but dams on the river and its tributaries made it unlikely that it would flood again as it did in 1927, and the altered chemical content of the water presumably lessened the likelihood of a hard freeze of the river such as occurred in 1940.

Foul air and water and an inadequate sanitary sewer system contributed greatly to Nashville's health problems during and after the war. Tuberculosis and polio were not uncommon then, and even such diseases as typhoid fever and typhus were reported occasionally. But by the end of the 1950s, vaccines and antibiotics—including some developed with the aid of Vanderbilt University medical researchers—had made most such communicable diseases rare, if not nonexistent. Programs of health care, training and research at Vanderbilt and at Meharry Medical College had not only helped to improve the general health of the city but also enhanced Nashville's reputation as an important national medical center. Among medical practitioners, there was an apparent consensus that the eradication of communicable diseases and improvements in air and water quality and waste removal were the most significant developments in Nashville in the 1940s and 1950s.

Nashville's higher education institutions enjoyed unprecedented growth during the 1950s, partly as a consequence of the influx of returning war veterans. By the end of the decade, the city had thirteen colleges and universities which awarded baccalaureate or higher degrees, and their diversity was impressive—Vanderbilt and Peabody, Fisk and Meharry, Lipscomb and Trevecca, Scarritt and Tennessee A&I, and these in addition: American Baptist Theological Seminary, a predominantly black institution; Free Will Baptist Bible College; Belmont College, a

When Nashville's economy rebounded in the 1950s, labor strikes sometimes resulted in violence—as when a trucker's windshield was riddled with bullets during a walkout in 1957.

Baptist liberal arts school built around Adelicia Acklen's old mansion; the law school of the YMCA; and a night-school branch campus of the University of Tennessee. In addition to its many church colleges, the city came to have so many churches, religious publishing enterprises, and denominational headquarters that in some ecclesiastical circles it was referred to as "the Protestant Vatican."

Colleges and churches were not the only fast-growing institutions in Nashville. Government at all levels—city, county, state, and federal—began an expansion after World War II that would continue through the 1970s. In time, the number of public employees would be greater than in any classification of private enterprise.

Suburbia was growing, too, beyond the

Noted American artist Georgia O'Keeffe and collector Carl Van Vechten (extreme left) came to Fisk University in 1947 when Van Vechten donated a collection of O'Keeffe paintings to the university. Fisk enhanced its reputation in art and music in the postwar years under the leadership of Charles S. Johnson (left), its first black president. At the Fisk Music Festival in 1949, the premiere performance (below) of "Golgotha is a Mountain" brought a standing ovation for (from left) soloist Charles Coleman, author Arna Bontemps, choir director John Ohl, and composer John W. Work.

Shortly before minor league baseball collapsed in Nashville, a crowd of more than 5,000 filled Sulphur Dell for the opening game of the 1960 season, when Jim Turner was managing the Nashville Vols.

fondest expectations of real estate developers and county government officials. All around the edge of the old city—and in more distant communities such as Donelson and Madison—subdivisions seemed to pop up overnight. A shopping center that opened in Madison in 1956 was called by its developers "the largest in the country"—yet within a decade, it would be dwarfed by the first of many completely enclosed and air-conditioned shopping malls that would threaten the future of consumer buying in downtown Nashville.

The 1960 census dramatized the continuing shift of population from the city to the county. For the first time in its history, Nashville's population declined (to 170,000)—and for the first time in a century, more people lived in Davidson County outside Nashville than within it. The city and county combined had just under 400,000 residents. Nashville's dwindling share of the total was a hint of serious economic and political consequences to come.

Along with the loss of people and business, the downtown area was in danger of losing some of its identity. The Nashville Vols seemed almost finished after more than a half-century of minor league play, and their home park, Sulphur Dell—the oldest baseball field in America— would finally be torn down. The demise of Union Station as a busy rail terminal was delayed by World War II, but only temporarily. It would come to be a relic of the past, worth preserving only for its architectural qualities and its symbolic importance to the city. To some, the thought of Nashville without baseball or trains was too terrible to contemplate.

In the postwar changes that affected Nashville so profoundly—technological innovation, urban renewal, developments in health and education, suburban growth, urban decay—it was ironic that a city with so many economic assets should be losing population and worried about its future. Nashville at the close of the 1950s resembled more than ever the urban communities of the South and the nation. It was an old town with new problems, a new city with old problems. In a nation that was between wars and full of great expectations, it was preoccupied with unfinished business at home.

Among its preoccupations were three matters of paramount importance. They, too, came into sharp focus in the 1950s and lasted far beyond those years, and they, too, permanently altered life in the city. One concerned development of the music industry, a presence in Nashville for decades but a potentially strong economic force only since the war. Another had to do with divisions and inequities between the city and the county, and the need for a unified metropolitan government.

The third issue that demanded attention was an age-old social problem that would not go away: racial segregation, discrimination, and inequality.

FROM THE VERY FIRST—from the days of James Robertson's scouting party and John Donelson's flotilla—Nashville had borne the dilemma of race in its flesh and blood. The contradictions of skin color, of freedom and slavery, of equality and segregation, had never been absent from the minds and lives of its people.

In the first unofficial enumeration of Davidson Countians, roughly one-fifth were black; two hundred years later, the proportion of blacks living in the county would be about the same. Between 1870 and 1960, non-whites in the city of Nashville constituted about one-third of the population, but they were always relegated to an inferior place in the governance and guidance of the community.

When "Black Bob" Renfroe ran the most popular tavern on the Public Square in the 1790s, Andrew Jackson and the other leading lights who enjoyed the hospitality of his "never disorderly place" must have known that he embodied an irreconcilable contradiction. Renfroe was a free man; he could vote, he could buy and sell land, he had certain standing in courts of law, he competed with whites on an equal basis for trade. But most of his fellow men and women of color were slaves. They had no rights; they were property, the same as cattle and sheep.

The contradiction begged correction. In a nation proclaiming all men to be created equal, logic demanded that the black minority must either be accorded the barest minimum of basic rights, as Bob Renfroe appeared to have, or the rights of the Bob Renfroes would have to be abolished.

In time, the white majority chose the latter course—in practice if not in law. The nation's highest court declared that slaves were not citizens and thus had no rights, and by a variety of legal and social maneuvers the rights of free blacks were effectively made meaningless. The pattern of economic and political and sexual exploitation of blacks continued. Even when a civil war was fought to resolve the issue of freedom and slavery, there was no place in America where blacks were accorded in every particular the same rights and privileges as whites.

Nashville was a house divided in that war, as surely as the nation was. In the aftermath of the conflict, it was possible for black men in Nashville and elsewhere to vote, hold office, and enjoy certain other constitutional rights. But whites never yielded their advantage; laws and ordinances and unwritten social codes steadily eroded the rights of black citizens. By the beginning of the twentieth century, after the United States Supreme Court had sanctioned the practice of "separate but equal" treatment of the races, pervasive and inequitable segregation had become a way of life, and it remained so for more than fifty years.

Black Nashvillians protested against the segregation of streetcars in 1905, but to no avail. They were excluded from all schools, churches, and public accommodations except those designated for blacks only. Their right to vote was so limited by poll taxes and other restrictive devices as to be nonexistent. Their presence in public office ended in 1913, and almost forty years passed before any black candidate won an election in the city.

In all those years, the legal right to vote was never taken away from Nashville's black citizens, but few of them voted, not even after the state's poll tax law was repealed in 1943. Of the ones who did, most were carefully controlled by ward heelers, men who kept incumbent politicians in office and their constituents in line by delivering blocs of votes in return for favors granted. Under such a system, apathy permeated the electorate, and in the absence of aggressive leadership, blacks could look only to such ward heelers as W.D. "Pie" Hardison and Henry "Good Jelly" Jones for political leverage. They were as effective as their white counterparts, but even so, there was a disparity: The white ward bosses (Gene "Little Evil" Jacobs being the most notorious) tended to hold seats on the city council. Hardison was put on the city payroll as a deputy coroner in 1941, but the shrewd and powerful "Good Jelly" ran his fiefdom from his alley cafe off Jefferson Street.

When black veterans came home from World War II there was a stirring of discontent with the continuing indignities of racial discrimination, and soon a few cracks began to appear in the wall of segregation. The first black patrolman was added to the police force in 1948, and in the early 1950s, Coyness L. Ennix, an attorney, was the first black to be appointed to the city school board. Fisk University also got its first black president, Charles S. Johnson, after the war.

But the most important sign of change was the election of two black lawyers, Z. Alexander Looby and Robert Lillard, to the city council. Lillard had long been active in ward politics in the city; Looby, more independent, had been a practicing attorney in Nashville since 1928. Once they gained office in 1951, the two men were able to give black voters at least a modicum of political power.

And then came *Brown*—the 1954 decision of the United States Supreme Court that threw out the "separate but equal" doctrine and outlawed segregation in public education. On September 1, 1955, a few months after the Supreme Court issued an order implementing its decision, a black barber named A.Z. Kelley took his oldest son, Robert, to East Nashville High School and sought to enroll him. The white principal, William H. Oliver (later to be superintendent of the school system), politely turned the Kelleys away.

Three weeks later, Robert Kelley's name headed a list of twenty-one plaintiffs in a federal court lawsuit calling for an end to segregation in the Nashville schools. The attorneys who filed the suit were Thurgood Marshall, chief legal counsel of the National Association for the Advancement of Colored People (now a United States Supreme Court justice); Avon N. Williams, a black attorney from Nashville (now a state senator from Davidson County); and Z. Alexander Looby, who was then completing his first term on the city council.

The city board of education, with Coyness

Z. Alexander Looby (right) had been a Nashville attorney for more than twenty-five years and a member of the city council for four years when he and his law partner, Avon N. Williams, represented black plaintiffs in a desegregation lawsuit against the city school board in 1955. Twenty-five years later, the case was still on the federal court docket and Williams was still the plaintiffs' attorney.

Mahlon Griffith (center), his wife Mary (lower right), and Harold and Roberta Street (behind Griffith) leading their children to Glenn School in East Nashville on the first day of public school desegregation, September 9, 1957.

After the *Brown* decision, my wife Mary tried to enroll our daughter Belinda at Glenn School near our home in East Nashville, but they wouldn't admit her. That was in 1955. So we became plaintiffs in the lawsuit against the Nashville schools. In 1957, when desegregation began, we took our daughter Jacqueline to Glenn. A lot of whites were there trying to stop us, but we got her enrolled. Nashville claimed to be the Athens of the South back then, but when John Kasper came to town, he destroyed that myth. He brought out the worst in a lot of white people, and it was ugly, and frightening.

Belinda never attended a desegregated public school. Jacqueline went on to finish at Cameron High, which was still a black school. Our son Steven, who started at Glenn a year after Jacqueline, later graduated at Overton.

My wife was fired from her job with the Pet Milk Company after we got involved in the schools. I was a clerk at the post office, and they tried to fire me, but I got backing from Washington. I was president of the National Alliance of Postal Employees, a black union, and in the years I worked at the post office in

Nashville—1949 to 1965—I did everything I could to break up segregation there. The postmaster told me I'd never be promoted as long as I stayed there, and I wasn't—but I'm proud of what I accomplished.

Looking back on all that happened in those years, I think middle-class blacks have made a lot of progress, but the poor—and they're still the majority—haven't gained much.

It's a vicious circle—blacks lose their schools, their teachers and administrators; they go into majority-white schools where they're made to feel isolated and unwanted; they become alienated, resentment builds up, discipline and learning problems increase; they're suspended or drop out, and without skills or jobs or hope, they get into crime and dependency, they prey upon middle-class blacks and whites, and the cycle repeats itself. After all these years, we haven't learned much—we're still creating our own problems as a society.

Nashville never was nearly as bad as most Southern cities, and it has made a lot of progress. It's a city where things can be done to make life better for

everybody. But there's still so much that isn't the way it ought to be. When you see how poor people live, white and black, you have to wonder what the turmoil of the fifties and sixties was all about. I can't say whether what we have is worth what we had to go through to get it—I just can't say.

But I'll tell you this: I'd do it again. I would take my children through the mob to give them a fair chance to have the education and equal opportunity they're entitled to—in Nashville or anywhere else.

MAHLON GRIFFITH, in a 1979 interview

Court-ordered busing to eliminate racial segregation in Nashville's public schools was protested by white parents and their children at many schools, including Glencliff Elementary, in September 1971. In spite of the protests, thousands of children rode the buses to and from school.

Ennix dissenting, voted to continue segregation for a year while it studied the court's desegregation order, and the county school board did the same. It took two years for the city board to offer and reluctantly to implement a court-approved "stair-step" plan by which desegregation would begin with the first grade and continue a grade at a time for twelve years.

When the plan was put into effect in the fall of 1957, organized white protest groups appeared at five formerly all-white schools where thirteen black children were scheduled to enroll. John Kasper, a white man already under indictment for his involvement in racial agitation in the schools of Clinton, Tennessee, was the principal organizer of the Nashville protesters. Threatening phone calls and the circulation of anti-black and anti-Jewish literature accompanied the protest, and shouts and scuffling marred the enrollment of the black first-graders on September 9, but serious violence was averted.

Sixteen hours later, in the post-midnight darkness, a dynamite explosion ripped Hattie Cotton School in East Nashville, where one black child had enrolled with 390 whites the previous day. No one was ever arrested for the bombing, or for a second blast at Nashville's Jewish Community Center, an agency which an anonymous caller termed "the center of integrationists in Nashville."

In an atmosphere of intimidation and fear, only a handful of black parents continued to enroll their children in all-white schools. By 1960, the number of black students in desegregated schools had reached only forty-four in the city (there still were none in the county schools)—but there were more than 15,000 black students in the two school systems.

In 1963, the two systems were merged when Nashville and Davidson County established a metropolitan government. Desegregation inched

onward with the prodding of the plaintiff attorneys and the court. In 1970 a more comprehensive desegregation plan was finally ordered, and the following year another white protest, led by Metro Councilman Casey Jenkins, failed to block implementation of the plan, which required an increase in busing but left more than thirty schools in the outlying sections of the county unaffected.

By the end of the 1970s, white enrollment in

the public schools had fallen by about twenty-five percent, and private schools in the area—including more than a dozen recently established ones—had approximately tripled in size. Some public schools were still virtually all-white; others had resegregated and were majority-black again. Some of the desegregated schools had become stable and productive centers of learning; others were still preoccupied with racial problems. Protests by parents, white and black, had abated. A new status quo had been reached, and it was marked by lingering dissatisfaction and a sense of resignation among many people of both races. In 1979, *Kelley v. Board of Education* remained an unsettled case on the federal court docket, twenty-four years after it was first filed. Nashville still struggled with the legacy of school segregation.

Racial issues also had far-reaching consequences for higher education in Nashville. Another court suit, involving Tennessee State University and the University of Tennessee at Nashville, was initiated in 1968, and eleven years later, the University of Tennessee was still pursuing an appeal to prevent merger of its majority-white Nashville campus into the structure of traditionally black Tennessee State. The unusual lawsuit had pitted one branch of public higher education against another and placed the state in a costly legal conflict with itself. The unprecedented outcome in the lower federal courts introduced an array of desegregation issues that no other higher education institutions in the nation had faced.

Education was only one arena in which grievances against segregation and racial discrimination came to the surface. Within a short time after public school desegregation began, protest demonstrations spread into other areas of the community, and throughout the decade of the 1960s, tense confrontations between blacks and whites took place repeatedly in

public accommodations that whites claimed were reserved for their use only. The tactic of nonviolent protest by blacks and some white supporters, inspired by the leadership of Martin Luther King Jr. and led by a growing cadre of black Nashvillians, was met with sullen hostility and at times with violence from whites determined to resist the desegregation movement.

The first serious clash occurred in February 1960, when students from Fisk and Tennessee State universities and the American Baptist Theological Seminary took seats at the lunch counters of three downtown chain stores. They were taunted and cursed by white youths who gathered, and when the blacks did not respond, the insults erupted into physical attacks. Police moved in, the whites fled, and eighty-one nonresisting students who had taken seats and asked for service were arrested and jailed on charges of disorderly conduct.

There were instantaneous repercussions. The black community strongly supported the conduct of the sit-in by the students; black lawyers—and some whites—volunteered to defend the arrested protesters in court; local government officials formed biracial committees to mediate the dispute; and the students vowed to continue nonviolent sit-in demonstrations until segregation was ended. One of their leaders, a black Methodist minister and divinity school student at Vanderbilt University named James M. Lawson Jr., was expelled by the executive committee of the university's governing board—a committee dominated by old-line Nashville businessmen—and the action caused deep fissures in the university community that took years to heal.

The crisis dragged on through long months of confrontation and negotiation. By 1963, segregation barriers had fallen in most of the city's public accommodations and facilities, and local leaders of both races were beginning to think the

THIS IS THE CITY whose integration plan has been called a model for other Southern cities; where white mobs were quickly and cleanly handled during school openings, where Negroes have voted and enjoyed justice in the courts, where bus segregation was ended by quiet agreement between city and Negro leaders, where the racist demagogue John Kasper is now meditating in the county jail.

It is a good city. Yet early this month, in the words of a photographer who had just watched white hoodlums stuff cigarette butts down the collars of Negro college students, it was "a good city gone ugly." For the sit-in demonstrations of Negro students at a lunch counter have turned Nashville into one of the South's most explosive racial areas.

As I write this, a special biracial citizens' committee is trying to solve the dilemma, and a temporary cease-fire has been announced. But the damage is already staggering: city court trials have been a farce; seventy-seven Negro and three white college students were convicted and fined fifty dollars each for (non-violent) disorderly conduct; sixty-three more will soon be tried; the original eighty have been rearrested on state charges; mass meeting of Negroes follows mass meeting; rumor follows bomb threat. And the end is not in sight.

DAVID HALBERSTAM, in
The Reporter, **March 31, 1960**

Picketers protesting lunch-counter segregation file past a Church Street restaurant under the watchful eyes of policemen during a 1964 demonstration.

turmoil was ending. But in the spring of 1964, new demonstrations were staged at a few hold-out restaurants that still refused to serve blacks, and the protest took an ugly turn: Some of the blacks returned the aggressiveness of police and angry whites with an aggressiveness of their own, charges and countercharges of "police brutality" and "inciting to riot" were exchanged, and when it was all over, both the city's claim of moderation and enlightenment and the black protest movement's devotion to nonviolence had been seriously eroded.

The last half of the 1960s might have been a positive turning point for Nashville. The city had accomplished more social change with less violence than most Southern cities. It had influential citizens, white and black, who were capable of uniting the community. With a new and promising metropolitan government and a strong economy, Nashville had the necessary resources to move forward as an integrated society. Perhaps with better luck—and a little more vision and will—it might have brought its disparate racial and religious and socioeconomic groups together in a reconciling and transforming way.

But that did not happen. Instead, radicalism gained adherents and nonviolence declined. White resistance to further desegregation hardened. Black power and black separatism replaced integration as the goal of many civil rights activists. The Vietnam War intervened. Acts of violence bred acts of repression and reprisal.

In April 1967, three nights of rioting followed a controversial visit to Nashville by firebrand black power advocate Stokely Carmichael. A year later, the assassination of Martin Luther King Jr. in Memphis sent shock waves reverberating through Nashville and dozens of other cities. Just when Nashville might have been nearing a resolution of its racial problems, it experienced instead the worst night in a decade of discord as a spasm of violence and counterviolence gripped the city. Units of the Tennessee National Guard, armed for combat but ill-prepared for that prospect, were called in, and a curfew was imposed. When the grim and traumatic night finally ended, black and white Nashvillians faced yet another painful period of adjustment and recovery.

The 1970s were quieter years. After the anti-busing protest mounted by whites against the school system in 1971, race-related demonstrations were more widely spaced, shorter in duration, and less heated than they had been

Hundreds of people, black and white, joined hands at the Metro Court House on the Public Square in a demonstration to protest racial segregation in Nashville in 1964.

256

The Reverend Martin Luther King Jr., head of the Southern Christian Leadership Conference, inspired thousands of citizens in Nashville and elsewhere to protest segregation. At a Fisk University rally in 1964, he was joined on the podium by Lester McKinnie, a local protest leader, and John Lewis, formerly a student at American Baptist Theological Seminary and then a student at Fisk.

Through much of the 1960s, black students marching in protest against segregation were a common sight on the streets of Nashville. This march on James Robertson Parkway below the capitol took place in 1964.

257

Months after Dr. Martin Luther King was assassinated in Memphis in April 1968, James Earl Ray was arrested and charged with the killing. Police authorities escorted him in handcuffs to the federal courthouse in Nashville, where he pleaded guilty and was sentenced to life in the Tennessee Penitentiary.

Dr. Mitchell addressing the Chamber of Commerce.

. . . you tell us education is the answer to the problem; the Negro is unprepared! . . . No, education is not the answer. Education plus opportunity is the answer! And until the opportunity is created, and until the Negro student can feel assured that it is not just an illusion, the school dropout rate will continue to dismay us, and college students will continue to pour off their campuses in protest movements . . . .

But times are changing, we are told on television! And we tell you we have seen them change before . . . . Negroes need jobs NOW! If they are unlearned, teach them! If they are unskilled, train them! Do not hide behind test scores that have no relevance to the job to be performed but rather measure social values of the majority culture.

•

We cannot imagine what manner of Negro man you feel lives here in Nashville when you continue to ignore the examples of [strife in other cities] as though Nashville's time is not coming.

Gentlemen, Nashville is indeed fashioning a new face . . . . But tall buildings which allow you to gaze outward upon the green grass of suburbia cannot long shelter you from the despair, frustration and bitterness that continue to build around you.

In a city that unites its governments but leaves its people divided . . . a cruel mockery is made. But sitting as they are in the midst of all this proverty, your businesses are just such a mockery to so many.

What brave and unthinking men you are!

DR. EDWIN H. MITCHELL, chairman of the Metro Human Relations Commission, in a speech to the Nashville Area Chamber of Commerce, October 11, 1967

National Guard tanks rumbled through the intersection of Broadway and Twelfth Avenue in Nashville in April 1968 after rioting broke out in the wake of Martin Luther King's murder. A curfew had virtually emptied the streets when this photograph was taken.

previously. Protests as a means of effecting social change had become a part of the culture, though, and the tactics of the civil rights movement would be used frequently—in Nashville and elsewhere—by such diverse groups as women, college students, prison inmates, environmentalists, pacifists, homosexuals, Ku Klux Klansmen, labor unions, foreign students, the handicapped, the poor.

The issue that started it all—racial segregation—was finally finished as a matter of law. But segregation as a matter of fact was still visible. Whether from prejudice or economic necessity or preference or force of habit, white and black Nashvillians still tended in the main to live their lives more separate than united—and in that, they resembled the preponderance of Americans. The dilemma of race endured.

Whites and blacks had belonged to the same Baptist church in Nashville until sometime in the 1840s, when there was established a colored mission. It had a white superintendent, but the Reverend Nelson Merry became the first black person to be in charge of the mission in about 1852. He had been a slave, and I understand that his freedom was purchased by the white church, where he worked as a janitor. The pastor, R.B.C. Howell, prepared him for ordination and placed him over the mission church. Reverend Merry served under the auspices of the mother church until after the Civil War, when the worshipers at the colored mission submitted a petition to the white church asking for freedom and independence. The separation took place in 1865, and the First Colored Baptist Church came into being.

In 1965, when we observed our 100th anniversary, we changed our name to First Baptist Church, Capitol Hill. On that occasion, I delivered a sermon to our congregation which took the form of a letter to the white First Baptist Church on Seventh Avenue. The burden of what I said was that these two churches ought to get together to talk about our common

history. I recognized that while we had a common history, we were not really one. We were never one—we were always two—but at the time, we were both talking about building new structures, and it seemed to me appropriate that we should consider becoming one church. I said here we are, five blocks apart, with a common history, claiming allegiance to the same kingdom, the same Christ, the same Bible, the same Father—and we are separated. I talked about the importance of keeping alive our respective traditions and heritage, but I said we should seek to be truly Christian. I think both Nelson Merry and R.B.C. Howell, had they been alive in 1965, would have approved of such a union.

Not everyone in my congregation liked the suggestion. Some felt we would be in great danger of losing our identity completely; others didn't know quite what to make of it.

I sent a copy of the sermon to Franklin Paschal, the pastor of the white church, and through friends I learned that there was much informal discussion of it—though as far as I know, it was never brought up officially.

It was a long time before I got an

answer. Finally, Dr. Paschal wrote, thanking me for my letter. He said that in these turbulent times, we need more—not fewer—good churches. He made it clear that he had no interest in forming any sort of union with our congregation.

And that was the end of it—nothing happened after that. I had simply wanted conversation in both churches on this subject, and to an extent, I think that happened. But we have gone our separate ways.

THE REVEREND KELLY MILLER SMITH, in a 1979 interview

IF ITS REACTION to racial issues had been typical of the nation's, Nashville's response to the pervasive crisis in urban government was far more imaginative, more comprehensive, and more successful. Long neglect of local needs was the factor that finally forced attention on the problems of city-county government here, but once the needs and the problems were acknowledged, Nashville and Davidson County addressed them in a novel way.

Prior to World War II, the separate governments of the city and the county operated independently but compatibly according to traditions that had not changed appreciably for more than a century. Nashville was an urban political jurisdiction governed by a mayor and a city council; surrounding Davidson County was a rural expanse of farms and country villages administered by a county judge and a quarterly court. The two entities had in common a few basic interests and needs, but not enough of either to make formal union a serious consideration.

But the postwar years brought an array of unprecedented problems—urban decay and suburban expansion, inequitable taxation, a decline in public services, factional political rivalries. Five areas of the county became incorporated towns in the 1950s, joining Belle Meade, the oldest such jurisdiction, which had incorporated in 1938. Nashville, having annexed virtually no county land since 1927, grew hardly at all in the 1940s, while the rest of the county experienced a tremendous increase in population—and with the shift in people there began a shift in needs, interests, and political power.

The spillover into suburbia extended urban complexities into the countryside. Sanitary sewers were needed, but the resources to provide them were not at hand. Fire protection, provided on a subscription basis by private companies, left much to be desired. Law enforcement, streets and highways, water lines, schools, and health care all were inadequate to meet the growing demands. Charges and countercharges of "suburban freeloading" and "city tax-grabbing" mounted as the problems grew year by year, and the rival political and governmental forces shifted blame and avoided action.

Early in the 1950s, Nashville elected a new mayor, Ben West, and Davidson County voters chose Beverly Briley to be county judge. The two men and their political forces maintained a delicate balance of power that dictated caution in their handling of metropolitan problems, but the problems had become so acute that major adjustments were unavoidable.

The first tentative step toward change was a comprehensive study of the city-county impasse. A commission created by the state legislature took up the matter, and its report in 1952 recommended an extension of Nashville's boundaries into the suburban fringes and a transfer of city health, education, and welfare functions to the county. West and Briley neither supported nor opposed the recommendations, and four years passed with little change. In 1956 another study was made, and from it came a "Plan of Metropolitan Government" that was carefully designed to gain the support of Briley, who seemed to favor city-county consolidation, and West, who leaned toward large-scale annexation of county land by the city.

In essence, the plan called for immediate annexation that would lead eventually to a single metropolitan government. The *Nashville Tennessean* reacted favorably, and Briley expressed cautious approval. Mayor West was noncommittal, but the *Nashville Banner*, which generally supported his administration, came out in favor of the study proposals, and with that shift in the balance of power the movement toward governmental consolidation gained momentum. When the legislature passed an

260

Nashville Mayor Ben West (left) and Davidson County Judge Beverly Briley stood together in support of local government consolidation when the issue was first put to the voters in 1958, but the proposal was defeated. Four years later, with Briley leading the proponents of merger and West opposing it, the electorate said yes to Metro.

Ten Nashville and Davidson County citizens made up the first commission appointed in 1957 to draw up a charter for local government consolidation; four years after the charter was voted down, eight of the ten commission members were reappointed to try again, and their second effort succeeded. Members of the original commission were (seated from left) Rebecca Thomas, R.N. Chenault, G.S. Meadors, and Thomas E. McGrath; (standing from left) Z. Alexander Looby, K. Harlan Dodson Jr., Edward Hicks, Cecil Branstetter, Victor S. Johnson, and Carmack Cochran, the chairman. In 1961, Joe Torrence and Charles Warfield replaced Hicks and McGrath.

enabling law in 1957 and authorized the creation of a commission to draw up a metropolitan government charter, it was clear that a formal attempt to resolve the Nashville-Davidson County division would be made.

The charter commission, made up of five members appointed by the mayor and five named by the county judge, took a year to complete its work, and on June 17, 1958, the charter was presented to the voters for their judgment. The *Banner* and the *Tennessean*, laying aside their customary roles as adversaries, cam-

paigned vigorously for approval of the document, and both Briley and West decided to do the same. Additional support came from the Nashville Chamber of Commerce, the Nashville Trades and Labor Council, the League of Women Voters, and many professional and civic organizations. The black community was divided. Since the city was more than one-third black but the rest of the county was more than ninety percent white, some blacks (including Robert Lillard, the councilman) feared that merger would dilute their growing political

Tennessean cartoonist Tom Little drew these two conflicting caricatures of Metro Mayor Beverly Briley to show him opposing a local tax on automobiles in 1963 and favoring such a tax in 1968. Briley and the Tennessean had both supported city-county government merger, but later the newspaper was a frequent critic of the mayor. Tom Little won a Pulitzer Prize for his cartooning in 1957, and in 1962, Tennessean writers Nat Caldwell and Gene S. Graham won the Pulitzer Prize for national reporting.

strength. Others listened to Z. Alexander Looby, who had been one of two blacks on the charter commission and who urged approval of the charter at the polls.

When the votes were counted, the city had approved the charter by a margin of three to two, but the county had rejected it by a similar proportion. The delicately constructed coalition of political forces, newspapers, business interests, racial groups, and special-purpose organizations had almost accomplished a structural reorganization unprecedented in American urban society—but in the end, an alliance of rural and suburban interests and ward politicians in the city had prevailed.

Soon after the charter was rejected, the city council used its strong annexation powers for the first time to take in two large areas of county territory. Mayor West approved of the first because it was largely industrial land, but he vetoed the second—a residential annexation—because it did not provide for a referendum. He was promptly overridden, and some county officials charged that the mayor had privately engineered the council's action. Then, when West and the council levied a tax on all automobiles using the city streets—a thinly veiled means of drawing new revenue from county residents—the movement for metropolitan government was revived.

West and the council, having gained new strength through annexation, no longer favored consolidation, but many county officials did, and so did the local legislative delegation, and they managed to get new enabling legislation passed in 1961. A local referendum calling for creation of a new charter commission was approved in a light but surprisingly favorable vote in the summer of 1961, and the commission, made up of seven men and one woman from the original body and two new appointees, went promptly to work. They made few changes in the original document. Then, on June 28, 1962, the voters of Nashville and Davidson County were given a second chance to merge their governments.

Judge Briley and the *Tennessean* again led the pro-consolidation forces, and a broad-based "Citizens Committee for Better Government" organized a door-to-door campaign. Mayor West campaigned vigorously against the charter, and his critics charged that his opposition stemmed from a personal calculation that his chances of being elected mayor of the new government were not good. The *Banner*, apparently seeing the referendum as a political choice between West and Briley, stuck with West and advocated rejection of the charter. The *Tennessean* also saw the vote in political terms, calling it an opportunity for the voters to oust "the mayor's political machine."

Divisions on the issue cut confusingly across political, ideological, racial, residential, and socioeconomic lines, and the campaign was heated and divisive. The outcome was surprising: a clear victory for consolidation. In the city, the vote was roughly 21,000 to 15,000; in the rest of the county, it was about 15,000 to 12,000. For the first time in the nation, a metropolitan community had won the approval of an urban-suburban electorate for government merger.

In the fall of 1962, the voters elected Beverly Briley over the county's tax assessor, Clifford Allen, to be mayor of the new government. Ben West, for reasons that were never clear, chose

262

On April 1, 1963, the Metropolitan Government of Nashville-Davidson County was officially established, and Beverly Briley (center) was sworn in as the first mayor of the new government. Vice Mayor George H. Cate Jr. (right) and forty members of the Metropolitan Council also took office. With Briley and Cate on the platform was attorney Charles Warfield, a member of the Metro Charter Commission.

TWO VIEWS OF METRO GOVERNMENT:

In almost every phase of government, from the schools to the rural road program, the people of Davidson County are facing crises which could be wiped out almost overnight with the adoption of the charter for consolidated government. We can only look for further trouble and confusion unless consolidation is put into effect. As we stand now, people who have absolutely no voice in the government of the city can be annexed . . . taxed with green stickers . . . taxed with service charges . . . and they have no recourse. Under the proposed charter, all the people will have a voice in government. Today is an historic day in our lives—if the people turn out and vote.

BEVERLY BRILEY,
Davidson County Judge,
in the *Nashville Tennessean*,
June 28, 1962

We are called upon to decide by our votes whether we will continue with the known and tested structure of our present city and county governments—imperfect as they may be—or embark on an attempted "consolidation" of these two governments with a metropolitan charter which is novel, untried, untested, and the constitutionality of which is yet to be ascertained. Metro is presented as a cure-all for the ills of local government, a magic formula that will bring more services, yet cost less money—a Utopian system that would bring a new wave of unity and harmony to Nashville. You know human nature better than that.

BEN WEST,
Mayor of Nashville,
in the *Nashville Banner*,
June 21, 1962

More than a decade after the Capitol Hill urban renewal project was completed, some Nashvillians still occupied shacks such as these on Tenth Avenue, just a few blocks from the capitol. Nashville Congressman Richard Fulton (center), Chamber of Commerce president David K. Wilson (left foreground) and businessman Inman Otey (in background, interviewing resident) were among a group of local leaders touring the area.

not to be a candidate. A forty-one-member metropolitan council—including a vice mayor, George H. Cate Jr.—was also elected. Legal challenges to the new structure were unsuccessful, and on April 1, 1963, the Metropolitan Government of Nashville-Davidson County, Tennessee, was formally inaugurated.

Because the government could not immediately deliver all services on an equitable basis, it designated for purposes of taxation an urban services district, in which all government departments operated, and a general services district, in which fire protection, sewers, water drainage, street lighting, and refuse collection remained a private responsibility. Incorporation of areas into the urban services district would take place gradually as the full range of government support could be provided. In a concession to the satellite cities in Davidson County which had been incorporated prior to the charter vote, the communities of Belle Meade, Berry Hill, Forest Hills, Goodlettsville, Lakewood, and Oak Hill were allowed to retain their charters and were made a part of the general services district.

Under Metro, as the new government was soon called, all departments of the old city and county governments were merged and con-solidated, and a more responsive and efficient operation replaced the fragmented, duplicative, and inequitable systems of the past. The worst fears of Metro's opponents did not materialize: Nashville did not lose its identity, nor did the more than two dozen incorporated and unincorporated towns, villages, neighborhoods, and districts that had long given the larger community much of its diverse character and quality. From Joelton to Antioch, from Old Hickory to Bellevue, from Bordeaux to Donelson, there remained as much cohesiveness and familiarity as before—and Nashville, at the center, was stronger and more prosperous and more attractive than it had ever been. It was also the envy of many an American metropolis crippled by government fragmentation, and the model for some cities which chose in time to follow Nashville's example.

Metro was no instant panacea for the urban ills of Nashville and Davidson County. The problems had not arisen overnight, and they could not be swept away by a single act, however dramatic or extraordinary. But the community's willingness to consider a new approach to local government—and the endorsement of such an endeavor by the voters—set

264

With Air Force One and a battery of photographers in the background, President John F. Kennedy (left) leaves the Nashville airport for a speaking engagement at Vanderbilt University. Seated with Kennedy in the limousine are Tennessee Governor Frank Clement and Senators Albert Gore Sr. and Estes Kefauver. A few months after his Nashville visit, Kennedy was assassinated while riding in a limousine in Dallas, Texas.

Nashville apart from other cities in the nation and gave it a certain distinctiveness. Among urban administrators, politicians, and scholars of American cities, Nashville was recognized as a pacesetting community. Beverly Briley, in his twelve years as mayor, was a vigorous proponent of metropolitan government as a modern approach to urban problems; former Congressman Richard Fulton, who succeeded Briley in 1975, further advanced the reputation of the government as he led Nashville to the observance of its two hundredth birthday.

In 1780, the first settlers who came into this river valley from North Carolina signed their names to the Cumberland Compact, an informal document which was intended as a statement of regional self-government. Three years later, before the town of Nashville was formally named, the North Carolina legislature created Davidson County and gave it jurisdiction over much of the mid-Cumberland region. One hundred and eighty years after that, the formation of Metropolitan Nashville-Davidson County represented a return of the modern urban community on the Cumberland to its original status—a voluntary union of diverse people in a system of regional self-government. No doubt James Robertson would have been pleased.

For all its pride in metropolitanism, however, Nashville's recognition in the nation and the world in the 1970s did not derive from its contemporary form of local government. Neither was it universally celebrated as the home of Andrew Jackson, nor as the site of the last major Civil War battle, nor as the Athens of the South. Its national and international reputation was not political or military or academic or religious, though it claimed a certain distinction in all those areas.

Instead, Nashville's claim to fame was musical. From the Deep South to the Far West to the Canadian border, from Tokyo and Sydney to London and Moscow, Nashville was known as the Mecca of Country Music, the motherland of an art form that had become internationally recognized. Nashville was Music City, U.S.A.

FOR A QUARTER of a century after radio station WSM started broadcasting the Grand Ole Opry in 1926, the weekly program of music and entertainment gradually built a large and widely scattered audience over a vast area of the country. In the Virginia mountains, the Carolina low country, the Texas plains, the Dakota hills—wherever the station's powerful signal reached—a diverse group of people found solace in plaintive vocal laments of hard times on the land and skillful instrumental renditions of familiar old-time tunes. Not until after World War II did that audience begin to emerge as a potentially cohesive and potent force—and that is when music set in motion an economic and physical metamorphosis in Nashville.

In its first decade on the air, the Opry provided exposure and a base for a handful of musicians who laid the foundation for the contemporary country music industry. It was not called country music then—the more common labels were hillbilly music, or simply old-time music—but those who heard the fiddles and banjos and mandolins and guitars did not need a name for the harmonious sounds they made. From the hills and hollows of Appalachia to the delta of the Mississippi, myriad versions of that music had been played and sung on the porches and in the churches and at the crossroads country stores for longer than the oldest family patriarchs could remember. It was the music of the rural South, of hard-pressed country people. The gift of radio was to spread it, to give it a far-flung mass audience.

WSM was not the only station to broadcast old-time music in the early days of radio, nor was it the first. (It was not even the first in Nashville; a small station, WDAD, beat WSM to the air with fiddle and string-band music in 1925.) But WSM beamed the Grand Ole Opry a greater distance for more years than any other station, and the Opry in turn put country songs—and Nashville—on the musical map. The first line of credits for those accomplishments went to two young men who were not musicians: Edwin W. Craig and George D. Hay.

It was Craig, the thirty-two-year-old son of National Life and Accident Insurance Company President C.A. Craig, who got the company into broadcasting, and it was Hay, age thirty, who as station manager and chief announcer introduced "barn-dance" music to WSM's program format.

National Life created WSM, it was said, because Edwin Craig was far more interested in the new invention of radio than he was in the insurance business—and as the heir apparent to the company presidency, it seemed important to keep him happy. If WSM was thus more of an experimental toy than an investment for profit, it was an expensive one; though the station increased its power from 1,000 watts in 1925 to 50,000 seven years later, though it became an early affiliate of the NBC network, though it claimed to have the tallest radio tower in the world, and though its clear-channel signal could be heard in much of the United States and Canada, the station accumulated a deficit of almost a million dollars in its first decade of operation.

But while the station lost money, the insurance company did not. Even in the leanest years of the Depression, National Life's sales increased an average of five or six percent a year, while the insurance industry as a whole suffered heavy losses. One explanation for that anomaly was that National Life's main business was selling so-called "industrial" or "weekly-premium" insurance to farmers and wage-earners of limited means—and it was just such people who listened to WSM radio in general and the Grand Ole Opry in particular.

George Hay was the first to recognize the connection. The owners of the company tended at

Long before he became known as "the solemn old judge," George D. Hay was WSM Radio's first general manager and chief announcer. It was Hay who convinced skeptical WSM officials that old-time fiddling and "country bumpkin" shenanigans would attract a large audience—and sell a lot of insurance.

first to see WSM in cultural rather than commercial terms, but Hay drew on his radio experience in Memphis and Chicago to demonstrate the powerful new station's influence in a much broader listening area. The owners were content to offer light classical music, lectures, dance bands, and studio orchestra performers—all catering to the sophisticated tastes of well-to-do Nashvillians; Hay agreed, but he also put a bearded fiddler named Uncle Jimmy Thompson on the air, and when phone calls and telegrams of enthusiastic approval poured into the station, the bond between the company's insurance business and its radio music was forever sealed. The cultured citizens of Nashville would have to take a few hoe-downs with their waltzes and operatic arias.

WSM did not even advertise insurance until early New Deal optimism seemed about to turn the Depression around. It did not need to advertise; the connection between the Opry, WSM, and National Life was advertisement enough to open the doors of receptive buyers. Lovers of the music bought lots of insurance. Agents in the field enjoyed a special advantage as representatives of "the Grand Ole Opry Insurance Company." George Hay delighted in presenting the

Opry musicians as ignorant hayseeds, mountaineer moonshiners, and clowning hillbillies. The musicians themselves—most of whom were not mountaineers at all, but Nashville-area salesmen, factory workers, repairmen, and even classically trained musicians—benefited from the opportunity to earn money from their instrumental and vocal talents. And the owners of the company and its radio station took special satisfaction in the profits they reaped—thanks in large measure to the Opry connection.

In the home office and the board room of National Life, there was considerable distaste for the music, and in the upper-class sections of Nashville there was embarrassment and alarm that the Opry was making the city a national laughingstock as "the hillbilly capital of the nation." But it was also helping to make a good many of the company's stockholders wealthy, and in the interest of good business, the Opry came to be seen as an asset too valuable to be discarded.

The earliest of the old-time music artists to gain recognition—such people as Uncle Dave Macon, the Carter family, Sam and Kirk McGee, and Fiddlin' John Carson—embraced a wide range of instruments, moods, and styles with their music. Their ballads, folk songs, fast instrumental numbers, and gospel songs were far more serious than humorous; it was George Hay's packaging, as much as anything else, that added humor and buffoonery to the radio mixture. For example, Hay took a versatile musical group organized by Humphrey Bate, a Vanderbilt-educated physician, replaced their business suits with overalls and straw hats and brogans, and billed them as a country band called "the Possum Hunters."

Most of the musicians were interesting and colorful enough without the hayseed packaging. Banjoist Dave Macon, born in a country hamlet called Smart Station, lived as a teen-ager in

Clowning, colorful, eccentric Uncle Dave Macon was the Grand Ole Opry's mainstay in its first decade, and he played on as the show's revered elder statesman until his death in 1952.

During and after the years of World War II, the Grand Ole Opry enjoyed nationwide popularity as the original stars of the show were joined by a second generation of headliners. Among them were these three: comedian Rod Brasfield, cowboy singer Red Foley, and Cousin Minnie Pearl of Grinder's Switch—and Ward-Belmont College.

downtown Nashville, where his father ran a hotel; a clever and skillful entertainer, he had worked in vaudeville and made records and public appearances before the Grand Ole Opry first went on the air. Jimmy Thompson, born and raised in rural Tennessee, was past seventy-five when he first fiddled on the air for WSM, and his fondness for whiskey later got him in trouble with Hay.

In the 1930s, numerous changes came to the Opry. Hay's tenure as station manager ended (though he remained as the Opry's announcer). More professional musicians were brought in—most of them, for the first time, from outside the Nashville area. A booking agency was set up to promote tours and arrange public appearances as a supplement to the musicians' incomes. A wider variety of acts was added to the show's format, including cowboy music and Western swing, made popular by the movies. NBC put a half-hour of the Opry on its Saturday night schedule, most of the show's performers also made records, and a Hollywood movie called "The Grand Ole Opry" was produced,

starring a young fiddler named Roy Acuff. Fans crowded the WSM studio in such numbers that the show had to be moved several times, finally ending up in the three-thousand-seat Ryman Auditorium in 1941.

In a decade of economic depression and poverty, the Grand Ole Opry paradoxically rose to a higher level of professionalism and commercialism, adding thousands of new enthusiasts as it went. During the war, the Opry's music was spread farther to military bases throughout the nation and overseas by traveling entertainers from Nashville, and by 1950 its popularity had spawned a "second generation" of stars and given Nashville itself much visibility as the home base of a thriving American art form.

The new wave of headline entertainers—Pee Wee King, Red Foley, Ernest Tubb, Eddy Arnold, Kitty Wells, Bill Monroe, Lester Flatt, Earl Scruggs—broadened the range of styles in which the music was sung and played. Because of the Opry they were identified with Nashville, but not many of them were in fact Nashvillians (Kitty Wells was one of the few), and even Ten-

Nashville's reputation as the home of country music and a major American entertainment center began to grow after the war, and Nashville characters playing starring roles in motion pictures added to the reputation. Among them were (clockwise from upper left) Claude Jarman Jr., Tex Ritter, Johnny Cash, Kris Kristofferson, Dinah Shore, and Pat Boone.

nessee was new to many of them. (Nashville did claim Opry comedienne Cousin Minnie Pearl; in private life she was Sarah Ophelia Colley Cannon, a longtime resident of the city and an alumna of stylish Ward-Belmont College.) But whatever their origins or their individual talents, the postwar crop of Opry celebrities created an

arresting phenomenon in Nashville. They represented "new money" in an "old-money" town, and they resembled the established rich only in their wealth and their conservatism. Beyond that, they were often colorful and conspicuous, in contrast to the discreet anonymity of the old guard. (The musicians were also con-

With its back door opening on the alley beside the Ryman, Tootsie's Orchid Lounge was a favorite hangout of Opry stars, would-be stars, fans, and lower Broadway beer drinkers. Tootsie Bess, the proprietress, found space on the walls for just about everybody's picture.

When the Opry played at the Ryman Auditorium, the scene could best be described as organized chaos: musicians and an assortment of fans, officials, and hangers-on milling about onstage and backstage while members of the Opry company performed under the spotlight.

Through the window of a music shop on lower Broadway, a young man looks covetously at a steel guitar on display. Before the Opry moved to its new quarters, thousands of fans filled the streets around the Ryman Auditorium each weekend.

troversial at times—as in 1957, when Ernest Tubb fired pistol shots in the main lobby of the National Life building.)

Old Nashville still shunned the Opry and its big-name entertainers, even when the music became a fifty-million-dollar industry in the city in the 1950s. Not even Roy Acuff's Republican candidacy for governor in 1948 or Tex Ritter's run for the United States Senate in 1970 were enough to remove completely the social barrier that separated the Opry's fortunes from those of Belle Meade.

The city took a little more pride in some of its native celebrities in the movies and popular music after the war—"Hit Parade" crooner Snooky Lanson, comedian Phil Harris, actress-vocalist Dinah Shore, and bandleader-composer Francis Craig, whose recording of a song called "Near You" was a national smash hit in 1947—but they were only a few compared to the Opry's many, and they were also distant, whereas the country music world's bright lights and shiny guitars were here to be seen and heard.

Still another turn in the evolution of Nashville music came with the arrival of a young song-writer and performer named Hank Williams. Writing and singing songs of loneliness and lament—country blues—he produced one hit after another, and his "honky-tonk" style of music not only became the dominant form among country performers but also attracted many pop singers to the field. There had been country singers who recorded popular songs— Eddy Arnold was one—but until Williams

When you say "music industry" in Nashville you mean country music, of course, even though Columbia Records does 10 percent of its pop recording there . . . . Nashville is and always has been the spiritual home of country music, "hillbilly heaven," a fact properly noted in more than one country song, and it is never so evident as on a warm weekend, when the crowds pour into town for the Friday- and Saturday-night Opry performances—coming in from an average of 500 miles away by every means imaginable, living out of campers in downtown parking lots, strolling up and down Opry Place and Broadway in their Western clothes, nosing through the souvenir and record shops, having a beer at Tootsie's Orchid Lounge, taking one of the tour buses from the Opry House so they can see Music Row and Hank Williams' old home ("That 1952 Cadillac in the driveway is the one Hank died in on January 1, 1953") and the Biltmore Courts Motel ("Right there's where Don Gibson wrote 'Oh Lonesome Me'"), and finally squatting on the curb in front of the ugly red-brick Grand Ole Opry House three hours before the doors open, sitting there emptying a box of Minnie Pearl's Fried Chicken and trying to figure out a way to get in for a show that was sold out seven weeks in advance. "When I die," says the old guitar picker, "I'm going to Nashville."

PAUL HEMPHILL, in
*The Nashville Sound: Bright
Lights and Country Music* (1970)

271

Atkins performing for the Vanderbilts at Cheekwood.

ALL THOSE VANDERBILTS HOLD A FAMILY REUNION

By Roy Reed
Special to The New York Times

NASHVILLE, March 18 [1973]—Why would the Vanderbilts, who are usually associated with Newport and the more expensive reaches of Manhattan, hold a family reunion in Tennessee?

The answer is not difficult.

The university here that bears their name is celebrating an important anniversary and they were asked to come down and join in. More than a hundred of them came.

The university and its chancellor, Dr. Alexander Heard, a Georgian who became a distinguished political scientist before coming here in 1963, arranged two days of entertainment for the visitors. It ranged from a lavish dinner party last night at Cheekwood, a country estate turned into an arts center and botanical garden . . . to a tour of Andrew Jackson's home today.

If the Vanderbilts learned anything of consequence during their two days at the school, it might have been a lesson taught by an unlikely teacher named Chet Atkins, a former hillbilly.

He was introduced for a performance last night as one of the stars of that other, non-Vanderbilt world in Nashville, the music industry. Mr. Atkins plays the guitar better than nearly everybody else in the world.

He began with some classical picking that might have reminded Eastern visitors of Segovia. Then he paused to tune his guitar, and as he did so he told a little joke to fill in the silence.

"I think I'd been playing about 20 years before I found out I couldn't tune too well," he said, his bony face expressionless, his voice thick with the Southern hills. The crowd chuckled politely. Then he added, without looking up from his tuning, "By then, I was too rich to quit."

The Vanderbilts did not laugh much at that. Perhaps it had not occurred to them that Mr. Atkins was richer than some of them. He earned it all with his magic fingers.

He finished tuning, and then he laid some country music on them. About halfway through the "Black Mountain Rag," Newport toes began to tap and Park Avenue shoulders began to sway, and it appeared that the Vanderbilts had started to get a glimmer of what it was that made this hillbilly one of them. They clapped for a long time when he finished.

---

brought his music to Nashville, few pop artists had found "crossover" material in the country sphere. Williams's contributions were a foretaste of the greater musical fusion to come.

Along with the music, Williams also introduced a different personal style to the growing country music colony. He was a brooding loner, a rebel, a youthful misfit. Even the Opry did not know what to make of him. His personal problems—particularly with alcohol—seemed to match his somber taste in music. He was fired from the Opry in 1952 because of his drinking, and on New Years Day 1953 he died in the back seat of his Cadillac. In just five years in the limelight, the twenty-nine-year-old musician

had produced two dozen hit songs—and almost singlehandedly changed the course of country music.

By 1960, the recording industry in Nashville—studios, music publishers, artists, licensing organizations, talent agents, promoters, and other allied interests—had become a mainstay of the local economy. The Grand Ole Opry, nearing a half-century of continuous weekly broadcasting, was larger and more popular than ever. Through road shows, recordings, televison appearances, and related activities, many country music stars were earning more than $100,000 a year, and some of them were millionaires. Rock and roll had slowed the growth of country

With instructions and a little body English from Roy Acuff, President Richard M. Nixon tries to yo-yo on the stage of the Grand Ole Opry. Nixon was present for the first show in the new Opry House in 1974, during which he played the piano.

music, but only temporarily—and even as new forms proliferated, Nashville recording companies picked up some of the business.

In the atmosphere of creativity and ferment that surrounded the industry in Nashville early in the 1960s, musicians began to speak reverently of a mystical quality called "the Nashville Sound." It was heralded as a musical miracle drug, an elixir that revived old performers and lifted new ones to stardom, and Nashville came to be thought of by some artists as music's Mayo Clinic. The Nashville Sound was never given a precise definition, but there was general agreement that it was not so much a sound as a style. In studio recording sessions, highly skilled backup musicians under the direction of producers such as Owen Bradley or Chet Atkins displayed a matchless ability to improvise arrangements. In a relaxed and informal atmosphere free of intense pressure, the musicians achieved high quality and productivity—and the featured artists got the full benefit of their talents. Whatever the Nashville Sound meant to the many and varied artists who promoted it as a unique musical quality, it made Nashville the favorite recording site of an array of entertainers, from pop crooner Perry Como to folk-rock artist Bob Dylan.

Another blossoming of the Nashville music industry accompanied the renown of the Nashville Sound. Throughout the 1960s, new stars emerged in the country field—Johnny Cash, Chet Atkins, Porter Wagoner, Dolly Parton, Loretta Lynn, Marty Robbins, Tammy Wynette, Tom T. Hall, Charley Pride—and the Opry, though still the mother church of country music, was no longer the only path to glory. Recordings, television, music festivals in the nation and abroad, and the lucrative (though physically exhausting) routine of traveling one-night stands generated a volume of activity great enough to make Nashville the leading national entertainment center between New York and Hollywood. Pop-country entertainers, the most visible being Glen Campbell, turned to television to gain superstar status, and Johnny Cash did the same by pairing his country music repertoire with such non-country artists as Ray Charles and Bob Dylan.

With Cash came others who contributed to the continuing evolution of country music—such artists as Kris Kristofferson, Waylon Jennings, Willie Nelson, and Merle Haggard. Many of them were independent of the Opry, but their roots were in country music, and their broad appeal as entertainers strengthened Nashville's reputation in the music world.

On Sixteenth and Seventeenth avenues south of Broadway, parallel strips of music industry

273

The Opry's last night at the Ryman Auditorium, March 15, 1974

. . . in 1943 . . . the Grand Ole Opry chose the Ryman for its permanent quarters. There was logic in the choice, of course. For the same people who had come to hear Billy Sunday were just as likely to come hear Hank Snow and Roy Acuff and Sam McGee. They felt comfortable there, and for upwards of 30 years they arrived in droves.

But March 15 [1974] marked the end of that era. It was the Opry's last performance in its old home . . . . Johnny Cash in his ruffled white shirt and long-tailed coat—looking like a Civil War vintage U.S. senator . . . was the closing act for Jimmy Snow's "Grand Ole Gospel Time," a popular Friday night feature of the Opry, and that night's show was one of the best. It featured the traditional gospel renditions of the LeFevres, the more upbeat compositions of a young Johnny Cash protege named Larry Gatlin, a rollicking, foot-stomping performance by country-rock singer Dobie Gray (who is one of the few blacks ever to appear on the Opry), and then the whole Cash clan.

By the time Dobie Gray was through it was late at night, and though it was cold and rainy outside, it was stuffy and humid within. The air was musty with mingled sweat fumes, and the people were tired. But they came abruptly to life, and the flashbulbs popped like a psychedelic light show when Cash appeared on stage. And when he led the entire cast through the country-folk classic, "Will the Circle Be Unbroken," even the hard-bitten newspaper reporters in the crowd had to admit they were probably seeing something special.

FRYE GAILLARD, in
Southern Voices, **May-June 1974**

businesses proliferated in what once had been a fashionable residential section of Nashville. The Country Music Hall of Fame was established there, and offices of the three major music licensing associations were opened. Tour-bus companies sprang up, taking music fans to see "the homes of the stars," and tourism became a Nashville industry in its own right, with such area attractions as the Parthenon and Andrew Jackson's Hermitage reaping the benefits along with the growing array of musical features. By the late 1970s, Nashville's booming music industry embraced a colony of artists, writers, producers, and auxiliary personnel numbering in the thousands. Among them, by conservative estimate, were close to a hundred music-made millionaires. The city not only profited from the exposure it received, but also from an estimated one hundred million dollars a year the industry pumped into the local economy.

Until the 1970s, WSM and its insurance company parent had been content to limit their involvement in Nashville's changing music industry to the Grand Ole Opry. But when the Ryman Auditorium could no longer withstand the weekly press of overflow crowds, National Life invested more than forty million dollars in a sprawling entertainment complex on the Cumberland River eight miles northeast of the city. Opryland, U.S.A., an amusement park proclaimed by its developers to be "the home of American music," was opened to the public in 1972, and within five years it was attracting more than two million visitors a year. The new

Opry House, located inside the park, was opened in 1974, and the spacious concert hall was soon drawing an annual attendance of almost one million. Meanwhile, Tom Ryman's old gospel tabernacle on Fifth Avenue was padlocked and shuttered, and only the advocates of its preservation as a historical landmark stood in the way of its demolition.

Music alone had not changed the face of Nashville; the strong and diverse economy that had favored the city since the 1940s was still vibrant. But it was music in all its variegated

Members of the Grand Ole Opry cast gather on the stage of the new Opry House in 1976 during the fiftieth anniversary performance of the celebrated music show.

The faces of the stars of "Nashville" were painted by Nashville artist Bill Myers for the titles and promotion of the film. Myers also appeared in the movie, as did many other local residents.

The filming of the movie "Nashville" at the Parthenon

REACTIONS TO ROBERT ALTMAN'S MOVIE, *NASHVILLE*

Songwriter-producer Billy Sherrill: "When you show the anatomy of a man, you should try to show something besides his tail."

Grand Ole Opry pianist Del Wood: "I've had enough. I'm not going to sit in a chair that long and be slapped in the face."

Buddy Killen, publishing company vice president: "I loved it. It had great depth. I was not offended in any way. It's a great piece of work."

Cousin Minnie Pearl: "I'm just too close to it. Part of it made me very sad, but sometimes I laughed so hard it hurt."

Singer Brenda Lee: "The only way it will be a big movie is for it to play a long time in the North. That's what the people up there think we look like anyway."

Songwriter-singer Larry Gatlin: "I think the acting was superb. I think the songs were horrible. I think it's a gross oversimplification of what our city's about."

Armando Gallo, correspondent for the Italian film magazine *Sorrisi E Canzoni:* "I don't understand why so many country music people are raving about this film, when it's so obviously anti-country. If I were a country music personality, I wouldn't be here."

Roy Acuff: "I haven't seen the film, but I've been hearing a lot of talk about it. I can see nothing but good come from it for Nashville and for country music."

from reports on the premiere of the movie, in the *Nashville Banner* and *Tennessean,* **August 9, 1975**

The Earl Scruggs band, blending the traditional music of banjoist Scruggs with the modern instrumental sounds of younger musicians (including his sons), performs before an enormous American flag in a concert at Vanderbilt University.

livelier, gaudier, less formal, more turbulent place. It had about it an aura of early-Hollywood extravangance, a dream-world quality that attracted hopeful young musicians with songs in their pockets and guitars on their backs. It was full of fanciful tales of bright new talent discovered in greasy-spoon cafes, of fortunes made overnight—and as quickly lost. It had a new dream of glory as audacious as the old—and if the old had never fully acknowledged the presence and the prominence of the new, the oversight no longer seemed to matter: Music City would keep on playing, with or without the blessing of Athens.

In the amalgamation of country music and other American musical styles, many traditional artists found cause to fear that their original art form would be modernized beyond recognition, with its treasures reduced to museum relics and its significance buried in dry academic treatises left to gather dust on library shelves. But whatever the consequences, there would be no pause in the quickening pace of change—for the music, or for Nashville.

In 1975, film-maker Robert Altman, seizing on the Nashville-as-Hollywood theme, produced a celebrated motion picture in which he portrayed Nashville and its music as metaphorical symbols of contemporary America. The movie, "Nashville," with its sharply contrasting images of glamour and gaudiness, decency and decadence, caused some to protest that the city had been unfairly maligned and others to say they recognized the real Nashville in the film.

The movie started more debates than it settled, and the real Nashville remained an elusive place. On the eve of 1980, another metaphor seemed appropriate: Nashville was an American song, an unfinished melody—a humming, throbbing, lilting, lumbering, harmonious, discordant, resonant piece of music. After two hundred years, it was still being composed.

forms that gave the city its visibility in the world. Nashville had not raised many of the stars of country music, but it had given them a place to shine, and wherever they went—to London and Tokyo, to New York and Los Angeles and a thousand stages across the United States—they took the Nashville mystique with them.

The Nashville of old—the quieter, more conservative city that had aspired to be the Athens of the South—was still here. Fragments of it could be glimpsed in the corporate board rooms of Union Street, the ivied cloisters of Vanderbilt, the suburban fastness of Belle Meade, the glittering elegance of Cheekwood's Swan Ball. But the Nashville of old was overlaid by another city—a

Nashville in the 1970s: An Album of Images

The Nashville skyline, photographed in June 1979 by Bill LaFevor

The Andrew Jackson Hotel, a Nashville landmark at Sixth Avenue and Deaderick Street for decades, was demolished in one thunderous minute on June 13, 1971, to make way for a new landmark: the James K. Polk State Office Building and Tennessee Center for the Performing Arts.

From 1846 until 1903, the congregation of Second Presbyterian Church met in this Greek-Revival edifice at Third Avenue and Gay Street; today, the building belongs to the makers of Nashville's most famous candy bar, the Goo-Goo.

As early as the spring of 1966, Nashvillians opposed to the war in Vietnam were demonstrating for a cease-fire in the conflict. Few men came home from the war to receive a hero's welcome, but one who did was a Navy pilot from Nashville, Captain William P. Lawrence (right), who survived six years in a North Vietnamese prisoner of war camp. Military and civilian officials alike gave him a standing ovation when he addressed the legislature soon after his return in 1973.

Six generations and 185 years after John Davis built a home on the Harpeth River in southwest Davidson County, descendants of the pioneer surveyor and militiaman still live in it. Edward D. Hicks II, a grandson of Davis, named the estate (above) Devon Farm. The brick home may be the only eighteenth-century residence in the county to be owned continuously by successive generations of the same family. The land on which Cleveland Hall (left) was built near the Hermitage in 1838 has belonged to the Donelson family since John Donelson acquired it in the 1780s.

Symbolic of Nashville's religious heritage, the Pentecost window in the Upper Room Chapel presents "an ecumenical interpretation of the work of the Holy Spirit through the Christian centuries." From its headquarters in Nashville, the United Methodist Church publishes The Upper Room, an interracial, international, interdenominational devotional guide with a circulation of two and one-half million copies in thirty-nine languages.

In the tradition of Sam P. Jones and Billy Sunday, traveling preachers whose Nashville appearances attracted huge crowds, evangelist Billy Graham returned to the city in 1979 after an absence of twenty-five years. More than 200,000 people attended the eight-night revival at Vanderbilt's Dudley Field.

282

Trees, lawns, and curving boulevards cover the hillside where slums once spread in downtown Nashville. More new structures have been added to the skyline since this aerial photograph was taken in 1976.

In 1885, when horse-drawn equipment was used to fight fires in Nashville, Engine Company Number Six operated out of a Victorian station on what is now Second Avenue South. The fire hall (above left) was named for James Geddes, a surveyor of the railroad line between Louisville and Nashville in the 1850s. The restored structure is now an art gallery and residence, one of many old Nashville buildings given new life through historic preservation. But deterioration and destruction still claim many more valuable structures even as some are saved. One example is this decaying Victorian house on Rutledge Hill (above). Another is the former governor's mansion on West End Avenue (left), which was demolished in 1979 to make way for a commercial fast-food outlet.

Two decades after she and five of her Tennessee State University Tigerbelle teammates participated in the 1956 Olympics, Wilma Rudolph could look back on a brilliant track career. She won three Gold Medals in the 1960 Olympics. TSU women's track coach Ed Temple (shown in the picture with his 1956 stars) has placed thirty-three girls on Olympic teams, and they have won eleven Gold Medals. Another TSU athlete, broad-jump star Ralph Boston, also was an Olympic Gold Medal winner in 1960.

For his discoveries concerning hormones—discoveries which were said to have "opened new paths of research into diabetes and cancer"—Vanderbilt University research biologist Earl W. Sutherland was awarded the 1971 Nobel Prize in medicine and physiology. Dr. Sutherland was the forty-third American—and the first Vanderbilt faculty member—to win the Nobel Prize in medicine, but two others came close: Dr. Ernest Goodpasture, for his work in the development of virus vaccines, and Dr. Amos Christie, for his discoveries concerning histoplasmosis.

Cheekwood, Leslie Cheek's palatial mansion in the southwestern suburbs of Nashville, was built during the Depression. Forty years later, Cheek's daughter, Mrs. Walter Sharp, gave the estate to the people of Nashville. Now it is the Tennessee Botanical Garden and Fine Arts Center, a private, non-profit facility featuring horticultural displays, a permanent art collection, and regular exhibitions, all open to the public.

Whenever Nashville has served as an international meeting ground, the Grand Ole Opry and Opryland have been principal attractions. The United Nations came to town in 1976 for its first meeting outside New York, and during the visit, UN Secretary General Kurt Waldheim and his daughter took an Opryland log flume ride with Tennessee Governor Ray Blanton (right, above). A year earlier, a historic Russian-American space hookup was recorded when astronauts and cosmonauts rode together on Opryland's Wabash Cannonball (above).

As Felix Grundy and numerous others did before him, Nashville attorney James F. Neal has earned a national reputation for his skill in the courtroom. As a prosecutor for the United States Department of Justice, Neal won a conviction of Teamsters Union leader Jimmy Hoffa for jury tampering in 1964. A decade later, he played a key role in the prosecution of top White House officials in the Watergate scandal. Another Nashville lawyer worked opposite Neal as a Watergate defense attorney.

286

The upside-down image of the Parthenon in Centennial Park's Watauga Lake is broken by the wake of a passing family of ducks. Though it is the best known, Centennial is only one of more than sixty-five Metro-area parks covering some sixty-five hundred acres.

The Nashville Symphony Orchestra and conductor Michael Charry, shown in rehearsal with operatic star Shirley Verett, performed in concert in War Memorial Auditorium during the 1978-79 season, the symphony's thirty-third.

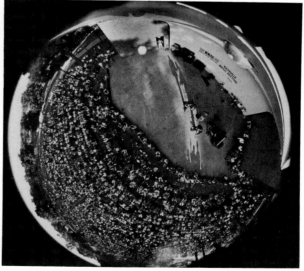

Photographed through a fisheye lens from directly overhead, musicians and their audience at the concert bandshell in Centennial Park seem bound together in the intimacy of a late afternoon in summer.

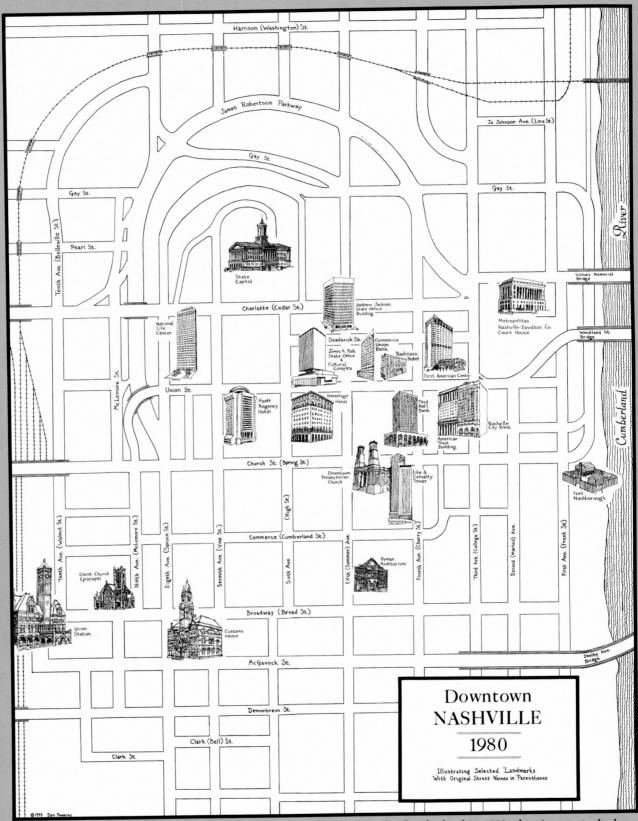

Since James Robertson and his companions built Fort Nashborough on the Cumberland in 1780, the pioneer stockade that grew to be a city has gone through many transformations. Dan E. Pomeroy's contemporary map highlights some of the downtown area's architectural features.

A revival of interest in the architecture and history of Nashville's older sections has been marked by restoration of many buildings and by street fairs to publicize the renewal effort. Crowds throng to the Market Street (Second Avenue) fair each fall (top). On Elliston Place (above), a thriving area of music clubs and shops, a 1979 street dance drew a couple from the crowd to the center of attention.

With Andrew Jackson looking on, former Congressman Richard Fulton was photographed at his desk in the courthouse soon after he was elected mayor of Metropolitan Nashville-Davidson County in 1975. Fulton won re-election in the summer of 1979.

With the Nashville recording industry now producing ninety percent of all country recordings and a fair share of other kinds of music, both the sound and the appearance of the artists and their songs have changed dramatically. The Nashville Sound is now a quarter-billion-dollar-a-year business employing more than four thousand artists, musicians, songwriters, and support personnel. Radio and television programs, festivals and shows, and tourist attractions related to the music industry add further to Nashville's claim as Music City, U.S.A. Uncle Dave Macon, showman though he was, would no doubt be astonished by the changes.

In twenty years as a public figure—legislator, attorney, judge, actor, entrepreneur—Charles F. Galbreath has seldom been far from the limelight. The flamboyant and unpredictable Galbreath, shown disco dancing with his wife Joyce, stirred a storm of protest in 1976 when he used official stationery of the Tennessee Court of Criminal Appeals, on which he served, to write a fan letter to a pornographic magazine.

At the stage entrance to Skull's Rainbow Room, a nightclub in Printer's Alley, an "exotic dancer" strikes a pose to match the sultry Nashville night. Since 1967, when the city's voters approved the sale of liquor by the drink, Nashville night life has spread far beyond the alley, but its clubs still maintain a brisk business.

290

Pari-mutual betting is only a memory, but horse racing does return briefly to Nashville each spring with the running of the Iroquois Memorial Steeplechase in Percy Warner Park. This is a scene from the 1979 race.

After an absence of more than fifteen years, minor league baseball returned to Nashville with a flourish in 1978 when the Nashville Sounds played their inaugural season before 380,000 fans—the largest minor league attendance in the nation. Larry Schmittou engineered baseball's return to the city in the new Herschel Greer Stadium on the south side of Fort Negley, and in the first half of the 1979 season, his team drew more paying customers than one major league club.

Nashville Banner.

VOL. C No. 253 — NASHVILLE, TENN., TUESDAY AFTERNOON, FEB. 1, 1977 — PRICE 15 CENTS

Judge Orders TSU
To Take Over UTN

By DAVID FOX
Banner Staff Writer

The University of Tennessee at Nashville Monday was ordered merged into Tennessee State University.

The "landmark" desegregation ruling by U.S. District Court Judge Frank Gray Jr. is the first such merger order in the country and is expected to have nationwide repercussions.

Calling the decision a "radical remedy," Gray ordered the two schools merged under the State Board of Regents, with the process to be completed by July 1, 1980. UTN at that time would cease to exist.

Although an appeal of the decision is likely, the 37-page memorandum could be the last act in a legal drama that began almost nine years ago.

In March 1968, a group of Nashville residents, represented by attorney George Barrett, sued the state to stop construction of UTN's new facility at 10th Avenue North and Charlotte Avenue.

The suit grew into a challenge of the alleged dual, segregated nature of the state's entire higher education system.

Gray ruled the accumulated evidence in the case led him to conclude "the only reasonable alternative is the merger of TSU and UTN into a single institution under a single governing board."

He further ruled TSU's status as a "land grant university with a 60-year history" makes it preferable to merge the two into TSU, with

UTN playing a "supporting" role during the three-year transition.

It was Barrett who first proposed a merger of the two schools in 1970. Also proposing merger was Nashville attorney Avon Williams Jr., who represented plaintiff intervenors Raymond Richardson, Sterlin Adams and a group called Tennesseans for Justice in Higher Education.

Barrett called the decision "a landmark case" which will strengthen the authority of the federal government nationwide in "dealing with states that have a dual, segregated system of higher education."

Less pleased with the decision was Dr. Charles Smith, chancellor

See TSU, Page 4

State Officials Ponder Appeal

By PHIL WEST
And JOHN BRITTINGHAM
Banner Staff Writers

An appeal was being considered today in the wake of a federal court ruling Monday requiring the merger of the University of Tennessee-Nashville into Tennessee State University.

The ruling evoked a wide range of reactions.

University of Tennessee and State Board of Regents officials voiced "disappointment" in U.S. District Court Judge Frank Gray Jr.'s ruling requiring the merger by 1980.

Dr. Charles E. Smith, UTN chancellor, called Gray's ruling "drastic" and indicated UTN officials may appeal the decision.

"We are cognizant that the same judicial process which gives some responsibility to federal judges also provides opportunity for appellate relief to those affected by decisions," Smith said in a statement released Monday night.

Meanwhile, a spokesman for UT President Dr. Edward Boling in Chattanooga, said UT officials will huddle today before releasing a statement on the ruling.

"I expect that we'll consider the possibility of filing an appeal, but nobody knows until we get to see it," said Beauchamp Brogan, legal counsel for the UT system and secretary of its board of trustees.

Students at both institutions Monday night had mixed reactions to the decision, and Dr. Frederick Humphries, TSU president, called the ruling "a very good decision on the part of the judge.

"I've always stated I thought a

See REACTION, Page 4

Please, Can I Come In?

— Banner Photo by Jack Gunter

Shivering in the cold, even with her smooth fur coat, Mrs. Johnny Thompson's cat, Bell, peers pleadingly through the door of her Brentwood home.

The Tennessean

VOL. 73—No. 345 — NASHVILLE, TENN., TUESDAY, MARCH 20, 1979 — 15 CENTS — 38 Pages

PEABODY, VU TO MERGE

By SAUNDRA IVEY

Peabody College's board of trustees unanimously approved a last-minute merger proposal from Vanderbilt University yesterday, under which the teachers college will become a professional school within Vanderbilt this fall.

The trustees did not discuss the proposal for merger with Tennessee State University submitted by the State Board of Regents March 10.

"A HISTORIC MOMENT has arrived," said Peabody's board chairman, Robert E. Gable, in announcing the trustees' decision to end more than a century of independence for the teachers college.

Looking for the Help He Knows Is There

Sunday Gas Flow Already Slowing

By ROBERT BURKHARDT

U.S. Said Giving
Israel $3 Billion
For Sinai Pullout

From WIRE REPORTS
WASHINGTON — Israeli Defense Minister Ezer Weizman said yesterday his country and the United States have agreed on $3 billion in American aid to finance Israel's pullout from the Sinai.

Alexander Hits
Auto Stalemate
With Lawmakers

By LARRY DAUGHTREY

Gov. Lamar Alexander's administration and key Senate administration leaders reached a stalemate yesterday on legislation aimed at allowing state automobiles.

After years of discussion, negotiation, and litigation, 1979 brought two major higher education mergers in Nashville. With its final appeal still pending in the United States Supreme Court, the University of Tennessee at Nashville was merged into Tennessee State University. George Peabody College for Teachers, its roots reaching back to Davidson Academy in 1785, was taken over by Vanderbilt University. Both mergers took effect on July 1, 1979.

WEATHER
NEAR 50°
60% Chance
See Page 18

The Tennessean

VOL. 73—No. 285 — NASHVILLE, TENN., THURSDAY, JAN. 18, 1979 — 15 CENTS — 76 Pages

INDEX
Page		Page

Alexander Sworn In;
Blanton Pushed Out

Somber Ritual on a Tumultuous Day

— Staff photo by J.T. Phillips

His hand resting on the 110-year-old family Bible, Lamar Alexander takes the oath of office from Chief Justice Joe Henry. Alexander's wife Honey holds the Bible as children Drew and Leslee place their hands on the pages. House Speaker Ned McWherter, Attorney General William Leech and Secretary of State Gentry Crowell watch. The Bible is open to the favorite verse of Alexander's father, II Timothy 2:15: "Study to shew thyself approved unto God, a workman that needeth not to be ashamed, rightly dividing the word of truth."

By LARRY DAUGHTREY and DOUG HALL

Lamar Alexander was sworn in as governor of Tennessee three days early last night after a federal prosecutor warned state leaders Ray Blanton might free convicts involved in a pay-for-freedom investigation.

Alexander, 38, a Republican who walked the state to gain public confidence, raised his right hand in a moment unprecedented in Tennessee history and repeated after Chief Justice Joe Henry:

Alexander, 38, a Republican who walked the state to gain public confidence, raised his right hand in a moment unprecedented in Tennessee history and repeated after Chief Justice Joe Henry:

"I, LAMAR ALEXANDER, do solemnly swear that I will perform with fidelity the duties of the office of governor of the state of Tennessee to which I am elected and which I am about to assume."

Seconds before, he told a crowd of friends, supporters and legislators in the Supreme Court's courtroom:

"It is not a happy day for me."

BLANTON, AT HIS new home on Jefferson Davis Drive, heard of what amounted to his ouster from office from a television news bulletin, and two hours later emerged from his house to talk with reporters.

"I am saddened and hurt for the state of Tennessee that this clandestine action has taken place this evening," he said. "There is such a thing as courtesy, and there was no courtesy extended to me today

"The thing that saddens me is that this action today leaves a blemish on Tennessee's record, and I have worked to promote Tennessee around the world.

"I HAVE NO BITTERNESS, and I won't have, because I have enjoyed serving the state of Tennessee. I am let down that an action of this kind has taken place."

Ray Blanton
"No bitterness"

Blanton complained he had been told he could not return to the Capitol last night to retrieve personal belongings. As Alexander representatives arrived to secure documents and offices, the door to the governor's suite was nailed shut.

But Tom Ingram, deputy to Alexander, said the governor was refused admission to the Capitol after his legal counsel, Robert Lillard, requested permission to take executive clemency papers to Blanton for his re-

Carter: Budget Deficit Lid At $29 Billion

Lillard, Freeland, 2 More Subpoenaed

By JOHN HAILE

Former Gov. Ray Blanton's legal counsel, his administrative assistant and at least two other close associates were subpoenaed late yesterday to

sial patronage operation for the past four years. Freeland, from Blanton's hometown, is one of Blanton's closest associates.

Bruce Purcell of Nashville,

Tommy Wilson of Brentwood, president of White Truck Sales and operator of a Chattanooga-to-Memphis trucking line.

Wilson said he is a friend of

It was also reported that Personnel Commissioner Ben Haynes was subpoenaed, but that could not be confirmed last night.

In a move unprecedented in Tennessee politics, Republican Governor-elect Lamar Alexander was sworn in three days before the expiration of Democratic Governor Ray Blanton's term on January 17, 1979, after a federal prosecutor warned state leaders that Blanton might free several convicts thought to be involved in an alleged pardons and clemency scandal. Alexander's early swearing in was called by some "a courageous act" and by others "an illegal seizure of power."

Overleaf: Two centuries old and still growing, an oak tree on a hilltop in northwest Davidson County dominates the Cumberland River and the distant Nashville skyline in David Wright's interpretation of the modern city in its natural surrounding. For all its urban growth, Metropolitan Nashville-Davidson County still shelters wildlife—including an estimated one thousand deer—and almost two-thirds of its 533-square-mile area is undeveloped.

WEATHER
PARTLY CLOUDY
80s
See Page 27

THE TENNESSEAN

VOL. 74—No. 89
Second Class Postage
Paid at Nashville, Tenn.

NASHVILLE, TENN., FRIDAY, JULY 6, 1979 15 CENTS 50 Pages

INDEX
| | Page | | Page |
Amusements 39-44 Living . . . 45-50
Business. . . 17-19 Obituaries . . 27
Classified . . 27-37 Radio-TV . 48,49
Comics. . . . 48,49 Sports . 21-26,38
Editorials . . 10,11 X-Word 50

TENNESSEAN, BANNER SOLD

Evanses Sell To Gannett; Staff To Stay

By CHARLES L. FONTENAY

Agreement was reached yesterday by the owners of the *Tennessean* and the *Nashville Banner* for the sale of the two daily newspapers.

Amon Carter Evans and his mother, Mrs. Silliman Evans Sr., owners, of the *Tennessean*, will receive approximately $50 million for the sale of their newspaper to the Gannett Co. Inc., owner of the *Nashville Banner*.

GANNETT AGREED to sell the *Nashville Banner* to John J. Hooker, Jr., Brownlee Currey and Irby Simpkins for approxi-

Ignore Old Ratios
Desegregation: Wiseman Says Find New Goals

By SAUNDRA IVEY

A federal judge told school officials yesterday they may ignore the black-white student ratios established in Metro's desegregation order and start planning for broader educational goals.

Saying his court "does not consider itself bound by determinations made eight years ago," U.S. District Judge Thomas A. Wiseman in effect told the educators to start from scratch in suggest-
ing remedies for lingering de-

Nashville Banner.

VOL. CIII No. 76   A GANNETT NEWSPAPER   NASHVILLE, TENN., FRIDAY AFTERNOON, JULY 6, 1979.   44 PAGES   ★   PRICE: 15 CENTS

Gannett Buys The Tennessean

Banner Returns To Local Ownership

By PETE BIRD
Business News Editor

Local businessmen Brownlee O. Currey Jr., John Jay Hooker Jr. and Irby Simpkins Jr. have agreed to buy the *Nashville Banner* from the Gannett Co. Inc. for $25 million.

At the same time, Gannett, a national communications company, announced an agreement in principle to buy the morning *Tennessean* for $50 million from Amon Carter Evans and the Silliman Evans family trusts.

James H. Jesse, president and

publisher of the *Banner*, a veteran newspaper executive who has served as publisher of 12 newspapers, was named president of Newspaper Printing Corp., the agency responsible for handling production, advertising and circulation functions for both newspapers.

The dramatic move caps weeks of speculation that a sale of the two fiercely competitive newspapers was imminent. The announcement was made Thursday night to both staffs.

The *Banner* will be sold to Music

City Media Inc., whose principals will have the following roles in the afternoon newspaper: Currey, chairman and chief executive officer; Hooker, publisher; and Simpkins, president.

Currey is vice chairman of Tennessee Valley Bancorp Inc., one of the state's largest bank holding companies. Hooker, a Nashville attorney and two-time Democratic gubernatorial candidate, has been involved in business enterprises ranging from video games to the STP Corp. Simpkins is president of

the Harpeth National Bank in Franklin.

The agreement, expected to become effective in 30 to 45 days after review by the U.S. Justice Department and the Federal Trade Commission, was concluded Thursday after a marathon negotiating session at a Nashville hotel.

Under antitrust laws, the same owner cannot retain both newspapers.

"We are pleased to place the *Nashville Banner* in the hands of a local group, preserving the mix of group and local ownership in this

exciting and competitive newspaper city," said Allen H. Neuharth, Gannett's chairman and president. "The roots of both newspapers shall remain buried deep in the soil of Middle Tennessee, and the commitment to free press and free enterprise shall continue to work for all in the community."

The new owners of the *Banner* said in a joint statement, "We are grateful, as a local group, to be given the opportunity to own the *Nashville Banner*. We understand and accept the enormous responsibility that goes with this opportu-

nity; the preservation of separate and vigorous editorial voices is fundamental to the health and prosperity of this region."

Neuharth said John L. Seigenthaler will continue as publisher of the morning newspaper while assuming the additional titles of president and editor under a "long-term contract."

Kenneth E. Morrell, editor of the *Banner*, will leave the newspaper and become a consultant to Gan-

See NEWSPAPERS, Page 4

For more than seventy years, the Banner and the Tennessean *had waged journalistic war. But on July 5, 1979, the family of Silliman Evans, owners of the* Tennessean *since 1937, sold the paper to the Gannett newspaper chain, which had bought the* Banner *from James G. Stahlman in 1972—and Gannett in turn sold the* Banner *to a group of Nashville businessmen headed by John J. Hooker. John Seigenthaler, publisher of the* Tennessean *under Amon Carter Evans, was retained by Gannett. Seigenthaler (left) and Hooker (right), longtime personal friends and political allies, thus became competitor publishers of Nashville's only two daily papers. Surprisingly, neither paper photographed the joint press conference of the friendly rivals, but all three local television stations recorded the meeting.*

I MAGES OF NASHVILLE in the two hundredth year of its life:

Almost a half-million people now live in Nashville-Davidson County. The 1980 census is expected to record a population of about 470,000—a modest gain of five percent since 1970. (In the six adjacent counties, which have become suburban extensions of the city, the combined population will total approximately 315,000, an increase of more than thirty-five percent in ten years.)

Who are the Nashville-Davidson Countians? Statistics, though deficient and inadequate as precise measures, are generally helpful in shaping a composite profile:

The overwhelming majority are native-born Americans, but an estimated ten thousand have come as immigrants from Asia, Africa, Europe, Latin America, and the Middle East, giving the city a taste of diversity it has lacked for most of this century. Of the native-born citizens, roughly eighty percent are white and twenty percent are black. A few American Indians, descendants of the original natives, have also come to dwell in this ancient hunting ground of their ancestors.

Nashville is predominantly a middle-class city. The average adult has completed at least twelve years of schooling. Among the approximately 125,000 households, the median annual income is almost $20,000. About two hundred thousand people are in the labor force, and more than ninety-six percent of them have jobs. One-fifth of the workers are employed by government—local, state, or federal—and one-tenth of the total are members of labor unions (including almost three thousand who belong to the American Federation of Musicians). Roughly one in every dozen families lives in poverty, while one in every hundred has enough assets to be accorded the designation "millionaire"; the remaining ninety percent are neither rich nor poor. If the numbers of telephones, television

sets, and motor vehicles in the city were distributed equally, every household would have at least two of each.

One-fourth of the total population is enrolled in schools and colleges. More than one-half are members of religious congregations. There are about 220,000 registered voters (but only 88,000 of them voted in the 1979 city elections). Democrats outnumber Republicans, and Protestants are far more numerous than Catholics and Jews. There are slightly more women than men and more adults over sixty-five than children under five.

For every four Nashvillians who get married, three get divorced. One in every five babies is born out of wedlock, and abortions are more numerous than live births. About fifteen hundred people die of heart disease in the city each year, and half as many more die of cancer. Accidents kill close to three hundred persons annually. Almost a hundred others are homicide victims, and about fifty commit suicide. There is one medical practitioner for every two hundred residents and one hospital or nursing-home bed for every seventy.

Nashville is finally rid of cholera and typhoid fever, and almost rid of tuberculosis—but not of venereal disease, which infects more than six thousand people a year, or of alcoholism, from which an estimated twenty thousand people suffer. There has also been a sharp increase in drug abuse and drug addiction since the late 1960s. Arrests for violations of narcotics laws totaled more than seventeen hundred in 1978, and there were about six thousand arrests for drunkenness and another fifty-three hundred for driving under the influence of intoxicants.

Images of Nashville:

Gasoline is approaching a dollar a gallon. Coffee is $2.38 a pound, milk is $1.03 a half-gallon, ground beef is $1.79 a pound. Tickets to the Grand Ole Opry, once free, now cost five dollars. A gallon of six-year-old Tennessee whiskey costs $37.29, and the average price of houses sold in Nashville in June 1979 was $61,470. The Metropolitan Nashville-Davidson County budget for fiscal 1980 is $307 million; sixteen years ago, the newly consolidated government had a budget of $65 million.

The Nashville airport, with 113 scheduled flights daily, handles two million passengers a year. The last remaining passenger train, Amtrak's *Floridian*, has been discontinued.

Growth and decay and revitalization constantly alter the physical face of the city. In the downtown area, soaring towers of steel and glass and concrete dominate the skyline—banks, insurance companies, hotels, government buildings, and the newest giant, the James K. Polk State Office Building, which will also house the Tennessee Performing Arts Center and the Tennessee State Museum. The long shadows of the skyscrapers fall across some architectural gems of a bygone age—the Ryman Auditorium, the Arcade, the Gay Nineties saloons on Fourth Avenue, the business houses of old Market Street (Second Avenue).

Union Station and the old United States Customs House on Broadway are being restored to new life and new purposes, raising hopes that the Ryman may also be saved from destruction. Lower Broadway still languishes and deteriorates, but Market Street is beginning to revive, and Church Street has a new brick surface. On First Avenue, there is a technological innovation: a thermal transfer plant, converting Nashville's garbage and trash into steam to heat and cool many downtown buildings.

The combination of innovation and renovation, of new ideas and old ones worth saving, is not in buildings alone. It can also be seen in the business world, where new firms handling products unheard of a decade ago operate compatibly with enterprises that have lasted for generations. More than two dozen Nashville firms that were begun in the nineteenth century and named for their originators are still operated under the same name by descendants of the founders. Among the names on that unusual list are these: Ambrose, Baltz, Beasley, Cline, Cohen, Creighton, Geist, Geny, Gerst, Gray, Harwell, Hill, Jamison, Joy, Levy, Lipscomb, Loventhal, Loveman, May, Mills, Norvell, Oman, Wallace, Werthan, Zibart.

As the rebuilding of downtown Nashville continues, three more development projects of major proportions are being considered—one in the railroad gulch between Church and Demonbreun streets, another along the riverfront, and a third in the bottomland where the Nashville Vols once reigned and the early settlers of the city watered their livestock.

The spirit of restoration and development reaches beyond the heart of the city. There is, for example, a surge of interest in the long-neglected qualities of some old neighborhoods: Edgefield (East Nashville), Germantown (North Nashville), Richland (West Nashville), Rutledge Hill (South Nashville), and the Belmont-Hillsboro district southwest of the downtown area. Directly north of the city center, on a riverbend plain where thoroughbreds once ran for high stakes, a multidimensional development known as MetroCenter is in progress. On a bluff nearby is the modern Maxwell House Hotel, its name recalling the elegant old hostelry at Fourth Avenue and Church Street where eight Presidents of the United States were guests.

East of the city, in another bend of the river, the Opryland, U.S.A. theme park and its companion attractions, the Opry House and the Opryland Hotel, have become a focal point of the booming tourist industry that attracts seven million visitors a year to Nashville.

In its perpetual state of change and continuity, Nashville faces challenges and opportunities that are both original and timeless. The rescue of the inner city from oblivion—a movement that can

be traced to the urban renewal dreams of Mayor Thomas Cummings almost forty years ago—is complicated by the rise of suburban shopping malls, manufacturing plants, housing complexes, and recreational attractions. Suburban development—indeed, all forms of expansion—is threatened by the national energy crisis and the related problems of inflation and recession. Even as it enhances its image as a thriving "New South" city in the nation's "Sunbelt," Nashville runs the risk of becoming a homogenized replica of the modern American urban metropolis, its distinctiveness lost in a sea of sameness. The national trend toward corporate conglomerates is shifting ownership of many local enterprises to executive offices in other cities. And finally, for all its prosperity, Nashville still has not fully resolved the social, economic, and environmental problems that have been present throughout its history.

There will be no lack of challenges—or opportunities—as Nashville enters its third century.

Images of the faces of two centuries:

The Mound Builders, the Shawnees, the Chickasaws; James Robertson arriving on foot, John Donelson on a flatboat, Andrew Jackson on horseback, General Lafayette on a steamboat; the remnant of Cherokees, walking to exile.

Union troops, marching up Broad Street in 1862; General Hood's war-weary army, advancing to its doom on the Franklin Pike; the Jubilee Singers, returning triumphant with the funds to save Fisk.

Crowds of visitors thronging to the Nashville Centennial in 1880 and the Tennessee Centennial in 1897; doughboys parading up Capitol Boulevard after World War I; the army of the unemployed, trudging in search of shelter from the Depression.

Country folks coming to town to shop, to work, to watch a broadcast of the Grand Ole Opry radio show; Franklin D. Roosevelt, bringing faith, hope, charity, and TVA; GIs and civilians celebrating the end of World War II.

Marching civil rights demonstrators, seeking freedom from racial discrimination; the voters of Nashville and Davidson County, deciding the second time around to reorganize their government; Dave Macon, Hank Williams, and a hundred harbingers of the Nashville Sound.

Protesters against the war in Vietnam; immigrants pursuing the American Dream; rhinestone cowboys walking the sidewalks of Music Row, hoping for a break, dreaming of stardom.

Arrivals and departures, faces in the crowd—people coming and going, staying and leaving, settling in and passing through. Shifting images of a place in America.

The curious old tunnel that legend has labeled Timothy Demonbreun's cave opens in a limestone palisade above the Cumberland River like a dark, unblinking eye. The *Belle Carol,* a little sternwheeler faintly reminiscent of the riverboats of old, churns past the cave and circles back beneath the bridges. It docks in the gathering dusk at the foot of Broadway, near the rustic replica of Fort Nashborough. The passengers come ashore, and presently the stillness of summer evening settles over the boat, the fort, the empty street.

And the river remains, a silent witness to the passing faces of two centuries. It is just where it has always been, and what it has always been—a slender, unbreakable cord weaving a crooked path across Nashville, binding a city on a bluff to the mountains and the sea.

Only the river has seen it all.

299

A Gallery of Nashville Commerce

By Louise Littleton Davis

Without its commercial enterprises, a city simply would not exist. They are essential to the ongoing of the community's social, civic, benevolent, political and religious affairs, as well as its economic life.

On the following pages are historical portraits of more than fifty Nashville businesses, some for-profit and some not-for-profit. Each of these firms was invited to participate in this gallery by the publishers and by the Mayor's Century III Commission.

They were carefully selected for inclusion here based on their firm's longstanding and productive contributions to the community of Nashville. Most have been in business during the greater part of the city's second century of life and, thus, have contributed in significant measure to the outstanding growth and progress the community has enjoyed during that period.

The space which each firm's biography occupies was purchased by that organization. They, therefore, made this volume commercially feasible through their support and confidence.

Aladdin Industries Incorporated

Aladdin Industries Incorporated, a dynamic force on the Nashville business scene for thirty years, would never have come here if it had not been for natural gas and a promise kept.

The influence of that move is incalculable in terms of Nashville's growth. Out of it has developed not only a multifaceted industry that employs more than two thousand people, but also the civic work of the company's president, Victor S. Johnson Jr., who helped establish Metro government here and had a strong hand in developing a bold new concept in city designing called MetroCenter.

The promise was made by his father, the late Victor S. Johnson Sr., Chicago businessman and founder of what is now Aladdin Industries. He had encouraged Wade V. Thompson in his effort to bring natural gas to Nashville and told him that if that project succeeded, Johnson would consider Nashville as site for a new Aladdin plant.

But before natural gas was finally piped here in June 1946, Johnson had died. His son, Victor S. Johnson Jr., had received his law degree from Yale University in 1941 and had every intention of returning to law practice as soon as his military service was finished. At his father's death, however, the board of directors of the company (then called Mantle Lamp Company of America) asked Victor S. Johnson Jr. to take over the presidency.

At that moment, an interesting turn in the company's affairs was developing. The company that his father had founded in 1908 to manufacture Aladdin lamps— kerosene lamps that shed a soft, white, incandescent light— was enjoying increasing success with another of its products: vacuum bottles, or insulated jugs, developed for the military during World War I. By 1946 Aladdin's 600 employees at the factory in Alexandria, Indiana, were spending fifty percent of their effort on production of kerosene lamps, twenty percent on production of vacuum bottles, and the rest on electric lamps.

Electricity was widespread by then, and Victor Johnson Jr. decided the time had come for the vacuum bottle market. Realizing that this meant building a new plant, he remembered his father's promise to look at the Nashville site. Not only did he build his new plant here, but by 1949 he had moved company headquarters from Chicago to Nashville, and all company manufacturing was moved here. He gave up any idea of returning to law and threw himself into building the new 130,000-square-foot plant on Murfreesboro Road—the first post-World War II plant to be built here.

From its world headquarters on Murfreesboro Road and in the stunning 850-acre MetroCenter development, Aladdin directs manufacturing plants, sales operations, licensees, and joint venture companies in over sixteen countries outside the United States. One of its subsidiaries, Temp-Rite International, markets its products in over fifteen countries. From its thermos bottle technology, the company developed trays for keeping hot foods hot and cold foods cold that have made it the world leader in institutional meal distribution systems.

One of Aladdin's divisions, Aladdin Electronics, produces a wide variety of electronic components used in everything from telephone systems to computers and space missiles. In the midst of all the technological pioneering, there is a renaissance of interest in the old-fashioned Aladdin lamp. Collectors treasure the early models, and models still being manufactured today are used for both decorative and emergency lighting.

Victor Johnson Jr. recently has chaired the Citizens Goal 2000 Committee which sought ways to preserve the quality of life in Nashville to the year 2000. Johnson, the man who came here to keep his father's promise, is still working Aladdin's magic.

This 1912 advertisement shows the product on which Aladdin Industries' reputation was built—the kerosene mantle lamp.

In 1948 Victor S. Johnson Jr. (center) broke ground for his company's new plant on Murfreesboro Road. The site, at the time, was considered to be out in the countryside.

Alley-Cassetty Coal Company

Alley-Cassetty Coal Company, bridging one hundred years of changing habits in fuel use, has seen coal drop from a favored position to least desirable and now soar as a treasured supplier of energy again.

In 1879, when James Cassetty began selling kindling and coal by the bushel, coal was highly regarded as a fuel because of its long-burning quality. And it was not until the 1940s and 1950s that disdain for soot and pollution turned the city away from coal and toward heating with electricity or natural gas.

When Cassetty opened his first coal yard on Clinton Street at Jo Johnston—a location now operated by Alley-Cassetty again—Nashville homes were heated by coal which sold for as little as $3 to $4 a ton.

For three generations—James Cassetty, his son Fred B. Cassetty, and grandson Fred J. Cassetty—Cassetty Coal remained a family business. But Fred J. Cassetty died just as his son, Fred J. Cassetty Jr., was graduated from Vanderbilt University as an electrical engineer in 1960. In 1964 the company merged with Frank H. Alley Coal Company to become Alley-Cassetty Coal Company.

Frank H. Alley's first contact with the coal business came in the early 1900s when he bought coal at wholesale from the yards in Nashville and peddled it from a house in North Nashville. Alley's first retail coal delivery yard was started in 1924 at 119 North First Street as part of a variety of business ventures. He had sold coal by the bushel, built wagons, manufactured ice, and operated a delivery service. By the 1930s, as electric refrigerators cut into Alley's ice manufacturing operation, he devoted more time to the coal business. And in 1934 Alley's son J.P. ("Pete") joined the company.

In 1943, when Pete Alley enlisted in the Navy, his brother-in-law, George W. West, was "drafted" into the family coal business. And after the war, a new type of coal called Number Eleven seam coal (an egg-sized, longer-burning, lightweight coal from Kentucky coal fields) brought new profits to the business. There were not only the thousands of residential customers still burning coal then but also sizable orders from commercial and government buildings.

When an urban renewal program razed some two thousand coal-burning buildings in East Nashville within three or four years and TVA began supplying more electricity to new electrically heated homes, coal companies felt the pinch. That, in addition to the fact that many homes and businesses turned to natural gas for heating after 1947, created problems for the coal business.

In the late 1950s, Pete Alley and G.W. West bought the business and began acquiring some twelve or fifteen small coal yards. In 1964, when they merged with Fred J. Cassetty, there were only ten or twelve coal dealers left in the city, and one of the largest was St. Bernard Coal Company. Alley-Cassetty took it over in 1968 and—luckily for them—the following two winters were so cold that the bank loan was quickly paid off. But the future of coal began to look uncertain, and Alley-Cassetty added a builders' supply business, Capitol Builders Supply, purchasing it in 1972. It was formerly the old W.T. Hardison Company located at the foot of the Shelby Street Bridge and South First Street. The two offices were, in 1973, consolidated at #2 Oldham Street, with the retail yard remaining at the 1040 Jo Johnston Avenue location.

Now, with the oil shortage, coal is in demand again, and Alley-Cassetty is dealing more in industrial and commercial coal. Among its industrial users are TVA (once a competitor in the energy market), Du Pont, state buildings, Vanderbilt University, Western Kentucky University, and various Tennessee state colleges. Coal that once sold for $4 to $8 a ton now retails for $58 to $72 a ton.

While Frank H. Alley (seated) was still primarily in the ice business, James E. Baird (standing) managed the coal company at 119 North First Street.

Fred J. Cassetty (left) and Fred B. Cassetty (right) stand with an unidentified company customer in front of the coal firm's offices at 816 Fourth Avenue North.

Baltz Brothers Meats

Robert Baltz, who entered the meat packing business when he was a teen-ager, has seen Baltz Brothers Meats grow from a two-man operation to an organization employing six hundred people in six plants that ship products throughout the eastern United States.

It was forty-six years ago that young Robert Baltz, son of a farmer on Elm Hill Pike, came upon a "commotion" on a neighbor's farm on a cold winter day and found that hogs were being butchered. The whole process took place outdoors with primitive equipment, but Robert was fascinated.

Baltz was even more interested when his neighbor, Louis McRedmond, explained the way he made a profit of two or three cents a pound on the sausage.

"For a young boy in the midst of the Great Depression, that seemed like a pretty good margin," Baltz said.

His father, Robert J. Baltz Sr., discouraged Baltz from going into the sausage-making business, but he did permit him to buy one sow and raise five pigs the next year. And in the fall, when he made his first sausage, he found that it was difficult business. He was discouraged until the following year, when he met Ed Unger.

"He was a brilliant man who knew all about the meat business," Baltz said. "He had the knowledge and equipment necessary for getting started. I added a 1932 Ford Roadster, which a blacksmith made into a truck, and my local contacts and sales ability."

In 1936 they went into business together, each investing $20. Unger processed the meat and Baltz sold it and made deliveries.

When Unger found out that his partner was only sixteen, he was concerned about his liability if Baltz—in his hurry to cover his territory in his improvised truck—were to become involved in an accident.

The only solution was for one of the partners to buy out the other, and Baltz became sole owner. But the going was tough without the skill of Unger, and Baltz had to turn to his father for help. The elder Baltz took out a loan on his farm, where the present plant is located, so that Robert could construct a building for the meat processing company.

To gain experience in the industry, Robert Baltz worked in a meat packing plant in Nashville, but World War II interrupted, and he had to work at war-oriented jobs during the war. He rented his new building to two other men who operated a packing plant there. At the end of the war, with the help of two uncles, Will and Louis Baltz, Robert Baltz was able to buy all of the equipment there and in October 1946 Baltz Brothers, meat packing plant, was founded.

In the beginning there were only four employees, but by 1950 there were almost seventy-five, and ten years later more than two hundred people worked for Baltz Brothers. It was only when a container salesman told Baltz that the name was "difficult to pronounce and spell" that Baltz began to think about another name for his product. Because the plant had always been on his father's farm on Elm Hill Pike, he decided to change the name to Elm Hill Meats.

Today, five Baltz brothers are partners in the ownership of Baltz Brothers Packing Company. Each supervises a different area of operation. Frank purchases all livestock; Martin serves as plant engineer; Dennis is supervisor of operations; Jack is in charge of sales; and Robert, as president, is responsible for overall management.

The original Baltz Brothers plant on Elm Hill Pike in Nashville is shown in this 1939 photo.

Baptist Sunday School Board

The Sunday School Board of the Southern Baptist Convention, a $96-million-a-year publisher and distributor of church materials, began in one man's mind and a borrowed office in 1891.

And now, in a city of churches and church publications, the Sunday School Board is the largest postal customer in Nashville, making Nashville second only to Washington, D.C., in the volume of second-class mail.

Today the eighty-eight-year-old industry, spread out over several blocks in downtown Nashville, employs fifteen hundred people and ships its books, magazines, films, records, and other educational material to 35,255 Southern Baptist churches with a total of more than thirteen million members in every state and ninety-two foreign countries.

But in 1891 when Dr. James M. Frost, a scholarly Kentuckian, founded the Sunday School Board almost single-handedly, his idea was coldly received. There had been earlier attempts that failed, and the denomination depended on educational material from the American Baptist Publications Society in Washington, D.C.

But miraculously Frost had convinced the Southern Baptist Convention that the need was "imperative," and he and his loyal wife left a pleasant pastorate in Richmond, Virginia, to establish the Sunday School Board in Nashville.

Six years after he arrived, he was able to buy a small residence at 167 Fourth Avenue North for his first office building. In 1903 he sold that house to buy a much larger residence at 710 Church Street for the Board's offices. In 1912 he was able to buy for $60,000 a lot that reached from 161 Eighth Avenue North to Ninth Avenue, location of part of the present Board. In 1914 the Board built a massive pillared building on the Eighth Avenue property, which later became known as the Frost Building.

Many additions to that building have been made, and it is being renovated now for use of seventy professional and eighty clerical employees. But most of the work of the Board is done in the complex of buildings that front on Ninth Avenue.

The Board operates no printing presses but prepares all editorial material and contracts with printers to do the actual printing. It publishes a hundred books a year, 140 monthly and quarterly publications, and 300 to 350 undated publications with a circulation of almost sixty-six million. Its books are published through the Broadman Press (which took its name from John A. Broadus and Basil Manly, who were influential in the Southern Baptist Convention in the 1800s).

Broadman Press also produces music and other supplies. Broadman Films began producing audio-visual materials in 1951, including films for television distribution. The Board and the Southern Baptist Radio and Television Commission jointly produce a weekly television and radio program, "At Home With The Bible," which airs nationally on commercial stations and cable systems.

Convention Press is the name under which the Board publishes books produced especially for Southern Baptists' use. The Board's sixty-five bookstores in twenty-four states sell the products of other publishers as well as those of its own imprints. Latest acquisition in the Board's publishing program is America's oldest Bible publisher, A.J. Holman. Grady Cothen, president of the Board, said he hopes the Board will become "the nation's largest denominational distributor of Scripture."

Not even the founder, Dr. J.M. Frost, who served as president almost without interruption from 1891 to 1916, could have hoped for so much.

This old house at 167 Fourth Avenue North served as the first home of the Baptist Sunday School Board from 1897 to 1903. It has long since been demolished.

Today the Board's offices encompass several city blocks in downtown Nashville. The headquarters tower is located on Ninth Avenue North.

Berry Wholesale Drug Company

Berry Wholesale Drug Company, rooted in Nashville's history of 145 years ago, was dispensing medication to Middle Tennesseans when Andrew Jackson was in the White House.

Through four generations of the Berry family, beginning with W.W. Berry Sr. in 1834 and continuing to his great-grandson, Allen D. Berry Jr., today, the Berry Drug Company has played a strong role in the city's business life.

Beginning on the Public Square and moving later to nearby sites on Second Avenue North (then Market Street), the company has never left its original neighborhood. That stability in location and family ownership is striking in a business that has watched medication evolve dramatically from the era of calomel and quinine to today's wide variety of antibiotics and vaccines.

In the beginning, in 1834, W.W. Berry and John Felix Demoville formed their wholesale drug company under the name W.W. Berry & Demoville Druggists, at Number Six Public Square. Berry's son, W.W. Berry Jr., and grandson, Allen D. Berry Sr., continued in the company, and as late as 1870 the firm was still doing business on the south side of the Public Square.

In those days of steamboat shipping, it was important for wholesale companies to have their warehouses near the river, and W.W. Berry & Demoville was one of the many that operated out of block-long buildings reaching from the front offices on Market Street to the huge back doors opening just above the river.

W.W. Berry & Demoville operated for a time from a building at the corner of the Public Square and Bridge Avenue. In 1908 the firm moved to 174 Second Avenue North. By 1929 the company had become part of McKesson, Berry & Martin Company, at 214 Second Avenue North. From 1934 until 1974, part of that company continued as McKesson & Robbins.

But in 1958 Allen D. Berry Jr., along with a number of key people from the old organization, left that company to form his own business at 128 Second Avenue North under the name Berry Wholesale Drug Company, thus continuing the family business established by his great-grandfather.

When Berry Wholesale Drug Company opened for business in 1958, Allen Berry had eighteen years' experience in the drug business (having worked during summers in the business as a youth). Many of his colleagues added years of experience in the field.

During the first year of the new business, politics within the industry, Berry said, prevented major suppliers from opening accounts with the company. But in 1959 Eli Lilly Company broke the ice by making the first shipment to Berry Wholesale Drug Company. This, along with other suppliers opening accounts, really got the young business going.

In the early days of W.W. Berry & Demoville Druggists, all orders were written by hand. Today they are relayed by a computer system. With fewer than one hundred employees, Berry Wholesale Drug Company handles eighty percent of its orders through its automated communications system. The company supplies pharmaceuticals, proprietaries (toothpaste, for instance), and sundries to hospitals, drugstores, and medical facilities within a hundred-mile radius of Nashville, including southern Kentucky and northern Alabama.

It is a matter of particular satisfaction, Berry said, that his company keeps on hand a large supply of drugs so that, in case of a community emergency, a quick supply is available. The company is growing at such a rate that it will soon have to move into a one-level warehouse designed for more sophisticated electronic equipment.

In 1959 Berry executives and employees greeted the first shipment of pharmaceuticals from Eli Lilly, one of the nation's largest pharmaceutical manufacturers.

W. W. BERRY & DEMOVILLE

WHOLESALE

DRUGGISTS,

NO. 6 PUBLIC SQUARE,

NASHVILLE, TENN.

Berry Wholesale Drug Company's predecessor was advertised in this 1860 City Directory.

John Bouchard & Sons Company

John Bouchard & Sons Company, in business in Nashville since 1898, has enjoyed a rare consistency. For all of those eighty-one years, there has been a John Bouchard as president of the company—a fourth generation now. And through all of those years, headquarters for the company have been at the same location, 1024 Harrison. From that location, the family-owned business has helped mechanize the city.

Part of the success of the business that grew out of a French Canadian's blacksmith shop is that it "rolled with the punches" as customs and materials changed, said John E. Bouchard III, now president of the company. As new needs for supplying water, heat, fire protection, and cooling systems developed through the years, John Bouchard & Sons has supplied new machinery and new services.

Now employing 150 people, the operation ranges from designing and making huge pumps and pipe for the Metro Department of Water and Sewerage to installing sprinkler systems in modern bank buildings. The versatile company has grown in sales volume from $117,000 in 1916, for instance, to $6 million per year in 1978.

When the first John Bouchard arrived in Nashville, much of the transportation was by horse and buggy or by wagons used for hauling merchandise from boat dock to warehouse or from train to store. Shoeing horses was a steady business, but it was a "dirty, sweaty job" that meant long hours and hard work.

As horse-drawn carriages gave way to automobiles and trucks, Bouchard changed his forges from shaping horseshoes to working with heavier industry. By 1913 the company was incorporated, and he was designing and manufacturing machine parts for a rapidly changing city.

Bouchard outfitted Nashville's earliest Coca-Cola plant and made many of the installations at Werthan Bag Company, May Hosiery Mill, Phillips & Buttorff, Vanderbilt University, and Avco. When air conditioning became available, Bouchard installed one of the earliest systems in the city in the old Loew's Theater on Church Street.

Bouchard installed and repaired boilers and steam heating plants in the 1920s, when steam heat by radiator was considered the best heat available. At the same time, Bouchard installed much of the equipment in ice plants (refrigeration and pipe work). Today, the company not only installs sprinkler systems but also operates as plumbing and electrical contractors, industrial suppliers, and machinists.

Bouchard operates a foundry of its own, established in the 1920s to produce steam engines for sawmills. The foundry, largest operation in the Bouchard company, has sixty employees and today produces components for the construction business by recycling scrap metal.

In its electrical division, Bouchard installs power service, power wiring and distribution, lighting, and control circuits for commercial and industrial installations. It also supplies hardware—pipes, valves, and fittings for both domestic and industrial use.

It is a matter of pride to Bouchard that the trials of the Depression never closed the doors, and the company never failed to meet the payroll. Some of the company's employees have spent all of their working years there. Two brothers recently retired, one having worked there fifty-four years and the other fifty-two years.

John Bouchard, founder of the company, was president from 1898 to 1917. John E. Bouchard, responsible for much of the diversification within the company, was president from 1917 to 1941. John E. Bouchard Jr., responsible for much of the work done for the military (including Fort Campbell), was president from 1941 to 1969. John E. Bouchard III became president in 1969.

John Bouchard, founder of the company bearing his name, sits among early employees in a 1910 photo (left). The second generation John Bouchard is at work at the desk in the rear left corner of the company's 1925 office (center). Standing among a group of plumbers on a housing project construction site, the third generation John Bouchard is wearing a white shirt and dark tie (right).

Braid Electric Company

In Braid Electric Company—founded in 1879 by a young Scotsman named James W. Braid who liked to tinker with telegraph, telephone, and telescope—is mirrored the immeasurable scientific adventure of the last one hundred years.

For electricity was the excitement of the 1870s, and Braid was one of the first to probe its possibilities. Braid arrived in Nashville in 1870 and set up a little shop at the back of a photographic studio owned by J.H. Van Stavoren, where Braid was employed as photographer.

Braid, familiar with Alexander Graham Bell's experiments, had already assembled a contraption of wires, magnets, and batteries for transmitting voices. In September 1877 at a meeting in Nashville of the American Association for the Advancement of Science, Bell gave a demonstration of his new invention: the telephone. In January 1878 Braid and his friend James S. Ross took the invention a step further. With the aid of Ross' father, who worked at the Western Union telegraph office here, they used the telegraph lines to make the first long distance call—between Nashville and Louisville. Bell, at that time, had used his telephone to talk as far as two miles. Braid and Ross made history by talking and singing to each other over some two hundred miles of wires.

The following year Braid founded his own business, Braid Electric Company. There, in an old building on Union Street, he manufactured and distributed batteries, telegraph instruments, call bells, burglar alarms, and other electrical devices.

Braid made many "firsts" here. In 1882 he introduced the incandescent light to Tennessee when he suspended a bulb from a window in the State Capitol. In 1890, before the city had any electric lighting facilities, Braid installed a generator in the Maxwell House Hotel for lighting the dining room, halls, and lobby. Soon his company was swamped with orders to wire the largest office buildings, schools, hospitals, and other public buildings in the region.

In 1890 Braid employed W.W. Gambill in his company, and ten years later Braid sold his interest in the company to Gambill. The company he founded had ceased its manufacturing operation and was concentrating on installing lighting and supplying electrical equipment to other contractors from 1900 to 1923. In 1923 Braid Electric discontinued contracting and devoted all efforts to distributing electrical supplies, lighting products, and appliances.

New inventions were opening new markets. The company that had begun with the telegraph and the telephone entered a new business: radio. Braid, along with Waldrum Drug Company, began operating one of the city's first radio stations, WBAW, in April 1926, and they ran the station for three years.

The big business then was in selling radios and radio parts. That, like the leap to television in the 1950s, created a new market for the electrical distributor. At the same time, other electrical inventions had stretched the company's role in new directions. Electric washing machines, refrigerators, stoves, and vacuum cleaners entered practically every home.

At the death of W.W. Gambill in 1933, his son, Ben S. Gambill Sr., succeeded him as president of the company. Under his leadership the company opened divisions in Chattanooga, Tennessee, and Bowling Green and Danville, Kentucky, expanded its territory to include not only Middle and East Tennessee but also parts of Kentucky, Georgia, and Alabama, and grew from a seven-man operation to employment of well over one hundred. Ben S. Gambill Sr. retired as chairman of the board in March 1977.

Now the third generation of the Gambill family leads the company into its second century. Ben S. Gambill Jr., president, and Thomas K. Gambill, executive vice president, have recently established operations in Cookeville, Shelbyville, and Clarksville, Tennessee, to distribute electrical supplies as well as commercial and residential lighting products.

Having celebrated its 100th Anniversary as "America's Oldest Independent Electrical Distributor," Braid Electric Company has played an unparalleled role in bringing electricity to Nashville and the Mid-South.

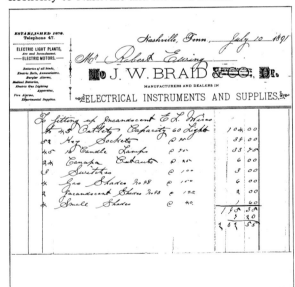

This 1891 invoice of J.W. Braid and Company, now Braid Electric Company, shows the wide variety of company products sold to Nashvillians at that time.

Brandau Craig Dickerson Company

Brandau Craig Dickerson Company, pioneer in color lithography and printing, was founded sixty-seven years ago. And today its products—including packaging materials, displays, color brochures and other commercial items—are distributed throughout the United States.

In 1912 A.G. Brandau—then a director of Brandon Printing Company, one of the largest in the Southeast—left that company with two of his colleagues, W.E. Craig and C.S. Dickerson, to take over Standard Printing Company. The new company, at 309 Fifth Avenue North, eliminated the office supply part of the business and confined itself exclusively to lithography and letterpress printing.

In those early days, artists on the staff engraved designs on fine-grained sandstone imported from Bavaria. The designs were transferred to metal plates and used for lithographing on paper. Much treasured are some of those surviving engraved stones—collectors' items today. When a later process, called photolithography, was developed, Brandau Craig Dickerson Company was one of the first to install the new process for reproduction.

In 1926 the company moved to a new and enlarged plant at 304 Tenth Avenue South, and today all phases of production are handled in that building.

Brandau Craig Dickerson played an interesting role in Nashville history in 1933, when all banks in the country were closed by order of the president. To prevent chaos in the area, Nashville banks decided to issue and guarantee face value of script, and that script was accepted (instead of money) by business houses and individuals.

Brandau Craig Dickerson Company designed and produced millions of dollars of this script in denominations of one dollar, five dollars, ten dollars, and twenty dollars. So accurate was the operation that no error or discrepancy was ever reported. When the state of Tennessee placed a tax on cigarettes, tobacco, and cigars, Brandau Craig Dickerson Company was given the contract to lithograph many millions of the revenue stamps.

A.G. Brandau, one of the founders of the company, died in 1931, and W.E. Craig succeeded him as president. In 1950 Seawell Brandau, Chester A. Roberts, and Thomas B. Walker purchased the interest of W.E. Craig. Seawell Brandau, son of one of the founders, became president, with Roberts as vice president and Walker as secretary-treasurer.

In 1960, following his graduation from Vanderbilt University and overseas service in the army, Seawell John Brandau, son of the president, joined the company. In 1969 Allen Roberts, son of the vice president, and three years later Perry M. Wilson, both graduates of David Lipscomb College, joined the company. Today Chester A. Roberts is chairman of the board, Seawell Brandau is president, Seawell J. Brandau is executive vice president, Allen Roberts is vice president, and Perry M. Wilson is secretary-treasurer.

By steady installation of new and improved equipment and by adoption of the latest methods, the company has kept pace with developments in the graphic arts industry. In addition to quality production of its volume products, the company offers such unusual specialties as dust bronzing, off-press die cutting, package insert folding, and spirit varnishing.

Founders of the company bearing their names were (from left) A.G. Brandau, W.E. Craig, and C.S. Dickerson. Many of the young company's best accounts were engraved on this early lithographic stone (below).

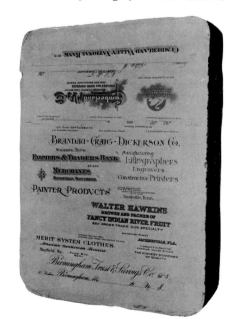

Capitol Engraving Company

Capitol Engraving Company, a leader in the photoengraving industry in the South, started out in 1909 on a shoestring and a $500 debt.

At that time, the process of etching plates for printers was a tedious one often involving hours of handwork by skilled craftsmen. Sunlight was used to expose photosensitive materials so that a cloudy day could be disastrous to a shop's schedule, and the chemicals used in etching the metal were a tempestuous blend that at times would tempt an oath from a preacher.

These were but a few of the difficulties faced by James H. O'Connell Sr. and his brother-in-law who founded Capitol in a building on Commerce Street between Sixth and Seventh avenues. After several months, O'Connell offered C.W. Bateman fifty percent of the business in return for $500. Bateman accepted, borrowing the money from his father and entering into what would become a forty-five-year investment in his trade.

The company enjoyed the boom economy following World War I, during which time Bateman traveled a great deal in order to establish a thriving trade in making engravings for college annuals. This, coupled with a local trade with such companies as Keith-Simmons, McQuiddy Printing, G.C. Dury, Brandau-Craig-Dickerson, Williams Printing, and the Methodist Publishing House, kept Capitol busy in those days.

The advent of the Depression brought an end to prosperity, and the burdens of debt were made more difficult by the death of O'Connell in 1930. Bateman found himself spending his Thursdays and Fridays "just trying to scrape up enough money to meet the payrolls."

Relief came in 1936 when Ernest Carroll, a former employee, bought a twenty-five percent interest in the business and began applying his considerable skills to catalog work for such companies as General Shoe (now Genesco). His experiments resulted in the first set of four-color process letterpress engravings ever made from a Kodachrome transparency. His process became a universal fixture in the industry.

Having survived the Depression and Prohibition when the company had to have a license to purchase the alcohol needed for the making of plates, Capitol was now faced with the copper and zinc shortage brought on by World War II. The shortage became so serious at one point that a special trip had to be made to Washington, D.C., to get enough copper to fill a large order.

As before, the postwar years were prosperous, and the business grew. Moving to its current location at 807 Clark Place in 1949, Capitol began making plates for offset lithography as a supplement to its traditional business in letterpress engravings. Beginning with black and white platemaking, after three or four years they began producing full-color work for lithographers.

In 1955 C.W. Bateman retired, leaving the business to his son, Fritz Bateman, who guided Capitol through twenty years of transition. The preparation of offset platemaking materials became the major portion of the business as letterpress printing declined. Trays and sinks once used for developing film and etching plates gave way to specially designed processors.

Technology in the form of electronic equipment, improved chemistry, and materials had begun to penetrate the industry. These innovations were costly and demanded further training for the craftsmen to develop new skills. During the 1950s and early 1960s, Fritz Bateman found ample business to support Capitol's needs in his almost daily visits to the Methodist Publishing House across the street on Eighth Avenue, but as the sixties waned, he realized that the business would have to be expanded to accommodate the increased expenses of the advancing technology.

In 1967 he was joined in his efforts by his son-in-law, Bill Mullins. Attention was given to markets in the North and East as well as in Nashville, and a full-time salesman was hired in the New York City area.

Bateman retired in 1975, relinquishing control to Mullins, who has since directed the continued growth of the company into a business six times the size it knew in the fifties. This growth has culminated with the complete remodeling and expansion of its existing facilities.

Capitol Engraving Company is now producing color separations in a matter of minutes on a computerized scanner, a single piece of equipment that costs several hundred times what the business was worth in 1909.

Today the company stands in tribute to seventy years of inspired leadership and dedicated craftsmanship. Its debts to the past are its gratitude for the present and the inspiration for a bright future.

Cummings Incorporated

Cummings Incorporated, one of the largest manufacturers of electrical signs in the world, has spread its designs throughout the United States and much of the world.

With sales at $28,863,000 in 1978, Cummings has designed, manufactured, installed, and maintained signs in all fifty states and Canada. Through its subsidiary, International Sign Service, Cummings has performed the same services from Belgium to Bangkok, from Argentina to Arabia. All Ford and Chrysler signs are manufactured by Cummings, along with signs for Conoco, Gulf, KFC, and many other nationally known companies.

Holiday Inn signs alone, designed and manufactured by the Nashville-based sign company, have spread the Cummings product to all states and many foreign countries. Fast-food products like Kentucky Fried Chicken, Captain D's Seafood, and Burger Queen and automobile dealers like Dodge and Chevrolet signal the public through the Cummings-made signs.

Thomas L. Cummings Jr., president and chairman of the board at Cummings Incorporated, 200 Twelfth Avenue South, says that leasing signs is a growing part of the business. The thirty-three-year-old business that he and a friend founded after World War II grew out of a college friendship. Cummings and Harold Balton of Memphis were fraternity brothers when they first thought of going into the sign business together. Balton's family had a similar business in Memphis.

Cummings had four years of service in World War II. Upon his return to Nashville in 1946, he and Balton put up $9,500 each to start the business. First operations were in an old Air Force gymnasium at Berry Field (the present airport). They called the company Balton and Cummings Incorporated.

In the first year, they did $48,000 worth of business, with $4,500 in earnings, and in the next three years, the volume of business doubled each year. At that time, the signs were neon tubing and porcelain enamel. Today the internally lit plastic sign is standard.

In 1951 executive offices for the company were moved to the present location. Beginning with local accounts, the firm created signs for automobile dealers, hotels, motels, and fast-food industries and soon spread to a national and international clientele.

In 1954 Cummings bought out Balton's share in the business, and it became Cummings & Company. In 1965 the International Sign Service was formed so that lighting and sign companies throughout the United States were licensed by Cummings & Company to install and maintain signs in a partnership agreement.

In 1967 the business went public. The company operates six manufacturing plants, in Memphis, Murfreesboro, and Nashville, Tennessee; Columbus, Ohio; Hurst, Texas; and Toronto, Ontario. Sales and service facilities are maintained in Detroit, Louisville, and Lachine, Quebec. The company employees 666 people.

When the company is designing signs for high-volume accounts, it coordinates all phases of a regional or national plan. The planning includes conducting a site survey to determine the best location for the sign and advising on code requirements and restrictions. Cummings coordinates all details of the production process, shipping, installation, and maintenance.

Five artists on the Cummings staff design the signs in collaboration with engineers. Custom manufacturing is done at all of the plants except the one at Murfreesboro.

Cummings, son of former Nashville Mayor Thomas L. Cummings, said one of the company's earliest customers was the H. Brown Furniture Company on Broadway. Among prominent signs in Nashville are the Tennessee Theater marquee and the twenty-five-foot L&C letters on the Life & Casualty Insurance Company tower.

In 1967 Board Chairman Thomas L. Cummings introduced a new logo for his company to emphasize the firm's expanding international operations.

311

Cutters Exchange

Cutters Exchange—a huge international business with headquarters in Nashville—grew out of one young man's idea in 1914.

John Walton Fite, a Nashville native, was twenty-two years old when World War I in Europe was troubling some Southeastern clothing manufacturers in 1914. Nervous about the outcome of the war, they decided to sell the piece goods they had on hand and go out of business. Fite, already an experienced auto salesman, was asked to handle the sale.

They were "cutters," with warehouses full of cloth to be cut. It occurred to Fite that he could set up a clearing-house for the "cutting" trade—selling the used merchandise to other cutters who wanted to start or expand businesses. Hence the name Cutters Exchange.

Fite opened his office at 202 Public Square, and Cutters Exchange was an overnight success. By the Depression years, Fite was a millionaire. He soon expanded his inventory to include every piece of machinery used in the business of cutting, sewing, and spreading. He sold not only to the apparel industry but also to companies that used office furniture and equipment. He was soon advertising that he could equip from his catalog any plant in the apparel industry, from front door to back.

Catalogs became the secret of his early success. A pioneer in the mail-order business, he distributed a series of weekly bulletins to the garment trade.

The catalogs grew out of the dictates of the day. Transportation over poor roads made it difficult for salesmen to cover much territory, and Fite decided to let the U.S. mail do the work for him. The 1,000-page catalogs became the standby of the trade, and today 50,000 of them are distributed twice a year throughout this country, Canada, Mexico, South America, and many European and Asian countries.

Fite's company not only supplies machinery, but it also sells and installs whole systems within a plant. But Fite's idea grew far beyond that. The company has the capability of securing a contract or contractor, securing a plant location, and even buying, selling, or leasing an entire plant.

Cutters Exchange includes Cutter Machine Company, which manufactures Cutline-Ajax spreading and cutting equipment for sale throughout the world; Cutters Electronics International, which designs and manufactures electronic and control systems for apparel and textile industries; and Commercial Interiors Division, which wholesales and retails office furniture and equipment.

A tornado in 1933 destroyed the original building at 202 Public Square. After several moves, the firm has been at 627 Nineteenth Avenue North since 1960.

Fite died in 1960 after seeing his company grow to an international, full-service catalog house where apparel manufacturers can buy everything they need to go into business—or to stay in business.

In the sixty-five years since John W. Fite began the business, the company has grown from "three or four employees" before World War I to 450 people today, in addition to a sales force of 125 men.

In 1946, when Fite's son-in-law, A.J. Rebrovick, joined the firm, the thirty-two-year-old company was well on the way to joining the ranks of family-owned businesses of long continuity. Rebrovick is president of the company now. His son, Art Rebrovick Jr., who joined the firm in 1973, continues the family tradition.

Besides the Nashville headquarters, with more than one-half million square feet, there are divisions of the company in Atlanta, Chicago, Dallas, Los Angeles, Miami, and Greensboro, North Carolina. Projected volume of business for 1979 is $40 million, with increased export business anticipated.

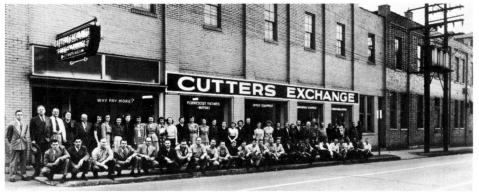

John Walton Fite (left) was only twenty-two when the idea for Cutters Exchange dawned on him in 1914. Employees of Cutters Exchange—by this time much larger and considerably more profitable—stand outside the company's offices at 901 Demonbreun Street in 1952 (right).

Foster & Creighton Company

Foster & Creighton Company, builders of many of the landmarks of Nashville for almost a century, have constructed bridges and streets, office buildings and industrial plants, hospitals and libraries and churches.

The fact that they built both the wood-and-plaster replica of the Parthenon in Centennial Park in 1897 and the permanent concrete replica on the same spot in 1931 ties the company to the city's history and cultural life. Because of that association, Foster & Creighton chose the Parthenon as their own emblem.

But Wilbur F. Foster and Robert T. Creighton had been building in Nashville long before they organized their firm in 1885 on a $1,500 investment. Creighton was the scion of a family of pioneer builders who raced horses with Andrew Jackson at Clover Bottom race track and employed Jackson as their attorney.

Foster & Creighton landscaped Capitol Hill, laid the foundation for the first building at Vanderbilt University, for Jubilee Hall at Fisk University, for the Tennessee state prison, and for Union Station. Foster & Creighton converted the city's dirt roads into paved streets, helped build the first street railway in Nashville, and constructed most of the bridges over the Cumberland River.

By 1895, when Tennessee began work on its gigantic celebration of its 100th birthday, the ten-year-old firm of Foster & Creighton was so well established that they were given complete authority for construction of all twenty-six buildings and the extensive landscaping for the grounds (site of present Centennial Park). Major Foster and Robert Creighton served successively as Director of Works for the Exposition, and that highly successful achievement played a pivotal role in the company's history.

In the early 1900s, Foster & Creighton continued their pioneering tradition, expanding operations throughout Tennessee and the South. They operated the first ready-mix concrete plant in Tennessee, built the first concrete arched bridge in the state, built the first concrete navigation lock on the Cumberland River, installed the first filtration plant in Nashville, and laid some of the first concrete-paved highways in the South.

Foster & Creighton have covered the range of Nashville history in their buildings—everything from the replica of the log fortress where the city began, Fort Nashborough, to the largest office building in the city, the First American Center.

A complete list of Nashville structures built, modified, or remodeled by Foster & Creighton would fill many pages, and a list of structures built by the company throughout the state, across the country and abroad would fill a book. Four generations of the Creighton family (founder Robert T. Creighton, Wilbur F. Creighton, Wilbur F. Creighton Jr., and Wilbur F. Creighton III) have led the company into its position as one of the largest building firms in the United States with branch offices in several states and overseas.

Among their recent achievements are the Nashville Thermal Plant, completed in 1974 (the first plant in the world to use solid waste as a fuel to heat and cool downtown buildings), and receipt of the Build America Award, presented to the company by Associated General Contractors of America in 1978 for construction excellence in its work as a major subcontractor on the New River George Bridge in West Virginia. Wilbur F. Creighton Jr., now chairman of the board, and Wilbur F. Creighton III, now president of the company, take special pride in the company's ninety-four years of helping build Nashville solidly and handsomely.

Two of Foster & Creighton Company's most impressive local construction projects are the full-scale, concrete replica of the Parthenon (completed in 1931) and the giant First American Center in downtown Nashville (completed in 1974).

Fidelity Federal Savings And Loan Association

Fidelity Federal Savings and Loan Association, forty-two years old and the largest savings and loan association in Nashville, reached more than $450 million in assets last year and is still growing. That growth is proof that ideas do have consequences.

It was at a Lions Club meeting in 1937 that W. Raymond Denney, a Nashville lawyer, heard a talk that set his head spinning. James M. Roundtree, then general manager of the Savings and Loan Division of the Federal Home Loan Bank Board, spoke to members of the club about the difficulty of getting a long-term loan for a home prior to the Federal Home Loan Bank Act of 1932.

When the Lions Club meeting adjourned that day, "several of the men assembled in a corner of the room and agreed informally to investigate this little-known and hardly heard-of business," Denney recalled years later.

After obtaining more information on the subject, the group met to discuss applying for a charter for what was to become Fidelity Federal Savings and Loan Association. In the organizing group were Denney, W.H. Browder, James G. Blakemore, C.M. Crow, W.H. Hailey, Virgil Hall, C.S. Ragland, Joe Wiles, Bernard Werthan, Sam Berger, and G.A. Harrington.

Harrington became the first president, Blakemore and Hailey vice presidents, and all of the group served on the first board of directors. The required $25,000 was raised with the required one hundred subscribers, and the charter was issued on April 6, 1937. The new company opened its doors for business on May 13, 1937, with its offices in what had been a small sandwich shop in the Brown Building on Union Street. Rent was $35 per month, and on opening day the office had no furniture, no secretarial help, and an obligation to pay dividends of four percent.

"Some of the directors hustled around and found $24,000 in mortgages," said Denney, who served as general counsel for the company for thirty-three years. Since his retirement in 1970, he has continued to serve on the advisory board. W.H. Browder, a founding director, became vice president in 1955, president in 1957, and chairman of the board in 1967. When he retired in 1974, he was elected to the advisory board and given the title chairman emeritus.

When the first secretary was hired, she brought her own typewriter and card table to work on. The old red brick building where the company first did business is said to have been the same building where Sam Houston, in 1819, studied law in the offices of Judge James Trimble.

In 1937, when Fidelity Federal opened its offices a few doors down from the corner, at 407 Union, the Depression was far from ended, and the great emphasis was on home loans. The savings and loan part of the business did not get a solid start until the post-World War II housing boom.

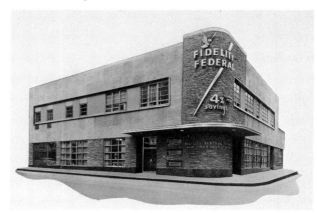

From 1955 to 1973 Fidelity Federal occupied the structure above at 401 Union Street. In 1973 this building was razed to make way for the association's striking new home office (right), located on the same site.

314

Those years immediately after World War II, along with the last five years, have marked the company's most dramatic growth. In 1955 the company moved into much larger quarters in the remodeled building at the corner of Fourth and Union. From 1973 to 1975, the company used a bank building at 226 Third Avenue North while its new office building was being built at its old corner, Fourth and Union. The company moved into that stunning new building in 1975.

Fidelity Federal was the first savings institution in Nashville to offer three percent savings, to increase it to four percent in 1955, and to four and one-half percent in 1969. In 1969 only one type of savings plan was offered, while today five and one-half percent is offered on regular passbook savings and eight percent on savings certificates held for ninety-six months. Ten savings plans are offered altogether.

Today Fidelity Federal is the largest savings and loan association in Middle Tennessee. Some indication of its forward push is that it opened its first branch in 1956 in Green Hills; installed its in-house computer program in 1962; offered Telefund services, moving funds from savings to checking, in 1976; offered prior approval loans and sponsored the first home loan advertising in fourteen years in 1977; and offered Money Market Certificates (now the primary savings investment in savings and loan associations and in banks) in 1978.

Fidelity Federal, with 182 employees and fourteen offices, showed a sixteen percent increase in 1978 over the previous year's assets, said Chairman of the Board and President Stanley D. Overton. In several areas, 1978 was a record year for the association.

Other members of the present board of directors include: Joe L. Hooper, executive vice president; Judson G. Collins, broadcasting; James L. Harper, James L. Harper & Associates; T.C. Summers, president, Cowan Stone Company; and Dan W. Denney, partner, Wilson County Motor Company.

First American National Bank

First American National Bank, ninety-six years old in 1979, is almost half Nashville's age and has roots reaching close to the city's founding.

Now the city's largest bank, in a $20 million office building towering twenty-eight stories above the spot where it began in 1883, First American is far removed from its small beginning. With thirty branches and thirteen hundred employees, the bank had assets of $1,251,284,000 in 1978.

But even when the bank was founded as American National Bank on July 6, 1883, its capital of $600,000 was impressive in a town so recently stripped of financial strength by the Civil War. That was only eighteen years behind them, and the twenty men who raised the $600,000 capital had to be among the city's wealthiest.

One of them, Colonel E.W. Cole, had won his rank in the Confederate army and had made his fortune with the Nashville, Chattanooga & St. Louis Railway. As one of the city's ablest businessmen and civic leaders, he had won the respect of the community since he arrived here in 1845, the year Andrew Jackson died and the work on building the capitol began.

Cole, first president of American National Bank, owned an office building, the Cole Building, that stood at Fourth and Union on the same spot where First American National Bank stands today. In that five-story brick Cole Building, the bank opened for business on September 1, 1883, and there it operated for the next five years.

Six months after American National Bank opened, it absorbed the old Third National Bank (not to be confused with today's bank of the same name), and John Kirkman, president of Third National, became president of the combined banks. At Kirkman's death in 1888, Edgar Jones became president. When Jones resigned to form Union Bank & Trust Company in 1891, W.W. Berry Jr. became president and served in that office for twenty-seven years.

First move of the bank came in 1888, when it bought a building at 235 College Street (now Third Avenue North). That building burned the following year but was rebuilt. It was not until 1911, when American National Bank absorbed Union Bank & Trust, that it moved into the handsome building occupied by the latter at the southwest corner of Third and Union (now American Trust Building).

After World War I, American National Bank expanded rapidly, absorbing Cumberland Valley National Bank in 1921 and Fourth and First National Bank in 1930. After the 1921 merger, it moved to the Stahlman Building and operated there for ten years. It was the merger with the larger but failing Fourth and First National Bank that led American National Bank back to its original site, on the northeast corner of Fourth and Union, in 1931. There, where the bank had opened forty-eight years earlier, it conducted business in marble-columned splendor until it moved into stunning new quarters on the same corner in 1973.

In the booming 1920s—in fact, from 1918 to 1927—P.D. Houston Sr. was president of American National. And when Paul M. Davis became president in 1927, the days of exciting growth were still in full swing. But it was during Davis' presidency that the Depression put banks over the nation to the test. In those rough years, when bank failures reached a national rate of 11.8 percent, American National had a strong hand in keeping Tennessee's rate of failure down to 9.7 percent.

By helping smaller banks in the area (correspondent banks) meet the threat of customers who might have withdrawn all of their deposits, American National gained a loyalty that remains to the present. That action also made American National's correspondent banking department one of the strongest in the bank, said Parkes Armistead, former president of the bank.

It was while Armistead was president that the bank added "First" to its name. To be "First" is a cherished title, and the bank had the right to use it from the day National American merged with Fourth & First Bank in 1930. But it was not until 1950 that American National became First American National Bank.

For a number of reasons, greatest growth for First American National Bank has come since World War II, beginning with the presidency of Paul Davis (1927 to 1948) and continuing with Parkes Armistead (1948 to 1957), P.D. Houston Jr. (1957 to 1960), Andrew Benedict (1960 to 1969), Scott Fillebrown (1969 to 1976), and Kenneth L. Roberts (since 1976).

Stressing its role as a corporate citizen, First American takes pride in the aid it was able to give Nashvillians when two disasters struck the city: once in 1916 when fire swept through much of East Nashville and destroyed 700 buildings, and again in 1933 when a tornado struck East Nashville and damaged fifteen hundred homes.

Now, as the largest bank in a holding company formed in 1969 and called First Amtenn Corporation, First American National Bank has widened its role as community developer. As part of a network of financial institutions offering financial and fiduciary services through much of the southeastern region of the United States, First American is affiliated with seven other banks in Tennessee; a Florida-based consumer finance company with business in Florida, Georgia, and Tennessee; and a commercial finance company and an investment advisory firm, both located in Tennessee. The corporation has a total of 111 banking and lending offices.

Not only do the bank and the subsidiaries of the corporation make substantial contributions to projects aimed at improving the quality of life in the areas served, but First American has a commitment to housing and urban redevelopment in the communities it serves. First American has been a leader in providing financial assistance to the Neighborhood Housing Authority, a program for improving homes in once-declining neighborhoods.

Thus, when First American National Bank began considering ways to expand its longtime headquarters building at Fourth and Union, in 1970, it decided to make it a telling move in restoring a rapidly deteriorating downtown area. Instead of merely adding an annex on the parking lot adjacent to its old building, it entered into a plan that would give new life and beauty to the whole block—the historic heart of the city's financial life, reaching from Fourth to Third, between Union and Deaderick. Union, the "Wall Street of the South," and Deaderick, named for Tennessee's first banker, seemed particularly appropriate entrances to the bank.

Outgrowth of that plan is the First American Center, dominated by a twenty-eight-floor office tower and open, pleasing vistas along a street-level plaza where fountains play and noontime strollers stop for concerts and art shows. The Equitable Life Assurance Society of the United States joined First American in the building venture, the first by any private business in the redevelopment of the downtown area.

The bank won an unequaled treasure in the process of building. There, excavators blasting for the bank's foundation found the remains of a prehistoric saber-toothed tiger in a cave. That find, displayed in the lobby, places the bank on the oldest known occupied real estate in Nashville.

Home offices of First American National Bank have included the American National Bank Building (left) at the corner of Third and Union (now the location of the American Trust Building); the Fourth and First National Bank Building (center) at the corner of Fifth and Union; and the bank's current headquarters (right), the First American Center, on the site of the now-demolished Fourth and First National Bank Building.

Fisk University

Fisk University, 113 years old in 1979 and one of the great black universities in the nation, has as dramatic a story to tell of its beginning and growth as any university can boast.

The fact that the tiny school—begun in abandoned Union army barracks and supported by mission groups—almost failed five years after its founding and was rescued by songs of old slave days is a story of rare triumph.

In October 1865, barely six months after the Civil War, the school began under auspices of the American Missionary Association of New York (now part of the United Church of Christ), which still assists the university, and with the help of Western Freedmen's Aid Commission of Cincinnati.

Men who had a part in the founding were John Ogden (first principal), the Reverend E.M. Cravath (first president of the university), and the Reverend E.P. Smith. General Clinton B. Fisk, former Union officer who became a director of the Freedmen's Bureau in Tennessee, helped secure quarters from the federal government for the school that was named in his honor.

On January 9, 1866, in barracks near Twelfth Avenue North, between Charlotte and Church, the school opened. The barracks were often cold and the food scarce in spite of efforts of sponsoring mission societies. Notwithstanding Spartan living and high ambition on the part of both faculty and students, the school seemed doomed to failure by 1871.

By that time, Adam K. Spence had succeeded Ogden as principal of Fisk School, and George L. White was both school treasurer and professor of music. He knew not only how desperate the school's finances were but also how rich the talents of some of the students were. It was his recognition of that talent that saved the school.

White's students worked hard at singing the formal music he taught them in class, but by accident he heard them singing in their own quarters. And the songs they sang among themselves were unlike anything he had ever heard. Slowly White coaxed them to share the stirring music that came to be known as spirituals.

He persuaded his students to share their songs with white congregations in Nashville churches who might donate to the struggling school. That effort was so successful that their fame spread to congregations in Boston and New York. Abolitionists like Henry Ward Beecher brought Fisk's plight to the attention of Northerners and arranged for the Jubilee Singers to give concerts in the North and East.

The name Jubilee itself touched the hearts of audiences. Taken from the biblical word describing the end of Hebrew bondage, Jubilee celebrated freedom for the ex-slaves with special poignancy.

So rich was the response of Northern audiences that in 1873 concert tours were arranged in England and Europe, and audiences there were particularly generous in support of the school. Queen Victoria summoned the singers to Buckingham Palace for a command performance and ordered the court artist to paint the portrait of the Fisk Jubilee Singers which hangs at Fisk today.

With funds from Fisk Jubilee Singers' concert tours, land for the present campus was bought, and Jubilee Hall—the first permanent building on the campus—was built in 1876. And through the years, later generations of Fisk Jubilee Singers have toured much of the world—to spread Fisk's fame and enrich her coffers.

Thus it was that Fisk Jubilee Singers introduced to the world the spirituals, a particularly appealing American art form, and around the Jubilee Singers grew the tradition of excellence in music and art at Fisk. Out of that tradition came emphasis on quality in all departments.

There were only three hundred students at Fisk in 1873 when the first Jubilee Singers began touring Europe. Even

Jubilee Hall was the first permanent building on any college campus in America built for the express purpose of educating black men and women. It was completed in 1876.

today Fisk is a small school, placing emphasis on individual training. But the rise from grammar school to high school, from there to "normal school" (teacher's training) to college and university has led over endless hurdles.

In 1930 Fisk became the first black college to gain full accreditation by the Southern Association of Colleges and Schools. Fisk was the first such college to be placed on the approved list of the Association of American Universities (1933) and the American Association of University Women (1948). In 1952 Fisk was granted a charter for establishment of a chapter of Phi Beta Kappa honor society.

More than fifty percent of Fisk's graduates go to graduate school, and within two or three years after graduation another twenty percent continue their education. Offering majors in humanities, fine arts, social sciences, natural sciences, and mathematics, Fisk confers the B.A., B.S., M.S., and B.Mus. degrees.

Students today come from forty states and six foreign countries, and there are alumni in forty-nine states. Fifteen percent of Fisk alumni become medical doctors, and Fisk has among its graduates nearly six percent of all black physicians in the United States. Another five to seven percent of Fisk graduates become lawyers, and nearly five percent of all black dentists and five percent of all black lawyers in the United States are Fisk alumni.

Caught in the economic squeeze that faces all private colleges and universities, Fisk is engaged in the constant struggle to keep top-quality educators on the faculty at competitive salaries.

Jubilee Hall has been designated a National Historical Landmark by the Department of the Interior. Recently the university has undertaken a program of renovation and beautification.

The eight former presidents of Fisk University have kept alive close ties with the community of Nashville: Erastus Milo Cravath (1875-1900); James Griswold Merrill (1901-1908); George Augustus Gates (1909-1912);

Fayette Avery McKenzie (1915-1925); Thomas Elsa Jones (1926-1946); Charles Spurgeon Johnson (1947-1956); Stephen Junius Wright (1957-1966); and James Raymond Lawson (1967-1975).

Johnson was the first black president of the university, and, as a sociologist of wide reputation, he established a Race Relations Insitutute at Fisk "for the confrontation of blacks and whites."

Since 1926 Fisk has received valuable endowments. President Thomas E. Jones helped Fisk win a million-dollar endowment that year, and thus Fisk became the first black university to receive so large an endowment. A $500,000 grant from the General Education Board was matched by donations from Julius Rosenwald, and many generous Nashvillians contributed.

As the 1950s and 1960s saw sweeping social changes, many black students sought white colleges. Suddenly Fisk was competing with white universities for the brightest black students. To help meet the problems, there was more competitive recruitment of students. Even so, Fisk was swamped in administrative and financial problems when Dr. Walter Jewell Leonard left an administrative post at Harvard University to become president of Fisk University in 1977.

Inaugurated on October 6, 1977, Leonard has fired students, faculty, and alumni to new effort to rebuild the university and its historic neighborhood in North Nashville.

Reflecting on the glory of 111 years of Fisk achievement, Leonard, at his inauguration, called the university a "slightly damaged Rembrandt."

"We can't allow this masterpiece to be destroyed," Leonard told the audience.

A moving force on the campus, Leonard has drawn to the university a group of young administrators determined to build Fisk to its full potential. Faculty, physical plant, and administrators are geared to draw more students than ever into a program that will strengthen the university built on Jubilee.

The original Fisk Jubilee Singers (left) were formed in 1871 as a desperate attempt to stave off bankruptcy for the young institution. Today the Singers (center) still travel worldwide as goodwill ambassadors for their school. Dr. Walter J. Leonard (right) became the president of Fisk University on October 6, 1977, and, since that time, he has attracted new students, administrators, and faculty members to the historic school.

Green Hills Market

Green Hills Market, celebrating its fortieth anniversary in 1979, has, in subtle ways, captured the best of two eras in grocery selling—the personal touch of the past and the wide assortment of elegantly displayed fresh foods available today.

A supermarket in size, it is an independent, family-owned store that became the nucleus for one of the most successful shopping centers in Nashville. The Green Hills Market, in fact, gave its name to the whole Green Hills Shopping Center.

It was Labor Day 1939 when partners A. Roy Greene and Roy T. Primm Sr. opened a grocery story at 3909 Hillsboro Road on property they had bought the spring before. The land was "nothing more than a cow pasture in the country" then, and they paid a total of $5,000 for the land and the first store they constructed there.

Greene, experienced in the retail grocery business, had been a partner in Richland Market, a quality store that emphasized personal service, at Thirty-First and West End Avenue. Primm had been a salesman for wholesale grocers Robert Orr and Company. After Greene was defeated in his race for mayor against Thomas L. Cummings, he and Primm pooled their resources to open their own store: Green Hills Market.

In 1941 Green Hills Market bought the drugstore next door and changed the name to Green Hills Pharmacy. When a new movie theater was opened in the area, the owners called it Green Hills Theater. With these three businesses—grocery, drugstore, and theater—named Green Hills, the name of the area was established.

Before World War II, Green Hills Market delivered groceries to the homes of customers. Orders were assembled in the store's basement, and five trucks made deliveries six days a week, covering an area from Vanderbilt University southward to the county line and from Trousdale westward to Harding Road.

In 1947 Roy T. Primm Sr. bought out Greene's interest in the business. In 1952, the year after the death of Roy T. Primm Sr., his son, Roy T. Primm Jr., became vice president of the company. W.D. Thweatt was president from 1952 to 1970, when Roy T. Primm Jr. succeeded him. Mrs. Roy T. Primm Sr. was chairman of the board until her death in 1978. Her daughter, Dorothy Primm Joyner, is vice president of the family-owned business.

Noted for its specialty items, Green Hills Market offers exotic, hard-to-find products, along with top-quality meats, vegetables, and fruits. Gourmet cooks turn to Green Hills Market for rare ingredients used in foreign recipes.

In a day when most supermarkets depend on self-service, Green Hills Market has seventy-five full-time employees and fifteen part-time employees to assist customers. Employees at the check-out counter offer special assistance to the sick and the elderly, often delivering an order by taxi.

With the rapid growth of the suburban Green Hills area after World War II, Green Hills Market was so crowded that it built a stunning new building in 1971—just behind the original store and twice its size. Next door is the new Green Hills Pharmacy. The store is in the process of installing an automated scanning system that "reads" the computer code on each package—a great help in record-keeping.

Primm says rising costs are rapidly changing the business, but the extra little services—like boning all roasts—keep the customers coming. That's one of the "unchangeables," Primm said. Service, personal contact, and quality—these made one independent grocery store the nucleus of a whole section of Nashville.

Roy T. Primm Sr. is shown here in 1944, only five years after he and A. Roy Greene founded Green Hills Market. The store would eventually lend its name to the entire neighborhood.

The original store, as seen here in 1960, was demolished in 1971 so that a modern structure could be erected.

Gresham And Smith

Gresham and Smith are so dynamically changing the approach to designing buildings that they have, in twelve years, established Tennessee's largest architectural firm.

In one year, they handle construction amounting to more than $100 million by assembling a team for each project—each team drawn from a staff of 164 professionals.

Founders of the company are Batey M. Gresham Jr. and Fleming W. Smith Jr. The buildings they design range from the historically significant rehabilitation of the Hermitage Hotel to the new Vantage Place office complex in MetroCenter to hospitals across the country and in Guatemala and Saudi Arabia.

"Partnership" is the key word in the whole operation, Gresham and Smith insist. When each is asked his title in the firm, the only answer is "partner."

The firm of Gresham and Smith was formed on April 1, 1967. Gresham's wife Ann agreed to act as secretary and bookkeeper. As the company developed, Gresham worked at getting contracts, and Smith "worked out solutions."

Both "did everything" when they opened their first office, a three-room corner suite on the eleventh floor of the Sudekum Building, on Church Street at Sixth Avenue. They were "nurturing" small accounts at first, but they had no "bread-and-butter" clients who could be counted on to pay the rent.

But in 1960 Mrs. Gresham had become a patient of Dr. Thomas Frist Sr. The Greshams and the Frists became friends, and through Dr. Frist, one of the founders of Hospital Corporation of America, Gresham and Smith received their first hospital contract: to design an addition to Metro General Hospital.

When Frist and his co-founders at HCA were ready to build their first hospitals, it was natural that they would turn to this young architectural firm. Gresham and Smith soon had their first three HCA contracts—for hospitals in Albany and Macon, Georgia, and in Chattanooga.

At that time, there were only four people at Gresham and Smith, but the firm had the three hospitals ready on schedule.

HCA gave Gresham and Smith contracts for hospitals from Florida to California and in 1972 asked them to design a hospital in Athens, Greece. Their most fantastic project was to design a 250-bed addition to the King Faisal Hospital in Saudi Arabia, and through that job came other contracts—to design high-rise apartment buildings, for instance, as well as two palaces.

In 1978 seventy percent of Gresham and Smith's total business involved designing medical facilities. In 1979 the firm works on 250 active projects per day. To meet that schedule, there are sixteen employees in the company's branch office in Charleston, South Carolina, and six in the Birmingham, Alabama, office, in addition to the 142 in Nashville.

To handle the company's rapid growth, Gresham and Smith have moved three times and are now crowded in a twelve-thousand-square-foot building of concrete and glass at 2222 State Street. A new building is being planned for the Nashville office.

Today the company includes four partners in addition to Gresham and Smith: Alexander C. Walker III, Albert A. Thweatt, Lloyd O. Gragg Jr., and James O. Hastings Jr. The average age for all employees in the company is thirty-five years, and that average puts them close to the youngest among Nashville's eighty-eight architectural firms. With projects totaling almost one-half billion dollars in construction value, Gresham and Smith take pride in their role of "improving the quality of our environment."

In 1967 Batey Gresham (above left) and Flem Smith (above right) began working as a team. By 1979 (below) their partnership carried them to worldwide projects and ownership of one of the largest architectural firms in the United States.

321

Herbert Materials Incorporated

Herbert Materials Incorporated, a brick manufacturer and building supply firm that serves builders and contractors throughout the South, was founded 112 years ago by a Confederate veteran who helped Nashville grow into a city.

William George Bush, founder of W.G. Bush and Company, left his native Cane Ridge community at age sixteen and traveled the twelve miles to Nashville to become an apprentice stone and brick mason under the guidance of his uncle, James Murrell, who was employed on the construction of the State Capitol.

Stories and recollections relating to W.G. Bush and his escapades as a member of the Nathan Bedford Forrest regiment during the Civil War earned him the honor, if not the rank, of Major in the Army of the Confederate States of America. At the end of the Civil War, Major Bush turned his early acquired masonry skills to the reconstruction of Nashville and Middle Tennessee.

By the time William G. Bush returned to Nashville after the Civil War, he was thirty-six years old, and he was convinced there was a better way to make brick. Before the war, most Nashville residences were constructed with brick made by hand at the job site, usually with the clay excavated from the foundation and cellar. However, with the devastating effects of war and the resulting reconstruction era, brick in Nashville was in great demand; therefore, the Major constructed kilns and mined clay for brick making at a central location on twelve lots costing $2,000 in North Nashville.

It was upon these early historic buildings and others in Nashville that W.G. Bush and Company built its base for 112 years of continued growth. From the early 1900s, W.G. Bush, in concert with his son-in-law, T.L. Herbert, expanded their building materials business which presently encompasses the manufacturing of clay face brick with two plants in Nashville and one in Gleason, Tennessee, with total annual production of eighty million brick.

In 1911 T.L. Herbert & Sons Incorporated was founded by Major Bush's son-in-law to furnish building supplies and sand and gravel dredged from the Cumberland River, while W.G. Bush and Company (incorporated in 1917) continued to supply brick. Today T.L. Herbert & Sons Incorporated dredges sand and gravel from the Tennessee and Cumberland rivers for its own ready-mix concrete plants and for resale, does commercial towing, markets building supplies, and operates a river fleet including two suction dredges, three towboats, four harbor tenders, and fifty-four barges.

Further expansion of business came with the acquisition of a concrete block manufacturing plant in Shelbyville, Tennessee, that also supplies masonry related building materials and operates a ready-mix concrete plant.

Major William G. Bush (left) founded his brick yards in the busy years following the Civil War. He was convinced there was a better way to make brick than on the building site itself, so he purchased twelve lots in North Nashville and proceeded to make brick on his property and then truck them to the site. Bush Lake, now part of MetroCenter, was formed when thousands of tons of clay were excavated (above) for Bush's brick.

In 1974 Herbert Marine Terminal opened to land and unload materials shipped into and out of Nashville by water. The river transportation companies operate towboats and barges on the Cumberland, Tennessee, Mississippi, and Ohio rivers, and a river marine terminal on the Cumberland River, Port of Nashville, and Tennessee River, Port of New Johnsonville.

For years, Bush operated the North Nashville brick yards and made brick and delivered them in mule-drawn wagons to the job sites The excavation left from digging tons of clay for brick eventually filled with water and became known as Bush's Lake (now part of MetroCenter). The original clay pit was filled in many years ago, and the City Sewage and Disposal Plant now occupies that site.

In 1850, when he was twenty-one, Bush married Agatha (Aggie) Sneed of Brentwood, and they had two children, Sarah (Sally) and W.C. Bush. In 1875 Sally Bush married Thomas Levens Herbert of Brentwood, and in 1879 W.G. Bush formed a partnership with his son and his son-in-law.

But by the time "Major" Bush retired as president of the company in 1900, his only son had died. His son-in-law, T.L. Herbert, succeeded Bush as president in 1900 and served until 1913. T.L. Herbert Jr. was president from 1917 until 1949, and his nephew, John S. Herbert, was president from 1949 until 1970. James A. Skinner Jr., grandson of R.D. Herbert and president since 1970, is the fifth generation of the family to operate the company.

W.G. Bush and Company and the Major contributed many Bush brick to Nashville's reconstruction growth as evidenced by such projects as the Maxwell House Hotel, repairs to the Downtown Presbyterian Church, the Union Gospel Tabernacle built by Captain Tom Ryman (later called Ryman Auditorium), early Vanderbilt University buildings, and the Tulip Street Methodist Church.

Today, W.G. Bush and Company produces more than 300,000 brick a day—a more modernized method than the 10,000 made by hand years ago—from all of their plants. The brick are delivered by a fleet of trucks with mechanized equipment capable of handling 50,000 brick per day. Herbert Materials now employs 415 people.

It was John S. Herbert's grandfather, T.L. Herbert, who put the company well ahead of the competition when he built sheds around his plants so that brick making could be a year-round business unaffected by the weather. With that advantage, W.G. Bush and Company had brick in stock in the early spring when the other brick makers were just firing up their kilns. It was Herbert's business skill that paved the way for rapid growth.

During the tenure of growth and the combined efforts of the same family, the name W.G. Bush and Company was changed to Herbert Materials Incorporated in order to encompass all the operations of the company and subsidiaries. After five continuous generations, the direct descendants of the Major remain the owners and active management of Herbert Materials Incorporated.

The "Major" would be proud.

The company entered the marine business rather inadvertently when it began to dredge sand and gravel from rivers throughout the South to be shipped to Nashville aboard the company's barges (above). Brick were handmade in the company's kilns in North Nashville (right) until 1968, when the process was automated.

323

Hospital Affiliates International

Hospital Affiliates International (HAI), one of the largest hospital management companies in the world, was founded in Nashville in 1968. HAI, largest in the world in terms of total hospitals and number of hospital beds managed under contract, originated the concept of managing hospitals for other owners.

Operating more than 140 hospitals in 1979—two-thirds of them by contract with the owners and the other third through HAI ownership—Hospital Affiliates today operates hospitals with revenues that have grown in less than ten years from $20 million to over $1 billion.

With regional offices primarily in the South, Southwest, and California, Hospital Affiliates recently opened an office in London to work more closely with HAI hospitals overseas. Most of the hospitals operated by Hospital Affiliates are in thirty-five states in this country and range in size from less than sixty beds each to more than four hundred beds.

Hospital Affiliates pools the knowledge of its experts in the diverse fields involved in providing quality health care to make it possible for individual hospitals to benefit from their skills.

In 1968 four Nashvillians, businessmen Baron Coleman and Richard Eskind and doctors Irwin Eskind and Herbert Schulman, founded Hospital Affiliates. "Its creation," said Chairman Jack Anderson," was based on an idea whose time had come."

"In forming Hospital Affiliates, the founders believed they could combine modern business management techniques with a genuine concern for quality health care and operate at a profit," said President George Van. "A well-run hospital is one whose staff uses its time and resources on patient care rather than on a series of administrative crises."

The founders also believed that a group of hospitals could acquire and share managerial talents and other resources that would be beyond the capability of any single hospital. At corporate headquarters in Nashville, appropriate standards of excellence in all facets of hospital operations are developed. The standards are then maintained through a decentralized organization responsible for supervising HAI's hospitals throughout the country. Experienced specialists based in Nashville also plan, design, build, equip, and staff new hospitals.

Hospital Affiliates draws on its many resources to find doctors interested in practicing in small communities that have had difficulty in attracting physicians. At the same time, HAI manages five teaching hospitals—among them the Tulane University Medical Center in New Orleans which the company also helped plan and develop.

In 1977 Hospital Affiliates was acquired by INA Corporation, parent company of Insurance Company of North America. INA, with over $12 billion in assets, has meant increased opportunities for expanding the number of owned hospitals, as well as the services HAI provides through management contracts. INA is a diversified financial services company with offices in 110 countries.

Medical Center Del Oro in Houston is a 270-bed hospital owned by HAI.

Interstate Construction Company Of Nashville Incorporated

Interstate Construction Company of Nashville Incorporated, a highway construction company founded in 1921, grew out of the automobile business as surely as did service stations and motels.

The first automobile came to Nashville in 1897, and by 1903 there were enough autos here—"about twenty"—to justify forming an automobile club. Driving an automobile then was considered a "delightful and exhilarating sport," and club members had races and put on automobile shows.

But by 1916 automobiles were so numerous over the state that a State Highway Department was established to provide a network of hard-topped roads throughout the state.

Fortunes were made and lost in the first burst of highway construction, and Walter E. Richardson Sr., working for a bonding company called Southern Surety Company, saw the wreckage of broken construction firms around him.

"As an employee of the bonding company, my father was often called on to finish the work which bankrupt companies were unable to complete," said Walter E. Richardson Jr., now president of Interstate Construction Company. "From this position, he was able to foresee the potential in the road-building business.

"He began his private business as a part-time venture and then went full time in 1921. At this time, he received Certification Number 14 for his small construction business—perhaps the earliest to be still doing business."

In 1921 a thousand shares were authorized at twenty-five dollars per share. According to company ledgers, first contracts were with the towns of Jackson and Bemis, Tennessee. Many city, county, and state contracts were to follow.

Until 1953 Interstate Construction Company had offices on the twelfth floor of the Independent Life Building, now J.C. Bradford Building, at Fourth Avenue and Church Street.

Interstate Construction originally used liquid asphalt surfacing which was mixed on the site of the paving. Eventually the state improved on this method, upgrading the specifications by using plant mix asphalt.

In 1937 Walter E.Richardson Jr. began work in his father's business, and after five years in the army (1941-1946), he returned home to take over the company from his ailing father. In 1952 the elder Richardson died.

The following year Walter E. Richardson Jr. expanded the business by founding Interstate Paving Company. The first asphalt mixing plant was opened in the Cedar Groves limestone quarry near Pulaski, and the company, with fifty employees, moved its offices to Harsh Avenue, off Murfreesboro Road.

Since 1953 ten plants have been established throughout Tennessee and Georgia. Since 1960 headquarters have been at 5610 Nolensville Road. In 1971 the third generation of the family came into the business when Walter E. Richardson III began working full time just before the company's fiftieth anniversary.

Over the years, Interstate Construction Company has paved roads throughout Tennessee, Georgia, Alabama, Virginia, and Mississippi. The company has built many of the roads for Nashville's satellite cities: Belle Meade, Berry Hill, Oak Hill, Forest Hills, and Brentwood. The company also provides snow removal service for these areas.

The early 1960s were the peak years in highway construction, and Interstate Construction Company got its share of the business. It recently completed the stretch of I-75 between Cartersville and Marietta, Georgia.

In the fifty-eight years since the business started, it has grown so rapidly that a $28 million volume is predicted for 1979, an amount that stands in striking contrast with figures recorded in company ledgers in the earliest years. Today, with three hundred employees, Interstate Construction Company is one of the fastest-growing highway construction companies in the state.

Walter Richardson Jr. (left) and Robert Armstrong (right) pause for a moment on a construction site at Trinity Lane in 1947.

Joy's Flowers

Joy's Flowers, Nashville florist for 102 years, has bloomed through more than a century, and its beauty still graces weddings, party tables, and endless notable occasions in the city's history.

The Joy Floral Company operates both a wholesale and a retail business, and branches of the company have served Middle Tennessee, Southern Kentucky, and Northern Alabama for generations.

Headquarters for the business now are at 2322 West End Avenue, with a branch at 200 Fourth Avenue North. Those retail stores, along with Joy's wholesale business at 1906 Church Street, have sales approaching $2 million a year.

Joy's Flowers grew out of Nashville's climate. An Englishman, Thomas Samuel Joy, had left his native land to settle in Port Albert, Ontario, on Lake Superior. There he became master of two sailing ships operating on the Great Lakes, and there he and his wife, Elizabeth Hawkins Joy, brought up their son and four daughters.

It was in 1877 that the seventeen-year-old son, Thomas Chaplin Joy, came south in search of a warmer climate. His letters from Nashville describing the rich land and mild climate convinced Thomas S. Joy and his wife that Nashville would be a good place for them, and in 1877 they moved here, bringing along their daughters Ellen, Victoria, Elizabeth, and Ann.

The Joys began their garden promptly and within a year had leased three acres in South Nashville for their flower and vegetable garden. The violets, pansies, and geraniums they grew—plus the vegetables—sold so well at the courthouse square market that they bought a horse and wagon to haul their products. In 1880 the Joys bought one hundred acres on Lischey Avenue in East Nashville where they built a small greenhouse that was eventually expanded to cover ten acres.

In the peak days of the tremendous greenhouse operation, the company had forty-three greenhouses, with four hundred thousand square feet under glass. Besides the greenhouses, there were nine acres under cultivation for summer cut flowers and twenty acres of field crops for soil supply for the greenhouses—the largest in the South. (Joy's has since sold its giant greenhouses.)

In 1886 the Joys opened their first retail shop in the old Jackson Building at Fifth and Church Street. Four years later they moved to larger quarters at 610 Church Street and later still to 606, 604, and 600 Church Street. In 1907 they moved to the Watkins Building at Sixth and Church, where they operated the business for forty-seven years. In 1954 they moved to the present West End location, across the street from Vanderbilt University and close to Baptist Hospital.

Since the death of Thomas C. Joy in 1916, the company has been continuously in the hands of his eight children or their children. Two of his sons, Tom Harvey Joy and Harold M. Joy, took charge of the businesses after the elder Joy's death. Often the daughters of the family, including Lillian Joy (beginning in 1937) and Ruth Joy (beginning in 1955), took administrative lead in the company. Mrs. Thomas Harvey Joy succeeded her husband as general manager of the retail stores until her death in 1969. Her daughter, Monica Joy Bramlett, is now vice president and treasurer. Her son, Tom S. Joy, served as president from 1955 until his death in 1973. Mrs. Harold M. Joy continues as honorary chairman of the board. Her daughter Ethel (Mrs. Russell Davis) is vice president, and Russell Davis is president.

In 1922 the wholesale part of the business was established, and in 1923 it became a full department. In 1954 the wholesale department moved to separate quarters at 1906 Church Street. Since World War II the increasing number of florist shops in small towns has given the wholesale business many outlets.

In 1914 four generations of Tom Joys posed for a portrait. The Joys purchased 100 acres on Lischey Avenue in 1880, and greenhouses were erected to cultivate the flowers and plants sold through the company's retail outlet.

Keith-Simmons
Company Incorporated

Keith-Simmons Company Incorporated, in its eighty-one-year history, has woven together so many elements in the city's hardware business that tracing its course is like reviewing Nashville's economic development.

In its sleek new building on South Seventh Street in East Nashville—a $1.75 million warehouse-office complex built in 1969—the solidly established old business reaches out for new markets.

Its merchandise—from horseshoes to plumbing fixtures, from garden tools to televisions, from building materials to food blenders—reflects the changing eras.

And the methods of selling and distributing merchandise stretch from the riverboat-traveling salesman of eighty-one years ago to computerized systems for receiving orders today. Salesmen now telephone their orders in at any hour, and the tape-recorded order is picked up by a monitor and processed within minutes.

The company began in 1898 when two young men, Walter Keith and William G. Simmons, built on the experience they had gained in an earlier hardware business here: J. Horton Fall & Company. In 1892 Fall had taken into his hardware company as junior partners both Keith and Simmons. But in June 1898 Fall dissolved the company and reorganized it under his sole ownership. Not discouraged at that development, his former partners organized their own retail store, Keith-Simmons & Company, and were soon open for business at 309 North College Street (now Third Avenue). Keith-Simmons & Company moved to 316-318 Union in 1903.

A quick succession of events soon put Keith-Simmons out front in the hardware business here. In 1910 J.H. Fall's store burned, and Fall retired from the retail business. Keith-Simmons added to their staff the employees who had worked for Fall, and the long tradition of "family ties" within the business began.

One of their strong competitors had been Gray & Dudley Hardware Company, and in 1916 Keith-Simmons purchased the entire retail and supply business of Gray & Dudley and consolidated it with their store, leaving Gray & Dudley in the wholesale business only.

The year 1916 marked several changes in Keith-Simmons' operation. For one thing, they moved to spacious quarters at 412-416 Union Street and operated their retail business there. They separated their retail and wholesale business and established the wholesale portion at Cummins Station, a huge warehouse complex back of Union Station.

Cummins Station alone marked a new era in Nashville's transportation. The steamboat had lost out to the railroad in the battle to ship freight. Cummins Station, built near the railroad station, gave easy access for loading and unloading freight shipped by rail.

Early salesmen found their biggest sales in harnesses, plows and parts, barbed wire, wagon parts, and blacksmith tools—sometimes selling as many as a thousand crosscut saws to one retail store at a time.

Today Keith-Simmons handles close to fifty thousand items, including major appliances, electronic parts and accessories, and floor coverings, in addition to hardware.

Through the years, Keith-Simmons has purchased many other hardware companies. Keith-Simmons itself became part of Washington Industries in the 1950s. In 1960 Keith-Simmons closed its Union Street store after forty-four years there, and in 1963 the company closed its last retail outlet.

In Keith-Simmons' eighty-one years, there have been only five presidents: Walter Keith, beginning in 1898, who bought Simmons' shares in 1928; William M. Parrish, beginning in 1933, who saved the company from bankruptcy during the Depression; Aubrey Carr, beginning in 1945; Donald E. Gentry, beginning in 1963, who had worked for the company since 1937 and is still vice chairman of the board; and David Bennett, beginning in 1977.

The 1970s have seen Keith-Simmons' major growth, Bennett said, with a twenty-one percent increase in 1974. In 1979, with two hundred employees, the company anticipates $29 million in sales.

In 1903 Keith-Simmons moved to this location on Union Street in downtown Nashville.

Levy's

Levy's, one of the best-known men's fashion stores in the Southeast, began at least 125 years ago, shortly after Zadoc Levy arrived in Nashville from his native Nassau province in Germany.

The growth of his store is part of the record of Nashville's awareness of fashion from its earliest days. In the 1850s, when the Levy family arrived here and Zadoc Levy opened his tailor shop on Market Street (now Second Avenue North), Southerners were the biggest customers that New York manufacturers of men's clothing had. And Nashville had more than its share of men's clothing shops.

Nashville—with forty-two clothing stores, eight wholesale clothing dealers, fourteen merchant tailors, and twenty tailors—had more clothing stores than any other city in Tennessee in 1860. And the men's clothing stores took pride in offering customers the latest merchandise from New York every season. Nashville was a "social town," and Southern gentlemen dressed to the hilt for the steady round of social events.

During the Civil War, Southern gentlemen refused to buy from New York manufacturers, and the latter suffered heavy financial losses until they received orders to make uniforms for the Union army.

But Zadoc Levy was well-established as a Nashville tailor by then. In Nashville's earliest city directory (1854-55), Zadoc Levy is listed as a "Custom Tailor." Zadoc's business is now run by the family's fifth generation and has expanded to five stores in the Nashville area.

Zadoc's son, Raphael Z. Levy, born in 1854, worked with him in the clothing business at 58 North Market Street as early as 1872, when he was eighteen years old. Throughout the early city directories, Zadoc and Raphael were listed in "clothing" or "general stores" or "clothing and gents' furnishings" or "clothier" categories.

After 1880, when Zadoc died, Raphael worked with his brothers Max and Solomon, in the business they called, after 1885, R.Z. Levy & Brothers. Their business was then at 39 North Cherry (Fourth Avenue North). The business changed location several times but remained on Fourth Avenue North for almost half a century. Eventually Solomon left the business, and R.Z. bought out his brother Max.

It was after R.Z. Levy's two sons Herbert (in 1918) and Alfred (in 1923) entered the business that the "Levy brothers" remembered by many Nashvillians today became prominent in the city's life. Raphael died in 1923, leaving the business in the hands of his sons. Alfred Levy died in 1948 and was followed in death a few years later by Herbert in 1956.

The fourth generation of Levys, Ralph (in 1946) and A.J. Jr. (in 1948), joined the family business after serving in the military in World War II. The company was changed from R.Z. Levy and Son to Levy's Incorporated in 1947.

In 1948, as the city's fashionable shops pushed in that direction, Levy's moved to its present downtown location at 212 Sixth Avenue North. The store's first branch shop opened in Madison in 1956 and later moved to Rivergate Mall. In 1967 another branch store opened in One Hundred Oaks. In 1977 a third branch opened in the Opryland Hotel, and in 1978 Levy's opened a Green Hills store and main office on Hillsboro Road in the Hillsboro Plaza Shopping Center.

Ralph Z. Levy died in 1976 and his son, David, came into the company early in 1977. He is now vice president and A.J. Levy Jr. is president. Levy's has made its mark in Nashville.

  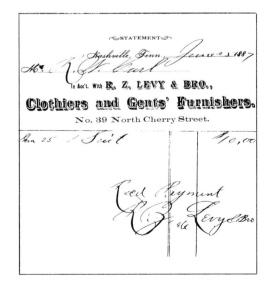

R.Z. Levy (left) worked with his father, Zadoc Levy, in his custom tailoring shop as early as 1872, when he was only eighteen years old. R.Z.'s sons Alfred (center) and Herbert (right) entered the business around 1920, and the "Levy's brothers" concept was born. An 1887 invoice (far right) shows a $10 charge for a suit.

Life & Casualty Insurance Company Of Tennessee

Life & Casualty Insurance Company, seventy-six years old and towering over much of downtown Nashville both in financial strength and in its thirty-one-story headquarters called L&C Tower, grew out of one man's obsession with thrift. Andrew Mizell Burton, twenty-four, had $1,000 to invest when he opened his own insurance company in September 1903 in a one-room office that he rented for $12.50 a month.

Burton had the help of a young woman, Helena Haralson (later Mrs. Thurston Johnson), who had worked at another insurance company with him and who also had $1,000 to invest in the new company. Their $2,000 plus $23,000 that Burton persuaded three other Nashvillians to invest (Dr. J.C. Franklin, Guilford Dudley, and P.M. Estes) made the necessary $25,000 capital to found the company. Charter was issued on September 8, 1903, and the first policy was sold on September 14. Burton swept out the office and built the fire every morning—in addition to handling a ready-made staff of fifty salesmen left over from a defunct company. Miss Haralson wrote the insurance policies, handled company correspondence, and kept the records.

The company that began by selling weekly "sick and accident" insurance for nickels and dimes soon began selling life and accident insurance, then added ordinary life and other coverages available on monthly and annual payment plans. L&C almost from its beginning invested heavily in real estate. (In 1979, L&C owns $48 million in real estate, nearly half in Davidson County.)

By 1909 L&C had outgrown its one-room office and bought the old Chamber of Commerce Building at 307 Church Street. It moved into the top floor and rented out the other seven floors. In 1910 L&C went public, offering five hundred shares within the company at $300 per share.

In 1910 the company also extended its territory to Mississippi and by 1912 had added Arkansas, Louisiana, and South Carolina. That was the beginning of operations that have expanded over nineteen states and Washington, D.C., with 3,300 field personnel working out of 144 district offices.

World War I dealt the company a blow, both in loss of personnel and in the influenza epidemic that took thousands of lives. In 1917 L&C paid more than $100,000 in claims—a considerable amount for a small firm. Yet the company prospered enough to build its own office building at 159 Fourth Avenue North in 1925, and Burton saw to it that the cornerstone had chiseled on it the words: "Thrift—the Cornerstone." Just a few years later, in the early 1930s, the perilous times of the Great Depression provided management its greatest challenge up to that time.

In 1950, when he was seventy-one, Burton retired, and Paul Mountcastle succeeded him, serving as president for two years and then as the chairman until 1966. In 1952 Guilford Dudley Jr. became president, and he held that job until he resigned in 1969 to become U.S. Ambassador to Denmark.

Under the initiative of Mountcastle and Dudley, the thirty-one-story L&C Tower was completed in 1957 at the corner of Fourth and Church. At that time the Tower was the tallest building in the southeastern United States, and these L&C leaders are given major credit for the impetus in maintaining a vital and viable downtown Nashville. Ten years later, L&C built another skyscraper across the street, the $8 million, twenty-story Third National Bank Building.

In 1968 Life and Casualty joined the American General Group of companies and assumed the management of the "home service" operations of the Group. Allen M. Steele has been president since 1970, and, with the Nashville-based companies of the Group exceeding $9 billion insurance in force, the company started on nickels and dimes in a one-room office a half block away is now one of the major insurance and financial institutions of the South.

In 1925 the Life and Casualty Insurance Company of Tennessee had prospered enough to construct its own home office building (left) at 159 Fourth Avenue North. In 1957 the company moved into the spectacular tower (right) it occupies today.

David Lipscomb College

David Lipscomb College, a four-year college supported by individuals and congregations from the church of Christ throughout the country, traces its beginnings to 1891.

On its sixty-two-acre campus on Granny White Pike, some 2,200 students are enrolled, and half of them are from other states and foreign countries. Approximately 1,500 are boarding students, and about ten percent of the student body are not from church of Christ backgrounds.

But there are 130 church of Christ congregations in Nashville alone, and from this stronghold of faith have come leading contributors to the college from the first. It was, in fact, in 1889 when a church of Christ evangelist, James A. Harding, was conducting a series of revival services here that he and his Nashville host, David Lipscomb, first discussed opening a Bible school here.

Their idea was to open a school where the Bible would be the textbook "to prepare Christians for usefulness in whatever sphere they are called upon to labor." Students would also be taught "such additional branches as are needed in understanding the Bible and teaching it to others," and in that pursuit they were taught Latin, Greek, English, and, eventually, science.

In October 1891 nine young men enrolled in the first class—all planning to be preachers. The Nashville Bible School, as it was called until 1917, opened in a big two-story brick residence in South Nashville on what is now Hermitage Avenue, and it served as dormitory, classroom building, and home of Harding and his family.

The next year, the Bible School moved to South Cherry (Fourth Avenue South), and in 1893 they bought a group of old buildings on South Spruce (Eighth Avenue South) near the city water reservoir, where they had buildings for classrooms and dormitories for men and women students for the next ten years.

It was not until 1903 that the school moved to new buildings on part of the farm on Granny White Pike that founder David Lipscomb gave them. There, particularly since a major building program following World War II, a number of handsome classroom buildings, dormitories, library, administrative building, auditorium, and gymnasium have been added.

From its opening in 1891, the school has taught on elementary, high school, and college levels. For years the college department offered only two years' study, but since 1946 it has been a four-year college, accredited by the Southern Association of Colleges and Secondary Schools.

In 1917, after Lipscomb left his farm and other property to the school, the name was changed to David Lipscomb College. Since then there have been many generous benefactors, including A.M. Burton, an insurance executive who contributed approximately $3 million to the college.

Emphasis on the sciences—particularly through the influence of Dr. J.S. Ward—has turned many of the students toward pre-med study. E.A. Elam, early scholar and preacher, won strong support for the college, and Dr. Athens Clay Pullias, president from 1946 to 1977, steered the school through its years of greatest growth.

Mack Wayne Craig, vice president of institutional planning of the college, and Willard Collins, president, state that the school's strength in the sciences today is a direct outgrowth of Lipscomb's 1907 will, directing that his property be used to help the college develop as an "electrical, mechanical and scientific institute."

In this composite photo dated 1898, the original faculty of the Nashville Bible School is shown. The school's name was later changed to honor one of its founders, David Lipscomb.

330

Marshall & Bruce Company

Almost from Nashville's founding, printing has been a leading industry, and Marshall & Bruce Company has been a leader in the business during its entire 114 years.

Opening its doors on October 25, 1865, just six months after the Civil War ended, the company rapidly outgrew its quarters in eight successively larger buildings and now operates in space equivalent to a city block at 605 Twelfth Avenue South. Today the company does an annual business of $4 million and employs ninety people.

But when James H. Bruce and Andrew Marshall put up their shingle on the narrow, unpaved lane called Rue Deaderick (now Deaderick Street) near the courthouse, they had their eyes on printing and binding record books to keep county court records more efficiently.

Bruce was twenty-eight years old at the time he and Marshall founded Marshall & Bruce's Book Bindery. During their lifelong partnership, Bruce was the administrator, managing all details of production, and Marshall was in charge of sales, covering Tennessee, Alabama, and Georgia to open new accounts.

By top-quality production, they were on their way in 1869 when they bought "the small printing office" of John T.S. Fall, with presses for printing record books and calling cards. In 1870 they bought out William Gamble's interest in a bookstore called William Gamble & Company (A.J. Wheeler being the "company") on Union Street. Then they merged their bindery, printing office, and bookstore in one building, at 219 Fourth Avenue North, under the name of Wheeler, Marshall & Bruce.

In 1876 Wheeler withdrew from the company to devote full time to book selling, and Marshall & Bruce moved to new three-story quarters at 306 Third Avenue North. The next year their business had grown so that they bought another building, at 212 Union Street, which doubled their space.

In 1893 Marshall & Bruce Company was reorganized into a stock company, with a capital of $50,000. Bruce was elected president and Marshall secretary-treasurer. They had installed new machinery in their new building when disaster struck: On February 10, 1895, the entire building burned to the ground. They rebuilt on the same site.

In 1903 they organized the Middle Tennessee School Book Depository and acquired a building at 309 Second Avenue North for that operation. Still too crowded, they built an even larger building at 162-6 Fourth Avenue North and moved there in 1905. From 1904 to 1938 they printed all publications of the Baptist Sunday School Board.

In November 1938 the company began construction of a new building at 407 Twelfth Avenue South for its offices and stationery store. At the same time, it leased adjoining property for a printing plant. On that property, the company runs its complete printing and bindery operation today.

Andrew Marshall died in October 1912, and James H. Bruce died in December 1914. Bruce Shepherd, nephew of J.H. Bruce, succeeded Marshall as secretary-treasurer and in 1914 became president. Marshall Hotchkiss, nephew of Andrew Marshall, then became secretary-treasurer.

Hotchkiss died in 1940 and Shepherd in 1941, and Ernest M. Allen became president on May 15, 1941. He held that office until his death in 1945, when he was succeeded by G. Allen Rather. Allen's widow, Mrs. Lannie B. Allen, succeeded Rather as president in 1946. In 1950 R.J. Clay became president.

In February 1952 P.M. French and Associates purchased the entire capital stock of Marshall & Bruce Company, and that deal made it a part of Washington Industries. Today the officers are Robert L. Smith, president; Billy Sharber, vice president; and Hurst L. Kiser, secretary-treasurer.

The Marshall & Bruce retail store on Fourth Avenue North is shown here as it appeared in 1905.

Andrew Marshall   *James H. Bruce*

McDowell Enterprises
Incorporated

McDowell Enterprises Incorporated, an $82 million per year business that began by moving earth for highways, was founded shortly after World War II. Today the company that serves eight Southeastern states describes itself as a company supplying products and services related to energy, environment, highway maintenance, safety and heavy construction.

But on September 1, 1946, when Roscoe B. McDowell and two of his sons formed their business (first called McDowell & McDowell), they were looking for ways to make their skills pay off. Roscoe B. McDowell Sr. had fifteen years' experience with earth-moving equipment on a variety of construction jobs. Two sons, Charles W. (Charlie) and Robert A. (Bob), had worked with heavy equipment during their military service in World War II—Charlie with the Marine Corps Combat Engineers and Bob with the Navy Civil Engineer Corps.

Both sons had saved their military pay during the war, and they and their father put $12,000 into the new company. There was a shortage of construction machinery, and it was only because he was a veteran that Bob McDowell was eligible to bid on the surplus equipment that the army sold at auction.

McDowell set up headquarters in a tiny residence on Wyoming Avenue and began grading and drainage work. But as the company expanded—excavating for skyscrapers (including the L&C Tower in Nashville), building interstate highways and bridges, paving shopping centers and parking lots—the company kept moving to larger quarters. Today McDowell is headquartered in its own five-story building at Plus Park Plaza.

In 1956, when the nation began its forty-thousand-mile network of interstate highways, McDowell was ready for the challenge. The company already had subsidiaries experienced in grading and drainage and in highway construction and paving. McDowell got the first contract in Tennessee for building part of the interstate system.

A series of subsidiaries had been formed through the years to handle growing specialty jobs: a real estate corporation for developing subdivisions and industrial parks in 1951; a paving firm, which now operates eighteen plants, in 1952; a highway building firm in 1957, to do grading, drainage, heavy and highway construction, and drilling; a bridge-building firm in 1957; and a company supplying road construction materials in 1958 and still another in 1963.

In 1969 a major reorganization of the company consolidated the various McDowell-controlled companies and placed more emphasis on real estate and industrial development. At the same time, the company that had been incorporated as McDowell & McDowell in 1954 became McDowell Enterprises Incorporated, and Bob McDowell became president of the new holding company.

Today, Roscoe B. McDowell Sr. is chairman of the board, Bob McDowell is chairman and chief executive officer, and Charlie McDowell is assistant to the president. Their vast network employs twelve hundred people.

Now, twenty-three years after the first interstate highway was built, forty-two percent of McDowell's work is in the maintenance and repair of existing roads. Severe winters have had a part in that situation, but McDowell has grown, the company says, by looking forward to the next challenge—whether from weather or a rapidly expanding economy.

McDowell Enterprises began operations in a small frame house on Wyoming Avenue in West Nashville. Today the company's activities span the continent and are headquartered in a modern office building located in the company's own office complex, Plus Park Plaza.

MetroCenter

MetroCenter, a handsomely planned office-convention-residential community within ten minutes of downtown Nashville, is a phenomenon marking the two-hundredth birthday of the city in a unique way. The 850-acre area—set apart from the rest of Nashville by its wide sweep of curving boulevards and landscaped open spaces—represents a new frontier in the city's growth. Its striking new buildings are rising in a three-mile curve of the Cumberland River where flooded mud flats had turned investors away until eleven years ago.

It was Robert C.H. (Bob) Mathews Jr. who had the idea in 1968 for turning the flood-plagued land into a stunning community. Mathews, a Vanderbilt University engineering graduate who studies the "genealogy of land" to understand its possibilities, knew the area's history. From the time French fur traders swapped their wares with Indians there in 1710 to the horse racing days of Andrew Jackson's day to the airstrip runway there early in this century, it had been a flat land subject to flooding. When brick makers mined clay, water filled the pits, forming Bush Lake. It was largely a commercial turnip patch by the time Mathews drove out to inspect it in 1968.

On the day he went out to look over the flats, his car mired in the mud. While he waited for the wrecker, he walked along the river bank. "I saw that the land at the river's edge was high," Mathews said. "The frequent flooding had come not from the river itself pouring over its banks, but from two small creeks—backwaters from the river."

Mathews had a sudden idea: He could prevent flooding "just by damming up the two small creeks." A dike along the river's edge would hold the water back.

He discussed his idea with Victor Johnson, president of Aladdin Industries, known for his foresight and analytical powers. Johnson was so enthusiastic about the idea that Aladdin Industries became full partner in the undertaking in 1971. Today the partnership headquarters is in a notable concrete-and-glass structure called Nashville House, the first building completed at MetroCenter.

From that building, which has won architectural awards for its general design (including use of a peaceful waterfall shaded by young trees in the atrium), Mathews has directed the development of MetroCenter. It is all privately financed, even to the four-lane streets, with all utility lines underground.

To create the 850-acre stretch of land, Mathews put together two hundred tracts of land in what had been a neglected part of North Nashville. He and Johnson had the advice of Robert Lamb Hart, top architect-development planner from New York City.

Each builder in MetroCenter is encouraged to make generous use of trees in landscaping the buildings, and for that purpose MetroCenter has its own tree farm. All builders are urged to design buildings with energy efficiency in mind.

In 1979 about half of the area set aside for office buildings is occupied, and a new 302-room hotel called the Maxwell House offers a convention hall that seats 850. Near the hotel is a new motel and a 251-unit apartment building for retired teachers. Businesses in MetroCenter range from insurance and telephone to printing and carpeting.

Already the land that was producing $17,000 in taxes before MetroCenter is producing almost a million dollars in taxes. Mathews said it will take another five to seven years to finish this project, but Nashville is so full of opportunities that "the difficult thing is to figure out what to do next."

Bob Mathews (left) had the idea for MetroCenter in 1968 when it dawned on him that a flood-plagued area in North Nashville could be turned into a planned community of offices, shops, warehouses, and apartments. Nashville House (above) was the first building completed in MetroCenter and remains one of the city's most striking structures.

NLT Corporation

NLT Corporation, a Nashville-born insurance company with over $4.1 billion in assets and more than 10,600 employees, is Nashville's largest corporation. And its influence through WSM radio, television, and country music is incalculable.

A diversified insurance holding company with eight principal subsidiaries and net earnings of $117 million in 1978, NLT derives most of its earnings from life and health insurance. In fact, ninety-five percent of NLT's earnings in 1978 came from life and health insurance—all from the National Life and Accident Insurance Company and another subsidiary, the Des Moines-based Guardsman Life Insurance Company, acquired by NLT in 1976.

A giant among insurance companies, National Life, with $2.7 billion in assets in 1977, is ranked sixth among life insurance stock companies in the United States. The merger in February 1979 with Great Southern Corporation, a Houston-based holding company with subsidiaries of its own, added assets of $700 million to NLT.

But National Life, when it was founded in Nashville seventy-seven years ago, barely survived its first winter. C.A. Craig, who bought it at an auction on the courthouse steps on December 27, 1901, for $17,250, or $150 per share, knew little about selling insurance then. But Craig, who was deputy commissioner of insurance in Tennessee, outbid by twenty-five cents per share the man who was already president of the company, C. Runcie Clements. The company, then called National Sick and Accident Association, had been auctioned to settle an estate.

Ownership was transferred to Craig on January 3, 1902, and Craig was elected president of the company at a meeting of shareholders on January 7. W.R. Wills, another founder, became secretary and treasurer of the company. And Clements, who already owned eleven shares of the company, became assistant secretary and treasurer. In June 1902 the name of the organization was changed to National Life and Accident Insurance Company.

In the beginning, the only policies sold by the company were health and accident policies paid for by weekly premiums. For five cents a week (as premium), the insurance company would pay the policyholder $1.25 per week in case of sickness, $2 per week in case of disability from an accident, and $12.50 in death benefits. The weekly premium health and accident policy was the only plan offered by the company for many years.

The first home office was at 316 Cedar Street (now Charlotte Avenue), and there were five people on the staff. That number included the men who knocked on doors every week, collecting nickels from policyholders. And Craig never forgot that first winter, when disability claims ran high and there was hardly enough money in the treasury to cover the payments.

By January 1, 1902, the company had only about $23,000 in assets, and about half of that was in real estate, Craig said. Only $3,200 was in cash.

"Mr. Craig said there was a great question whether or not the company's meager funds would last until spring and the company could survive that first winter," William C. Weaver, chairman of the board in 1977, recalled on the company's seventy-fifth anniversary.

But the fact that both Craig and Wills had been deputy insurance commissioners of the state of Tennessee and that Clement had owned the company was a tremendous asset in itself. Each of the three top men—Craig, Wills, and Clements—had special insights to contribute to the development of the struggling company. Craig "set about establishing a relationship with the men in the field as soon as they got the company through that first winter,"

The founders of the National Life and Accident Insurance Company pose with their wives in an early photo (above left). Founders were (from left): C.R. Clements, C.A. Craig, W.R. Wills, Thomas J. Tyne, and Dr. R.E. Fort. Minnie Pearl and Roy Acuff (above right) are the unquestioned queen and king of WSM's Grand Ole Opry, today a thriving division of NLT Corporation.

Weaver said, and it turned out that he had a special understanding of their problems. Soon the company had sixty men in the field covering parts of Tennessee, Kentucky, and Alabama, and Craig trained them to establish the company as one that always lived up to its promises—not a universal practice in those days.

"Our policies call for dollars and cents," Craig told company salesmen in 1929. "But if we give nothing more, we fall far short of what our policyholders and the public have a right to expect. Money is cold. No warm blood courses its veins. There is no human sympathy in its touch. Yet we may give it heart by giving a part of ours with it. We can warm it with kindness and good will."

It was that personal touch in a world rapidly growing depersonalized that gave the company an edge over the competition, said R.L. Wagner, chairman and chief executive officer of the company today. Weaver gave Craig credit for setting the company on its philosophical course. Clements, "an extremely effective organizer, was the glue that held the home office together," Weaver said, and Wills was "the intellectual, easily the best analytical mind of the three."

All of them were Middle Tennesseans, devoted to their home community. By 1911 they had moved their headquarters into the former Leake residence at the northeast corner of Seventh and Union, and in 1924 the company moved into its handsome stone building just across the street, on the northwest corner of Seventh and Union. That imposing five-story building, still in use, was the first building erected for the home office and stands next to the stunning thirty-one-story National Life Center, the company's present home, completed in 1969.

In October 1925 National Life founded radio station WSM (We Shield Millions). The international fame that station won through one of its programs of country music, the Grand Ole Opry, stamped Nashville's future. Out of the Grand Ole Opry has grown Opryland.

Opened in 1972, it is the 217-acre entertainment park and setting for the Opry broadcasts. Close on its heels came the Opryland Hotel, a 615-room hotel and convention center completed in 1977 at a cost of $26 million. Altogether WSM and its phenomenal country music popularity have had a tremendous impact on Nashville's tourist industry and music business and have been a telling factor in making the insurance company known across the country.

In 1920 National Life opened its first life insurance department, with Edwin W. Craig as manager and Eldon B. Stevenson Jr. as assistant manager. For generations, the founding families continued to manage the company, with Jesse E. Wills, G.D. Brooks, William C. Weaver, and Walter S. Bearden among them.

In an effort to expand its market, National Life now offers a full range of insurance policies, ranging from whole life, endowment, and term policies. The company also offers group and individual life and health policies and has established a subsidiary, The National Property Owners Insurance Company, which provides homeowners coverage for both house owners and apartment dwellers.

In 1968 NLT Corporation was created as a holding company, with National Life as the principal subsidiary. Other subsidiaries of NLT are Guardsman Life Insurance Company, The National Property Owners Insurance Company, NLT Marketing Services Corporation, WSM Incorporated, Intereal Company, NLT Computer Services Corporation, Great Southern Life Insurance Company, and State Savings and Loan. They are active in a variety of insurance fields, in real estate, in hotel and amusement park businesses, in computer service business, and savings and loan business. But it is the voice of WSM's radio and television stars that has spread Nashville's fame and influence to distances and in directions no money could buy.

Over the years National Life has occupied several home offices, each larger and more elaborate than its predecessor. Shown here are the company's offices at the northeast corner of Seventh Avenue North and Union Street (left), the company's first custom-constructed building at Seventh and Union (center), and the giant thirty-one-story NLT Center (right) which serves the firm as its headquarters today.

Metropolitan Nashville Airport Authority

Metropolitan Nashville Airport Authority, guiding the city's facilities for air transportation, ties the Middle Tennessee region to the nation's and the world's markets as no other means of transportation can.

In countless ways, Nashville's air facilities for handling both passengers and freight have pushed the city into a position of prominence out of all proportion to its population, said James S. Graham, director of Metropolitan Nashville Airport Authority.

Serving sixty-four cities (on direct flights from Nashville), the Nashville airport had the busiest year in its forty-two year history in 1978. During calendar year 1978 passenger volume exceeded 2.3 million, an increase of nearly seventeen percent over the same period a year earlier. Number of landings and take-offs increased to 227,359, a four percent increase.

"Nashville airport is entering 1979 with a fifty percent increase in passenger flow in the past five years," Graham said. "And the greatest potential gateway to the economic growth of Metropolitan Nashville and Davidson County is the Metropolitan Airport."

The growth includes air freight, use of private planes both by companies and individuals, charter planes, commuter planes, mail shipment, and military aircraft, as well as commercial airline passenger planes.

In the forty-three years since Metropolitan Airport was opened, the era of air travel has reshaped distances, communication, habits of travel, and business. The growth of Nashville since 1937, when the first commercial flight came through Nashville's municipal airport, is intimately tied to the expansion of airport facilities.

But Nashville's fascination with flying dates almost

Nashville aviators returning home from World War I wasted no time in forming the 105th Observation Squadron. It was not until 1920, however, that the squadron had its own field, Blackwood Field, located near what is today Lebanon Road.

from the beginning of air transport in this country. Not even counting the demonstration of flying by balloon at Tennessee's Centennial celebration in 1897 or the first airmail (also by balloon, from Nashville to Gallatin and Lebanon) in 1877, Nashvillians have been flying enthusiasts from the first.

World War I offered the first dramatic opportunity to prove some of the possibilities of flying—in combat, observation, and transportation—and the pilots who survived those adventures came home to test flying for peacetime possibilities.

But even before the war, in 1916, a flat pasture lying approximately where Hampton Avenue is today—a two-thousand-foot stretch of grassy land between Woodmont Boulevard and Golf Club Lane—served as Nashville's first airfield. Edgar Lee Hampton raised cattle there, and the airport was called Hampton Field.

During World War I transient military planes landed at Hampton Field, but there was "no hangar and never more than a half-dozen planes at once, all transient."

When Nashville aviators in World War I returned home late in 1918, they wasted no time in organizing what became the 105th Observation Squadron and would have qualified as the first in the nation if they had had a proper airfield. Among the organizers were Lieutenant Wamp Hinton, Major J.C. Bennett Jr., Charles Blackard, Justin Potter, Herbert Fox, and Walter M. Williams. The federal government approved the airport and recognized the 105th Squadron in 1920.

The 105th Squadron trained new pilots and attended annual summer encampments over the nation, and in 1929 they participated in aerial maneuvers of the entire American Air Force. But the state provided no financial assistance, and for years there was no hangar, no housing for the 105th.

In 1920 H.O. Blackwood, Nashville tire dealer, led the way in obtaining a new airport by contributing $1,000 to the fund, and other businessmen followed. The new airport, some twelve miles from Nashville on the Lebanon Road, was named Blackwood Field. And for the first time the 105th Squadron had a hangar of its own.

There, on June 29, 1924, the biggest air show ever staged in the South was held. Aviators across the nation flew in to take part in the "Dixie Air Meet."

One month later, on July 29, 1924, Lieutenant Vincent J. Maloy and Captain Herbert Fox—both instructors with the 105th Squadron—flew the first airmail out of Nashville to Chicago.

Two years later, when the flooding Cumberland River cut off travel between Nashville and Old Hickory, Lieutenant Brower McConnell of the 105th Squadron made the mail delivery by air. A few months later, McConnell lost his life while on duty with the army at Langley Field, and when Nashville,, in 1927, bought a

336

111-acre site for an airport in West Nashville (where McCabe Park is today), it was named McConnell Field.

McConnell Field, in use from 1927 to 1936, saw airmail inaugurated through Nashville via Interstate Airlines on December 1, 1928. Interstate was later absorbed by American Airways (predecessor of American Airlines).

In 1929, to accommodate larger commercial planes, McConnell Field was deserted for Sky Harbor Airport at Murfreesboro. Dedicated on October 14, 1929, Sky Harbor was used by both American and Eastern Airlines until Berry Field opened. In 1929 Nashville Flying Service was established to serve the ever increasing number of private aircraft and passengers. That company is still in business today.

If the Depression had not brought about the Works Progress Administration—with its funds for building airports—Nashville might have waited years to get its present airport. But a mighty effort by the city's business and civic leaders resulted in selection of the present airport site. In 1936 construction began on the original 340 acres.

Colonel Harry S. Berry, state WPA director, directed the work of the hundreds of men who transformed the slight hills and valleys into an airport "flat as a tennis court." And when the airport was dedicated on October 9, 1939, it was named Berry Field in honor of Colonel Berry.

Berry Field was hardly in operation before World War II threatened, and soon Berry Field became an active military base. The Air Transport Command, which ferried men and planes over much of the world, added equipment for the control tower, built an auxiliary administration building, and extended and improved runways, hangars, barracks, and other facilities for the military.

When the war was over in 1945, the military returned Berry Field—then grown to fifteen hundred acres—to the city of Nashville. In 1946 Capitol Airways was founded here and has grown to be one of the most successful non-scheduled airlines in the nation.

During the 1950s and 1960s, the city's airport grew larger and larger. Size was increased to 2,800 acres; runways were added and extended, with a new Terminal Building dedicated in 1961. The city's added investment at the airport totaled $12 million.

In 1970 the Metropolitan Nashville Airport Authority was created so as to better guide the city's aviation programs. Costs of airport operations were removed from the city's tax rolls as it was decided that it could be operated on a "pay as you go" basis, applying business practices common to private industry.

Since creation of the Airport Authority an additional $30 million has been spent on improvement of airport facilities. Metropolitan Airport has grown in size (4,000 acres). Smyrna Airport (formerly Sewart Air Force Base) is being used for air freight processing, serving of general aviation (privately owned aircraft), and headquarters for Capitol International Airways.

A third airport is planned for construction within the "Cockrill Bend" area of Metropolitan Nashville-Davidson County on land acquired in 1973. In addition, an entirely new terminal complex is expected to be built at Metropolitan Airport during the early 1980s.

The Airport Authority is responsible for encouragement of commercial and industrial development through promotion of air transportation. Having adequate airport facilities available to meet the community's present and future needs is the objective.

The Airport Authority is governed by a seven-member board who serve without compensation. Members of that board are: Harold J. Black, P.E.; James T. Fulghum; H. Miller Lanier; R.C.H. Matthews Jr.; John C. Tune; C.D. Walling Jr.; and David K. Wilson.

In 1937 "Berry Field's" Terminal was opened. It compares to the present passenger Terminal complex opened in 1961 and rebuilt-renovated in 1977.

Nashville Area Chamber Of Commerce

The Nashville Area Chamber of Commerce, founded in 1847, has helped shape the development of the city in a variety of ways—everything from settling difficulties "arising among masters of steamboats and the shippers of freight" in 1847 to helping bring new roads and bridges to the area in the 1920s.

Goals are shifting now. Emphasis is on improving the quality of life—not just expanding the volume of business. The importance of cherishing the central city so that it throbs around a revitalized downtown business area shapes the long-range planning.

The goal is no longer just to bring in new industry, but to "use greater selectivity . . . in the prospects solicited to come into our area," Chamber president Joe Thompson Jr. said in 1979. One goal, from the beginning, has been to "collect and record such local and general statistical information relating to commerce and manufacturing as may promote the interests of Nashville, and generally to protect and advance the welfare of the commercial and manufacturing classes, to promote just and equitable principles in trade, and establish uniformity in the commercial usages in Nashville."

Those purposes have remained for 132 years, but the Chamber of Commerce disappeared during the Civil War and was not revived until 1869, under a new name: "The Board of Trade." The name has changed several times—from 1913 to 1921 the organization was known as the Commercial Club—but most of the time it has been the Chamber of Commerce. In 1960 it became theNashville Area Chamber of Commerce.

In 1958, for the first time in its 109-year history, the Chamber moved into a new building of its own—a bright and cheery contemporary structure of glass and aluminum at 310 Union Street. But the Chamber was there only thirteen years when the building had to be razed to make way for a new bank building, the First

American Center, that covers a block. In 1971 the Chamber moved to its present home at 161 Fourth Avenue North, next to the L&C Tower.

In any one decade, the Chamber's role in pushing Nashville forward has shown foresight. In the 1920s, the Chamber helped push through Congress the bill that was responsible for using the dam at Muscle Shoals and thereby preparing the way for the Tennessee Valley Authority, which opened new doors for the South.

The Nashville Area Chamber of Commerce organized all Chambers in the state to back better health care in the 1920s, suggested Governor Austin Peay's reorganization of state government, led the effort to convert the World War I power plant at Old Hickory into a synthetics manufacturing operation, and established the agency now know as the United Way.

The Chamber was a strong leader in the campaign to merge the old city and county governments into our present consolidated Metropolitan Government, developed and engineered implementation of legislation creating the Airport Authority, and supported sensible land planning and use by promoting the comprehensive zoning ordinance.

That small fraction of Chamber activity indicates the variety of its interests. In 1979, with 3,047 firm and professional accounts and 4,028 individual members, the Chamber concentrates on new jobs and capital investment through economic development, stimulating and servicing tourist and convention business for the city, monitoring federal, state, and local legislation for the benefit of the community, and watching over the financing and structure of local government. Through its research programs, the Chamber provides a degree of management for the unending changes which take place in all metropolitan areas.

Originally the Vanderbilt University Law and Dental Building (left), this structure at 314 Fourth Avenue North was the home of the Chamber of Commerce from 1916 to 1950. The Chamber moved into its first real home (right) at 310 Union Street in 1958.

Nashville CityBank & Trust Company

Nashville CityBank & Trust Company, celebrating its ninetieth birthday in 1979, is the fourth largest bank in Nashville and is rapidly becoming a top-earning institution here.

Founded in 1889 as Nashville Trust Company, the bank has gone through many mergers and changes in name since its establishment. But since 1968 it has taken on new direction. Now a full-service commercial bank with twelve offices, Nashville CityBank has attracted some of the best business minds in the city to its board of directors and its management team.

Building its staff from outstanding career and professional bankers, Nashville CityBank recently topped $150 million in deposits. Since August 1973, James A. Webb Jr., president and chairman of the board, has led the bank in a plan that has resulted in dramatic improvement in earnings, growth, services, personnel, and general welfare of the bank.

Strong emphasis on the involvement of officers and staff of the bank in the city's business, civic, and social life has brought impressive results. At the same time, the bank has established a Young Executives' Council, made up of thirty-four outstanding young men and women in Nashville who assist the bank and the community by their suggestions.

It was that same emphasis on community service that led Herman Justi, a public-spirited young man of many interests ninety years ago, to take the lead in founding the bank on July 3, 1889. He, along with Charles Nelson, Dr. Walter M. Dake, General Gates P. Thruston, and Joseph Phillips, organized the bank with a capital of $250,000. The bank's chief purpose then was to administer trusts and estates.

On September 3, 1889, Nelson was elected president, and the bank opened on September 9, 1889, in temporary quarters. A few days later, the bank leased space in a four-story stone building on Fourth Avenue North, between Union and Deaderick, where Vanderbilt University operated its law school.

In 1903 the bank moved into its own building at 233 Third Avenue, near Union, and part of today's bank is on that same site. In 1926 the bank moved into a new building at 315 Union, and that building, recently renovated, is occupied by the bank today.

The strength of the bank was greatly enhanced in 1933 when Horace G. Hill purchased control of the bank and gave it new life. He was president from 1933 to 1936 and chairman of the board from 1936 until his death in 1942. Mr. Hill was followed as chairman of the board by his son, Horace G. Hill Jr., who provided personal leadership until the bank was merged with Third National Bank in 1964.

In 1968 the bank was separated from Third National Bank, and the new bank, then called The Nashville Bank and Trust Company, continued to do business at 315 Union—its home today. In 1970 another influential businessman, Jack Massey, was drawn into the bank's future when he assisted in the merger of Capitol City Bank with The Nashville Bank and Trust Company. The new name of the combined banks became the Nashville City Bank and Trust Company.

In 1971 the bank became part of a holding company, United Tennessee Bancshares Corporation, but on December 31, 1976, the bank separated from the holding company and became an independent financial institution, under the name Nashville CityBank & Trust Company.

The bank today dates its rebirth from 1968, when businessmen of the stature of Joe T. Howell Jr. and M.S. Wigginton began to play key roles (Howell as president and Wigginton chairman of the board). After many changes in direction through its almost century of life, the bank has set its course as a major independent bank, and its recent rapid growth has come partly from the fact that young men and women of ability are encouraged to use their maximum talent.

In its handsomely renovated main office, where the architecture of 1924 underscores the continuity of the ninety-year-old business, Nashville CityBank combines the soundness of the old with the vigor of the new.

Members of the founding board of directors of Nashville CityBank were listed on the company's original stock certificates.

The bank's downtown lobby was a beehive of activity when this picture was made in 1930.

339

Nashville Board Of Realtors

The Nashville Board of Realtors, the largest and one of the oldest professional trade associations in Nashville, is the primary spokesman for the property owners in Metropolitan Nashville today. It is an organization of over three thousand qualified and carefully screened real estate agents who are committed to a strict Code of Ethics.

Originally chartered on July 16, 1911, as the Nashville Association of Real Estate Boards, the local board is one of the oldest Realtor organizations in the country.

Nashville was one of the first cities to initiate such a local organization, which originated in the 1890s as the Nashville Real Estate Exchange. A forerunner of the present organization, this group was instrumental in initiating the movement for a national organization.

Thomas T. Wright of Nashville was honored in a formal resolution of 1891-1892 as the originator of the idea of the National Real Estate Association. This short-lived organization, which was terminated by 1894, was nevertheless significant as its membership, its objectives, and its whole working life made it the forerunner of the National Association of Real Estate Board, later known as the National Association of Realtors.

In the early days anyone could sell real estate. There was no training available, no laws established to govern conduct of agents, and no standard practices established for salesmen to follow. The resulting confusion made the need for an organization of agents apparent.

By banding together, agents could eliminate many of the problems that had arisen by a lack of standardization and upgrade the industry as a whole. They wanted to firmly establish their business as a respected profession by encouraging legislation to protect the public, providing education of agents and promoting ethical conduct.

By 1908 there were local boards over the nation beginning to form state associations and to form the National Association. In 1913 the National Association wrote its Code of Ethics and registered the term Realtor (with a captial R) to identify those agents who subscribed to this standard.

In 1920 Nashville hosted twenty-eight representatives of real estate boards from Chattanooga, Memphis, Nashville, Watertown, and Tullahoma at a meeting to form the Tennessee Realtors Association, later called the Tennessee Association of Realtors. The state association, chartered and supervised by the National Association, is a voluntary, nonprofit association which serves as an advisor, consultant, and coordinator for local board activities.

The first half-century of Nashville Board activity was characterized by a concerted effort of members to make the public aware of their goals and functions and to protect the industry and the public by taking a stand on any legislation or federal regulation they determined to be not in the best interest of either. Regular monthly meetings were held in various places to discuss matters of concern. In the mid-fifties those meetings were held in the old Noel Hotel and drew a crowd of fifty to seventy-five Realtors. Today some four to five hundred attend regular monthly meetings.

A major milestone was achieved in 1951 when, after years of effort on the part of Realtors throughout the state, the state legislature passed a law requiring all real estate agents to be licensed. This law established the Tennessee Real Estate Commission to administer a written examination which must be passed in order to obtain a license.

All of those who are licensed to practice real estate, however, are not Realtors. Realtors are committed formally to a more rigid set of requirements both ethically and educationally.

Becoming a Realtor or a Realtor-Associate takes a lot of time, hard work, and dedication. Besides earning an affiliate-broker's license—which involves passing the Tennessee Real Estate Commission's exam and completing one three-hour (quarter or semester hour), state-approved real estate course within a two-year period—a Realtor-Associate candidate must take a five-session course, three hours per session, and pass the Realtor's Code of Ethics examination. After holding the affiliate-broker's license for two years, a second exam and three additional three-hour (quarter or semester) courses are necessary to acquire a broker's license. (The broker's license entitles a person to own his own company.) In Nashville, to become a Realtor, a candidate must hold a real estate license and pass a strict Realtor's exam.

At the time the licensing law was first passed, there were not more than one hundred members of the Nashville Board. During that decade membership began to climb and the number of women Realtors increased considerably. In 1957 these women formed the Nashville Chapter of the Women's Council of Realtors, whose purpose is to provide its members with further educational opportunities to expand their knowledge of principles of practice and to develop their capacity for leadership.

Through the National Association of Realtors, a number of affiliated institutes, societies, and councils have been formed in Nashville to keep pace with the constantly growing trend toward specialization in today's complex real estate field and also to assist members with specialized interests.

A Court of Arbitration was established to guard against abuse of the Board's Code of Ethics and to ensure that all members uphold the high standards set by the Board. Five Board members are elected to serve on this Court, which ensures ethical conduct between members as well as protects the homebuyer. It offers an avenue of recourse for any homebuyer who feels he has been unfairly treated or misled in any way. In fact, according to local sources, the court has often ruled in favor of the homebuyer so as to avoid any hint of wrongdoing on the part of a Board member.

The decade of the sixties was an eventful one for the Board, which by this time was well-established and respected. A new charter was issued on May 9, 1967, changing the name of the organization from Nashville Real Estate Board to Nashville Board of Realtors.

This was the same year the Board moved into new offices in the Nashville Bank and Trust Company Building, which included a library, conference room, two private offices, and a reception area. Prior to this, the Board's first executive officer, Evelyn Haston, had occupied a single-room office on the same floor of the Trust Building for many years.

Realtors and homeowners alike started reaping the benefits of the Nashville Multiple Listing Service Incorporated (MLS) in 1967. The MLS catalog, published weekly with daily supplements, lists almost all the residential property in the area for sale by subscribing Realtors. Members have the option of subscribing.

Multiple listings mean increased benefits to both the Realtor and homeowner. It means more Realtors trying to sell each house. To the Realtor, it means sales cooperation with a fellow Realtor who lists the home; to the homeowner, it means the possibilty of hundreds of people working to sell a home rather than just one Realtor. In 1979 this service was computerized, increasing the speed and efficiency of the system.

After the death of Miss Haston, who had served the Board of Realtors for over twenty years, Grace Fairbanks became executive vice president and serves in that capacity at this writing.

The next decade was one of substantial growth in membership. In 1969 there were five hundred members and in just ten years the membership has grown to over three thousand.

With the increase in membership and additional services being offered, the Board staff also began to grow. In 1973 the Nashville Board bought their own office building at 500 James Robertson Parkway, where they remain today. This facility contains classrooms in which the many seminars and educational activities offered by the Board are held to improve the profession of real estate sales and management.

The Board office also houses the Evelyn Haston Memorial Library, where books, periodicals, films, 16mm projectors, slide presentations, carousel projectors, and cassette tapes are made available to members.

The Nashville Board of Realtors has through the years, by hard work and exemplary conduct, achieved their goal of making the term Realtor connote to Nashvillians competence, fair dealing, and high integrity resulting from adherence to a lofty ideal of moral conduct in business relations.

Although there were no real estate agents in Nashville during its early days, today there are more than 3,000 brokers and agents here, handling thousands of sales, transfers of title and examinations annually.

341

Nashville Electric
Service

Nashville Electric Service, which supplies electricity to a city with more electrically heated homes than any other city in the world, has the challenge now of encouraging Nashvillians into conserving electricity.

And that switch in roles—from selling electricity to conserving it—is a striking example of the nation's energy plight.

From 1882, when James W. Braid, founder of Braid Electric Company, turned on a light in a window of the State Capitol to demonstrate to visiting scientists in convention here how a light bulb worked, Nashville has hungered for electricity.

In 1897, when Tennessee celebrated her 100th birthday with a six-month extravaganza spread out over sixty acres in what has been called Centennial Park ever since, the twenty-six exhibition buildings—all painted white to reflect the bright lights—were lighted with thousands of electric lights powered by the Centennial exposition's own generating plant. The grounds were dazzling in the white light of electricity, and Nashvillians found that electricity was one of the great excitements of the Centennial.

Just six years later, in June 1903, electricity came to Nashville when Nashville Railway & Light Company was incorporated as a successor to the Nashville Railway and Cumberland Electric Light & Power Company (which had begun operating electric streetcars from Fourth Avenue to what is now Centennial Park in 1889). Nashville Railway & Light Company was formed not only to operate streetcars but also to provide light and other electric power. All current was generated by steam engines.

The growth of the city toward suburbia was tied to development of electric streetcar lines. Glendale Park and Zoo, on some sixty acres now in the Glendale area of the city, was owned and operated by the Railway & Light Company from 1903 to entice visitors to the zoo to travel by streetcar. Subdivisions in the Glendale and Belle Meade areas were developed so that residents there would use streetcars to travel to work or downtown shopping.

In 1930 Nashville Railway & Light Company became a part of Tennessee Electric Power Company, which had been incorporated in 1922. By 1939 Tennessee Electric Power Company was serving 52,384 customers in the Nashville area.

Mayor Tom Cummings applied for and received a state charter to supply electric energy to Nashville. Subsequently, he appointed the first Electric Power Board in 1939. The board issued $15 million in revenue bonds and purchased TEPCO in August of the same year. The operating name became Nashville Electric Service. The board sets all policies and appoints the managerial positions which are directly responsible for NES operations. It buys TVA power at a wholesale rate and selects resale rates so that it can pay operating costs and expenses.

To meet the city's postwar boom in use of electricity—both in suburban areas and in industry—NES built a new electric center on a twelve-acre site at Thirteenth and Church in 1950-1952. Later they bought adjoining property to bring the total to more than fourteen acres, and all administrative offices, along with most operating functions, are housed there.

In the postwar years, practically all new homes were built for electric heat. Central air conditioning was included in many of those homes. But in late 1972, a severe energy crisis turned NES toward conservation. Coal strikes and a shortage of oil imports made it necessary to concentrate on cutbacks in use of electricity.

Nashville is still called "Electri-City" and is the tenth largest public electric utility system in America. In 1979 the company had a thousand employees serving two hundred thousand customers in Metropolitan Nashville and six surrounding counties. J. Dudley Phillips is chairman of the board, and Paul P. Hembree is general manager.

The Nashville Railway and Cumberland Electric Light & Power Company ran electric streetcars (above) from Fourth Avenue to what is now Centennial Park. The company was to become a part of the Tennessee Electric Power Company (right) in 1922.

Electric appliances were introduced into the Nashville area by Nashville Electric Service's predecessor. Today the city has more electrically heated homes than any other community in the world.

Nashville Gas Company

Nashville Gas Company, which has supplied gas to Nashville for 128 years, played a strong role in the community's growth from frontier town to prospering city.

The men who brought gas to Nashville, headed by the distinguished Washington Barrow (former minister to Portugal, congressman, and editor of a Nashville newspaper), made varying contributions to the city's development. In 1849 John Kirkman, Samuel R. Anderson, N.E. Alloway, and William T. Berry founded Nashville Gas Light Company.

The company was ready to light the first gas street light in Nashville on February 13, 1851, and a hundred street lights were installed. That same year, Barrow, as a promotional gimmick, offered a "beautiful silk dress" to the first lady who would have her home lighted by gas. The John Bass home was the first, and by the end of the year there were 285 customers using gas.

By 1855, when the State Capitol was finished, visitors were impressed with the tremendous bronze chandelier hanging in the House of Representatives. That chandelier, made in Philadelphia and designed with buffalo, Indians, corn, and tobacco symbolizing the state's history and products, had cost $1,500 and had forty-eight gas burners. (Later generations of backwoods legislators were so fearful of the chandelier's great weight that they had it removed from the building.)

The gas company's offices moved many times during its rapid growth—beginning at 35 Public Square and gradually working its way up Fourth Avenue North and Church Street to its present location at 814 Church Street in 1950. At the same time, the gas plant itself and its service department had many additions. In its first ten years, the company's facilities doubled, and by 1860 it had two hundred street lights and between eight hundred and nine hundred meters, along with eighteen miles of gas mains.

During the Civil War when Union forces held Nashville, Washington Barrow, a Confederate sympathizer, was thrown into prison. Samuel Watkins, brick manufacturer and benefactor of the city, was made president of the company.

After the war, the invention of the "blue flame," which produced an intensely hot flame, and the "gas mantle," which produced a white light, brought a new era to the gas industry. The blue flame paved the way for cooking, heating homes, and powering many household conveniences. The white light meant better illumination for many homes and businesses. By 1890 the company had three thousand customers and forty-five miles of gas mains. By 1894 there were fifteen hundred gas ranges in Nashville kitchens.

In 1900 the company was reorganized as the Nashville Gas Company, and in 1911 it was purchased by a Philadelphia-owned company and renamed the Nashville Gas and Heating Company. In 1945 that company was bought by Tennessee Natural Gas Lines Incorporated. At a ceremony at Twenty-Eighth Avenue North and Buchanan Street on August 5, 1946, Mayor Thomas L. Cummings turned the valve that started the first flow of natural gas from Texas wells into Nashville. Standing beside the mayor was Wade V. Thompson, president of Tennessee Natural Gas Company Lines, who fought for years to introduce natural gas and cheaper rates to Nashville.

Today the network of gas mains is spread over Davidson, Cheatham, Williamson, Sumner, and Wilson counties, reaching a total of 62,521 customers.

W.H. Ligon, president of the company for twenty-five years and now a member of the board, and John C. Bolinger Jr., current president, state that the greatly expanded capacity keeps gas flowing through 1,374 miles of mains now, a flow uninterrupted since 1851.

Nashville Gas and Heating Company employees serviced thousands of Nashville customers from vehicles like this one during the first two decades of this century.

Mayor Thomas L. Cummings turned the wheel and opened the valve to introduce natural gas to Middle Tennessee on August 5, 1946.

Nashville Sash And Door Company Incorporated

Nashville Sash and Door Company Incorporated, wholesale supplier of windows, doors, blinds, and glass, is one of the longtime businesses on Nashville's picturesque Second Avenue North—the row of Victorian warehouses celebrated in recent years in the Market Street Fair.

Today two of its owners, the brothers Sidney S. and John D. (Jack) McAlister (the third partner is Thomas J. McMeen), are selling millwork products close to the same spot on Second Avenue North where their great-grandfather, Harry Hill McAlister Jr., sold windows and doors eighty-seven years ago.

But the business has changed radically since then. No windows or doors are manufactured there any more. Instead, all products arrive at the company's seven warehouses along Second Avenue North already semi-fabricated. The mellowed look of the historic buildings gives no clue to the fact that Nashville Sash and Door Company did over $10 million worth of business in 1978, for instance. The company's fleet of seventeen trucks that back up to the old storefronts along Second Avenue North are a familiar sight to strollers along the historic way.

Today's company, with headquarters at 148-160 Second Avenue North, includes buildings where windows and doors have been manufactured since 1908. It includes 152 Second Avenue North where Harry Hill McAlister III operated the business in 1926. It is the same lot where a great-uncle, James A. McAlister, operated a cotton warehouse in 1843.

Harry Hill McAlister Jr. was listed in the 1892 City Directory as secretary-treasurer of the Riddle Company, manufacturer of sashes, doors, and glass. That company included a shop where windows and doors were made to order—in contrast to today's business of selling mostly stock items already manufactured and ready for delivery.

In 1915, when the Riddle Company closed and H.H. McAlister Jr. left Nashville to manage Cole Manufacturing Company in New Orleans, his son, H.H. McAlister III, remained in Nashville and continued in the sash and door business. A former salesman for the Riddle Company, H.H. McAlister III formed a partnership with Ben Patterson to found the Southern Door and Glass Company, with headquarters at 200 Second Avenue North.

In 1926 H.H. McAlister III and colleagues Wallace Green and W.L. Robertson sold their interests in the firm to Patterson and founded the present Nashville Sash and Door Company Incorporated, with headquarters at 152 Second Avenue North. Early in the 1930s, they purchased the Atlanta Sash and Door Company but kept it only briefly.

In 1936 Thomas J. McMeen joined the firm of Nashville Sash and Door Company as secretary to Harry McAlister. Today he is a full partner in the business. The other two partners in the business—both sons of Harry Hill McAlister III—are Sidney S. McAlister and Jack McAlister. Sidney joined the family business full time in 1946, and Jack followed in 1951.

The seven warehouses, covering approximately 180,000 square feet, store not only windows, doors, and millwork, but also hardware and other supplies as varied as sinks, mirrors, and skylights.

Though the wholesale company serves contractors in the Nashville and Davidson County area, it also supplies dealers and lumber yards throughout Tennessee, Southern Kentucky, and Northern Alabama.

The fifty-two-year-old business has experienced its greatest growth since World War II. One of its largest orders recently was to supply most of the windows and doors for the huge and handsome Opryland Hotel.

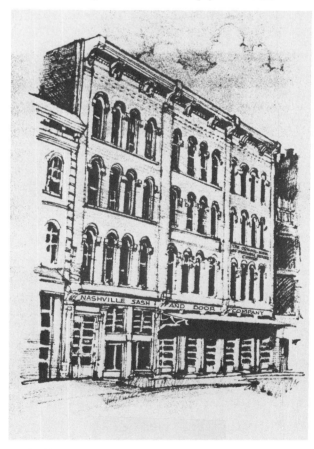

Nashville Sash and Door Company occupies one of the most historic buildings on Nashville's Second Avenue.

344

Norvell & Wallace Incorporated

Norvell & Wallace Incorporated, retail lumber dealer and one of the oldest businesses in Nashville today, has supplied much of the lumber for the building of this city during the last century.

In the last two decades of the nineteenth century, Nashville was one of the outstanding hardwood centers of the nation and the largest in the South. The Cumberland River made the industry possible. Some of the finest tracts of cedar, oak, ash, poplar, beech, walnut, and hickory in the United States grew in a half-dozen counties along the upper Cumberland in the 1870s to 1890s, and timber men there floated huge rafts of logs to Nashville sawmills and lumber yards. When the log rafts were pulled out of the river at Nashville lumber yards, they poured $8 million a year into the city. Norvell & Wallace was one of the twenty companies that shared in handling the eighty-four million feet of lumber here in 1884 alone.

The story began with William E. Norvell & Company, which for three years had operated on the northeast corner of Broad and Seventh. In 1880 Mr. Norvell joined forces with Mr. W.J. Wallace, who had been the bookkeeper for Spain & Hawkins Lumber company. From this association, Norvell & Wallace was founded.

After the company's first ten years in business, the bountiful hardwood from the upper Cumberland began to disappear, and Norvell & Wallace was the first to import Southern yellow pine into Nashville. The yellow pine, from Georgia and other Southern states, was shipped here by railroad.

The transition in transportation and materials had begun. Today Richard Norvell, president of the company and grandson of one of the founders, says that a majority of the lumber used in buildings is yellow pine, and the typical carload is 50,000 board feet, as compared with 9,000 board feet per carload on the earliest freight cars.

By 1893 Norvell & Wallace, while maintaining a sales office at Sixth and Broad, moved its flourishing business to larger yards on Hamilton Avenue in South Nashville. In 1946 the sales office and yard office merged to the Hamilton Avenue location, where Norvell & Wallace still maintains its business operations today.

In 1893 the second generation of the Wallace family, W.J. Wallace Jr., joined the firm. He was followed by the third generation of the Wallace line with Hamilton Wallace in 1922, W.J. Wallace III in 1924, and J.E. (Ned) Wallace in 1939.

In 1915 the second generation of the Norvell family entered the business when Richard Norvell became a part of the firm, and he was followed by his two sons, Richard (Red) Norvell in 1941 and W.E. Norvell II in 1949. Red Norvell's son, Owen M. Norvell, joined the company in 1978 as did Elizabeth Owen Norvell, daughter of W.E. Norvell II, that same year, thus bringing the fourth generation of the Norvell family into the company.

In 1967 a major change in the management of the company came when J.E. Wallace, Richard Norvell Jr., and W.E. Norvell II bought out the other partners and began operating under the name of Norvell & Wallace Incorporated.

In 1978 Richard Norvell and W.E. Norvell II bought full interest in the corporation and now operate the company as its principals.

Norvell & Wallace takes great pride in the long tenure of its employees and the true loyalty they have shown over the past years. This loyalty and one hundred years of sharing the growth and prosperity with Nashville and the business community have made Norvell & Wallace what it is today. They are proud of buildings their lumber has helped construct, which is a significant contribution that has changed the whole skyline of Nashville, Tennessee.

*Marion Hamilton
Wallace
1900-1970*

*William Joseph
Wallace
1846-1905*

*William Edmund
Norvell
1847-1922*

*William Joseph
Wallace Jr.
1876-1961*

*Richard Owen
Norvell
1893-1944*

Office of NORVELL & WALLACE,

GENERAL

LUMBER DEALERS,

Rock City Machine Company

Rock City Machine Company was founded seventy-seven years ago when farmers and suburban residents had to pump water from their own wells. Today, its customers are often plumbers, contractors, and small industry owners with large problems to tackle.

Rock City Machine Company for years had a machine shop that was the scene of innovative solutions to a variety of mechanical problems. Established in a day when Nashville's limestone base gave the city her nickname "Rock City," the company welcomed new challenges.

The company was founded in 1902 by Julian D. and F.C. Stone, and their first shop, at 134-136 North College Street, was listed as "Stone's" in the city directory of that year. In 1903 it was listed as Rock City Machine Company, at 117 North College Street. The Stone brothers owned Rock City Machine Company until 1954, supplying generators for operating shaft-driven pumps.

In 1927 Gilbert W. Lovell Sr. went to work for the Stone brothers, and he began devising new parts for machinery. Some of his inventions were patented, including a book-creaser that the company still manufactures. In 1958 Lovell invented a base and top guide for submerged pumps, and in 1959 he invented Lovell's level well cover. In 1960 he invented a pie-slicer for industrial use. He designed and built bat testing machines and a machine for closing the ends of aluminum baseball bats made by one of the nation's largest manufacturers of bats. In World War II, the company tooled the dies for bomb casings that were manufactured by Nashville firms.

In 1946 Gilbert W. Lovell Sr. purchased one-fifth ownership in the company, and in 1954 he purchased the remaining interest. In 1944 his son G. Ward Lovell Jr. had begun working there part time after school, and he was working there full time by 1954. He purchased the company after his father's retirement in 1976.

G. Ward Lovell Jr. became president of the company in 1976, and his wife Caroline became secretary of the firm. Their two sons Gilbert Ward III and John Charles—just out of college—are already members of the firm.

The two sons of G. Ward Lovell Jr. began working at the company during summer vacations from school. Gilbert Ward Lovell III, with a business degree from Vanderbilt University, works in the sales area, while his brother, John Charles Lovell, with a mechanical engineering degree from Tennessee Technological University in Cookeville, is interested in reopening the machine shop where his grandfather's inventiveness made unique contributions to the community.

Since 1905, selling F.E. Myers pumps has been part of the operation. Pump sales, installation, and servicing, along with well supplies, have been major activities of the company for almost seventy-five years. Since 1960 Rock City Machine Company has added machinery for lawn and garden cultivation. Today it is a Nashville dealer for John Deere lawn and garden machines. Rock City Machine Company also handles air compressors, chain saws, and chlorination and laboratory equipment.

With twelve employees and restoration of some of the custom-built machinery, the company maintains a flexibility that has made it strong for seventy-seven years.

G.W. Lovell Sr. and F.C. Stone (standing left and right in photo at left above) were early partners in the distribution of Myers pumps. Today's generations of Lovells (standing left to right, John, G. Ward, and Gilbert in photo at right above), current owners of Rock City Machine Company, distribute and service everything from pumps to lawn and garden implements to laboratory equipment and supplies.

Joe M. Rodgers & Associates

Joe M. Rodgers & Associates, contractors and engineers, dramatically illustrates a new breed of business people in today's Nashville. Seizing on a formula for a quality product, they multiply it into a fortune.

Joe M. Rodgers, only thirty-three years old when he invested of $250 in his own company in 1966, has built it into a $95 million per year business in this country alone—not counting the $20 to $30 million annual volume in overseas construction.

Seven years after receiving his degree in engineering, he came to Nashville to work for his brother, Ed Rodgers, in his Dixie Concrete Pipe Company. Joe Rodgers decided after three years there to form his own company.

Through his work for his brother's company, Joe Rodgers met Bob McDowell, whose company (now McDowell Enterprises) specialized in highway construction. Rodgers encouraged McDowell and other members of that company into investing $125 each, while he invested $250 in a new corporation to be called Joe M. Rodgers & Associates. That company would subcontract for McDowell—handling small jobs like erecting highway signs, guardrails, and landscaping.

Through a chance meeting in 1968, Joe Rodgers met the man who would change his whole career: Dr. Thomas Frist Sr. Rodgers and Frist were soon talking about Frist's plans (along with Jack Massey and Henry Hooker) to build a chain of hospitals for Hospital Corporation of America. Frist asked Rodgers if he would be interested in doing the construction work on the hospitals. Three weeks later, Rodgers was inspecting the site for the first of the hospitals, a $650,000 unit to go up in Erin, Tennessee.

That was the beginning of a long business relationship, full of challenges. Rodgers still handles a substantial portion of HCA's construction. Because of the rapid expansion of HCA, Rodgers' volume of business went from $9 million to $27 million in one year (1970). Rodgers' reputation for finishing a job on the scheduled date, or sometimes sooner, placed him in demand with many builders.

It was through HCA that Rodgers extended the company's work to overseas construction. HCA had agreed to manage and staff the King Faisal Specialist Hospital in Saudi Arabia, but the project was bogged down for years through construction problems. HCA called Rodgers' top men in for consultation, and they made recommendations that helped solve the problems.

Consequently, he expanded his overseas operations through a subsidiary called Joe M. Rodgers and Associates Limited. A reorganization of the company later put Rodgers International B.V. in charge of various subsidiaries, with thirty people in the Amsterdam office to handle the international work.

In Nashville, Rodgers has built the Opryland Hotel guest rooms, Hickory Hollow Mall, McKendree Manor additions, Central Parking on Deaderick Street, Olin Engineering Hall on the Vanderbilt campus, the HCA home office, and the McDowell Enterprises office. He also developed International Plaza.

With a thousand employees working on construction jobs in twenty-five states, Rodgers shaves days off construction time by coordinating work with that of architects and builders. A staunch believer in "merit shop" (in contrast with union shutdowns), the company stakes its reputation on getting the job done right and getting it done on time.

Joe M. Rodgers invested $250 to launch Joe M. Rodgers & Associates in 1966. Today the company has operations worldwide and handles more than $100 million of construction annually.

Rudy's Farm Country Sausage

Rudy's Farm Country Sausage, cooked in kitchens in thirty states, is a multimillion dollar business that grew out of one Nashville family's smokehouse skill.

With almost five hundred employees and $65 million worth of business this year, Rudy's Farm is one of the major employers in the Nashville area. It began with the grandfather of the present owners, and today brothers Frank and Dan Rudy operate the business on the same land where the family has lived and worked for generations. The ninety-one acre farm of green hills tucked in the Pennington Bend of the Cumberland River has recently been split by Briley Parkway, and Opryland is just across the road.

It was the problem of poor refrigeration in their grandfather's day that made sausage production a cold weather project so the Rudys spent most of the year farming. But Daniel Rudy was so expert at sausage making that he would "custom slaughter" hogs for neighbors when cold weather struck.

The Rudy recipe for making sausage came from their German ancestors, the Rudys and the Clees, and Daniel Rudy's son, Jacob L. Rudy, built his first small "sausage house" near a spring on the farm to make water hauling easier.

At first they hand-ground the sausage, later using a grinder powered by a one-cylinder gas engine. To refrigerate their product, they packed it in an icebox that held six hundred pounds of ice. And they wrapped the sausage in corn shucks.

When Jacob Rudy died in 1936 leaving a $3,000 debt, his sons were still teen-agers. They have never forgotten that they were able to continue their business because Sam Fleming, then a loan officer at Third National Bank, let them borrow their first money ($600). As collateral, they had a "warehouse of stored wheat."

But the business was hardly launched when World War II stopped their plans for expansion. The Rudys put all of their effort into farming, and Dan was deferred from military service to produce badly needed food on a 1,012-acre farm nearby.

It was not until the war was over that the Rudy brothers decided to make a new try at the sausage business, and they formed Rudy Sausage Company. Refrigeration created year-round "hog-killing weather," and they were the first here to buy refrigerated trucks to deliver their products.

When one of the first customers, the commissary of the army classification center here, requested a spicier sausage, Rudy's began a new service: a choice between "hot" and mild sausage, an innovation standard in today's sausage industry.

In the 1950s the company changed its name and trademark to emphasize its unique farm operation. The name of the company became Rudy's Farm Country Sausage, and the dinner bell ("the one Dan had down at the house") was the new emblem.

In 1961 they replaced the old "sausage house" with a new plant. A model of gleaming tile walls and stainless steel equipment, the new plant shines in spotless efficiency, and all employees wear freshly laundered white coats. In 1979 it is already three times as large as it was in 1962, and the fleet of trucks has grown from six in 1962 to forty today.

In 1971 the company merged, through an exchange of stock, with Consolidated Foods Incorporated of Chicago, but no change in operation was made. Today Dan Rudy is chairman of the board, and Frank Rudy serves as consultant. Bill Hardison, an employee of the company for twenty-five years, is president.

It's a far cry, the Rudy brothers say, from their first output of a few sausages per day, wrapped in corn shucks down by the spring on the farm.

At one time, Frank Rudy's children traveled nationwide, singing and promoting their father's increasingly popular sausage.

Marking the opening of the company's new plant in 1961 were (left to right): a USDA representative, Frank Rudy, Frank Rudy Jr., Governor Buford Ellington, and Dan Rudy.

348

Service Merchandise
Company Incorporated

Service Merchandise Company, Inc., a catalog-showroom business with national headquarters in Nashville, grew out of a chain of stores that Harry and Mary Zimmerman founded in Pulaski in 1934.

With total revenues rising steadily from $726,000 in 1960 to $528 million in 1979, the company has ninety-one catalog showrooms operating in twenty-one states ranging from Alabama and Oklahoma to Maine and Massachusetts, and ten more showrooms will be opened in 1979.

Service Merchandise Company employs 6,500 people today, with 5,000 employees in the showrooms and the remainder in company offices and warehouses. Mr. and Mrs. Zimmerman take pride in the fact that they and their son, Raymond Zimmerman, along with four other employees, made up the whole work force of the company when they opened for business in 1960.

But the romance of the business began in 1934, when Harry and Mary Zimmerman—both born in Memphis in 1911 and both graduates of Memphis' Central High School—decided that he should give up his work as an insurance agent to enter the mercantile business.

With no experience in merchandising, they borrowed $2,800 to open a Five and Ten Cent Variety Store in Pulaski, and that soon developed into a chain of ten stores—at Union City, Humboldt, Fayetteville, Lawrenceburg, Lewisburg, Camden, Waverly, Dickson, and Goodlettsville.

After serving in the U.S. Navy from 1944 to 1946, Harry Zimmerman returned to his business, which by then had moved headquarters to Nashville. In 1947 he entered the wholesale field, selling to variety stores, drugstores, and general stores. Soon he sold his retail stores, mainly to Kuhn's Variety Stores in Nashville.

Harry Zimmerman stated that in 1960 it occurred to him that the wholesale business was doomed as a method of distribution of merchandise. One day he called his wife and son in to announce that he was liquidating the present business and would enter what he considered the business of the future—catalog showrooms, catering directly to the public.

The idea behind the business is to mail what is now a 500-page catalog (but not so large then) showing some 10,000 items and to invite customers to come to the nearest showroom to make their selections. There everything from jewelry to toys, tableware to luggage, sewing machines to tennis rackets is sold, and the customer examines what he has seen in the catalog.

However, when he opened the new business, Service Wholesale Company, at 305 Broadway, his two daughters assembled the first mailing list, and he soon had his first catalog in the mail. The Company's name was later changed to Service Merchandise Company. "At that time," Mr. Zimmerman stated, "there were few like us in this new business—mostly in smaller communities and with local catalogs serving modest-sized territories." Harry Zimmerman wanted to get in on the ground floor and help develop this new method of merchandising—the key to which is—all merchandise in the catalog is in stock and immediately available to customers. "We received enthusiastic acceptance by the public as far back as 1960," recalled Harry Zimmerman.

In today's environment, costs are kept at a minimum to compete with the same merchandise sold through regular department stores. Service Merchandise mails approximately eight million catalogs a year, along with smaller supplements. To support sales, each showroom has an adjoining warehouse with an inventory of merchandise purchased from 1,300 suppliers. Less than one percent of the business is done by mail order, and overhead costs are kept low with no-frills showrooms and much self-service.

Today, Service Merchandise is publicly held, with its stock actively traded over the counter (NASDAQ:SMCH), but the family is still active in the business. Harry Zimmerman is chairman of the board, Raymond Zimmerman is president and Mary K. Zimmerman is secretary. Their leadership in the civic and religious life of the community has kept pace with their rapidly expanding business.

Harry Zimmerman (left) and Raymond Zimmerman (center) join with Third National Bank executive John Clay (right) to finalize a major loan agreement in 1973.

St. Thomas Hospital

St. Thomas Hospital, built on eighty-one years of devoted care of the sick, today provides its services in a five-year-old, $29 million building that towers over one of the most delightful sections of the city, on Harding Road at Bosley Springs Road.

The first patients were moved to that historic hilltop site from the old Hayes Street hospital on December 30, 1974, and already the new building with 410 beds is so crowded that a new 161-bed unit is being added. In addition, a thousand-space parking pavilion on the twenty-eight-acre site has just been completed.

In open-heart surgery alone, the hospital showed an increase of eighteen percent in 1978 over the previous year. At the same time, there was a 103 percent increase in neurosurgical procedures, a thirty-three percent increase in vascular procedures, and a twenty percent increase in orthopedic work. To accommodate these new demands, the new 161-bed addition will include adjunct facilities—laboratories, surgical suites, recovery room and critical care areas.

The building itself, handsomely designed to combine efficiency and personal care, is so arranged that patients—all in private rooms—are cared for by a staff freed of every task that automation can do. An automated monorail transportation system, for instance, delivers all meals, supplies, and medication to the proper destinations. A comprehensive communications system includes a computerized pneumatic tube system for delivering laboratory specimens, X-ray reports, and other items.

On the medical staff alone, there are 516 doctors, including twenty-one honorary, 181 active, 160 courtesy staff members, and 154 consultants. Vanderbilt School of Medicine provides twenty-nine members of the house staff (interns and residents). Also there are six fellows—specialists pursuing their study in six fields of medicine.

In 1897, when Bishop Thomas S. Byrne of the Catholic Diocese of Nashville (including all of Tennessee) set about the task of founding a Catholic hospital here, he was thinking in terms of buying one of Nashville's finest homes, the antebellum home of Judge J.M. Dickinson (later to become Secretary of War under President Taft).

The original St. Thomas Hospital building, opened in 1902, featured the most modern facilities of its time. The fifty-bed hospital was built at a cost of $200,000.

A Daughter of Charity renders nursing care, as depicted in the catalog commemorating the grand opening of the St. Thomas Hospital building in 1902. Hospital rates began at a dollar a day.

That home, with its eight-acre grounds covering a city block on Church Street, between Twentieth and Twenty-First Avenues, was, through Bishop Byrne's request, bought by the Daughters of Charity of St. Vincent de Paul, with headquarters at Emmitsburg, Maryland.

The Sisters of Charity, who were already running thirty-five other hospitals in the United States, bought the Dickinson home in December 1897 for $50,000, and on March 3, 1898, two sisters arrived to begin converting the house into a combination hospital and dormitory for the nurses. On Easter Monday, April 11, 1898, at the formal opening, the hospital was named in honor of Bishop Thomas Byrne's patron, St. Thomas the Apostle. The first patient was the wife of a Baptist minister.

The going was hard at first, and in January 1899 an auxiliary society, the St. Thomas Relief Society, was formed to help pay off the debts. That valuable organization bore many of the burdens of helping finance the fledgling institution. But by March 1899, with twenty-two patients in the hospital, the building was overcrowded, and a new hospital was built on the grounds at a cost of $200,000. The first wing was formally opened on January 29, 1902. As the needs grew, a second wing was added in 1917 and a third in 1957.

The fantastic electronic equipment available to hospitals through knowledge gained in space exploration in the 1960s made earlier hospitals obsolete. Aids in diagnosing, monitoring, and treating patients brought hope in conditions that were formerly incurable. To offer patients the most sophisticated equipment and treatment, St. Thomas Hospital had to design an innovative new building.

In January 1972 excavation for the building on Harding Road began, and in December 1974, when the first patients arrived, a new era had begun. Few today can remember the days when the charges at the old St. Thomas were $1 a day and horse-drawn ambulances transported patients. And nobody arriving by helicopter at the new hospital's own FAA-approved helicopter landing pad would swap eras. Expensive as today's technology is, St. Thomas administrators say few patients would give it up to lose their lives.

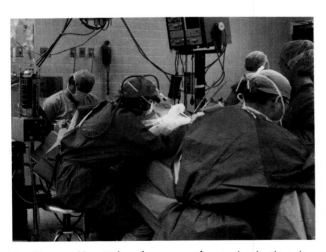

St. Thomas Hospital ranks among the top institutions in the nation with regard to cardiac and vascular procedures. More than 1,200 open-heart operations are performed at St. Thomas each year.

The new St. Thomas Hospital, opened in 1974, serves as a referral center for patients from throughout the mid-United States. The current expansion program will increase the capacity of the 410-bed hospital by one-third.

Shoney's Incorporated

A phenomenon in the food business, Shoney's calls its restaurants "the main feeders of Nashville," where its growth has set a spectacular pace in twenty years since it came here. At least two factors contributed to its growth: Americans are eating out in greatly increasing numbers and Shoney's found the formula for serving consistently good food at reasonable prices in pleasant surroundings.

Shoney's had its beginning in California. In 1936 Robert Wian Jr., a young man in Glendale, California, opened a hamburger stand near the high school where he had graduated two years before. He had worked for a restaurant chain, learning every phase of the business, and it was his ambition to turn out the best hamburgers in the most spotlessly clean surroundings anywhere.

Three things would be invariable in his hamburger stand, Bob Wian determined: top-quality food, cleanliness, and quick, friendly service. He called his first hamburger stand Bob's Pantry, but when success brought a more varied menu in his growing chain of restaurants he sought an emblem: A chubby little boy carrying aloft a huge double-deck hamburger. He named his chain of restaurants Bob's Big Boy, and the symbol became familiar in southern California and Arizona in the next twenty years.

In 1951 Alex Schoenbaum of Charleston, West Virginia, purchased a franchise to operate Big Boy Restaurants in ten states in the Southeast, and he promoted a contest to see what his Big Boy Restaurants should be called. The winner was a shortened version of Schoenbaum—"Shoney's—and the prize was an automobile.

In 1958 Ray Danner and James Craft moved from Louisville, Kentucky, where they had been in several business ventures together, to Nashville, Tennessee. They opened their first Shoney's Big Boy Restaurant in Madison, a suburb of Nashville. This was the tenth Shoney's Big Boy of the fledgling chain. The first week's volume was only $3,000, but by the end of the first year they had managed to triple that weekly volume. That restaurant is still open, although the original building was replaced in 1979 with a totally new facility. That restaurant, from its humble beginnings, has consistently been a member of the Million Dollar Club.

In the second year of business, Shoney's were opened on Thompson Lane, Murfreesboro Road, Donelson Plaza, and Clarksville, Tennessee, and during 1965 Ray Danner bought out his partner, James Craft. In 1966 Shoney's took the franchise for Kentucky Fried Chicken in Louisville. By 1979 the company had developed twenty units in the greater Louisville market. These stores have consistently been some of the highest volume stores in Kentucky Fried Chicken.

In April 1969 Danner Foods became a publicly owned company. In August, Danner Foods opened the first Mr. D's, later to be changed to Captain D's, in Donelson, Tennessee. This project was quarterbacked by Dave Wachtel, who had joined Shoney's as a busboy while in high school and is now the company's president. Captain D's had grown to over 290 units by the end of 1979.

In 1971 Ray Danner merged Danner Foods with Alex Schoenbaum's company to form Shoney's Big Boy Enterprises Incorporated (later shortened to Shoney's Incorporated), and the headquarters was moved to Nashville. This meant that Shoney's Big Boy Enterprises became the franchisor for Shoney's Big Boy Restaurants throughout the Southeast and opened many avenues for growth.

In order to supply the restaurants, Shoney's operates commissaries in Nashville and Charleston, West Virginia. The objectives of the commissaries are to provide the highest quality food, the best service to the individual restaurants, and to maintain price stability to the store. The commissary includes a meat plant, bakery, and extensive food preparation departments.

By the end of 1979, the Shoney's chain of restaurants will number over 630 units system wide in a twenty-one-state area with sales exceeding 400 million dollars a year. Of these, 257 restaurants are company owned and 373 are franchised, and they fall into five categories: the "full service family restaurants" with varied menus called Shoney's Big Boy; the fast seafood restaurants called Captain D's; twenty-two Kentucky Fried Chicken outlets in Louisville; three Town and Country Restaurants (an upscale Shoney's); and seven restaurants classified as dinner houses that go by the names of Sailmaker and Fifth Quarter.

The company with 9,500 employees has headquarters at 1727 Elm Hill Pike, where operations for the huge network are coordinated.

Alex Schoenbaum (left) and Ray Danner (right) are the founders of a company which today operates 543 restaurants in a twenty-one state area with sales exceeding $300 million per year.

352

A. J. Smith Company

A.J. Smith Company, dealers in lumber and builders' supplies since 1901, began accumulating experience in the field almost a century ago. And the company's story is so entwined with that of Tennessee railroads and cedar that the three are inseparable.

It began in the 1880s when Tennessee Central Railroad cut a path eastward to the Kentucky coal fields and, along the way, ran its tracks across the farm of Fleming W. Smith Sr., near Commerce, Tennessee. Smith and his son, Andrew J. Smith, contracted with TCR to haul crossties for the railroad with their farm mules, but they soon realized that it would be more profitable to cut timber and saw crossties themselves.

By 1901 Andrew J. Smith had experience enough in operating his own sawmill to establish A.J. Smith Lumber Company in Murfreesboro. Cedar trees were plentiful in the area, and the company was formed to produce cedar lumber for pencil blanks, cedar chests, caskets, and fence posts.

By 1913 the company operated nineteen sawmills. Railroad facilities in Nashville sped shipments so that A.J. Smith moved the sales office and "concentration yard" to Twenty-Fifth Avenue North in Nashville. It was there, during World War I, that the company saw drastic changes in its products. In the first place, steel companies began manufacturing mechanical pencils, caskets, and fence posts, thereby eliminating the market for cedar.

Also, a construction boom in Nashville provided an opportunity for supplying building materials, especially dimension lumber and millwork. The company's sawmills were converted to planing mills to be used in dressing lumber. Moulders and joiners were added, and A.J. Smith turned its sales efforts from the worldwide market to Middle Tennessee markets.

In 1933, in the midst of the Depression, Fleming W. Smith—the third generation of the family in the lumber business—joined his father in the company. In 1935 the company moved to its present location at 3100 Charlotte Avenue. Soon the company expanded its sales to include hard goods (cement, masonry materials, pipe, roofing).

During World War II, Fleming W. Smith entered the Navy and his father, Andrew J. Smith, came out of retirement to manage the business. Fleming W. Smith became commanding officer of the Pacific Lumber Division at Pearl Harbor, serving the Navy's needs throughout the Pacific operation. Out of that experience came many of the ideas for efficient material handling procedures used in the company today.

During the late 1940s and the 1950s, A.J. Smith Company became a wholesale distributor of many brand-name materials that appealed to home builders and commercial contractors in Nashville. The company began shipping those materials to Middle Tennessee, Southern Kentucky, and Northern Alabama.

In 1964 the fourth generation of the family, Gilbert N. Smith, now president of the company, joined his father in the firm. In 1972 an Olympic prestaining plant was erected to produce prefinished exterior siding. In 1974 a new facility across the street at 3001 Charlotte Avenue gave the firm space to prehang doors, fabricate roof and floor trusses, and build wall panels and subcomponents.

The cedar that was once the firm's mainstay—the Tennessee Red aromatic cedar—is hardly used any more for anything but closets, cedar chests, and shavings. The lumber sold today includes everything from Southern pine from Alabama and Georgia to plywood from Finland.

And there's an odd twist in the company's history: A large part of its present Nashville property was purchased from Tennessee Central Railroad when the latter went out of business—the same railroad that put the Smith family in the lumber business in the 1880s.

Andrew Smith stands atop one of his company's first loads of timber. He is holding the right hand of his son, Fleming. Andrew's father is standing on the ground in shirtsleeves.

South Central Bell Telephone Company

South Central Bell Telephone Company, 102 years after the first telephone conversation in Nashville, has a history as romantic as conquering space.

For the men who first experimented with the telephone in Nashville—a young electrician named James W. Braid and his partner in an electrical supply company, dentist James S. Ross—strung wires and devised "talking boxes" almost from the time Alexander Graham Bell's invention was announced in 1876. Braid, already experienced in manufacturing telegraphic instruments, and Ross were among those present on September 1, 1877, when Bell gave a demonstration of the telephone in Nashville at a meeting of the American Association for the Advancement of Science. Later they set up a demonstration in the parlor of the widowed Mrs. James K. Polk so that she could talk to a friend a block away.

Braid, who had seen Bell's published models for the telephone, had been experimenting with similar instruments, and he and Ross would spend exciting Sunday afternoons stringing wires between houses to hear each other's voices. In January 1878 Braid and Ross used the telegraph lines to make the first long distance call between Nashville and Louisville.

Later that year Ross gave up dentistry to devote full time to the telephone business, and in June 1883 the Cumberland Telephone and Telegraph Company was formed, with exchanges in Kentucky, Louisiana, Mississippi, Tennessee, and parts of Illinois and Indiana. By 1884 the company had 2,698 customers in twenty-six exchanges it owned, and in Nashville alone there were six hundred "talk boxes"—still considered a fad by many.

In 1883 businessman James E. Caldwell, whose office was next door to the telegraph office, witnessed an attempt to transmit the human voice to a telephone in Evansville, Indiana. It was successful enough to convince Caldwell of the telephone's future, and in 1890 he bought a controlling interest in Cumberland T&T.

Caldwell persuaded Leland Hume, manager of the telephone office in Memphis, to come to Nashville to operate the office here, and, under the direction of these two strong-minded men, the Nashville office soon dominated the area. In 1884 the first long distance lines in the South were constructed between Nashville and Memphis.

Meanwhile, Caldwell, rivaling the Atlanta-based Southern Bell Telephone Company, bought so many independent telephone companies to add to his system that Nashville seemed destined to dominate the industry in the South. But in 1912 American Telephone and Telegraph bought controlling interest in Cumberland T&T, and in 1926 a merger between the Nashville system and Southern Bell Telephone shifted headquarters for the South-wide operation from Nashville to Atlanta.

At that time, there were 25,000 telephones in Nashville. Since then, there have been vast technological developments, making obsolete in a few years the equipment for handling calls and completely revolutionizing habits—both social and business.

On July 1, 1968, Southern Bell Telephone Company's nine-state area was split into two companies, and Tennessee, Kentucky, Alabama, Louisiana, and Mississippi were incorporated into the South Central Bell Telephone Company, with headquarters in Birmingham.

From the 1,525 telephones in Nashville in 1890, when the population was approximately 40,000 and all calls were handled by telephone operators (called "Central"), to today's approximately 500,000 telephones, with most calls handled by automation, the growth and variety of services has been phenomenal. And Nashville—once a center of telephone systems for most of the Southeast—is well into its second century of rapid change.

In 1895 executives of what is today South Central Bell gather for the inauguration of long distance service from Nashville to Chicago and New York.

The Southwestern Company

The Southwestern Company, publisher of Bibles and other reference books for some 118 years, sells its products largely through college students during summer vacation, and it is the development of these students that delights company officials.

"Our product is developing young people," said Spencer Hays, president and chief executive officer of the company. "Southwestern sales managers, who work directly with the students, have a personal interest in each young person that goes far beyond teaching them to sell. A sales manager's greatest joy is seeing college students learn principles of successful living that will go with them long after their summer profit is spent."

Over the past five years, more than thirty thousand students representing six hundred colleges and universities have knocked on doors over the nation selling Southwestern products, and in 1978 the average profit per month for all student salesmen was $1,344.

Hays himself started as a student salesman in the Southwestern program twenty-four years ago, joined the firm full time in 1960, and by 1972 had worked his way up to the job as president.

Carefully recruited students come to Nashville at their own expense for a week's training early every summer and then set out to work their sales areas on foot, by bicycle, or by car. The students work six days a week, twelve to thirteen hours a day, and the company encourages them to talk to thirty to forty potential customers a day.

The immediate financial rewards derived from a summer of hard work on the bookfield cannot be overlooked. Yet far more significant is the impressive list of Southwestern "alumni"—giants in every profession, community leaders—who attribute their success in life to principles ingrained in them during their college days by their Southwestern sales manager. Learning to meet and deal with people; to sell themselves and their ideas; to meet, face, and overcome difficulties; to value hard work; to be self-reliant; to serve—these are the gains of lasting importance associated with the Southwestern program.

The whole idea came out of post-Civil War poverty in the South, when the war-ravaged region had little money for sending young men to college. The Reverend J.R. Graves, a Baptist minister who had been printing religious pamphlets in Nashville since the 1840s, called his company The Southwestern Publishing House in the 1850s and wrote on religion and politics in a publication he called "The Tennessee Baptist."

It was not until the Civil War cut the South off from all Bible publishers (all located in the North until that time) that Graves determined to publish Bibles. Managing to get plates for Bibles smuggled into the South, Graves published the South's first Bibles in 1861, in Nashville.

Graves fled Nashville during Union occupation of the city, and Southwestern continued publishing the Bible in Memphis to 1879. But the company had its offices back in Nashville in 1878. Today The Southwestern Company, a subsidiary of Times Mirror Company (a huge conglomerate of publishing and television operations), has its offices at I-65 and Moore's Lane, near Franklin.

Graves retired from The Southwestern Company in 1871, but in 1868 he inaugurated the program of having the company's Bibles and other books sold door-to-door by college students. And Nashville—long associated with churches and religious publications—spread Southwestern's products through the West as the nation grew.

P.B. Jones, president and general manager of The Southwestern Company, works at his desk in 1903. By the time this photograph was made, the company was already fifty years old.

Student booksellers for The Southwestern Company prepare to leave Nashville's Union Station at the beginning of the summer of 1903. The company's basic sales method remains virtually unchanged to this day.

Sunday School Publishing Board, National Baptist Convention, U.S.A. Incorporated

The Sunday School Publishing Board of the National Baptist Convention, U.S.A., Incorporated has the three-dimensional responsibilty of publishing and distributing curriculum materials for the spiritual nurture of Baptist young people and adults, of promoting a program of Christian Leadership Education among National Baptist constituents, and of fostering the development and growth of Sunday Schools throughout the nation and the world.

Its publications are sent to more than 26,000 churches in the United States and to missions in Africa, Central America, and the West Indies.

Nashville is a city of thirteen religious publishing houses. The Sunday School Publishing Board ranks third in the volume of printed materials shipped through the post office.

The story of the Sunday School Publishing Board is deeply rooted as an integral part of the history of National Baptists. Dr. E.C. Morris became president of the National Baptist Convention in 1894. He was a great advocator of building a publishing house where the growing needs of National Baptist churches could be met.

Dr. R.H. Boyd became the first editor-in-chief and pioneered in issuing the first publications on January 1, 1897. The idea and the publications produced were well received, and there was born the great publishing enterprise among black Baptists in the United States of America.

Today there are two great publishing houses in Nashville serving a large number of National Baptists throughout the world—the Sunday School Publishing Board of the National Baptist Convention, U.S.A., Incorporated and the National Baptist Publishing Board of the National Baptist Convention of America. The

Sunday School Publishing Board, U.S.A., Incorporated stands at the corner of Fourth and Charlotte Avenues. It is at this location that the Old Commercial Hotel once stood, a site where slaves were sold.

Dr. A.M. Townsend, executive secretary and builder of the new building, captured the pioneer spirit of black baptists and led them in contributing funds through the theme "To Serve Is Sacrificing; To Sacrifice Is Serving." "The Memorial 300" who contributed the funds to purchase and demolish the Old Commercial Hotel led the way in building the present structure which has become the base for sending forth printed materials which now help to free the total man for right relationships with God and man.

The cornerstone of the Morris Memorial Building, named for Dr. E.C. Morris, then president of the National Baptist Convention, U.S.A., Incorporated, was laid on May 18, 1924; the building was dedicated on April 25, 1929. The mortgage on this, the largest religious publishing house owned and operated by blacks in the world, was burned on December 11, 1942.

Dr. J.H. Jackson, president of the National Baptist Convention, U.S.A., Incorporated, has given support and guidance to this production arm of the national body. Dr. A.M. Townsend passed away in 1959 and was succeeded by Dr. D.C. Washington, who gave dynamic leadership until his death in 1974.

In 1975 Mrs. C.N. Adkins was the first woman to be elected executive director. Her leadership and expertise have brought the Sunday School Publishing Board to new heights of achievement. "Building On The Basics And Beyond As Foundations For Higher Ground" is the working theme for 1978-1979.

In 1975 Mrs. C.N. Adkins (right) was the first woman to be elected executive director of the Sunday School Publishing Board.

When James Robertson Parkway was completed, the Morris Building, originally completed in 1925, received a new veneer for its Parkway facade.

Earl Swensson Associates Incorporated

Earl Swensson Associates Incorporated, a firm of architects, planners, and interior designers, has fashioned its business to grow as diversely as the city has grown.

The firm's buildings—office buildings, hospitals, apartment buildings, luxury hotels, condominiums, college buildings, high school buildings, industrial plants—are helping change the face of Nashville.

After he received his advanced master's degree in architecture from the University of Illinois, Swensson gained valuable experience in the three years he worked in Chicago with the nationally known architectural firm of Perkins & Will.

At the end of that time, he decided it was time to found his own business in Nashville and in 1961 took the leap. He returned to Nashville, borrowed the necessary funds from his father, and opened a two-man office in the basement of the 1719 West End Building. Swensson's wife worked as secretary in the new firm, and his father acted as secretary-treasurer.

Two years later the firm had grown so that it moved to larger offices at 1714 Hayes Street and by 1967 occupied its own specially designed office building at 2104 Sunset Place. Seven years later, in 1974, the firm built its present facility—a five-story office building at 2303 Twenty-First Avenue South.

Swensson said the growth of the firm from 1961 to 1970 was directly related to the boom in business which Nashville and the nation experienced during that time. In particular, the firm participated in three major growth markets: housing, educational facilities, and office buildings. During this period, the firm designed apartment buildings (Imperial House and Windsor Towers), the University of Tennessee at Nashville, the Tennessee Baptist Convention Headquarters, and the office building and studios for television station WTVF.

After 1970 another field of growth was in medical facilities, and a major portion of the work was to design various types of medical buildings throughout the Southeast.

Since 1975 the firm has taken a new turn. Rather than tie their business to one market boom, the firm is emphasizing diversification. In these four years, they have designed the Opryland Hotel and Convention Center, Whites Creek Comprehensive High School, the new Miller Clinic, Chowning Square Apartments, the Metropolitan Development and Housing Agency's new high-rise apartment building for the elderly, D.A.B. Industries' new local plant facility, and new additions to Broadcast Music Incorporated and the Country Music Hall of Fame.

Earl Swensson Associates, registered to practice in thirty states, is owned by Earl S. Swensson, A.I.A., chairman of the board; Richard L. Miller, A.I.A., president; Joe D. Crumpacker, vice president; and Raymond M. Pratt, vice president.

Earl Swensson's design projects include the Opryland Hotel (above) and the University of Tennessee at Nashville (below), now Tennessee State University's downtown campus.

The Tennessean

The Tennessean, only morning newspaper and only Sunday newspaper in Nashville since 1937, traces its history to 1812, when one of its antecedents, *The Nashville Whig*, was founded.

The Tennessean today has evolved through fifteen mergers and sales—the last of them completed on August 19, 1979, when Amon Carter Evans and his mother, Mrs. Silliman Evans Sr., owners of the paper, sold it to an eighty-one-paper chain, Gannett Company Incorporated, for approximately fifty million dollars.

Gannett, with headquarters in Rochester, New York, announced the purchase of *The Tennessean* on July 6, 1979, after its merger with Combined Communications Incorporated, of Phoenix, Arizona. Purchase of *The Tennessean* was negotiated by Karl Eller, chief executive officer of Combined Communications.

Under the new ownership, John L. Seigenthaler, publisher of *The Tennessean* since 1973, remains publisher and adds the duties of president and editor.

"In keeping with Gannett's policy of local autonomy, Seigenthaler will have full responsibility for all news and editorial matters," said Allen H. Neuharth, chairman and president of Gannett. "With Gannett's additional resources and under Seigenthaler's direction, we expect *The Tennessean* to become an even more effective voice throughout Tennessee and the South."

With a daily circulation of 141,000 and a Sunday circulation of 252,500, *The Tennessean* circulates in fifty-one counties in Tennessee, Kentucky, and Alabama.

Gannett had hoped to buy *The Tennessean* in 1972, but when the Evans family refused to sell, Gannett bought *The Tennessean's* only rival, the *Nashville Banner*, for fifteen million dollars. Because of federal regulations designed to promote diversity in media ownership, Gannett sold the *Nashville Banner* in August 1979 in order to purchase the more influential *Tennessean*. Music City Media Incorporated, whose owners are Brownlee O. Currey, Irby Simpkins, and John J. Hooker Jr., bought the *Nashville Banner* for twenty-five million dollars.

Neuharth said that he expects *The Tennessean* to continue "the traditions and the very best of the many good things the Evans family . . . have brought to this great newspaper."

Published under many names in its 167 years, the paper rose to wide influence as *The American* from 1875 to 1907.

In 1907 Colonel Luke Lea—flamboyant soldier, senator, financier, and publisher—founded *The Nashville Tennessean*, and it was the *Tennessean's* editor, Edward Ward Carmack, who was shot to death in 1908 as a result of editorials he wrote attacking an alliance between liquor forces and the state administration.

In 1911 Lea took over *The American*. At first he called the morning editions of the combined papers *The Tennessean American* and the afternoon editions *The Evening American*. In 1919 he combined the two as *The Tennessean*, with morning and afternoon editions.

But Lea, caught in the collapse of the Rogers Caldwell financial empire in the Depression in the early 1930s, was found guilty by a North Carolina court of an investment irregularity, and *The Tennessean* was forced into receivership on March 3, 1933. Littleton ("Lit") J. Pardue, a lawyer with considerable newspaper experience, was appointed receiver and, in spite of short funds and dilapidated equipment, *The Tennessean* increased its circulation from 50,062 to 76,275 in four years.

However, the paper was still losing money when Silliman Evans, a Texan of wide newspaper and financial experience, bought *The Tennessean* at auction for $850,000. The sale was made on March 3, 1937, and

Four-year-old Amon Carter Evans (top) is held by Amon Carter of Texas as his father, Silliman Evans Sr., and other Tennessean *executives look on. Nearly five decades later, on August 23, 1979,* Tennessean *Publisher John Seigenthaler (second from left in photo above) stands with Allen H. Neuharth (second from right), chairman of the Gannett Company, as they announce completion of the sale of the newspaper to the Gannett chain. Offices for both Nashville newspapers are located at 1100 Broadway (right), although they are separately owned.*

Evans took possession on April 17, 1937. His imprint on the paper made it a power to be reckoned with in city, county, and state affairs.

Evans had the financially ailing paper showing a profit in forty-five days after he took control. And he suggested to James G. Stahlman, publisher of the *Nashville Banner*, that the two papers form a third corporation, the Newspaper Printing Corporation, to handle production, advertising, and circulation for both papers.

Since both papers had been operating in makeshift quarters with broken-down equipment, they could meet their needs jointly by sharing a new building and equipping it with new presses. Evans had already selected the site at 1100 Broadway, where the two papers have operated side by side ever since. Over the years, the buildings have been enlarged. After Gannett purchased the *Banner*, the two papers replaced the equipment with computerized systems. The idea for the NPC remains so successful that it has become a model for papers in other cities.

The arrangement in no way altered the separate ownership of the two papers and in no way lessened the fierce competition between them. Under the Evans family, *The Tennessean* took the lead in promoting agricultural improvement, commercial expansion, and industrial development.

The Tennessean fought for TVA and against the poll tax, along with its mammoth fight to rid Tennessee of the political dictatorship of "Boss" Ed Crump.

"Silliman Evans woke up the region," Seigenthaler said.

Evans died on June 26, 1955, and his son, Silliman Evans Jr., succeeded him as publisher. After young Evans' death in 1961, John H. Nye became publisher. In 1962 Amon Carter Evans, son of Silliman Evans Sr., became publisher, and Seigenthaler became editor. In 1973 Amon C. Evans became president, and Seigenthaler became publisher.

Amon Evans, like his father and brother, participated in community affairs, serving as chairman of the board of Memorial Hospital and as chairman of the Century III Steering Committee, the organization set up to plan and execute Nashville's celebration of her two-hundredth anniversary.

Under the aggressive leadership of Evans and Seigenthaler and with the cooperation of Gannett Company (then owners of the *Nashville Banner*), a new building was constructed in 1972, adjoining the original 1100 Broadway headquarters. The new building, to meet expanding needs, moved the papers toward computerized production. With its purchase of *The Tennessean*, Gannett committed its national resources to making the paper an even more dynamic publication.

Seigenthaler, who has spoken widely about the necessity of newspaper groups' keeping their roots deep in each paper's community, sees his role in the same light.

"I am here to nurture the roots, to keep the paper a part of the hometown," Seigenthaler said. Seigenthaler himself was born in Nashville and lived here most of his life, except for the time he worked in Washington as an officer in the Justice Department during the administration of President John F. Kennedy.

Seigenthaler, who has served as reporter, editor, and publisher in his thirty years on *The Tennessean* staff, has roots with the paper that reach even farther. His uncle, Walter Seigenthaler, began work as an office boy to *Tennessean* owner Luke Lea the year *The Tennessean* was founded and was an executive in the circulation department of the paper for fifty years. Another uncle, Louis Seigenthaler, was a veteran of *The Tennessean* press room when John Seigenthaler began work as a reporter there.

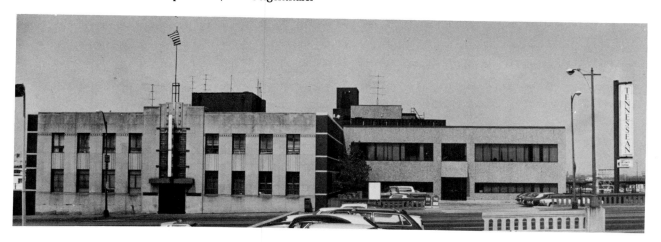

Third National Bank

Third National Bank, now in its fifty-second year, has spread its influence across Tennessee and much of Kentucky, Alabama, and Mississippi. With its thirty branches and 1,385 employees, it ranks 135th among the fourteen thousand banks in the United States. Its assets have long passed the billion-dollar mark.

Frank Mitchell Farris, thirty-five years old at the time he founded the bank in 1927, had fifteen years of banking experience—first with Cumberland Valley National Bank and then with American National Bank, after its merger with Cumberland Valley National Bank. Farris became cashier at American National Bank, and there he worked closely with Walter J. Diehl, branch manager.

It was Diehl to whom Farris first confided his idea for starting a new bank. Farris had worked out plans for the new bank while he was at home recovering from influenza in January 1927.

Farris and Diehl knew which businesses in town would be potential customers. They knew where to turn for investors in the new bank. In less than a week, Diehl decided to join Farris in the venture. Together they sought the counsel of their friend Charles Sykes, a "sage businessman," who served as chairman of the organization committee.

Plans were to capitalize the new bank at $500,000, but Nashvillians were so enthusiastic about the proposed bank that the initial capitalization was $600,000 with a surplus of $120,000. To supply the original capital, 444 stockholders purchased six thousand shares of stock at $120 per share. Hoping that the 444 shareholders would open accounts at the new bank, Farris and Diehl purposefully limited the average shareholder to ten shares.

Space for the new bank was rented on the ground floor of the Independent Life Building (now J.C. Bradford Company building), and the opening date was set for July 18, 1927.

Greeting customers and visitors in the flower-decked lobby on opening day were the carefully selected officers and staff of the new bank: C.A. Craig, chairman; N.A. Crockett, honorary vice president; Watkins Crockett, president; Frank M. Farris, executive vice president; S.S. McConnell, vice president and cashier; Walter J. Diehl, assistant cashier; J.E. Walsh, general counsel; D.W. Johnston, note teller; W.G. Birdwell, savings teller and bookkeeper; Claude Jarman, teller; Wirt Armistead and Ben Ewing, bookkeepers; P.D. Wileman and S.H. Hunt, transit clerks; and James McAdoo, porter.

Farris, founder of the bank, had decided that because of his youth, it would be wise for him not to seek a higher office in the bank. Not until 1935, when he was forty-five years old, did Farris become president.

On opening day, deposits exceeded $1 million, and by the end of that year, deposits had risen to almost $3 million.

Farris, "a shrewd selector of men," began an aggressive campaign to bring in business. "Sins of commission he could tolerate," one of his staff said, "but woe to the officer or employee who failed to speak pleasantly to a customer, large or small, who entered the bank."

By July 1937, when the bank celebrated its tenth anniversary, deposits had reached more than $28 million. But the achievement of that decade was surviving the Depression. The whirlwind of bank failures that struck Nashville in the fall of 1930 closed sixteen state banks and three national banks in November and December. Much older and larger banks than Third National were saved only through mergers.

Third National Bank located its first offices in the old Independent Life Building at the corner of Fourth and Church, the same intersection where the bank's home office tower now stands.

Third National Bank was not quite six years old in 1933 when President Franklin D. Roosevelt closed all banks in the nation for a "holiday" to sort out those institutions sound enough to continue in business. Third National was permitted to reopen without any restriction. It was one of four in Nashville that survived.

When Farris became president in 1935, Watkins Crockett became chairman of the board. That same year, when most investors were shying away from bank stock, an offering of four thousand shares of Third National stock at $125 a share was so popular that stockholders were asked to waive their rights to one-half of the stock so that it could be made available to other customers.

In 1936 Third National Bank was growing so fast that larger quarters were necessary. The bank bought the Independent Life Building and the vacant lot behind it to make room for expansion. On the vacant lot, the bank built a twelve-story addition to the original building to provide more attractive and efficient accommodations for the increasing number of customers and staff. The new quarters, with a banking room nearly five times as large as the previous one, were ready for occupancy in 1938.

After World War II, Third National Bank followed the city's expansion with new branches built in quick succession. Now the bank has twenty-nine branches, in addition to the main office. Ten of those branches are managed by women.

Since 1971, through its holding company, Third National Corporation, the bank has broadened its role in developing the whole region. That holding company, made up of eight commercial banks serving the three divisions of Tennessee plus non-banking affiliates,

provides financial services throughout the region.

Reaching out to serve farmers of the state, Third National has helped make the now highly mechanized agribusiness the Number Two industry in the state. Through its network of financial institutions, Third National has helped finance a variety of businesses—from the tourist industry in the Smoky Mountains and the country music business in Nashville to manufacturing all over the state.

To meet new demands for operating space, Third National Bank moved into new quarters in 1968, in the impressive twenty-story building that stands where the historic Maxwell House Hotel stood until it burned in 1961. In 1950, at age fifty-seven, Frank Farris died, and Sam Fleming succeeded him as president. Walter Diehl became chairman of the board, and D.W. Johnston became executive vice president.

After Sam Fleming's retirement in 1970, John W. Clay Sr. became president. Following him in that office were Roscoe Buttrey in 1972 and Charles J. Kane in 1975. Kane also was elected chairman and chief executive officer in 1976, and Charles W. Cook Jr. was named president in 1979. In this, its fifty-second year, Third National Bank is a "billion-dollar corporation."

Officers of the bank gathered in 1937 for this photo (above) made on the occasion of the firm's tenth anniversary celebration. Walter Diehl is seated to the far left. Frank Farris is also seated, fourth from the left. Standing directly behind Farris is Sam Fleming, later to become the bank's president. In 1938 the bank moved into newly remodeled quarters in the Independent Life Building (right).

Tree International

Tree International, world's largest publisher of country music, is a giant in Nashville's newest industry of worldwide influence: country music.

In a somewhat Spanish-type headquarters building at 8 Music Square West, where fountains play in the courtyard and a million-dollar recording studio has been set up for making demonstration records, Tree International brings together writers and musicians who work together to produce a hit record.

Tree International searches constantly for songs worthy of recording and takes pride in having under contract 104 of the top songwriters in the country. The company matches songs to musicians and acts as agent to push those products to record manufacturing companies. In the fiercely competitive industry that measures success by the number of records sold, Tree International in 1979 had fifty-five songs "in the charts" (among the top ten sellers), with seven songs that ranked Number One in that group. The influence of Tree International on the country music world is incalculable, and the money earned in Nashville is difficult to estimate. But Tree International recently turned down an offer of $40 million for the business.

Founder of the phenomenal business, with more than ten thousand songs on file and an endless search for new songs and new talent, is Jack Stapp, who succeeded in a variety of jobs in radio before he established Tree (later called Tree Music and then Tree International) in 1951. At that time, he was program manager of radio station WSM in Nashville, and that included the famous country music program, the Grand Ole Opry.

Born in Nashville, Stapp had moved to Atlanta when he was nine years old and had begun work as an announcer for radio station WGST there when he was seventeen. In two years, he was in New York, working for Columbia Broadcasting System—first as producer, then as assistant production manager, then acting production manager. It was not until Nashville's radio station WSM offered Stapp a job as program manager that he returned. While he was there he began, as a part-time business, publishing country music.

Country music, introduced to the nation through WSM, had caught the ear of thousands of homesick soldiers during World War II, and skilled promotion nourished its popularity in the following years. It was then, in 1951, that Stapp and Lou Cowan, who knew the country music writers and performers and had a sharp eye for talent, established Tree, a company that would acquire copyrights to new songs and share the royalties on the songs it promoted.

Cowan soon left Nashville to become president of CBS-TV in New York, and Stapp bought Cowan's stock in Tree. In 1953 Stapp added to his Tree staff Buddy Killen, a young bass player in the Grand Ole Opry. Killen, who wrote some successful songs himself ("Forever," for instance), was also skilled at spotting exceptional talent. Stapp later made Killen a partner.

Since matching songs and talents is a vital part of the publisher's business, Stapp is particularly proud of fostering the work of performers like Jim Reeves, Marty Robbins, Johnny Cash, Porter Wagoner, Faron Young, Chet Atkins, Carl Smith, Jean Shepard, Ferlin Husky, Ray Price, and Hawkshaw Hawkins. And Killen has guided many unknown talents (like Roger Miller and Dolly Parton) to stardom. Both Stapp and Killen look on one of their early recordings, "Heartbreak Hotel," as their first big success.

Since the first foreign office of Tree International opened in London in 1965, profits from foreign markets have doubled every year, and now Tree has offices in sixty-six foreign countries. Stapp, now chairman of the board, was succeeded as president by Killen in 1975.

Jack Stapp founded Tree International in 1951 and recently turned down an offer of $40 million for the business.

The United Methodist Publishing House

The United Methodist Publishing House, almost 200 years old and one of the most influential businesses in developing the cultural and economic life of Nashville, now operates the largest church-owned printing plant in the world.

And the struggle that Southern Methodists had in establishing the Publishing House here in 1854 and maintaining it through crushing hardship during the Civil War underscores the suffering of the South.

Tracing its beginning to Philadelphia in 1789, the year that George Washington was inaugurated president, the Publishing House in its history has in many ways paralleled the nation in its unfolding. Based on the belief of John Wesley, founder of Methodism, that reading is a valuable step in gaining understanding, the Publishing House operates for "the advancement of the cause of Christianity through the printed word."

The fact that the Southern Methodism won the right in 1854 to have its own Publishing House (after a fight that went to the Supreme Court) and that Nashville was selected as site for that Publishing House (winning over Louisville, Atlanta, Memphis, New Orleans, and other cities) is a story of rare courage and determination in itself.

The force of one man, the dynamic John B. McFerrin, editor of the most influential church paper in the South, was telling in that struggle. When Southern Methodists began their Publishing House in a one-time sugar warehouse on Nashville's public square in 1858, it was a triumph for the region.

But they had hardly begun their work when the Civil War emptied Nashville of many of her leading citizens and brought much of the city's life to a standstill. Under Union army occupation, Nashville was deprived of most of her business, and the Publishing House was used by Federal forces. Not until 1870 did the Publishing House begin the long climb back to pre-Civil War status.

Today the Publishing House does its work through three divisions: Abingdon and Graded Press (publishers), Cokesbury (distributors), and Parthenon Press (manufacturer of the material).

Abingdon Press, which publishes some one hundred books each year—notably scholarly reference volumes and outstanding books for children—also prepares audiovisual material. Graded Press publishes all of the denomination's church school literature. Abingdon Press took its name from Methodism's first institution for higher education, Cokesbury College in Abingdon, Maryland.

And Cokesbury, the retail division of the Publishing House, took its name through combination of the names of two pioneer Methodist leaders, Thomas Coke and Francis Asbury. Today's Cokesbury operation, through a chain of thirty-three bookstores and six mail-order centers in twenty-two states, distributes all books, audiovisual material, and church supplies for the Publishing House.

Through its Parthenon Press, which does all of the actual printing and manufacturing of books for the Publishing House, some 150 million separate items a year are produced. That number includes "The Upper Room," a devotional guide distributed in many languages around the world, with almost three million copies printed every other month.

The Publishing House employs sixteen hundred people and has a sales volume of $50 million per year. More importantly, the scholarly and gifted editors, writers, and artists in many fields who have come from all regions of the nation to work for the Publishing House have enriched Nashville immeasurably. Through the books and other materials they produce, they take Nashville's name in richest connotation to all sections of the earth.

The Southern Methodist Publishing House used this brick building (above) on the public square in downtown Nashville as its headquarters during the Civil War. Methodist circuit riders (below) were the first to distribute Methodist publications widely in this country.

Since 1789

Vanderbilt Medical Center

Vanderbilt Medical Center, nationally recognized hospital, medical school, and research center, is on the threshold of new achievement. With a $48 million, 514-bed hospital under construction, the new Rudolph A. Light Hall for medical education, the adjoining 1,200-seat auditorium, and the 1,402-car parking garage already in use, Vanderbilt Medical Center is making the biggest leap forward since 1925.

That year, 1925, was the dividing line between the fledgling school that began in South Nashville, when Vanderbilt took over the medical school of the old University of Nashville, and the "new" Vanderbilt medical school that moved to its present site at Twenty-First Avenue South and Garland. It is there that research was done that has improved the health of hundreds of thousands of people around the world.

In the Twenty-First Avenue medical school laboratories, for instance, Dr. Ernest Goodpasture, in the 1920s and 1930s, showed that the fertile chicken egg could be used to study viruses, to develop vaccines, and to do both inexpensively. Through that one dramatic discovery, medical researchers have found ways to vaccinate massive populations against polio, measles, yellow fever, and many other diseases.

Through the research of Dr. Earl Sutherland, member of the Vanderbilt medical school faculty when he received the Nobel Prize in 1971, some of the mystery about normal and pathological conditions attendant to disease was solved. His discovery has led to further investigations in physiology, biochemistry, endocrinology, diabetology, molecular biology, and microbiology.

But a comparatively small percentage of physicians trained at Vanderbilt Medical Center devote their lives to research. Approximately seventy-eight percent of all graduates practice medicine. The others teach in medical schools or are engaged in research.

Just entering Vanderbilt medical school has become a tremendous hurdle, as evidenced by only 103 vacancies in the student body last year and almost six thousand applications.

From 1875 to 1895, Vanderbilt medical school had little control over admission requirements, curriculum, or standards for graduation. But in 1895, in a new building in South Nashville, the medical school was reorganized with such improvement that, in 1910, the Carnegie Foundation's Flexner Report singled out Vanderbilt as "the institution to which the responsibility for medical education in Tennessee should just now be left."

Massive grants from Carnegie, Ford, and Rockefeller Foundations not only lifted the Vanderbilt school of medicine to a new level of teaching and research but also set a pace for the rest of Vanderbilt University.

The Flexner report called the 1925 medical school "the best arranged school and hospital in the United States," and that facility became the nucleus for what is now the Vanderbilt Medical Center. Today a full-time faculty of 391 in the medical school teach 400 medical students and, along with 433 part-time faculty members, provide care for 18,000 inpatients and 173,000 outpatients from the Middle Tennessee region and throughout the United States.

Vice President for Medical Affairs Dr. Vernon E. Wilson is responsible for the overall administration of the Medical Center, which is self-supporting and employs nearly four thousand people. Working with him are Dr. John E. Chapman, dean of the school of medicine, and Mr. William Kreykes, executive director of the hospital. Children's Hospital, which is within Vanderbilt Hospital, is an outgrowth of the pediatric department. Dr. David Karzon, chairman of pediatrics, is also medical director of Children's Hospital.

The Vanderbilt Medical Center has had the awesome responsibility of training the brightest minds to do research, to teach, and to provide care for the sick and injured. This challenge continues to be met.

The new $48 million, 514-bed Vanderbilt Medical Center was nearly complete when this photograph was made in the summer of 1979.

Vanderbilt University

When in 1873 Commodore Cornelius Vanderbilt gave a million dollars to found a university, the one that would bear his name was already fixed upon a course toward excellence. Seeking to establish "an institution of learning of the highest order," Bishop Holland McTyeire of the Methodist Episcopal Church South had led conferences in Tennessee, Alabama, Mississippi, and Louisiana to obtain a charter for "Central University," to be operated under Methodist auspices. The South was still struggling to rebuild its war-shattered economy, however, and the necessary funds for Central University could not be raised.

Bishop McTyeire thus turned to Commodore Vanderbilt. (The wives of the two men were cousins.) The Commodore, a shipping magnate and founder of the New York Central Railroad, took an interest in the project, and upon his gift to the bishop, the name of the proposed university was changed to honor him. Part of the funds were used for the original buildings and endowment. Vanderbilt University offered its first instruction in 1875 and conferred its first baccalaureate degree in 1876. It became nonsectarian in 1914.

Today, more than 1,600 faculty members, associated with the nine colleges that compose Vanderbilt University, enable it to offer a wide range of basic and advanced studies in the major fields of human knowledge. George Peabody College for Teachers of Vanderbilt University is the newest of its nine schools. The merger of Peabody and Vanderbilt on July 1, 1979, was the most important educational event on the two campuses in at least half a century.

Since 1879, when Miss Kate Lupton became the first woman to receive a Vanderbilt degree, the university has enrolled women as well as men, and their numbers are approximately equal in the present student body. Its eight thousand members come from fifty states, sixty nations, and myriad backgrounds.

Vanderbilt alumni include the present governor of Tennessee, Lamar Alexander, and James Sasser, now serving in the United States Senate. Among its distinguished former students have been James McReynolds, attorney general of the United States under President Wilson and appointed by him to the U.S. Supreme Court; John Nance Garner, vice president under Franklin Roosevelt; Pulitzer Prize winner Robert Penn Warren; Nobel laureate Stanford Moore; Grantland Rice, America's most famous sportswriter; entertainment personality Dinah Shore; and twenty-eight Rhodes Scholars. In the 1920s and '30s, the campus was the home of the group of writers known as the Fugitives and the Agrarians. Their novels, poems, and social criticism are among the most influential writings in American literature of the twentieth century.

Vanderbilt University is the largest private employer in Nashville, with about six thousand employees and an annual payroll of more than $60 million. It is estimated that expenditures in Nashville by the student body of the university total at least $15 million each year.

Some direct services to the community offered by Vanderbilt include the annual Middle Tennessee Science and Engineering Fair, legal aid for low-income persons, the Vanderbilt Environment Group recycling center, and a university-wide Speakers Bureau, available for use by community organizations. Vanderbilt also participates in the Chamber of Commerce and the United Way.

The university has long associated itself with other institutions of higher learning. In 1969 it joined with Fisk University, Meharry Medical College, Scarritt College, and George Peabody College to form the Nashville University Center. Vanderbilt University belongs to the Southern College and University Union, and, on the national scene, it is one of only forty-eight major research universities in the United States that hold membership in the Association of American Universities.

When Vanderbilt University's various schools conferred degrees in the spring of 1979, the university was completing its 106th school year.

Washington Manufacturing Company

Washington Manufacturing Company, a major manufacturer of Western and casual wear for men, women and children, was founded in Nashville sixty-six years ago. Today its products—ranging from dress shirts to overalls, from suits and blouses to Fun Fashion Jeans—are sold in every state and many foreign countries.

With twenty-five thousand accounts over the world, including many leading department stores, Washington Manufacturing Company operates eighteen plants scattered over Tennessee, Kentucky, and Mississippi which employ more than five thousand people.

In its transition from work clothes to "fun clothes" and casual wear, Washington Manufacturing reflects the nation's changes in habits and social customs. The overalls that were a farmer's badge in 1913, when the company was founded, are today colorful play clothes for girls of all ages.

But when Robert Wickliff Comer and W.H. Dodd merged their business to found Dodd-Comer Manufacturing Company in 1913, it was a sterner era. Dodd was already manufacturing suspenders, garters, sleeve bands, and handkerchiefs, and for the first year Dodd-Comer continued that operation in an old residence on Charlotte Avenue, in West Nashville.

In that house, fourteen employees made and sold all of the company's products and handled warehouse and office duties. And when Comer bought out Dodd's interest in the company in 1914, he liked the company's initials, D-C (for Dodd-Comer), so well that he made Dee-Cee the name of one of the company's major brands. Comer decided it would be more impressive—and patriotic too—if D.C. were preceded by Washington. From that came two names: Washington Manufacturing Company and Dee-Cee brand work clothes.

By 1928 the company had become a nationally known manufacturer and distributor of "the now famous Washington Dee-Cee brand of workshirts and overalls," a newspaper article of the day stated. The Dee-Cee brand soon grew to be a top name in men's and boys' sports, utility, and Western wear. Eventually "Dee-Cee for Gals" was added to the line.

By the early 1930s, the company was manufacturing coats, jackets, and matching pants and shirts. During the 1930s, jeans (then called dungarees) began to be popular, and the stage was set for their stealing the fashion scene.

During the Depression of the 1930s, Washington Manufacturing came through the trying years with only one year showing a loss, and that loss amounted to $532. During World War II, the company acquired additional plants to manufacture uniforms for the armed forces, and after the war the plants were used to manufacture uniforms for industrial use.

Expansion into the ladies sportswear market came in the 1950s, beginning with jeans and tops and growing rapidly with addition of skirts, dresses, blouses, jackets, and sportswear of wide variety.

Under the management of R.W. Comer and his sons, Mont Bliss Comer and Guy Leon Comer, and the latter's son, Wickliff Comer, Washington Manufacturing Company had become a multimillion dollar business with many subsidiaries by the 1960s.

In 1966 Washington Industries was formed, and Washington Manufacturing Company became the largest of the many subsidiaries owned by Washington Industries.

First headquarters building for Washington Manufacturing Company was at Fifth and Cedar, where the Andrew Jackson State Office Building stands today. By 1934, the company had moved headquarters to 208-210 Public Square, and in 1936 they moved into the big brick building on historic Market Street—now 224 Second Avenue North, a landmark in the area. Occupying a row of six buildings, most of them five stories high and a block long, Washington Manufacturing Company has refurbished them in keeping with the street's revival as a site of historic interest.

In 1914, in this combination office/warehouse/factory (left), four sewing machines and fourteen employees were used to turn out (and sell) garters, suspenders, and handkerchiefs for the Dodd-Comer Manufacturing Company. Although the business would later become one of the leading apparel manufacturing companies in America, the company's early products were largely garters and suspenders (center). R.W. Comer (right) founded what would later be Washington Manufacturing Company along with his partner, W.H. Dodd.

Williams Printing Company

Williams Printing Company, sixty-eight years old this year, is the largest home-owned and -operated printing company in Nashville—a city where printing is a major industry.

Specializing in publications and general commercial printing, the company produces in excess of $5 million worth of printing per year. Fletcher L. Williams Jr., chairman of the board, says it is unique in that it offers its complete manufacturing service under one roof, at 417 Commerce Street (in addition to a storage and shipping facility on First Avenue).

Williams Printing Company was founded on August 23, 1911, by two brothers, Fletcher L. Williams Sr. and his younger brother, Roy F. Williams. The two had worked for some time at McQuiddy Printing Company where Fletcher was bookkeeper and Roy was a traveling salesman. The two bought Folke-Keeling Printing Company (formerly B.L. Foster Company) in 1911 and changed the name to Williams Printing Company, with Roy as president and Fletcher as treasurer.

Courthouse supplies were some of their chief products at first, but Williams soon began producing greeting cards and hot-dish mats. Around 1917 the Williams brothers founded the American Engraving Company to handle the production of greeting cards, and from then until 1926 that part of the business was "big and prosperous."

In those brisk days, approximately 250 salesmen worked for the company, and Williams shipped greeting cards as far away as Washington state. But the bottom fell out of the greeting card business in 1925. Williams Printing Company had to close its American Engraving Company.

Also in 1926, Fletcher L. Williams Sr. had to leave the business because of illness, and in 1929 Roy Williams, the other founder, died. J.R. Overall, E.A. Bergstrom and others operated the business, with Bergstrom as president until 1960. Overall was president from 1960 to 1966.

The company was located at 162 Fourth Avenue North until 1933. Reorganization of the company came on October 30, 1933, when all stock was called in. Bergstrom consolidated the company's assets and concentrated on printing instead of the combination of printing, office supplies, and equipment.

Through the trying years, another of the Williams brothers, Robert H. Williams, vice president of Travelers Insurance Company, gave important financial backing to the printing company. A fourth brother, Thomas A. Williams, the "company artist," was vice president for several years. A sister, Ruth O. Williams, was bookkeeper.

During the Depression when the company handled only one or two jobs a day (compared to four hundred a day now), a few major accounts stood by the wavering company. Life & Casualty Insurance Company ordered one million calendars at fifteen cents each and is still a treasured customer. The Methodist Publishing House gave Williams a contract to print one of its major publications: "The Missionary Voice."

At the same time, orders kept coming from George Peabody College, Vanderbilt University, the Order of the Eastern Star, First American National Bank, White Way Laundry, David Lipscomb College, the Twentieth Century Christian Publishing Company, and many others. Later the Baptist Sunday School Board became a valuable account.

In 1933 the company moved to its present location on Commerce Street. In 1938 Paul W. Moore began a tenure with the company that ran until early 1979 when, because of ill health, he was forced to retire. He had served as artist, salesman, and finally as vice president of the corporation.

In 1939 F.L. Williams Jr. began working part time for the company. He worked there full time from 1946 and in 1966 succeeded Overall as president. In 1977 Williams became chairman of the board and chief executive officer, and Bob Johnson, who came with the company in 1974, became president. Current officers of the corporation, in addition to Williams and Johnson, are: Dudley L. Fortner, executive vice president; John T. McNeal, vice president—manufacturing; Dave L. Cantrell, vice president; John R. Sanders, vice president—purchasing; Pete T. Mitchell, vice president; and Julia Brown Jackson, controller.

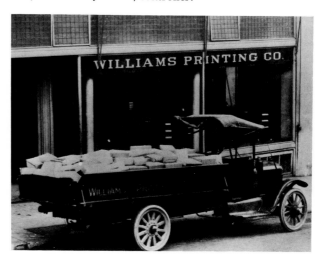

Williams Printing Company delivery vehicles have been a familiar sight on downtown streets since the early part of this century, when the company was founded.

Index

Acklen, Adelicia 152-154, 247
Acklen, Joseph A.S. 152-153
Acuff, Roy 268, 271, 273, 274, 276
Adams, John Quincy 76, 80
Adelphi Theater 61, 94, 121
★Aladdin Industries Inc. 302
Alden, Augustus E. 131-134
Alexander, Lamar 292
Allen, Clifford 262
Allen, John 87
★Alley-Cassetty Coal Co. 303
Altman, Robert 277
Ambrose family 298
American Baptist Theological Seminary 247, 254
American Protective Association 157
Andrew Jackson Hotel 280
Antioch 49, 93, 150
Arcade 172, 173, 205, 297
Arnold, Eddy 268, 271
Arnow, Harriette Simpson 16
Asbury, Francis 57
Atkins, Chet 272, 273
Attakullakulla 15
Ayers, J.P. (map by) 85, 100
Bailey, DeFord 223
★Baltz Brothers Meats 304
Baltz family 297
Bandy, William 207, 208, 210
Bank of Nashville 56
Bank of Tennessee 105
Baptist, First Church 60, 100, 155, 259
Baptist, First Church Capitol Hill 259
Baptist, First Colored Church 189, 259
★Baptist Sunday School Board 305
Baptists 72, 89, 99, 159, 175
Barnard, Edward Emerson 137
Barnum, P.T. 94
Bass, John M. 133
Bate, Humphrey 267
Baxter, Jere 166-168, 170, 171, 227
Beasley family 297
Beazley, Johnny 241
Beeler, Henry 50
Bell, Alexander Graham 137
Bell, John 83, 90, 112, 114, 128
Bell, Montgomery 84, 85, 101
Belle Meade 152, 240, 242, 260, 264
Belle Meade Plantation 38, 95, 128-130, 151
Bellevue 93, 150
Belmont 95, 152, 153
Belmont, August 165
Belmont College 247
Belmont Junior College 148
Bennett, Robert A. 237
Benton, Jesse 70
Benton, Thomas Hart 70, 71, 76, 236
Bernhardt, Sarah 158
Berry Field 224
Berry, Harry S. 224
Berry Hill 264
★Berry Wholesale Drug Co. 306
Berry, William T. 60, 94, 106
Bess, Tootsie 270
Big Salt Lick 21
Bingham, George Caleb (portrait by) 88

Blanton, Ray 286, 292
Bledsoe, Issac 14
Blount, William 39, 65
Bob Taylor's Magazine 175
Bomar, Lynn 211
Bontemps, Arna 219, 233, 248
Boone, Pat 269
Booth, Edwin 61
Booth, John Wilkes 122
Bordeaux 154
Boston, Ralph 285
★John Bouchard & Sons Co. 307
Bowling, William K. 101
Boyd, Henry Allen 189
Boyd, J.B. 180
Boyd, R.F. 189
Boyd, Richard Henry 189, 191, 192, 227
Bradford, Benjamin 52
Bradley, Owen 273
★Braid Electric Co. 308
Braid, James 137
★Brandau Craig Dickerson Co. 309
Bransford, John S. 127
Branstetter, Cecil 261
Brantz, Lewis 36
Brasfield, Rod 268
Briggs, William T. 101
Briley, Beverly 260-263, 265
Brooks, Cleanth 210, 215
Brown, Aaron V. 92
Brown, Neill S. 92, 127, 133
Brownlow, William G. 124, 131, 132
Buchanan family 21
Buchanan, John 19, 40, 41, 44, 84
Buchanan, Sally Ridley 25, 41
Buchanan's Station 41
Buell, Don Carlos 113, 119
Buford, Ed 195
Burch, John C. 127
Burch, Lucius 215
Burch, Mrs. Lucius 181
Burke, E.M. 181
Burnett, Peter H. 106
Burr, Aaron 56, 67
Burton, A.M. 202
Buttrick, Daniel 89
Byrd, William 30
Byrns, James 43
Byrns, Joseph W. 225
Caesar (tavern keeper) 51
Cain-Sloan 172, 241
Caldwell, James E. 227
Caldwell, Mary French 186
Caldwell, Nat 240, 262
Caldwell, Rogers 68, 215, 218, 227, 229-232
Calvit, Frederick 17
Campbell, Blanche 222
Campbell, George W. 48
Campbell, Glen 273
Candyland 176
Cannon, B.B. 88
Cannon, Sarah Ophelia Colley (see Minnie Pearl) 268, 269
★Capitol Engraving Co. 310
Carmack, Edward Ward 177-181, 191, 227-229
Carmichael, Stokely 256
Carnegie, Andrew 172, 173
Carpenter, F.B. 119
Carroll, William 70, 73, 76
Carson, Fiddlin' John 267
Carter family 267

Cartwright, Marcus 154
Caruso, Enrico 158, 222
Cash, Johnny 269, 273, 274
Castner-Knott 172, 241
Cate, George H. 263, 264
Catholic, Church of the Assumption 138
Catholic, St. Cecilia's 138
Catholic, St. Mary's Church 100
Catholics 72, 100, 159
Catlin, George (portrait by) 68, 87
Catron, John 127, 174
Centennial Exposition, Nashville 140, 141
Centennial Exposition, Tennessee 161, 163, 170
Centennial Park 161, 163, 171, 287
Central Tennessee College (Walden University) 110, 144, 145, 148
Chambers, J.S. 135
Chaplin, Charlie 221
Charles, Ray 273
Charry, Michael 287
Charleville (French trader) 13
Cheatham County 56
Cheatham, Richard B. 113, 114
Cheatham, William Archer 154
Cheek, Joel Owsley 174
Cheek, Leslie 226, 285
Cheekwood 226, 272, 285
Chenault, R.N. 261
Cheney, Brainard 214, 231
Cheney, Frances Neel 214
Cherokee Park 158
Cherokees 13, 15, 28, 32, 34, 86-89
Chickamaugas 41
Chickasaws 13, 15, 28, 30, 32
Children's Museum 240
Childress, George C. 87, 106
Childress, Joel 50
Choctaws 13, 69
Christian, Spring Street Church 99, 100
Christie, Amos 246, 285
Church of Christ 99, 202
Citizens Savings Bank & Trust Company 173
City Hotel 85
Civil, Jack 25
Claiborne, Thomas 103
Clark, Cannon 211
Clark, George Rogers 17, 30
Clark, Lardner 32
Clark, Saville 211
Clarion & Tennessee State Gazette 57
Clement, Frank 265
Cleveland Hall 281
Cline family 297
Clover Bottom 28, 56, 95
Cobb, William 208
Cochran, Carmack 261
Cockrill, Ann Robertson Johnston 25
Cockrill family 72
Cockrill, Mark Robertson 95, 128
Cohen family 297
Cole, Edmund W. 139, 168, 173, 227
Coleman, Charles 248
Coleman, Joseph 52
Colyar, Arthur S. 133
Commerce Union Bank 197
Como, Perry 273

Confederate Veteran 175
Consolidated Vultee Aircraft Corporation (Avco) 237, 238
Constitutional Union Party 112, 114
Cooper, Duncan B. 177, 179-181, 227
Cooper, Robin 179-181
Cooper, W.F. 92
Cooper, Washington 72, 119, 152
Cooper, Washington (portrait by) 53, 70, 72, 73, 77, 85
Couchville 93
Country Music Hall of Fame 274
Cox, John I. 191
Crabb, Alfred Leland 14, 241
Crafts, David 84
Craig, C.A. 266
Craig, Edwin W. 223, 266
Craig, Francis 222, 223, 271
Craighead, John 85
Craighead, Lavinia Robertson 85
Craighead, Thomas B. 34, 44, 47, 52, 98, 100
Cravath, Erastus M. 110, 146
Creeks 13, 28, 41, 69, 70
Creighton family 297
Cumberland College 52, 77, 78, 98, 99, 144
Cumberland Compact 26-29, 265
Cumberland, Duke of 14
Cumberland Presbyterians 99
Cumberland River 14, 36, 56, 58, 73, 82, 83, 299
★Cummings Inc. 311
Cummings, Thomas L. 238-239, 240, 241, 299
Currier & Ives (lithograph by) 95
Curry Field 148
Curry, Walter Clyde 207, 209
★Cutters Exchange 312
David Lipscomb College 202, 247
★David Lipscomb College 330
Davidson Academy 34, 47, 52, 144, 292
Davidson College 52
Davidson County Courthouse 85, 135
Davidson, Donald 204, 206, 207, 209, 211, 214, 218, 219
Davidson, William 30
Davis, John 281
Deaderick, George M. 55
Deaderick, Mary 55
DeLuca, Gaetano S. 222
Demonbreun, Timothy 13, 17, 25, 32, 46, 54, 78, 84, 299
Dempsey, Jack 200
Devon Farm 281
Dickey, James 219
Dickinson, Charles 65, 67
Dikinson, Jacob McGavock 174
Dickson, William 48
Disciples of Christ (Christian) Church 99, 100
Dix, Dorothea L. 59
Dodge, Grenville M. 122
Dodson, K. Harlan 261
Donau (horse) 175
Donelson 93, 150, 249
Donelson, Andrew Jackson 68, 83, 129
Donelson, Emily 83
Donelson family 281
Donelson, John 16, 18, 19, 21, 24, 25, 26, 28, 30, 32, 34, 36, 48, 281

Donelson, John II 36
Donelson, Rachel 25, 65
Dougherty, Edward 221
Douglas, Aaron 203
Douglas, Josephine Hutton 197
Douglas, Mary Stahlman 201
Drake, Benjamin 19
Draughon, J.F.B. 148
Driver, William 113, 126, 127
Dromgoole, Will Allen 195
DuBois, William E.B. 145
Dudley, Anne Dallas 185, 186, 188, 227
Dudley Field 223, 282
Dudley, Guilford 185
Dudley, William L. 204
Duncan Hotel 137
Dunham, Daniel 38
DuPont 195, 196, 237
Dury, George 102, 137
Dury, George (painting by) 92, 96
Dylan, Bob 273
Earl, Ralph E.W. 56, 72, 78, 89
Earl, Ralph E.W. (portrait by) 63, 64
East High School 237
East Nashville 37, 198, 298
Eaton, Amos 19, 21
Eaton, John H. 76
Eaton's Station 25, 28, 34, 56
Edgar, John Todd 98
Edgefield 73, 92, 93, 113, 138, 150
Edison, Thomas 137
Eichbaum, William A. (maps by) 54, 100
Ellington Argricultural Center 231
Elliott, William Yandell 209, 211
Elliston, Joseph 52, 53
Ennix, Coyness L. 251, 253
Episcopal, Christ Church 79
Episcopalians 159
Evans, Amon Carter 293
Evans, Silliman 228, 229, 240, 293
Eve, Paul F. 99
Everett, Edward 112
Ewing, Andrew 128
Fairfield 47
Fall, Philip 99
Featherstonhaugh, G.W. 82
★Fidelity Federal Savings & Loan Assn. 314-315
Fields, W.C. 221
First American National Bank 173
★First American National Bank 316-317
Fisk, Clinton B. 109, 110, 145, 146
Fisk University 110, 144-147, 192, 202, 247, 248, 251, 254, 257
★Fisk University 318-319
Fitch, John 124
Flatt, Lester 268
Fogg, Francis B. 102, 126, 127
Fogg, Henry 126, 127
Foley, Red 268
Forest Hills 264
Forrest, Nathan Bedford 116, 119, 135
Fort, Cornelia 237
Fort Donelson 115
Fort Negley 126, 137
Foster and Creighton 162
★Foster & Creighton Co. 313
Foster family 72
Foster, Rebecah 55
Foster, Wilbur 136
Frank, James M. 209, 210
Franklin College 93
Franklin, Isaac 152
Free Will Baptist Bible College 247

Freeland, George 17, 21, 37
Freeland's Station 25, 29
French Lick 9, 13, 16, 21, 24, 28, 33
Frierson, William 209, 211
Fry, Patsey 43
Fulton, Richard 264, 265, 289
Gaillard, Frye 274
Galbreath, Charles F. 290
Gale, W.D. 124
Galli-Curci, Amelita 222
Garland, Landon C. 148
Garrett, W.A. "Bully" 231
Gary, "Uncle Bob" 230
Gatlin, Larry 274, 276
Gaul, Gilbert (painting by) 172
Geddes, James 284
Geist family 297
General Shoe Corporation (Genesco) 237
Geny family 297
George Peabody College for Teachers 109, 144, 174, 203, 292
Gerst family 297
Gerst, William 160, 175
Giers, C.C. and Otto 139, 149, 151
Gimre, Gerald 240
Glen Cliff 93
Goater, Walter 141
Gompers, Samuel 176
Goodlettsville 93, 150, 264
Goodpasture, Ernest W. 204, 285
Gordon, Caroline 214
Gore, Albert Sr. 265
Gowdy, Charles C. 191
Gower family 72
Graham, Billy 282
Graham, Gene S. 262
Grand Ole Opry 266-277, 273, 275, 286, 296, 297
Grant, Ulysses S. 122
Gray, Dobie 274
Gray family 297
Green, Bob 129
★Green Hills Market 320
★Gresham and Smith 321
Griffen, Booker 48
Griffith, Mahlon (family) 252
Grimes, John C. (portrait by) 40, 98
Grundy, Felix 76, 77, 84, 87, 89, 90, 286
Guild, Josephus C. 77, 133
Gustav, William 157
Haggard, Merle 273
Halberstam, David 255
Hall, Tom T. 273
Halsey, Leroy J. 98
Hampton Field (Stokes Field) 201
Hanley, James 17, 37
Hardin, Lizzie 116
Harding family 72
Harding, Henry 189
Harding Light Artillery 130
Harding, William Giles 95, 128-130
Hardison, W.D. "Pie" 251
Harris, Isham G. 114, 115
Harris, Phil 271
Harris, S.P. 192
Harvey, Fred 241, 242
Harwell family 297
Hatcher, Joe 232
Hay, George D. 222, 223, 266-268
Hayes family 72
Hayes, Oliver Bliss 152
Hayes-Kiser House 49
Head, James M. 165-167, 170, 227
Heard, Alexander 272

Heiman, Adolphus 60, 94, 96, 97, 99, 128
Hemphill, Paul 271
Henderson, Richard 15, 16, 26, 28, 30, 42
Henkel, F. Arthur 222
Henry, Patrick 30
★Herbert Materials Inc. 322-323
Hermitage, The 66, 67, 76, 77, 81, 83, 93, 130, 152, 274
Hermitage Hotel 172, 174
Herschel Greer Stadium 291
Hicks, Edward 261
Hicks, Edward D., II 281
Hill family 297
Hillsboro 93
Hillsboro Village 159
Hippodrome arena 238
Hirsch, Nathaniel 209
Hirsch, Sidney Mttron 209, 211
Hoffa, Jimmy 286
Holley, Horace 77
Holley, Luther 77
Holston River 15
Holt, Ben E. 237
Hood, David 17
Hood, John B. 122, 124
Hooker, John J. Sr. 232
Hooker, John J. Jr. 232, 293
Hooper, Ben W. 182, 186
Hoover, Herbert 224
Horn, Stanley F. 27
Horton, Henry 227, 230
★Hospital Affiliates International 324
Houston, Eliza Allen 86, 87
Houston, Sam 84, 86, 87, 88, 90, 106
Howell, R.B.C. 60, 129, 259
Howse, Hilary 182, 185, 186, 227, 238, 240
Hume, Alfred 59, 101, 102
Hume, William 98, 101
Hume-Fogg School 101
Ingraham, J.W. 102
Inston, John 47
★Interstate Construction Co. Of Nashville Inc. 325
Iroquois Memorial Steeplechase 291
Jackson, Andrew 55, 59, 61, 63-90, 94, 129, 140, 141
Jackson, Andrew Jr. 68, 69, 130
Jackson, Andrew III 130
Jackson, Howell E. 174
Jackson, Rachel 25, 66, 67, 69, 70, 77, 80, 81, 129
Jackson, William H. 127, 130, 151
Jacobs, Gene "Little Evil" 251
James, Jesse and Frank 154
James K. Polk State Office Building and Tennessee Center for the Performing Arts 280, 297
Jamison family 297
Jarman, Claude Jr. 241, 269
Jarman, Rufus 244
Jarrell, Randall 218
Jenkins, Casey 253
Jennings, Obediah 98
Jennings, Waylon 273
Jews 99, 138, 139, 159
Joelton 154
Johnson, Andrew 106, 109, 117, 119, 122, 124, 128, 131, 133
Johnson, Charles S. 248, 251
Johnson, Ike 154
Johnson, James Weldon 202, 203, 219
Johnson, Mary Hannah 173
Johnson, Stanley 209
Johnson, Victor S. 261
Johnston, Albert Sidney 114-116

Joiner, Jemima 43
Jones, Henry "Good Jelly" 251
Jones, Sam P. 157, 158, 282
Joy family 297
★Joy's Flowers 326
Jubilee Hall 110, 147
Jubilee Singers 110, 146, 147
Kasper, John 252, 253, 255
Keeble, Marshall 202
Keefe, Jack 240
Kefauver, Estes 265
★Keith-Simmons Co. Inc. 327
Kelley, A.Z. 251
Kelley, Robert 251
Kennedy, John F. 265
Kenny, Catherine Talty 186
Killen, Buddy 276
King, Martin Luther Jr. 254, 256-259
King, Pee Wee 268
Kinney, Belle 221
Kirkland Hall 147
Kirkland, James H. 147, 203, 213
Kirkman, Van Leer 151
Kristofferson, Kris 269, 273
Ku Klux Klan 135, 137
Lafayette, Marquis de 78, 79
Lakewood 264
Lanier, Lyle 214
Lanson, Snooky 271
Lawrence, William P. 280
Lawson, James M. Jr. 254
Lea, John M. 127, 133, 134, 178
Lea, Luke 178, 179, 182, 183, 215, 218, 224, 227-231
Lee, Brenda 276
LeFevre family 274
Lentz, John 240, 246
Levy family 297
★Levy's 328
Lewinthal, Isadore 139
Lewis, Eugene C. 162, 163, 165, 170, 171, 179, 227
Lewis, John 257
Lewis, William B. 76
Lewis, William T. 34, 47
Life & Casualty Insurance Company of Tennessee 172, 185, 246
★Life & Casualty Insurance Co. of Tennessee 329
Lillard, Robert 251, 261
Lincoln, Abraham 114, 117, 119
Lind, Jenny 61, 94
Lindsey, Isaac 14
Lindsley, John Berrien 99, 109, 110, 127, 133, 134, 137, 147
Lindsley, Maggie 123
Lindsley, Philip 78, 98, 99, 101, 109, 149
Lipscomb, David 148, 203
Lipscomb family 297
Little, Tom 262
Loiseau, Joseph 105
Looby, Z. Alexander 251, 261, 262
Louis-Philippe, Duke of Orleans 46
Louisville and Nashville Railroad 108, 140, 163, 165-171
Loveman family 297
Loventhal family 297
Lurton, Horace H. 174
Lyncoya 69
Lynn, Loretta 273
Lytle, Andrew 210, 214
Macon, Uncle Dave 267, 268, 290
Macpherson, Joseph 222, 223
Madison 37, 93, 150, 249
Mansker, Kasper 14, 17, 21, 25
Mansker's Station 25, 28
Marling, John Leake 104

Marr, John 55
★Marshall & Bruce Co. 331
Marshall, Goodrum 48
Marshall, Sally 51
Marshall, Thurgood 251
Mathews, A.F. (sketch by) 94
Maxwell House Hotel 137, 138, 172, 173, 297
May family 297
McAlister, Hill 225, 227
McCarn, Jeff 180
★McDowell Enterprises Inc. 332
McFerrin, John B. 127
McGaugh, Robert 43
McGavock, David 37
McGavock family 39
McGavock, Randal 127, 128
McGee, Sam & Kirk 267, 274
McGill, Ralph 207, 210
McGovern, George 225
McGrath, Thomas E. 261
McGugin, Dan 174
McKellar, Kenneth D. 183, 188, 228
McKendree, William 99
McKenzie, Fayette A. 192
McKinley, William 161
McKinnie, Lester 257
McKissack family 192, 193
McNairy, Boyd 70, 72, 78
McNairy, Francis 127
McNairy, John 63, 65, 66
McReynolds, James C. 174
McTyeire, Holland N. 111, 147
McWhirtersville 93
Meadors, G.S. 261
Meharry Medical College 110, 145, 148, 194, 202, 247
Meigs, Return J. 127
Melrose 240
Melton, James 222
Mero District 39
Merry, Nelson 189, 259
Methodist, Barth Memorial Church 197
Methodist, McKendree Church 100
Methodists 47, 72, 89, 99, 100, 159, 175, 282
MetroCenter 94, 297
★MetroCenter 333
★Metropolitan Nashville Airport Authority 336-337
Mills family 219, 297
Mims, Edwin 205, 215
Minnie Pearl 268, 269, 276
Mitchell, Edwin H. 258
Molloy, Sophia 51
Molloy, Thomas 32, 51
Monroe, Bill 268
Monroe, James 56, 71
Montfort, Richard 165
Montgomery Bell Academy 101
Montgomery County 39
Moore, John Trotwood 175, 210
Moore, Merrill 209, 210, 219
Morgan, John Hunt 119
Morton, Marmaduke Beckwith 201
Moss, Charles 207, 210, 214
Mott, William 113, 116
Mound Builders 13
Mount Olivet Cemetery 152
Mulherrin family 21
Mulherrin, James and John 19
Murrell, John 171
Myers, Bill 276
★NLT Corp. 334-335
Naff, Lula 222
Napier, James Carroll 190-192, 227
Nash, Abner 26
Nash, Francis 27, 28, 33

Nashborough 28-33
Nashville American 170, 177, 179, 182
★Nashville Area Chamber of Commerce 338
Nashville Banner 137, 139, 170, 175, 179, 188, 192, 228, 229, 240, 242, 260, 261, 262, 293
Nashville, Battle of 123
Nashville Bible School 148
Nashville Bicycle Club 155
★Nashville Board of Realtors 340-341
Nashville Bridge Company 237
Nashville Centennial Exposition Hall 140
Nashville and Chattanooga Railroad 108, 168
Nashville, Chattanooga & St. Louis Railroad 163, 165, 166, 167, 168, 170, 171
★Nashville CityBank & Trust Co. 339
Nashville Daily News 170, 200
★Nashville Electric Service 342
Nashville Female Academy 56, 84, 94, 126, 148
"Nashville" (film) 276, 277
★Nashville Gas Co. 343
Nashville Globe 192, 194
Nashville Inn 47, 48, 85
Nashville Medical College 148
Nashville Medical Society 72
Nashville Normal and Theological Institute 144
Nashville Race Track 94
Nashville Railway and Electric Company 173
Nashville Republican Banner 137
★Nashville Sash And Door Co. Inc. 344
Nashville Sounds 291
Nashville Symphony Orchestra 287
Nashville Tennessean 175, 179, 188, 192, 200, 240, 242, 260, 261, 262, 293
Nashville Theater 121
Nashville Turf 56
Nashville, University of 61, 109, 110, 117, 126, 134, 144, 147, 148, 174
Nashville Vols 173, 297
National Baptist Publishing Board 194
National Life and Accident Insurance Company 172, 266, 267, 274, 275
Neal, James F. 286
Neely, William 17, 37
Nelson, Willie 273
Nixon, Richard M. 225, 273
Noel, Jeanette 163
North Nashville 37, 138, 297
Norvell, C.C. 89
Norvell family 297
★Norvell & Wallace Inc. 345
Oak Hill 264
O'Connor, Flannery 219
Oconostota 15
Ogden, John 110
Ohl, John 248
O'Keeffe, Georgia 248
Oliver, William H. 251
Oman family 297
Opryland Hotel 297
Opryland, U.S.A. 275, 286, 297
O'Reilly, Henry 83
Otey, Inman 264
Overall, William 17, 37
Overton, John 44, 66, 67, 76, 84, 89, 137, 138
Overton, John W. 195

Owsley, Frank 214, 216
Owsley, Harriet 216
Paderewski, Ignace 222
Paragon Mills 93
Paramount Theater 226
Parthenon 162, 163, 274, 287
Parton, Dolly 273
Paschal, Franklin 259
Paschal, Hattie 223
Patterson, Malcolm 179, 181, 182, 183, 185, 227
Pearl, Joshua F. 101, 127
Pearson, Josephine 187
Peay, Austin 227
Peck, Gregory 241
Penitentiary 82, 84, 258
Percy Warner Park 129, 291
Peyton, Balie 127
Peytona (horse) 94, 95
Pinckard, Mrs. James 187
Piomingo 30-32
Ploughboy (horse) 56
Polk, James K. 83, 84, 89, 90, 92
Polk, Sarah Childress 92, 129
Pomeroy, Dan E. 288
Pope Pius XII 241
Possum Hunters 267
Potter, Edward 197
Prentis, Noble L. 144
Presbyterian, First Church 71, 84, 96, 100, 151
Presbyterian meeting house, Spring Hill 47
Presbyterians 71, 72, 84, 89, 96, 98, 100, 159, 175, 280
Pride, Charley 273
Priest, J. Percy 239
Priestly, James 52
Printer's Alley 240, 290
Protestant Orphan Asylum 60
Public Square 47, 48, 70, 78, 83, 85, 93
Pyle, Howard 125
Rains, John 19, 54, 84
Ransom, Harry Howe 232
Ransom, John Crowe 204, 205, 206, 209, 211, 213, 216, 218, 219
Ray, James Earl 258
Reed, Roy 272
Reese, Gil 211
Renfroe, "Black Bob" 51, 250
Renfroe's Station 51 .
Rice, Grantland 200, 229
Riding, Laura 209
Ritter, Tex 269, 271
Riviere des Chauouanons (Cumberland River) 13
Robards, Lewis 66
Robbins, Marty 273
Roberts, Alfred H. 186, 188
Robertson Academy 101
Robertson, Charlotte 19, 21, 25, 31, 52, 54, 84, 85
Robertson County 39
Robertson, Felix 17, 34, 52, 60, 72, 99, 126
Robertson, James 16-54, 66, 68, 288
Robertson, Jonathan 20
Robertson, Mark 17, 20, 37
Robertson, Sterling 87, 106
Robinson, Francis 222
Robinson, Thomas H. Jr. 241
★Rock City Machine Co. 346
★Joe M. Rodgers & Associates 347
Roger Williams University 110, 144, 203
Rogers, Will 221
Roland, Harold 226
Roosevelt, Eleanor 225
Roosevelt, Franklin D. 224, 225

Roosevelt, Theodore 158, 173, 174, 191
Rosecrans, William S. 120
Royall, Ann 58
Rudolph, Wilma 285
★Rudy's Farm Country Sausage 348
Russell, Fred 200
Rutledge, Henry M. 72
Rutledge Hill 284
Rutledge, Mary Middleton 126
Rutledge, Septima Sexta Middleton 72
Rutledge's Artillery 115
Ryman Auditorium 222, 268, 270, 274, 275, 297
Ryman, Tom 157, 158, 168, 171
St. Cecilia Convent 138
St. Mary's Orphanage 60
★St. Thomas Hospital 350-351
Sappington, John 99
Satsuma Tea Room 176
Scarritt College 202, 247
Schmittou, Larry 291
Scruggs, Earl 268, 277
Sears, Roebuck and Company 226
Seigenthaler, John 232, 293
Seminoles 70
★Service Merchandise Co. Inc. 349
Sevier, John 48, 66, 67
Sharp, Alf 211
Sharp, Mrs. Walter 285
Shawnees 13
Shelby, John 72, 73
Shelby Medical School 73, 148
Sherman, William Tecumseh 122
Sherrill, Billy 276
Shoat, Ruth 43
★Shoney's Inc. 352
Shore, Dinah 269, 271
Shy's Hill 125
Silver Dollar Saloon 155
Singleton, J.B. 194
Skalowski's Ice Cream Parlor 176
★A.J. Smith Co. 353
Smith, Beasley 222, 223
Smith, Daniel 42
Smith, E.P. 110
Smith, Gipsy 198
Smith, Kelly Miller 259
Smith, Margaret Bayard 81
Smith, Thomas 43
Snow, Hank 274
Snow, Jimmy 274
Snow, Marshall S. 128
★South Central Bell Telephone Co. 354
South Nashville 101, 138, 297
Southern Agriculturalist 175
Southern Lumberman 175
Southern Methodist Publishing House 120
Southern Motor Works 196, 197
Southern Turf saloon 154
★The Southwestern Co. 355
Spencer, Thomas Sharpe 14, 17
Stahlman Building 172
Stahlman, Edward B. 170, 179, 188, 227-229
Stahlman, James Geddes "Jimmy" 201, 228, 229, 240, 293
Star, Reese 88
Starr, Alfred and Milton 209, 214
Stevenson, Alec B. 209
Stevenson, Vernon K. 127, 139, 140, 167, 168, 227
Stewart, A.P. 124
Stone, Uriah 14
Street, Harold and Roberta 252
Strickland, Francis 135
Strickland, William 60, 96

371

Stritch, Samuel 241
Stuart, Jesse 219
Stump, Frederick 19, 25, 38, 39, 44, 84
Sudekum, Tony 173
Sulphur Dell 148, 156, 200, 249
Sulphur Spring 21
Sumner, Charles 79
Sumner County 39
Sunday, Billy 156, 198, 274, 282
★Sunday School Publishing Board, National Baptist Convention, U.S.A. Inc. 356
Sutherland, Earl W. 285
Swanson, Edward 17, 25, 37, 54
★Earl Swensson Associates Inc. 357
Sycamore Shoals 15

Taft, William Howard 173, 174
Tannehill, Wilkins 59, 72, 76
Tarkington, Joseph 54
Tate, Allen 204, 208, 209, 210, 211, 214, 219, 220
Tate, W.K. 171
Taylor, Peter 199, 219
Taylor, Preston 191, 192
Taylor, Robert Love 175, 179, 182, 227
Temple, Ed 285
★The Tennessean 358-359
Tennessee Botanical Garden and Fine Arts Center 285
Tennessee Central Railroad 166-171
Tennessee County 39
Tennessee Gazette 52
Tennessee Historical Society 141, 162
Tennessee State Capitol 96, 113
Tennessee State Fairgrounds 225
Tennessee State Normal College 144, 203
Tennessee State University (A&I) 192, 203, 247, 254, 292

★Third National Bank 360-361
Thomas, George H. 122. 124
Thomas, Philip 51
Thomas, Rebecca 261
Thompson family 72
Thompson, T. Leigh 148
Thompson, Thomas 19
Thompson, Uncle Jimmy 267-268
Thuss, Andrew Joseph 157
Tootsie's Orchid Lounge 270
Torrence, Joe 261
Traveller's Rest 44
★Tree International 362
Trevecca Nazarene College 202
Trimble family 72
Trimble, John 127
Trimble School 101
Troost, Gerard 59, 101
Trotwood's Monthly 175
Truesdail, William 120
Truman, Harry S. 241
Truxton (horse) 56
Tubb, Ernest 268, 271
Tulane Hotel 185
Turner, Jim 249
Union Gospel Tabernacle (Ryman Auditorium) 156-158, 170
Union Station 163, 165-171, 297,
★The United Methodist Publishing House 363
United States Customs House 155, 297
University of Nashville 78, 94, 96, 98, 99, 101
University of Tennessee-Nashville 247, 254, 292
Upper Room Chapel 282
Van Buren, Martin 82
Vanderbilt, Cornelius 111, 147
Vanderbilt family 272
★Vanderbilt Medical Center 364
Vanderbilt University 111, 144, 147-150, 174, 203-220, 246, 247, 254, 264, 277, 292

★Vanderbilt University 365
Van Vechten, Carl 248
Vauxhall Garden 61, 83
Verett, Shirley 287
Vertrees, John J. 185
Vine Street Temple 139

WDAD radio 266
WSM radio 266, 267, 268, 274
WSM television 244
Wade, John Donald 214, 215
Wagoner, Porter 273
Wakefield, Hek 211
Waldheim, Kurt 286
Walker, Sam Swan (portrait by) 86
Walker, Seth 188
Walker, Thomas 14
Walker, William 106
Wallace family 297
War Memorial Building 220, 226, 287
Ward-Belmont College 148, 202, 269
Ward's Seminary 148, 202
Warfield, Charles 261, 263
Warioto River (Cumberland) 13
Warner, Edwin 224
Warner, Kate Burch 186
Warner, Percy 224
Warren, Robert Penn 204, 205-221
Washington, Booker T. 158, 191
Washington, George 39, 78
★Washington Manufacturing Co. 366
Watauga River 14, 15
Watkins family 72
Watkins Institute 148, 151
Watkins, Samuel 127, 148
Watterson, Henry 137
Watts, Lee (portrait by) 203
Wauford, James A. 237
Wells, Haydon 19
Wells, Kitty 268

Werthan Bag Company 237
Werthan family 297
Werthan, Joe 239
West, Ben 240, 260, 261, 262, 263
Western Military Institute 99
Wheat, C. Roberdeau 79, 107
Wheat, John Thomas 79
White, George L. 146
White, Hugh Lawson 82
White, James 34, 99
White, Lucinda "Granny" 152
White, Zachariah 17, 37
White's Creek 34, 93
Whitsett, James 99
Williams, Avon N. 251
Williams, Daniel 19, 32
Williams, Hank 271, 272
★Williams Printing Co. 367
Williams, Sampson 19
Williamson County 43
Wills, Jesse 209, 220
Wills, Ridley 208-211
Wilson, Mrs. Beverly 181
Wilson County 43
Wilson, David K. 264
Wilson, Woodrow 186
Winter, Lewis 189
Wood, Del 276
Work, John W. 248
Wynette, Tammy 273
YMCA law school 247
York, Alvin 231
Zerfoss, Tom 215
Zibart family 219, 297
Zollicoffer, Felix K. 104, 127
Zorthian, Jirayr H. (painting by) 25, 28, 93

★Individuals associated with business and institutions in the Gallery of Nashville Commerce are not indexed separately.

Credits

Appreciative acknowledgement and credit are due to the photographers, artists, owners, curators, and others who provided the more than four hundred illustrations in this book. A consecutive listing of the illustrations by page is given below.

Frontispiece 1783 seal in the Tennessee Historical Society collection, housed in the Tennessee State Museum; Metro seal courtesy of the Mayor's Office; photographed by Bob Schatz
11 Courtesy of the Tennessee Committee for the Humanities; photographed by Roy Neel
12 The Cumberland River photographed from McMinn Bluff by Bill LaFevor, August 13, 1979
15 Courtesy of the Smithsonian Institution
16 Copyright 1977 by David Wright
18 Courtesy of a Donelson descendant; photographed by Bill LaFevor
19 Copyright 1979 by Dan E. Pomeroy
20-21 Courtesy of Mrs. E.A. Blair
22-23 Copyright 1979 by David Wright
24 Tennessee Historical Society collection, housed in the Tennessee State Library and Archives; reproduced by Leslie Pritikin
25 Mural in the Tennessee State Capitol; photographed by Dave Damer
26-27 Tennessee Historical Society collection, housed in the Tennessee State Library and Archives; reproduced by Leslie Pritikin

28 Mural in the Tennessee State Capitol; photographed by Dave Damer
29 Courtesy of William C. Cook
31 Tennessee State Museum; photographed by Bill LaFevor
33 Tennessee Historical Society collection, housed in the Tennessee State Museum; photographed by Bill LaFevor
35 Copyright 1979 by David Wright
37 Tennessee Historical Society collection, housed in the Tennessee State Library and Archives; reproduced by Leslie Pritikin
38 (top) Photographed by Mack S. Prichard
38 (bottom) Photographed by John Egerton
39 Photographed by John Egerton
40 Tennessee Historical Society collection, housed in the Tennessee State Museum; photographed by Bill LaFevor
41 Tennessee Historical Society collection, housed in the Tennessee State Library and Archives; reproduced by Leslie Pritikin
42-43 Courtesy of James C. Kelly; reproduced by Leslie Pritikin
44-45 Photographed by Bill LaFevor
46 French National Archives portrait, re-

produced by Leslie Pritikin from *Diary of My Travels in America*, by Louis-Philippe (Delacorte Press, New York, 1977)
47 Courtesy of Mrs. Warren W. Taylor; photographed by Dave Damer
48 Tennessee State Library and Archives; reproduced by Leslie Pritikin
49 Photographed by Bill LaFevor
50 Tennessee State Library and Archives; reproduced by Leslie Pritikin
52 Tennessee State Library and Archives; styled by Harriette Bateman
53 Portrait courtesy of Mrs. James Sartor Jr., photographed by Dave Damer; silver courtesy of Jean F. Prueher, photographed by Bill LaFevor
54 Tennessee Historical Society collection, housed in the Tennessee State Library and Archives; reproduced by Leslie Pritikin
55 Owned by Christine S. Farrar, in the care of the Tennessee State Museum; photographed by Bill LaFevor
56 Tennessee State Library and Archives; styled by Harriette Bateman

57 Tennessee State Library and Archives; reproduced by Leslie Pritikin

58 Tennessee State Library and Archives; reproduced by Leslie Pritikin

61 Courtesy of the University of Tennessee at Nashville

62 Collection of Brooks Memorial Art Gallery, Memphis Park Commission purchase

64 Courtesy of the Ladies Hermitage Association; photographed by Bill LaFevor

65 (top) Courtesy of the Ladies Hermitage Association; photographed by Dan Quest

65 (bottom) Courtesy of Colonel James S. Corbitt

67 Courtesy of the Colonial Dames, housed at Travellers' Rest; photographed by Bill LaFevor

68 Courtesy of Dr. and Mrs. Benjamin F. Byrd Jr.; photographed by Bill LaFevor

70 Tennessee Historical Society collection, housed in the Tennessee State Museum; photographed by Bill LaFevor

71 (top) Tennessee Historical Society collection, housed in the Tennessee State Library and Archives; reproduced by Leslie Pritikin

71 (bottom) Courtesy of the Ladies Hermitage Association; photographed by Bill LaFevor

72 Tennessee Historical Society collection, housed in the Tennessee State Museum; photographed by Bill LaFevor

73 (left) Tennessee Historical Society collection, housed in the Tennessee State Museum; photographed by Bill LaFevor

73 (right) Nashville Room, Metropolitan Nashville-Davidson County Public Library; photographed by Bill LaFevor

74-75 Copyright 1979 by David Wright

76 Courtesy of the Masonic Grand Lodge of Nashville; photographed by Bill LaFevor

77 (left) Tennessee State Library; reproduced by Leslie Pritikin

77 (right) Tennessee Historical Society collection, housed in the Tennessee State Museum; photographed by Bill LaFevor

78 (left) Courtesy of Mrs. Granberry Jackson; photographed by Bill LaFevor

78 (right) Courtesy of William Ridley Wills II; photographed by Bill LaFevor

79 Courtesy of Silvio A. Bedini

80 Tennessee State Museum; photographed by Bill LaFevor

83 Tennessee Historical Society collection, housed in the Tennessee State Library and Archives; reproduced by Leslie Pritikin

84 Courtesy of James A. Hoobler; reproduced by Leslie Pritikin

85 (top left) Tennessee Historical Society collection, housed in the Tennessee State Museum; photographed by Bill LaFevor

85 (top right and bottom) Tennessee Historical Society collection, housed in the Tennessee State Library and Archives; reproduced by Leslie Pritikin

86 Tennessee State Museum; photographed by Bill LaFevor

87 Courtesy of the R.W. Norton Art Gallery, Shreveport, Louisiana

88 Courtesy of Stanley F. Horn; photographed by Bill LaFevor

89 Tennessee State Library and Archives; styled by Harriette Bateman

91 Tennessee Historical Society collection, housed in the Tennessee State Museum; photographed by Bill LaFevor

92 (top) Tennessee State Museum; photographed by Bill LaFevor

92 (middle) Courtesy of Dr. and Mrs. Benjamin F. Byrd Jr.; photographed by Bill LaFevor

92 (bottom) Tennessee State Museum; photographed by Bill LaFevor

93 (top) Courtesy of the Public Library of Cincinnati and Hamilton County, Ohio

93 (bottom) Mural in the Tennessee State Capitol; photographed by Dave Damer

94 (top) Tennessee State Museum; photographed by Bill LaFevor

94 (bottom) Courtesy of C. William and Sarah H. Green; reproduced by Leslie Pritikin

95 Nashville Room, Metropolitan Nashville-Davidson County Public Library; photographed by Bill LaFevor

96 (top) Courtesy of Stanley F. Horn; photographed by Bill LaFevor

96 (bottom) Tennessee State Museum; photographed by Bill LaFevor

97 (top) Tennessee State Library and Archives; reproduced by Leslie Pritikin

97 (bottom) Courtesy of Stanley F. Horn; photographed by Bill LaFevor

98 Tennessee Historical Society collection, housed in the Tennessee State Museum; photographed by Bill LaFevor

99 (left) Tennessee State Library and Archives; reproduced by Leslie Pritikin

99 (right) Courtesy of Margaret Lindsley Warden; reproduced by Leslie Pritikin

100 (all) Tennessee Historical Society collection, housed in the Tennessee State Library and Archives; reproduced by Leslie Pritikin

102 (left) Tennessee Historical Society collection, housed in the Tennessee State Museum; photographed by Bill LaFevor

102 (right) Tennessee State Library and Archives; reproduced by Leslie Pritikin

104 Tennessee State Library and Archives; styled by Harriette Bateman

105 Tennessee Historical Society collection, housed in the Tennessee State Library and Archives; reproduced by Leslie Pritikin

106 (left) Tennessee State Library and Archives; styled by Harriette Bateman

106 (right) Tennessee State Library and Archives; reproduced by Leslie Pritikin

107 (left) Tennessee Historical Society Collection, housed in the Tennessee State Library and Archives; reproduced by Leslie Pritikin

107 (right) Tennessee State Library and Archives; styled by Harriette Bateman

108 (top) Tennessee State Library and Archives; styled by Harriette Bateman

108 (bottom) Courtesy of the Louisville and Nashville Railroad

111 Courtesy of Fisk University

112 Tennessee State Library and Archives; photographed by Bill LaFevor

114 Tennessee State Library and Archives; reproduced by Leslie Pritikin

115 Tennessee Historical Society collection, housed in the Tennessee State Library and Archives; reproduced by Leslie Pritikin

116 Photograph by Giers, courtesy of C. William and Sarah H. Green; reproduced by Leslie Pritikin

117 Tennessee Historical Society collection, housed in the Tennessee State Library and Archives; reproduced by Leslie Pritikin

118 Tennessee Historical Society collection, housed in the Tennessee State Museum; photographed by Bill LaFevor

120 (left) Courtesy of the Tennessean; reproduced by Billy Easley

120 (right) From The Annals of the Army of the Cumberland (1864), reproduced by Leslie Pritikin

121 (top and bottom) Tennessee State Library and Archives; reproduced by Leslie Pritikin

123 (top) Nashville Room, Metropolitan Nashville-Davidson County Public Library; photographed by Bill LaFevor

123 (bottom) Tennessee State Library and Archives; reproduced by Leslie Pritikin

125 (top) Courtesy of Stanley F. Horn; photographed by Bill LaFevor

125 (left) Tennessee State Library and Archives; reproduced by Leslie Pritikin

125 (right) Tennessee State Museum; photographed by Bill LaFevor

127 (left) Courtesy of the Smithsonian Institution

127 (right) Tennessee Historical Society collection, housed in the Tennessee State Library and Archives; reproduced by Leslie Pritikin

128 Courtesy of Hamilton Gayden Jr.; photographed by Bill LaFevor

129 (top) Courtesy of William Ridley Wills II; photographed by Bill LaFevor

129 (bottom) Tennessee State Library and Archives; reproduced by Leslie Pritikin

130 (top) Courtesy of William Ridley Wills II; photographed by Bill LaFevor

130 (bottom) Tennessee State Library and Archives; reproduced by Leslie Pritikin

132-133 Courtesy of William Ridley Wills II

132 (left) Courtesy of Robert M. McBride; reproduced by Leslie Pritikin

132 (right) Tennessee Historical Society collection, housed in the Tennessee State Library and Archives; reproduced by Leslie Pritikin

134 (top) Tennessee Historical Society collection, housed in the Tennessee State Museum; photographed by Bill LaFevor

134 (bottom) Courtesy of Margaret Lindsley Warden; reproduced by Leslie Pritikin

135 (top and bottom) Tennessee State Library and Archives; reproduced by Leslie Pritikin

136 Courtesy of William Waller; photographed by Bill LaFevor

137 Courtesy of the Tennessean; reproduced by Billy Easley

138 (left) Tennessee State Library and Archives; reproduced by Leslie Pritikin

138 (right) Tennessee State Library and Archives; styled by Harriette Bateman

139 (top left) Photograph by Giers, courtesy of C. William and Sarah H. Green; reproduced by Leslie Pritikin

139 (bottom left) Courtesy of the Jewish Temple, Congregation Ohabai Shalom

139 (top right) Courtesy of the Nashville Banner

139 (bottom right) Tennessee State Library and Archives; reproduced by Leslie Pritikin

140 (top) Courtesy of C. William and Sarah H. Green; reproduced by Leslie Pritikin

140 (bottom) Tennessee State Library and Archives; styled by Harriette Bateman

141 (top) Courtesy of William Ridley Wills II; photographed by Bill LaFevor

141 (bottom) Tennessee State Library and Archives; reproduced by Leslie Pritikin

142-143 Copyright 1979 by David Wright

144 From The City of Nashville, Illustrated; reproduced by Leslie Pritikin

145 (top) Photographed by Bill LaFevor

145 (bottom) From History of Davidson County; reproduced by Leslie Pritikin

146 (top) Courtesy of Fisk University; photographed by Bill LaFevor

146 (bottom) From The Story of the Jubilee Singers With Their Songs, by J.B.T. Marsh (Boston, 1880)

147 (left) Portrait by Jared B. Flagg, 1875, courtesy of Vanderbilt University; photographed by Bill LaFevor

147 (right) C.C. Giers photograph courtesy of Vanderbilt University Photographic Archive

148 Courtesy of Vanderbilt University Photographic Archive

149 (top) Nashville Room, Metropolitan Nashville-Davidson County Public Library; reproduced by Bill LaFevor

149 (left) Photograph by Giers, courtesy of C. William and Sarah H. Green; reproduced by Leslie Pritikin

150-151 From the Giers collection owned by C. William and Sarah H. Green; reproduced by Bill LaFevor

151 (lower left, top) Photograph by Giers, courtesy of C. William and Sarah H. Green; reproduced by Leslie Pritikin

151 (lower left, bottom) Tennessee State Library and Archives; reproduced by Leslie Pritikin

151 (right, top) Photograph by Giers, courtesy of C. William and Sarah H. Green; reproduced by Leslie Pritikin

151 (right, bottom) Tennessee State Library and Archives; reproduced by Leslie Pritikin

152 (top) Courtesy of Oscar F. Noel; photographed by Bill LaFevor

152 (bottom) Photograph by Giers, courtesy of C. William and Sarah H. Green; reproduced by Leslie Pritikin

153 Courtesy of the Tennessee Fine Arts Center at Cheekwood; photographed by Bill LaFevor

154 Photograph by Giers, courtesy of C. William and Sarah H. Green; reproduced by Leslie Pritikin

155 (top left and right, bottom left) Tennessee State Library and Archives; reproduced by Leslie Pritikin

155 (bottom right) Courtesy of the Tennessean; reproduced by Billy Easley

156 (top) Courtesy of the Tennessean library

156-157 From Thunderbolts, by Sam P. Jones; reproduced by Leslie Pritikin

157 From the Byrd Douglas papers, Tennessee State Library and Archives; reproduced by Leslie Pritikin

157 (middle) Photograph by Giers, courtesy of C. William and Sarah H. Green; reproduced by Leslie Pritikin

158 (top) Photograph by Giers, courtesy of C. William and Sarah H. Green; reproduced by Leslie Pritikin

158 (bottom) Courtesy of the Tennessean library

159 From Art Work in Nashville (1894); reproduced by Bill LaFevor

160 (top) Courtesy of the Gerst House; photographed by Bill LaFevor

160 (bottom) Courtesy of David Marshall Stewart; photographed by Bill LaFevor

161 Courtesy of Margaret Lindsley Warden; reproduced by Leslie Pritikin

162 From The Official History of the Tennessee Centennial Exposition (1897); reproduced by Leslie Pritikin

163 Tennessee State Library and Archives; reproduced by Leslie Pritikin

164 Nashville Room, Metropolitan Nashville-Davidson County Public Library; photographed by Bill LaFevor

166 (top) Tennessean library

166 (bottom) Nashville Room, Metropolitan Nashville-Davidson County Public Library; reproduced by Leslie Pritikin

167 Tennessee State Library and Archives; reproduced by Leslie Pritikin

168 Giers photograph, Tennessee State Library and Archives; reproduced by Leslie Pritikin

169 Copyright 1979 by David Wright

170 Tennessee State Library and Archives; reproduced by Leslie Pritikin

171 Photographed by Custis L. Stamp; reproduced by Leslie Pritikin

172 (top) Courtesy of Stanley F. Horn; photographed by Bill LaFevor

172 (bottom) Nashville Room, Metropolitan Nashville-Davidson County Public Library; reproduced by Bill LaFevor

173 (all) Nashville Room, Metropolitan Nashville-Davidson County Public Library; reproduced by Bill LaFevor

174 (top) Courtesy of George Peabody College for Teachers; reproduced by Leslie Pritikin

174 (bottom) Nashville Room, Metropolitan Nashville-Davidson County Public Library; reproduced by Bill LaFevor

175 (top) Courtesy of the Gerst House; photographed by Bill LaFevor

175 (middle) Portrait by Willie Betty Newman, in the Tennessee State Museum collection; photographed by Bill LaFevor

175 (bottom) Portrait by a Mrs. McClellan, in the Tennessee State Museum collection; photographed by Bill LaFevor

175 (lower right) Nashville Room, Metropolitan Nashville-Davidson County Public Library; photographed by Bill LaFevor

176 Tennessee State Library and Archives; reproduced by Leslie Pritikin

178 (both) Tennessee State Library and Archives; reproduced by Leslie Pritikin

179 (top and bottom) Tennessee State Library and Archives; reproduced by Leslie Pritikin

181 Tennessee State Library and Archives; reproduced by Leslie Pritikin

182 Nashville Room, Metropolitan Nashville-Davidson County Public Library; reproduced by Bill LaFevor

183 Courtesy of Mary Louise Lea Tidwell and Laura Lea Knox

183 (right) Tennessee State Library and Archives; styled by Harriette Bateman

184 Tennessee State Library and Archives; reproduced by Leslie Pritikin

186 Photographed by John Egerton

187 Tennessee State Library and Archives; reproduced by Leslie Pritikin

188 Cartoon by Ray McGill, in the Tennessee State Library and Archives collection; reproduced by Leslie Pritikin

189 Courtesy of the National Baptist Publishing Board; reproduced by Leslie Pritikin

190 Courtesy of Special Collections, Fisk University Library; reproduced by Bill LaFevor

193 Courtesy of DeBerry and Sam McKissack; reproduced by Leslie Pritikin

194 (top) Courtesy of J.B. Singleton; reproduced by Leslie Pritikin

194 (bottom) Photographed by John Egerton

195 Tennessee State Library and Archives; reproduced by Bill LaFevor

196 (top) Courtesy of Jim and Harriette Bateman

196 (middle and bottom) Tennessee State Library and Archives; reproduced by Leslie Pritikin

197 (left) Nashville Room, Metropolitan Nashville-Davidson County Public Library; reproduced by Bill LaFevor

197 (right) Photographed by John Egerton

198 (all) Tennessee State Library and Archives; reproduced by Leslie Pritikin

199 (both) Nashville Room, Metropolitan Nashville-Davidson County Public Library; reproduced by Bill LaFevor

200 (top) Photographed by Kay Russell

200 (bottom) Photographed by John Egerton

201 (top) Courtesy of Mary Stahlman Douglas

201 (bottom) Photographed by John Egerton

202 (top) Nashville Room, Metropolitan Nashville-Davidson County Public Library; reproduced by Bill LaFevor

202 (bottom) Tennessee State Library and Archives; reproduced by Leslie Pritikin

203 (top) Portrait by Laura Wheeler Waring, courtesy of the National Portrait Gallery, Smithsonian Institution

203 (bottom) Portrait by Lee Watts, courtesy of David Lipscomb College; photographed by Bill LaFevor

203 (right) Courtesy of Vanderbilt University Photographic Archive; reproduced by Leslie Pritikin

204 Photograph by Barr-Hime, courtesy of Vanderbilt University Photographic Archive

205 Photographed by John Egerton

210-212, 217, 219 Wills collection of Fugitive-Agrarian materials, housed in Special Collections, Joint University Libraries, Nashville; photograph on page 219 by Joe Rudis

221 Tennessee State Museum; reproduced by Bill LaFevor

222 (top) Nashville Room, Metropolitan Nashville-Davidson County Public Library; photographed by Bill LaFevor

222 (bottom) Dustjacket for Caruso: His Life in Pictures, by Francis Robinson (Studio Publications, New York, 1957)

223 (top) Tennessee State Library and Archives; styled by Harriette Bateman

223 (bottom) Vanderbilt University Photographic Archive

224 Courtesy of the Airport Authority of Metropolitan Nashville-Davidson County

225 (left and right) Nashville Room, Metropolitan Nashville-Davidson County Public Library; reproduced by Bill LaFevor

225 (bottom) Tennessean library

226 (left) Tennessean library

226 (right) Courtesy of Leslie Cheek Jr.; reproduced by Leslie Pritikin

226 (bottom) Nashville Room, Metropolitan Nashville-Davidson County Public Library; reproduced by Bill LaFevor

227 Tennessean library

228 (left and right) Courtesy of Mary Stahlman Douglas; reproduced by Leslie Pritikin

229 Courtesy of Mary Louise Lea Tidwell and Laura Lea Knox

230 Nashville Room, Metropolitan Nashville-Davidson County Public Library; reproduced by Bill LaFevor

231 Photographed by John Egerton

232 Tennessean photograph by Elred Reaney

235 Courtesy of Vanderbilt University

236 Copyright 1975 by the Country Music Foundation Incorporated

238 (both) Tennessee State Library and Archives; reproduced by Leslie Pritikin

239 (both) Courtesy of Mrs. Jack Kuhn; photographs by John E. Hood

240 Photographed by John Egerton

241 (left) Tennessean library

241 (middle) Photographed by Jack Corn

241 (right) Courtesy of the George J. Flanigen collection, Aquinas Junior College

242 (left) Tennessean library

242 (right) Tennessean photograph by Joe Rudis

243 Tennessean library

245 (both) Courtesy of the Metropolitan Development and Housing Authority

246 Photographed by John Egerton

247 Tennessean library

248 (all) Courtesy of Special Collections, Fisk University Library

249 Tennessean photograph by Bill Preston

251 Tennessean library

252 (top) Photographed by Jack Corn

252 (bottom) Photographed by Mary Griffith

253 (top) Photographed by Jack Corn

253 (bottom) Tennessean photograph by Nancy Warnecke

255 Photographed by Joe Zinn

256 Photographed by Joe Zinn

257 (both) Photographed by Joe Zinn

258 (both) Photographed by Jack Corn

259 (top) Tennessean photograph by Robert Johnson

259 (bottom) Photographed by John Egerton

261 (both) Tennessean photographs by Jack Corn

262 Special Collections, Joint University Libraries

263 Photographed by Joe Zinn

264 *Tennessean* photograph by Frank Empson
265 Photographed by Jack Corn
267 Courtesy of WSM; photograph by Powell Stamper
268 *(both)* Courtesy of WSM; photographs by Powell Stamper
269 *(all)* Courtesy of Denver Sherry; photographed by Bill LaFevor
270 *(both)* Photographs by Al Clayton
271 Photographed by Al Clayton
272 Vanderbilt University Photographic Archive; photograph by J. Clark Thomas
272 Photographed by Jack Corn
274 Photographed by Slick Lawson
275 Photographed by Bill LaFevor
276 *(top)* Painting by Bill Myers; photographed by Bill LaFevor
276 *(bottom)* Photographed by Kit Luce
277 Photographed by Al Clayton
278-279 Photographed by Bill LaFevor
280 *(top left)* Courtesy of the Metropolitan Development and Housing Agency
280 *(top right)* Tennessee State Library and Archives; reproduced by Leslie Pritikin
280 *(middle)* Photographed by Bill LaFevor
280 *(bottom left)* *Tennessean* photograph by Dale Ernsberger
280 *(bottom right)* *Tennessean* photograph by Joe Rudis
281 *(both)* Photographed by Bill LaFevor
282 *(top)* Courtesy of the Upper Room Chapel
282 *(bottom)* *Tennessean* photograph by Bill Welch
282-283 Photographed by Slick Lawson
284 *(top and bottom)* Photographed by Bill LaFevor
284 *(right)* Photographed by Charles F. Bryan Jr.
285 *(top left)* Photographed by Joe Zinn

285 *(right)* Photographed by James A. Hoobler
285 *(bottom left)* Courtesy of *Vanderbilt Alumnus* Magazine
286 *(left)* Photographed by Bill LaFevor
286 *(right)* Photographed by Jack Corn
286 *(bottom)* *Tennessean* photograph by Frank Empson
287 *(top)* Photographed by John Egerton
287 *(bottom left)* Holder-Kennedy photograph, courtesy of the Nashville Symphony Guild
287 *(bottom right)* Photographed by Slick Lawson
288 Copyright 1979 by Dan E. Pomeroy
289 *(top)* Photographed by Bob Schatz
289 *(bottom left)* Photographed by George Walker III
289 *(bottom right)* *Tennessean* photograph by Frank Empson
290 *(top)* Photographed by Bill LaFevor
290 *(bottom left)* *Tennessean* photograph by Frank Empson
290 *(bottom right)* Photographed by Jack Corn
291 *(top)* Photographed by George Walker III
291 *(bottom)* Courtesy of the Nashville Sounds; photographed by Robert Johnson
292 *(all)* The *Banner* and the *Tennessean*
293 *(top and middle)* The *Tennessean* and the *Banner*
203 *(bottom)* Courtesy of WNGE
294-295 Copyright 1979 by David Wright
298 The Cumberland River and the Nashville skyline, photographed on August 17, 1979, by Bill LaFevor
317 *(center)* Courtesy of John Hardcastle
341 *(right)* Photographed by Slick Lawson
343 *(bottom)* Photograph by Edwin P'Poole

352 Photograph by Jack Gunter
363 *(top)* Photograph courtesy of United States War Department
364 Photograph by Ginger Carnahan
365 Photograph by David Burnside
All other photographs in the Gallery of Nashville Commerce were provided by the participating businesses and institutions.

In addition, appreciation is expressed for permission to quote herein, on the pages indicated, from the following published works:

14 Alfred Leland Crabb, *Nashville: Personality of a City* (Bobbs-Merrill, New York, 1960)
16 Harriette Simpson Arnow, *Seedtime on the Cumberland* (Macmillan, New York, 1959)
46 Louis-Philippe, *Diary of My Travels in America* (Delacorte Press, New York, 1977)
116 *The Private War of Lizzie Hardin*, G. Glenn Clift, editor (Kentucky Historical Society, Frankfort, 1963)
123 *Maggie Lindsley's Journal* (M.D. Mackenzie, Southbury, Connecticut, 1977)
135 John Sharpe Chambers, *The Conquest of Cholera* (Macmillan, New York, 1938)
171 *Speaking of Union Station*, Deborah Cooney, editor (Union Station Trust Fund, Nashville, 1977)
199 "Nerves," a short story by Peter Taylor, in *The New Yorker*, September 16, 1961
220 "Remembrances," a poem in *Nashville and Other Poems*, by Jesse Wills (Fantasie Press, Nashville, 1973)
271 Paul Hemphill, *The Nashville Sound* (Simon and Schuster, New York, 1972)

Appreciation

The evolution of this book from an idea to an accomplished reality in just nine months was aided immeasurably by the timely assistance of the more than two hundred people whose names are listed below. Their contributions, large and small, were indispensable. The final word of thanks belongs to them.

Hubert Adams
Martha Adams
Pat Alderman
Anne Anderson
James Anderson
Yeatman Anderson III
Harriette S. Arnow
Catherine P. Avery
Mike Barich
Anne Battle
Kay Beasley
Paul H. Beasley
Wesley O. Beazley
Silvio A. Bedini

Bob Bell Jr.
Marylin Bell
Vic Bellos
John Bissinger
Nancy Blackwelder
Gary Bogle
Jowain Braddock
J. Robert Bradley
Theodore Brown Jr.
Edith H. Bryan
Allison Caldwell Byrd
Benjamin F. Byrd Jr.
Nat Caldwell
Mary French Caldwell

Will D. Campbell
Sam Cameron
Charles B. Castner
George H. Cate Jr.
Steven A. Channing
Brainard Cheney
Amos Christie
Jo Church
Herman Clark
Harry D. Claybrook
Mary Melbourne Clements
L.M. Collins
John L. Connelly
Carol Cook

William C. Cook
James S. Corbitt
William Corum
Steve Cox
Alfred Leland Crabb
Kendall Cram
Wilbur F. Creighton Jr.
Isaiah T. Creswell
Nathaniel A. Crippens
Gene Crosswhite
Estella T. Crutcher
Ann L. Cummings
Ricky Curtis
Jack Custer

Francis Davis
J. McGavock Dickinson
Wilton Dillon
John Dobson
Josephine Hutton Douglas
Mary Stahlman Douglas
Alice Duncan
Jean Dyer
Francis Eagle
Luke Easter
May Dean Eberling
Ann B. Egerton
Zainab El-Berry
Jimmy Ellis
Sandy Evans
Nell Fisher
Jane Fleming
Dudley Fortner
Fedora Small Frank
Maxine Fuqua
Jennifer Galloway
Jack Gannon
Noel Gentry
Don Goad
Harry Gore
G.T. Granbery Jr.
John P. Graves
C. William Green
Sarah Hicks Green
Mahlon Griffith
Cheryl Hamberg
Herbert Harding
Josephine L. Harper
Minerva H. Hawkins
Mary Henard
Troy Henry
Mary E. Higgs
May Buntin Hill
Owen M. Hines Jr.
Paula Lovell Hooker
Stanley F. Horn
Beth House
Albert W. Hutchison Jr.

Stanley Idzerda
Johnnie Jones
B.G. Johnson
Victor S. Johnson
Kathy Joyner
Linda Keeton
James C. Kelly
Chester Kielman
James King
Myron King
James Knight
Laura Lea Knox
Elsie Kolar
Heloise Kuhn
Peter LaPaglia
Jerry Livingston
John Love
Judith Lowder
Betsy MacPherson
Mary Lou Mahaffey
William Marlin
John Martin
Robert M. McBride
Selene McCall
James L. McDonough
Robert A. McGaw
Millie McGhee
Frances McLester
Diane McNabb
John McNeal
Max Mendelsohn
Frances Meeker
Catherine Mims
Eugene Moore
Harold Moredock
Eleanor F. Morrissey
J. Emerick Nagy
Maurine F. Newell
Karen Nicely
Bob Oermann
Genella Nye Olker
Flem B. Otey II
Mary W. Parrent

Robert H. Paslay
Hershel Payne
Sheryl Peters
Edgar M. Pittenger
Leslie Pomeroy
William Pratt
Randy Prince
Jean F. Prueher
Gordon Publow Jr.
Sally Raye
Dorothy Richardson
Rich Riebeling
Nathaniel Roberson
Sandra Roberts
Bobby Robertson
Tommy Rogers
Thelma Rucker
Fred Russell
Bob Sanders
Kenneth Sanders
Fran Schell
Larry Schmittou
Fred Schmitz
James Schmitz
Marion Schow
Mingo Scott
John Seaman
Huldah Cheek Sharp
James Sharp
Larry Short
J.B. Singleton
Andrew Jackson Smith
Hugh Smith
Kelly Miller Smith
Paul Smith
W.O. Smith
Jim Sparks
Sarah Stamps
Martha Bridges Starlin
Martha Steele
Samuel E. Steele
David Marshall Stewart
Gladys C. Stewart

Butch Stinson
Virginia G. Stovall
Mildred Stoves
Elizabeth Street
Jackie Sullivan
Jane Sutherland
Mary Teloh
Harold Thompson
John Thweatt
Tom Tichenor
Leonard Tidwell
Mary Louise Lea Tidwell
Bobby Tignor Jr.
Mary Jean Turbett
Roger Turnbow
Bob Vaughn
George Vaughn
Robert Victory
Hugh Walker
Ellen Wallace
Margaret Lindsley Warden
James E. Ward
Fred Way Jr.
Lydia D. Weesner
R.W. Weesner
Shirley Welch
Clarence Wells
Betty Werthan
Esther White
William Ridley Wills II
Raleigh A. Wilson
John Windrow
Roland Wolfe
Marice Wolfe
Elizabeth Woosley
Eva Jean Wrather
Joe Wright
Linda Wright
Kyle Young
Kate Zerfoss
Carl F. Zibart